Surviving Chemistry

W9-DJI-046

Review Book

High School Chemistry

with

NYS Chemistry Regents Exams
The Physical Setting

E3 Chemistry Books
Student and teacher-friendly High School books to:
- ✓ Excite students to study
- ✓ Engage students in learning
- ✓ Enhance students understanding

Acknowledgement

Many thanks go to **Mr. Stephen Costanza,** Chemistry Teacher at Whitesboro High School in Marcy, NY. His superb editing has made this book better.

ISBN-13: 978-1512267259

ISBN-10: 1512267252

Printed in the United States of America

e3 Chemistry

E3 Scholastic Publishing

Survivingchem.com

(877) 224 – 0484

info@e3chemistry.com

Now on

NYC DOE Famis E-catalog

New York City Teachers

Our books are now listed on Famis E-catalog through Ingram

Vendor #: ING032000
Contract #: 7108108

Table of Contents

Topic 1: Matter, Energy, and Change........................... Pg 1 - 18
Lesson 1: Types of Matter
Lesson 2: Phases of Matter and Temperature
Lesson 3: Heat Energy and Heat Calculations
Lesson 4: Characteristics of Gases and Gas Law Calculations
Lesson 5: Physical and Chemical Properties of Matter

Topic 2: The Periodic Table..................................... pg 19 - 32
Lesson 1: Arrangement of the Elements
Lesson 2: Types of Elements and their Properties
Lesson 3: Groups of Elements and their Properties
Lesson 4: Periodic Trends

Topic 3: Atomic Structure .... pg 33 - 54
Lesson 1: The Historical Development of the Modern Atom
Lesson 2: The Atom
Lesson 3: Electron Location and Arrangement
Lesson 4: Valence Electrons and Ions
Lesson 5: Quantum Numbers and Electron Configurations

Topic 4: Chemical Bonding .... pg 55 - 72
Lesson 1: Stability and Energy in Bonding
Lesson 2: Types of Bonding and Substances
Lesson 3: Molecular Polarity and Intermolecular Forces
Lesson 4: Lewis Electron-dot Diagrams and Bonding

Topic 5: Chemical Formulas and Equations .... pg 73 - 86
Lesson 1: Interpretation of Chemical Formulas
Lesson 2: Types of Chemical Formulas
Lesson 3: Nomenclature
Lesson 4: Chemical Equations

Topic 6: Stoichiometry: Mole Calculations...................... Pg 87 - 102
Lesson 1: Mole Calculations in Formulas
Lesson 2: Mole Calculations in Equations

Topic 7: Solutions .... pg 103 - 120
Lesson 1: Properties of Solutions
Lesson 2: Solubility Factors
Lesson 3: Descriptions of Solutions and the Solubility Curves
Lesson 4: Expressions of Concentration of Solutions
Lesson 5: Vapor Pressure
Lesson 6: Effect of Solutes on Physical Properties of Water

Table of Contents

Topic 8: Acids, Bases and Salts.............................. pg 121 - 136
Lesson 1: Definitions of Acids and Bases
Lesson 2: Reactions of Acids and Bases
Lesson 3: Salts and Electrolytes
Lesson 4: Formulas and Names of Acids

Topic 9: Kinetics and Equilibrium .... pg 137 - 160
Lesson 1: Kinetics and Rate of Reactions
Lesson 2: Energy and Chemical Reactions
Lesson 3: Entropy
Lesson 4: Equilibrium

Topic 10: Organic Chemistry .... pg 161 - 182
Lesson 1: Properties of Organic Compounds
Lesson 2: Classes of Organic Compounds
Lesson 3: Isomers
Lesson 4: Organic Reactions

Topic 11: Redox and Electrochemistry .... pg 183 - 206
Lesson 1: Oxidation Numbers
Lesson 2: Oxidation and Reduction (Redox) Reactions
Lesson 3: Electrochemistry (Voltaic and Electrolytic cells)
Lesson 4: Spontaneous Reactions

Topic 12: Nuclear Chemistry .... pg 207 - 228
Lesson 1: Nuclear Transmutations
Lesson 2: Nuclear Energy (Fission and Fusion)
Lesson 3: Half-life and Half-life Calculations

Topic 13: Lab Safety, Measurements .... pg 229 - 235
     and Significant Figures

16 Days of Questions for Regents and .... Pg 236 -342
Final Exams Practice

Reference Tables .... pg 343 - 354

Glossary and Index .... pg 355 - 371

Answer Key Booklets.

This book has a separate Answer Key Booklet.

Answer Key Booklets to all
of our titles are available as pdf
eBooks and hard copy prints.
Since our books are used in
schools as instructional materials,
Answer Key Booklets can only
be purchased through us, the
Publisher.

Teachers

You can purchase the Answer Key Booklet to any of our title directly from
our website, **survivingchem.com**. Please use your school mailing address
as the SHP TO location so we can easily verify that you are a teacher.

Free Answer Key Booklets with all Class Orders.

All class orders made from our websites (**survivingchem.com or
e3chemistry.com**) will be shipped with 2 to 4 copies of the Answer Key
Booklet.

If you've made a class order of our book through Amazon or Barnes and
Noble, you'll have to contact us for free copies of the Answer Key Boklet.

Parents, students and tutors:

Before buying any Answer Key Booklet from our website, first send us an
email to request permission to do so. Send the request-email to
info@e3chemistry.com or use the Contact Us form on our website. Thanks.

Lesson 1: Types of Matter

Introduction:

Chemistry is the study of matter: its composition, structures, properties, changes it undergoes, and energy accompanying these changes.

Matter is anything that has mass and takes up space. Matter, in other words, is "stuff." Matter can be grouped and classified as pure substances or mixtures. In this lesson, you will learn about the different classifications of matter.

Types of Matter

Pure substances are types of matter composed (made up) of particles that are the same. Composition of a pure substance is uniform and definite in every sample. Elements and Compounds are classified as pure substances.

Elements are pure substances that are composed of identical atoms with the same atomic number. Elements cannot be decomposed (broken down) into simpler substances by physical nor chemical methods. Ca(s) and $Br_2(g)$ are examples of elements. All known natural and synthesized elements can be found on the Periodic Table of the Elements.

Compounds are pure substances composed of two or more different elements that are *chemically* combined. Properties and composition of a compound are definite (the same) in all samples of the compound. Compounds can be decomposed (separated) into simpler substances by chemical methods only. Properties of a compound are always different from those of the elements found in the compound. $CaBr_2(s)$, $H_2O(l)$, and $NH_3(g)$ are examples of compounds.

Law of definite composition states that elements in a compound are combined in a fixed and definite ratio by mass. For example, the composition (mass percentages) in every sample of water is always 89% O to 11% H. That means any 10-gram sample of water will always contain about 8.9 g of O to 1.1g of H.

Mixtures are types of matter that are composed of two or more different substances that are *physically* combined. Composition of a mixture may vary (can change) from one sample to another. A mixture can be separated into its components only by physical methods. A mixture always retains the properties of the individual component.

Diagrams of Matter given:

O　Ca atom

● Br atom

Ca

Br₂

elements Ca and Br

CaBr₂

a **compound** of Ca and Br

a **mixture** of Ca and Br

Homogeneous and Heterogeneous Mixtures

Homogeneous mixtures are mixtures that are uniformly and evenly mixed throughout. Samples taken within the same mixture have definite and fixed composition. Aqueous solutions are homogeneous mixtures that are made with water. Salt water, NaCl(aq), is an example of an aqueous solution.

Heterogeneous mixtures are mixtures that are not uniformly nor evenly mixed throughout. Samples taken within the same mixture have different and varying compositions. Soil and concrete are examples of heterogeneous mixtures

Classification of Matter Diagram

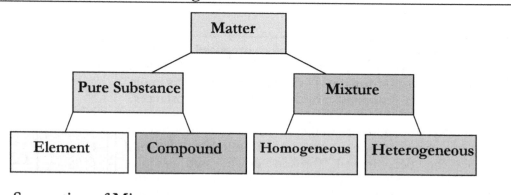

Separation of Mixtures

In a mixture, substances retain their unique physical properties. Depending on these physical properties, various physical methods can be used to separate each substance from the mixture.

Heterogeneous mixtures can be separated by simple physical methods.
Decantation is a process of pouring out the top component of a mixture that has separated into layers. An oil and water mixture can be separated this way.

Filtration is a process that can be used to separate a solid from a liquid. During filtration, the liquid or aqueous component of a mixture will go through the filter paper because particles of a liquid are always smaller than the holes of a filter. The solid component of the mixture will remain on the filter paper because particles of a solid are generally bigger than the holes of a filter.

Homogeneous mixtures (such as solutions) can be separated by more complicated physical methods.
Distillation is a process of separating a homogeneous mixture (solution) by using differences in the boiling points of the substances in the mixture. During distillation, a mixture is heated to vaporize (boil off) each substance in the order from lowest to highest boiling point. Each substance can be condensed and collected as it leaves the mixture. Water can be separated from salt in a salt-water mixture by simply boiling and evaporating the water off in a simple distillation apparatus. A mixture of hydrocarbons (methane, ethane, propane, etc.) can be separated through a more complicated distillation process.
Chromatography is another method of separating homogeneous mixtures. In this process, a mixture is dissolved in a solvent (mobile phase) that allows the components of the mixture to move though a stationary phase at different speeds. Data from chromatograph separation can be collected and analyzed to learn about the mixture.

Lesson 2: Phases of Matter, Energy and Temperature

Introduction

There are three phases of matter: solid, liquid, and gas. The nature of a substance determines the phase in which the substance will exist under normal conditions. Most substances can change from one phase to another. The nature of a substance also determines conditions necessary for the substance to change from one phase to another.

In this lesson you will learn about the three phases of matter. You will also learn about phase changes of matter and the relationship to temperature and energy.

Phases of Matter

Solid: A substance in the solid phase has the following characteristics:

. Definite volume and definite shape

. Particles arranged orderly in a *"regular geometric pattern"*

. Particles vibrating around fixed points

. Particles with strong attractive forces to one another

. Particles that cannot be easily compressed (incompressible)

particles arrangement

$H_2O(s)$

Liquid: A substance in the liquid phase has the following characteristics:

. Definite volume, but no definite shape (it takes the shape of its container)

. Particles that flow over each other

. Particles that cannot be easily compressed (incompressible)

$H_2O(l)$

Gas: A substance in the gas phase has the following characteristics:

. No definite volume and no definite shape (it takes volume and shape of its container)

. Particles that are less orderly arranged (most random)

. Particles that move fast and freely

. Particles with very weak attractive forces to each other

. Particles that can be easily compressed (compressible)

$H_2O(g)$

Phase Changes

A **phase change** is a physical change. During a phase change, a substance changes its form (or state) without changing its chemical composition. Any substance can change from one phase to another given the right conditions of temperature and/or pressure. Most substances require a large change in temperature to go through one phase change. Water is one of a few chemical substances that can change through all three phases within a narrow range of temperature changes.

Phase changes and example equations representing each change are given below.

Melting is a change from *solid* to *liquid*. $H_2O(s) ---> H_2O(l)$

Freezing is a change from *liquid* to *solid* $H_2O(l) ---> H_2O(s)$

Evaporation is a change from *liquid* to *gas* $C_2H_5OH(l) ---> C_2H_5OH(g)$

Condensation is a change from *gas* to *liquid* $C_2H_5OH(g) ---> C_2HOH(l)$

Deposition is a change from *gas* to *solid* $CO_2(g) -----> CO_2(s)$

Sublimation is a change from *solid* to *gas* $CO_2(s) ----> CO_2(g)$

Iodine, $I_2(s)$ and dry ice, $CO_2(s)$, are two substances that readily sublime at normal conditions. Most substances do not sublime.

Phase Changes and Energy

A substance changes phase when it has absorbed or released enough heat energy to rearrange its particles (atoms, ions, or molecules) from one form to another. Some phase changes require a release of heat by the substance, while others require heat to be absorbed.

Endothermic: describes a process that absorbs heat energy.
Fusion, evaporation and sublimation are endothermic phase changes.

Exothermic: describes a process that releases heat energy.
Freezing, condensation and deposition are exothermic phase changes.

The diagram below summarizes phase changes and the relationship to energy.

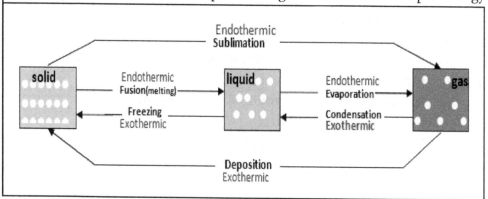

Phase Changes and Temperature

A phase change for a substance occurs at a specific temperature. Every substance has its own unique melting and boiling point.

Temperature is a measure of the average kinetic energy of particles in matter.

Kinetic energy is energy due to movement of particles in matter. The higher the temperature of a substance, the greater its kinetic energy. As temperature increases, the average kinetic energy also increases.

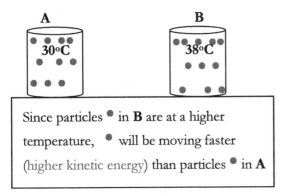

Since particles ● in **B** are at a higher temperature, ● will be moving faster (higher kinetic energy) than particles ● in **A**

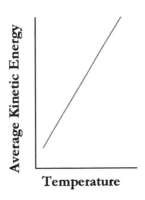

A thermometer is a piece of equipment that is used for measuring temperature.

Degree Celsius (ºC) and Kelvin (K) are the two most common units for measuring temperature.

Two fixed reference points are needed to create a thermometer scale:

The *freezing point (0ºC , 273K)* and the *boiling point (100ºC , 373K)* of water are often used as the two reference points in creating thermometer scales.

The mathematical relation between Celsius and Kelvin is given below.

$$K = ºC + 273 \quad \text{Table T equation}$$

According to this equation, the Kelvin temperature value is always 273 units higher than the same temperature in Celsius.

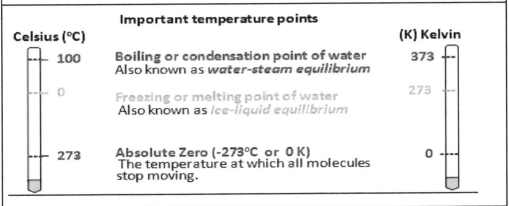

Important temperature points

Celsius (ºC)   (K) Kelvin

100   **Boiling or condensation point of water**
      Also known as *water-steam equilibrium*   373

0   Freezing or melting point of water   273
      Also known as *Ice-liquid equilibrium*

273   **Absolute Zero (-273ºC or 0 K)**   0
      The temperature at which all molecules
      stop moving.

Phase Change Diagrams

A **phase change diagram** shows the relationship between temperature and phase changes of a substance over a period of time as the substance is heating or cooling.

A **heating curve** shows a change of a substance starting with the substance as a solid. Changes represented on a heating curve are endothermic (heat is absorbed).

A **cooling curve** shows a change of a substance starting with the substance as a gas. Changes represented on a cooling curve are exothermic (heat is released).

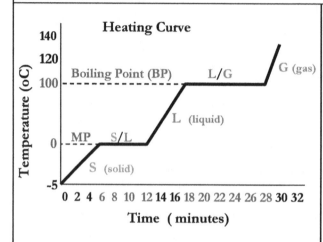

During segments S, L, G.
. One phase is present
. Temperature increases
. Kinetic energy increases
. Potential energy stays the same

During segments S/L and L/G
Two phases are present
. Temperature stays the same
. Kinetic energy stays the same
. Potential energy increases

The substance represented by this curve is likely water.

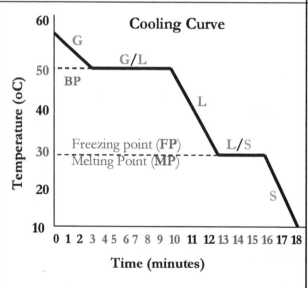

During segments G, L, S.
. One phase is present
. Temperature decreases
. Kinetic energy decreases
. Potential energy stays the same

During segments S/L and L/G
. Two phases are present
. Temperature stays the same
. Kinetic energy stays the same
. Potential energy decreases

The substance represented by this curve is not water.

Lesson 3: Heat and Heat Calculations

Introduction

Heat is a form of energy that can flow (or transfer) from one object to another. Direction of heat flow depends on the temperature difference. **Heat flows**
from an area or object of a *higher* temperature to an area or object of a *lower* temperature until equilibrium temperature is reached. The equilibrium temperature in the above diagram will be 18.5∘C (The sum of the two temperatures divided by 2).

During chemical and physical changes, heat energy is either absorbed or released.

Exothermic: describes a process that releases (emits or loses) heat.

Endothermic: describes a process that absorbs (or gains) heat.

Joules and **calories** are the two most common units for measuring heat. A **calorimeter** is a device that is used for measuring heat during physical and chemical changes.

Heat Constants and Heat Equations

The **specific heat capacity (C)** of a substance is the amount of heat needed to change the temperature of a one gram sample of the substance by just one degree Celsius (or one Kelvin). Specific heat capacity is different for different substances.

The specific heat capacity (C) for water is 4.18 J/g.∘K (See Table B). In other words, a one gram sample of water will absorb 4.18 Joules of heat to increase its temperature by one Kelvin, or release 4.18 Joules of heat to decrease its temperature by one Kelvin.

When the mass and specific heat capacity of a substance are known, the amount of heat absorbed or released by that substance to change between any two temperatures can be calculated using the **Table T** equation below.

Heat (q) = m x C x ΔT

    m   = mass of substance (g)

    C   = specific heat capacity (J/g.K)

    ΔT = difference in temp (K or ∘C)

    ΔT = High temp - Low temp

Example 1

How much heat is released by a 7 gram sample of water to change its temperature from 15 ∘C to 10 ∘C?

q = 7 x 4.18 x 5   *setup*

q = | **146.3 J** | *calculated result*

The **heat of fusion (H_f)** of a substance is the amount of heat needed to melt a one gram sample of the substance at constant temperature. The heat of fusion for water is 334 J/g (**See Table B**). In other words, a one-gram sample of water will absorb 334 joules of heat to melt, or release 334 joules of heat to freeze.

When the mass and heat of fusion of a substance are known, the amount of heat absorbed or released by the substance to change between the solid and liquid phases can be calculated using the **Table T** equation below.

Heat (q) = m x H_f

m = mass of substance (g)

H_f = Heat of fusion (J/g)

Example 2

What is the number of joules needed to melt a 16 g sample of ice to water at 0°C?

q = m   x H_f

q = 16   x   334   *setup*

q =   **5344 J** *calculated result*

The **heat of vaporization (H_v)** of a substance is the amount of heat needed to vaporize (evaporate) a one gram sample of the substance at a constant temperature.

The heat of vaporization of water is 2260 J/g. In other words, a one-gram sample of water will absorb 2260 joules of heat to vaporize, or release 2260 joules of heat to condense .

When the mass and heat of vaporization of a substance are known, the amount of heat absorbed or released by the substance to change between the liquid and gas phases can be calculated using **Table T** equation below:

Heat = m x H_v

m = mass of substance (g)

H_v = Heat of vaporization (J/g)

Example 3

Liquid ammonia has a heat of vaporization of 1.35 kJ/g. How many kilojoules of heat are needed to evaporate a 5 gram sample of ammonia at its boiling point?

q = m   x H_v *setup*

q = 5   x   1.35

q =   **6.75 kJ**

Solving a heat problem correctly depends on your understanding of the question, as well as choosing the right heat equation and substituting the correct factors into the equation. Keep the following key words or phrases in mind when deciding which of the three heat equations on Table T to use.

Two temperatures given, changes temperature from: *Use $q = mC\Delta T$*

To melt, to freeze, changes from liquid to solid, at 0°C :   *Use $q = mH_f$*

To boil, to condense, changes from liquid to steam, at 100°C: *Use $q = mH_v$*

Lesson 4: Gas Characteristics and Gas Laws

Introduction

Gas behavior is influenced by three key factors: volume (space of container), pressure and temperature. The relationships between these three factors are the basis for gas laws and gas theories. These laws and theories attempt to explain how gases behave.

In this lesson you will learn about the gas laws and theories as well as gas law calculations.

Kinetic Molecular Theory (KMT) of Ideal Gas

The **kinetic molecular theory** of an ideal gas is a model that is often used to explain the behavior of gases. This theory is summarized below.

- Gases are composed of individual particles
- Distances between gas particles are large (far apart)
- Gas particles are in continuous, random, straight-line motion
- When two particles of a gas collide, energy is transferred from one particle to another
- Particles of a gas have no attraction to each other
- Individual gas particles have no volume (negligible or insignificant)

An **ideal gas** is a theoretical (or assumed) gas that has all properties summarized above.

A **real gas** is a gas that actually does exist. Examples of real gases are *oxygen, carbon dioxide, hydrogen, helium, etc.*

Since kinetic molecular theory (summarized above) applies mainly to an ideal gas, the model cannot be used to predict exact behavior of real gases. Therefore, real gases deviate from (do not behave exactly as) an ideal gas for the following reasons.

. Real gas particles do attract each other.
  Ideal gas particles are assumed to have no attraction to each other
. Real gas particles do have volume
  Ideal gases are assumed to have no volume.

Real gases with small molecular masses behave most like an ideal gas. Hydrogen (H) and Helium (He), the two smallest real gases by mass, will behave more like an ideal gas than any other real gas.

Real gases behave more like an ideal gas under conditions of *High temperature and Low pressure.*

Helium, a real gas, will behave more like an ideal gas at 300 K and 1 atm. than at 273 K and 2 atm.

Gas Laws

Avogadro's Law states: Under the same conditions of temperature and pressure, gases of **equal volume** contain **equal number of molecules (particles).**

Containers A and B to the right contain the same number of molecules.

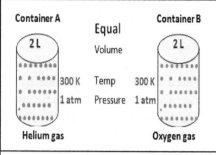

Container A　　Equal　　Container B

2 L　　Volume　　2 L

300 K　Temp　300 K

1 atm　Pressure　1 atm

Helium gas　　　　Oxygen gas

Dalton's Law of Partial Pressure states: The total pressure (P_{total}) of a gas mixture is the sum of all the partial pressures.

Partial Pressure (P) is a pressure exerted by an individual gas in a gas mixture

Total Pressure from Partial Pressures:

$$P_{total} = P_{gasA} + P_{gasB} + P_{gas\,C}$$

Example 4: What is the total pressure in the container given the partial pressures of the three gases below:

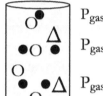

$P_{gas} \Delta = .2$ atm

$P_{gas} O = .4$ atm

$P_{gas} \bullet = .5$ atm

$\mathbf{P_{total}} = .2 + .4 + .5 = \boxed{\textbf{1.1 atm}}$

Total Pressure when gas X is collected over water:

$$P_{total} = P_{gas\,X} + VP_{H_2O} \text{ (at temp)}$$

VP_{H2O} is the vapor pressure of water at the given water temperature. See **Table H** for vapor pressure at different temperatures.

Example 5: Oxygen gas is collected over water at 45°C in a test tube. If the total pressure of the gas mixture in the test tube is 26 kPa, what is the partial pressure of the oxygen gas ?

26 kPa = Pgas O + VP_{H_2O} at 45°C

26 kPa = Pgas O + 10

$\boxed{\textbf{16 kPa}}$ = Pgas O

Partial Pressure of gas X from mole fraction:

$$P_{gas\,X} = \frac{\text{moles of gas X}}{\text{total moles}} (P_{total})$$

Example 6: A gas mixture contains 0.8 moles of O_2 and 1.2 moles of N_2. If the total pressure of the mixture is 0.5 atm, what is the partial pressure of N_2 in this mixture?

$$\mathbf{P_{gas}\,N_2} = \frac{1.2}{2.0} \times 0.5 = \boxed{\textbf{0.3 atm}}$$

Graham's Law of Diffusion states: The rate of diffusion (movement or spread) of a gas is proportional to its mass. In other words, a lighter gas will diffuse faster than a heavier gas.

Boyle's Law states: At **constant temperature**, the volume of a gas is inversely proportional to the pressure on the gas. In other words, as pressure increases, volume (space) of the gas decreases by the same factor. The Boyle's law equation given below can be used to calculate the new volume of a gas when pressure on the gas is changed at constant temperature.

$$P_1 V_1 = P_2 V_2$$

Example 7: At constant temperature, what is the new volume of a 3 L sample of O_2 gas if its pressure is changed from 0.5 atm to 0.25 atm?

$$(0.5)(3) = (0.25)(V_2)$$

$$\boxed{6 \text{ L}} = V_2$$

Charles' Law states: At **constant pressure**, the volume of a gas is directly proportional to the *Kelvin* temperature of the gas. In other words, as temperature increases, volume (space) increases by the same factor.
The Charles' law equation given below can be used to calculate the new volume of a gas when temperature of the gas is changed at constant pressure.

$$\frac{V_1}{T_1} = \frac{V_2}{T_2}$$

Example 8: The volume of a confined gas is 25 mL at 280 K. At what temperature would the gas volume be 75 mL if the pressure is held constant?

$$\frac{25}{280} = \frac{75}{T_2}$$

$$\boxed{840 \text{ K}} = T_2$$

Gay-Lussac's Law states: At **constant volume**, the pressure of a gas is directly proportional to the *Kelvin* temperature of the gas. In other words, as temperature increases, pressure increases by the same factor.
The Gay-Lussac's law equation given below can be used to calculate the new pressure of a gas when temperature of the gas is changed at constant volume.

$$\frac{P_1}{T_1} = \frac{P_2}{T_2}$$

Example 9: At constant volume, pressure on a gas changes from 45 kPa to 50 kPa when the temperature of the gas is changed to 340K. What was the initial temperature of the gas?

$$\frac{45}{T_1} = \frac{50}{340}$$

$$T_1 = \boxed{306 \text{ K}}$$

Combined Gas Law describes a gas behavior when all three factors (volume, pressure, and temperature) of the gas are changing: In the combined gas law, the only constant is the mass of the gas. The combined gas law equation below can be used to solve any problem related to the above three gas laws.

$$\frac{P_1 V_1}{T_1} = \frac{P_2 V_2}{T_2}$$

Table T equation

P = pressure
V = volume
T = Kelvin temperature
1 = initial condition
2 = new condition

Example 10: A 30 mL sample of H_2 gas is at 1 atm and 200 K. What will be its new volume at 2.0 atm and 600 K?

$$\frac{(1)(30)}{200} = \frac{(2.0) V_2}{600}$$

$$\boxed{45 \text{ mL}} = V_2$$

Pressure, Volume, and Temperature

Pressure

Pressure of a gas is a measure of how much force is put on a confined gas.

Units: atmospheres (atm) or Kilopascals (kPa)   1 atm = 101.3 kPa

Volume

Volume of a gas measures the space a confined gas occupies (takes up).
Volume of a gas is the space of the container in which the gas is placed.

Units: milliliters (mL) or centimeters cube (cm³) 1 mL = 1 cm³
1 L = 1000 mL

Temperature

Temperature of a gas is a measure of the average kinetic energy of the gas particles. As temperature increases, gas particles move faster, and their average kinetic energy increases.

Units: degrees Celsius (°C) or Kelvin (K) $K = °C + 273$

Standard Temperature and Pressure: STP

| Standard Temperature: **273 K** or **0°C** | **REFERENCE** |
| Standard Pressure: **1 atm** or **101.3 kPa** | **TABLE A** |

In some gas law problems, the temperature and/or pressure of the gas may be given at STP.
When a gas is said to be at STP in a gas law problem, the above values should be substituted into a gas law equation as needed. Be sure the unit of STP you choose is the same as the other unit in the given question.

NOTE: Always use Kelvin temperature in all gas law calculations.

Example 11

*Hydrogen gas has a volume of 100 mL at **STP**. If temperature and pressure are changed to 546 K and 0.5 atm respectively, what will be the new volume of the gas?*

$V_1 = 100$ mL $V_2 = ?$

STP { $T_1 = 273$ K $T_2 = 546$ K

$P_1 = 1$ atm $P_2 = 0.5$ atm

$$\frac{P_1 V_1}{T_1} = \frac{P_2 V_2}{T_2}$$

$$\frac{(1)(100)}{273} = \frac{(0.5)(V_2)}{546} \quad setup$$

400 mL $= V_2$ *calculated result*

Lesson 5: Physical and Chemical Properties and Changes

Introduction

Properties are sets of characteristics that can be used to identify and classify matter. Two types of properties of matter are physical and chemical properties.

In this lesson, you will learn the differences between physical and chemical properties as well as the differences between physical and chemical changes of matter.

A **physical property** is a characteristic of a substance that can be observed or measured without changing the chemical composition of the substance. Some physical properties of a substance depend on sample size or amount, and some do not.

Extensive properties depend on sample size or amount present. Mass, weight and volume are examples of *extensive properties.*

Intensive properties do not depend on sample size or amount. Melting, freezing and boiling points, density, solubility, color, odor, conductivity, luster, and hardness are *intensive properties.*

Differences in physical properties of substances make it possible to separate one substance from another in a mixture.

A **physical change** is a change of a substance from one form to another without changing its chemical composition.

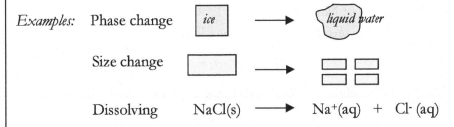

Examples: Phase change   ice ⟶ liquid water

Size change

Dissolving   NaCl(s) ⟶ Na⁺(aq) + Cl⁻(aq)

A **chemical property** is a characteristic of a substance that is observed or measured through interaction with other substances.

Examples:

It burns, it combusts, it decomposes, it reacts with, it combines with, or it rusts are some of the phrases that can be used to describe chemical properties of a substance.

A **chemical change** is a change in composition and properties of one substance to those of other substances. **Chemical reactions** are ways by which chemical changes of substances occur.

Types of chemical reactions include *synthesis, decomposition, single replacement, and double replacement.*

You will learn more about these reactions in Topic 5.

Practice Questions

Lesson 1: Types of Matter

Define the following terms and answer questions below.

1. Pure substance   2. Mixture 3. Element 4. Compound 5. Aqueous solution
6. Law of definite proportion   7. Homogeneous mixture
8. Heterogeneous mixture   9. Filtration   10. Distillation

11. Which property correctly describes all compounds?
    1) They are always homogeneous   3) They can be physically separated
    2) They are always heterogeneous   4) They cannot be decomposed

12. Bronze contains 90 to 95 percent copper and 5 to 10 percent tin. Because these percentages can vary, bronze is classified as
    1) A compound   2) A mixture   3) An element   4) A substance

13. When sample X is passed through a filter a white residue, Y, remains on the filter paper and a clear liquid, Z, passes through. When liquid Z is vaporized, another white residue remains. Sample X is best classified as
    1) An element   3) A compound
    2) A heterogeneous mixture   4) A homogeneous mixture

14. Which is a formula of a mixture of substances?
    1) $Cl_2(g)$ 2) $MgCl_2(s)$ 3) $H_2O(l)$ 4) $HF(aq)$

15. The formula $N_2(g)$ is best classified as
    1) A compound   2) A mixture   3) An element   4) A solution

Lesson 2: Phases of Matter

Define the following terms and answer questions below.
16. Solid   17. Liquid 18. Gas 19. Condensation 20. Evaporation 21. Sublimation
22. Deposition 23. Exothermic 24. Endothermic 25. Temperature
26. Kinetic energy   27. Potential energy   28. Ice/liquid equilibrium
29. Water/steam equilibrium   30. Phase change diagram   31. Absolute Zero

32. Particles in which phase are arranged in a regular geometric pattern?
    1) Solid   2) Aqueous   3) Liquid   4) Gas

33. Which formula correctly represents a substance that has a definite volume but no definite shape?
    1) $Hg(l)$ 2) $HCl(g)$ 3) $Na(s)$ 4) $H_2(g)$

34. Which equation is showing sublimation of iodine?
    1) $I_2(g) \rightarrow I_2(s)$ 3) $I_2(s) \rightarrow I_2(l)$
    2) $I_2(s) \rightarrow I_2(g)$ 4) $I_2(g) \rightarrow I_2(l)$

35. Which temperature of a solid substance will have particles with the highest kinetic energy?
    1) 273 K   2) 373 K   3) 170°C   4) 70°C

36. Which change in temperature of a sample of water would result in the smallest decrease in the average kinetic energy of its molecules?
    1) 25°C to 32°C   3) 15°C to 9°C
    2) 25°C to 29°C   4) 12°C to 2°C

Answer questions 37 and 38 based on the information and diagram below.
The graph below represents the uniform cooling of an unknown substance, starting
with the substance as a gas above its boiling point.

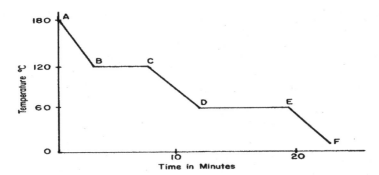

37. What is the melting point of the substance?
   1) 0°C   2) 60°C   3) 120°C   4) 180°C

38. During which segment is the substance's kinetic energy remaining constant?
   1) AB   2) BC   4) CD   4) EF

Lesson 3: Heat and Heat Calculations
Define the following terms and answer multiple choice questions below.
 39. Heat   40. Joules   41. Specific heat capacity   42. Heat of fusion
 43. Heat of vaporization   44. Calorimeter

45. The heat of fusion of ice is 334 Joules per gram. Adding 334 Joules to one gram of
   ice at STP will cause the ice to
   1) Increase in temperature
   2) Decrease in Temperature
   3) Change to water at a higher temperature
   4) Change to water at the same temperature

46. A solid material X is placed in liquid Y. Heat will flow from Y to X when the
   temperature of
   1) Y is 20°C and X is 30°C   3) Y is 15°C and X 10°C
   2) Y is 10°C and X is 20°C   4) Y is 30°C and X is 40°C

47. How many kilojoules of heat are needed to raise the temperature of 500 g of water
   from 15°C to 20°C?
   1) 4.20 kJ   2) 10.5 kJ   3) 32.0 kJ   4) 105 kJ

48. What amount of heat energy is needed to change a 20 g sample of water at 100°C to
   steam at the same temperature?
   1) 905 kJ   2) 0.200 kJ   3) 1.13 kJ   4) 45.2 kJ

49. What is the total number of joules of heat energy released by a 2.5 gram sample of
   water to change to ice at 0°C?
   1) 133 J   2) 8.4 J   3) 10.5 J   4) 835 J

50. What is the heat of vaporization of an unknown liquid if 5 grams of this liquid
   requires 22 kJ of heat to change to vapor at its boiling point?
   1) 4.4 J/g   2) 100 J/g   3) 4400 J/g   4) 11300 J/g

Lesson 4: Gas Laws and Gas Law Calculations

Define the following terms and answer multiple choice questions below.

51. Ideal gas   52.Kinetic molecular theory   53. Avogadro's law   54. Boyle's law
55.Charles' law   56. Gay-Lussac's law   57. Dalton's law of partial pressure

58. The kinetic molecular theory assumes that the particles of an ideal gas
    1) Are in random, constant, straight-line motion
    2) Are arranged in a regular geometric pattern
    3) Have strong attractive forces between them
    4) Have collisions that result in the system losing energy

59. Under which two conditions do real gases behave least like an ideal gas?
    1) High pressure and low temperature   3) High pressure and high temperature
    2) Low pressure and high temperature   4) Low pressure and low temperature

60. Which graph best illustrates the relationship between the Kelvin temperature of a
    gas and its volume when the pressure on the gas is held constant?

1) 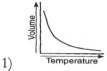   2)   3)   4)

61. Which gas is least likely to obey the ideal gas model under the same temperature
    and pressure?
    1) Xe   2) Kr   3) Ne   4) He

62. A real gas will behave most like an ideal gas under which conditions of
    temperature and pressure?
    1) 273 K and 1 atm   3) 546 K and 2 atm
    2) 273 K and 2 atm   4) 546 K and 1 atm

63. Under which conditions would a 2 L sample of O_2 has the same number of
    molecules as a 2 L sample of N_2 that is at STP?
    1) 0 K and 1 atm   3) 0 K and 2 atm
    2) 273 K and 1 atm   4) 273 K and 2 atm

64. A gas sample has a volume of 12 liters at 0°C and 0.5 atm. What will be
    the new volume of the gas when the pressure is changed to 1 atm and the
    temperature is held constant?
    1) 24 L   2) 18 L   3) 12 L   4) 6.0 L

65. At STP, a gas has a volume of 250 mL. If the pressure remained constant, at what
    Kelvin temperature would the gas have a volume of 50 mL?
    1) 137 K   2) 500 K   3) 54.6 K   4) 273 K

66. A gas has a pressure of 120 kPa and a volume of 50.0 milliliters when its
    temperature is 127°C. What volume will the gas occupy at a pressure of 60 kPa
    and at a temperature of -73°C?
    1) 12.5 mL   2) 50.0 mL   3) 100 mL   4) 200 mL

Lesson 5: Physical and Chemical Properties and Changes

Define the following terms and answer multiple choice questions below.

67. physical property
68. chemical property
69. physical change
70. chemical change

71. Which is a physical property of sodium?
    1) It is flammable
    2) It is shiny
    3) It reacts with water
    4) It reacts with chlorine

72. Which is a chemical property of water?
    1) It freezes   2) It evaporates   3) It boils   4) It decomposes

73. Which is a physical change of iodine?
    1) It can decompose into two iodine atoms
    2) Iodine can dissolve in water
    3) Iodine can react with sugar
    4) Iodine can react with hydrogen

74. An example of a chemical change is
    1) Boiling of water
    2) Dissolving of sodium bromide
    3) Burning of magnesium
    4) Breaking of sulfur into pieces

75. Given the particle diagram representing four molecules of a substance.

Which particle diagram best represents this same substance after a physical change has taken place?

1)    2)   3)    4)

Topic Mastery / Constructed Response

76. A 12 gram sample of water initially at 32°C loses 780 joules of heat. What is the new temperature of the water?

77. A 50 L sample of O_2 gas is at STP. When the temperature of the gas is changed to 64°C, the new volume of the gas is 20 L. What is the new pressure of the gas in kilopascals?

The graph below is showing the change in temperature of a 15 g sample of a substance from below its melting point as heat is added at a rate of 20 kJ/min.

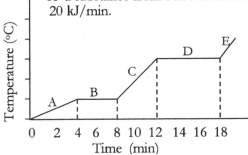

78. Calculate the heat of fusion of the substance.

79. a) How would the heat of vaporization of the substance compare to the heat of fusion?

b) Explain your answer using information from the graph.

Additional Materials

Ideal Gas Equation

The **ideal gas equation** relates all three factors (Pressure, Volume, and Temperature) of a gas, as well as the number of moles, n, of the gas. When three variables of a gas are known, the ideal gas equation below can be used to calculate the fourth variable.

$$PV = nRT$$

n = the number of moles of the gas

R = the universal gas constant,
  0.0821 L · atm /(mol·K)

T must always be in Kelvin

Graham's Law of Effusion

When speeds of two gases are compared the lighter gas will diffuse (spread out) faster than the heavier gas. But how much faster? **Graham's Law** states that under the same conditions of temperature and pressure, the rate (speed) at which gases effuse (escape through a pinhole) is inversely proportional to the square root of their molecular masses.

$$\frac{r_1}{r_2} = \sqrt{\frac{M_2}{M_1}}$$

r₁ = rate (speed) of Gas 1
r₂ = rate (speed) of Gas 2
M₁ = molecular mass of Gas 1
M₂ = molecular mass of Gas 2

The calculated result shows how much faster (or slower) one gas travels relatively to another gas.

Example 12

A 5.0 L sample of an ideal gas at 310 K exerts a pressure of 2.0 atm on the walls of its container. What is the number of moles of the gas?

$$n = \frac{PV}{RT} = \frac{(2.0)\,(5.0)}{(0.0821)\,(310)}$$

n = moles = **0.39 moles**

Example 13
How much faster does hydrogen gas, H₂, escape through a hole of a container than sulfur dioxide, SO₂ ?

$$\frac{r_{H2}}{r_{SO2}} = \sqrt{\frac{\text{mass of } SO_2}{\text{mass of } H_2}}$$

$$\frac{r_{H2}}{r_{SO2}} = \sqrt{\frac{64\text{ g}}{2\text{ g}}} = \boxed{\textbf{5.63 times}}$$

80. How many moles of an ideal gas take up 35 L of volume at 25°C and 1.5 atm?

81. 2.39 moles of an ideal gas at 300 K occupy 29.0 L . What is the pressure?

82. 0.105 moles of an ideal gas occupy 5.00 L at a pressure of 0.975 atm. What is the temperature of the gas in Kelvin?

83. Of these gases; SO_2, CO, HCl, and NO_2 .
    a) Which will travel the fastest?   b) Which will travel the slowest?

84. How much faster does NO(g) effuse in comparison to N_2O_5(g)?

85. Calculate the rate of effusion of NO_2 in comparison to SO_2 at the same temperature and pressure.

86. An unknown gas effuses 1.66 times more rapidly than CO_2. What is the molar mass of the unknown gas?

87. A sample of hydrogen gas effuses through a porous container 9 times faster than an unknown gas. Estimate the molar mass of the unknown gas.

Lesson 1: Arrangement of the Elements

Introduction

There are more than 100 known elements. Most of the elements are naturally occurring, while a few are artificially produced. The modern Periodic Table contains all known elements. These elements are arranged on the Periodic Table in order of increasing atomic number.

Important information about an element can be found in the box of the element on the Periodic Table .

In this lesson, you will learn about the arrangement of the elements on the Periodic Table.

Properties of the Modern Periodic Table

The modern Periodic Table, which was created by Dmitri Mendeleev, has the following properties:

. Elements are arranged in the order of increasing atomic number

. The three types of elements found on the Periodic Table are metals, nonmetals, and metalloids

. More than two thirds (majority) of the elements are metals

. The Periodic Table contains elements that are in all three phases (solid, liquid, and gas) at STP

. The majority of the elements exist as solids

. Only two (mercury and bromine) are liquids. A few are gases.

. An element's symbol can be one (O), two (Na), or three (Uub) letters. The first letter must always be capitalized. The second (or third) letter must be lowercase.

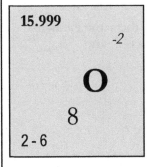

15.999	Atomic Mass	196.967
-2	*Selected Oxidation states (charges)*	+1 +2
O	**Element's symbol**	**Au**
8	Atomic number	79
2 - 6	Electron configuration	2 - 8 -18 - 32 -18 - 1

Information listed in the box for each element is related to the atomic structure of that element. Atomic Structure is discussed in Topic 3.

Groups and Periods

Groups are the vertical arrangements of the elements. There are 18 groups on the Periodic Table of the Elements. Group names are listed below.

Group 1 :   Alkali metals

Group 2 :   Alkaline earth metals

Group 3 – 12: Transition metals

Group 17:   Halogens

Group 18:   Noble (Inert) gases

Elements in the same group have the same number of valence electrons. Valence electrons are electrons in the outermost energy level of an atom. Elements in the same group have similar chemical properties and reactivity due to similarity in their number of valence electrons.

Periods are the horizontal rows of the Periodic Table. Elements in the same period have the same number of occupied electron shells. There are seven (7) Periods on the Periodic Table of the Elements.

The periodic Law states that: The properties of the elements are a periodic function of their atomic numbers. In other words, by arranging the elements in order of increasing atomic number, a new period of elements is formed so that elements with similar chemical properties fall in the same group.

Allotropes

Allotropes are different molecular forms of the same element in the same state.

Allotropes of the same element have different molecular structures.

Differences in molecular structures give allotropes of the same element different physical properties (color, shape, density, mass..) and different chemical properties (reactivity).

Examples of some common allotropes:

Oxygen allotropes: oxygen gas (O_2) and Ozone (O_3)

Carbon allotropes: Diamond, graphite, and buckminsterfullerene

Phosphorus allotropes: Red, Black, and White

Lesson 2: Types of Elements and their Properties

Introduction

There are three general categories of elements: metals, nonmetals and metalloids. Elements in each category have a set of physical and chemical properties that can be used to distinguish them apart from elements in other categories.

In this lesson, you will learn about the three different types of elements, their location on the Periodic Table, and their properties.

Location of metals, metalloids, and nonmetals

1	2	3	4	5	6	7	8	9	10	11	12	13	14	15	16	17	18
H		metals		metalloids		nonmetals											He
Li	Be											B	C	N	O	F	Ne
Na	Mg											Al	Si	P	S	Cl	Ar
K	Ca	Sc	Ti	V	Cr	Mn	Fe	Co	Ni	Cu	Zn	Ga	Ge	As	Se	Br	Kr
Rb	Sr	Y	Zr	Nb	Mo	Tc	Ru	Rh	Pd	Ag	Cd	In	Sn	Sb	Te	I	Xe
Cs	Ba	La	Hf	Ta	W	Re	Os	Ir	Pt	Au	Hg	Ti	Pb	Bi	Po	At	Rn
Fr	Ra	Ac	Rf	Db	Sg	Bh	Hs	Mt	Ds	Rg	Cn	Uut	Uuq	Uup	Uuh	Uus	Uuo

La	Ce	Pr	Nd	Pm	Sm	Eu	Gd	Tb	Dy	Ho	Er	Tm	Yb	Lu
Ac	Th	Pa	U	Np	Pu	Am	Cm	Bk	Cf	Es	Fm	Md	No	Lr

Properties of the Elements

There are several physical properties that are used to describe and identify the elements. Below are terms and definitions of these properties.

Malleable describes a solid that is easily hammered into a thin sheet.

Ductile describes a solid that is easily drawn into thin wire.

Brittle describes a solid that is easily broken or shattered into pieces when struck

Luster describes the shininess of a substance.

Conductivity describes the ability of heat or electricity to flow through a substance

Electronegativity describes an atom's ability to attract electrons from another atom during bonding.

Ionization energy describes an atom's ability to lose its most loosely bound valence electrons.

Atomic radius describes the size of the atom of an element.

Density describes the mass to volume ratio of an element

See **Table S** for values to these four properties

Ionic radius describes the size of the element after it has lost or gained electrons to form an ion.

Properties of Metals, Metalloids, and Nonmetals

Metal elements are located to the left of the Periodic Table.
All elements in Groups 1 – 12 (except hydrogen) are classified as a metal. The rest of the metal elements are found near the bottom of Groups 13, 14 and 15. The majority (about 75%) of the elements are metals.

General properties of metals are listed below.
- All metals (except Hg) exist as a solid at STP. Hg is the only liquid metal.
- Metals are malleable, ductile, and have luster
- Metals tend to have high conductivity due to their mobile valence electrons
- Metals tend to have low electronegativity values (because they do not attract electrons easily)
- Metals tend to have low ionization energy values (because they lose their electrons easily)
- Metals lose electrons and form a positive ion during chemical bonding
- Radius (size) of a metal atom decreases as it loses electrons and forms a positive (+) ion
- The size of a +metal ion (ionic radius) is always smaller than the size of the neutral atom (atomic radius)

Metalloids are the elements located between the metals and the nonmetals. Metalloid elements are located along the zigzag line of the Periodic Table.
General properties of metalloids are listed below.
- Metalloids tend to have properties of both the metals and nonmetals
- Metalloid properties are more like those of metals and less like nonmetals
- Metalloids exist only as solids at STP

Nonmetal elements are located to the right of the Periodic Table.
All elements in Groups 17 and 18 (except astatine, At) are classified as nonmetals. The rest of the nonmetals are found near the top of Groups 14, 15, and 16. Hydrogen is also a nonmetal.
General properties of nonmetals are listed below.
- Nonmetals are found in all three phases: solid, liquid, and gas.
- Most nonmetals are either a gas or solid at STP. Br is the only liquid nonmetal
- Solid nonmetals are generally brittle and dull (lack luster, not shiny)
- Nonmetals have low (poor) electrical and heat conductivity
- Nonmetals tend to have high electronegativity values (because they attract or gain electrons easily)
- Nonmetals tend to have high ionization values (because they do not lose their electrons easily)
- Nonmetals generally gain electrons and form a negative ion during bonding
- Radius of a nonmetal atom increases as it gains electrons and forms a negative (–) ion
- The size of the - nonmetal ion (ionic radius) is always bigger than that of the neutral atom (atomic radius)

Summary of Types of Elements and Properties

	Phases at STP	Physical properties	Conductivity	Electrone-gativity	Ionization energy	In bonding	Common ion	Ionic size (radius)
Metals	Solid Liquid	Malleable Luster Ductile	High	Low	Low	Lose electrons	+ (positive)	Smaller than atom
Nonmetals	Solid Liquid Gas	Brittle Dull	Low	High	High	Gain electron	- (negative)	Bigger than atom
Metalloids	Solid only	Properties of metals and nonmetals	Low	-	-	Lose electrons	+ (positive)	Smaller than atom

Properties of Groups

According to the Periodic Law, an element falls into a particular group based on its properties. Elements with similar chemical properties belong in the same group. Below is a table summarizing group names and general characteristics of each group.

Group number	Group name	Types of elements in the group	Phases (at STP)	Valence electrons (during bonding)	Common oxidation number (charge)	Chemical bonding (general formula)
1	Alkali metals	Metal	Solid (all)	1 (lose)	+1	XY with halogens (17) X_2O with oxygen (16)
2	Alkaline earth	Metal	Solid (all)	2 (lose)	+2	MY_2 with halogens (17) MO with oxygen (16))
3-12	Transition metals	Metal	Liquid (Hg) Solid (the rest)	(lose)	Multiple + charges	varies (form colorful compounds)
13	-	Metalloid Metal	Solid (all	3 (lose)	+3	LY_3 with halogens (17) L_2O_3 with oxygen (16)
14	-	Nonmetal Metalloid Metal	Solid (all)	4 (some share) (some lose)	vary	varies
15	-	Nonmetal Metalloid Metal	Gas (N) Solid (the rest)	5 (gain or share)	-3	varies
16	Oxygen group	Nonmetal Metalloid	Gas (O) Solid (the rest)	6 (gain or share)	-2	X_2O with alkali metals (1) MO with alkaline earth (2)
17	Halogens (Diatomic)	Nonmetal	Gas (F and Cl) Liquid (Br) Solid (I)	7 (gain or share)	-1	XY with alkali metals (1) MY with alkaline earths (2)
18	Noble gases (Monatomic)	Nonmetal	Gas (all)	8 (neither gain nor share)	0	Forms very few compounds. XeF_4 is the most common.

The Periodic Table of the Elements

Atomic Mass
Element's Symbol
Atomic Number
e- configuration

30.973	-3 +3 +5
P	Selected
15	oxidation
2 – 8 – 5	states

Metals
Metalloid elements
Nonmetals

Alkali metals (1)
Alkaline earth metals (2)
Transition metals (3-12)
Halogens (17)
Noble gases (18)

Group

Period 1

1																		18
1.007 +1 H 1 1																		4.002 0 He 2 2

Groups: 1, 2, 3, 4, 5, 6, 7, 8, 9, 10, 11, 12, 13, 14, 15, 16, 17, 18

Period 2

- 6.941 +1 Li 3 2-1
- 9.012 +2 Be 4 2-2
- 10.81 +3 B 5 2-3
- 12.011 +3 C 6 2-4
- 14.006 -3 +2 +4 +5 N 7 2-5
- 15.999 -2 O 8 2-6
- 18.998 -1 F 9 2-7
- 20.179 0 Ne 10 2-8

Period 3

- 22.989 +1 Na 11 2-8-1
- 24.305 +2 Mg 12 2-8-2
- 26.981 +3 Al 13 2-8-3
- 28.085 -4 +2 +4 Si 14 2-8-4
- 30.973 -3 +3 +5 P 15 2-8-5
- 32.06 -2 +4 +6 S 16 2-8-6
- 35.453 -1 +5 Cl 17 2-8-7
- 39.948 0 Ar 18 2-8-8

Period 4

- 39.09 +1 K 19 2-8-8-1
- 40.06 +2 Ca 20 2-8-8-2
- 44.9559 +3 Sc 21 2-8-9-2
- 47.88 +3 +4 Ti 22 2-8-10-2
- 50.9414 +2 +3 +4 V 23 2-8-11-2
- 51.996 +2 +3 +6 Cr 24 2-8-13-1
- 54.938 +2 +3 +6 Mn 25 2-8-13-2
- 55.847 +2 +3 Fe 26 2-8-14-2
- 58.933 +2 +3 Co 27 2-8-15-2
- 58.69 +2 +3 Ni 28 2-8-16-2
- 63.546 +1 +2 Cu 29 2-8-18-1
- 65.39 +2 Zn 30 2-8-18-2
- 69.72 +3 Ga 31 2-8-18-3
- 72.59 -4 +2 +4 Ge 32 2-8-18-4
- 74.921 -3 +3 +5 As 33 2-8-18-5
- 78.96 -2 +4 +6 Se 34 2-8-18-6
- 79.904 -1 +5 Br 35 2-8-18-7
- 83.80 0 Kr 36 2-8-18-8

Period 5

- 85.468 +1 Rb 37 2-8-18-8-1
- 87.62 +2 Sr 38 2-8-18-8-2
- 88.905 +3 Y 39 2-8-18-9-2
- 91.224 +4 Zr 40 2-8-18-10-2
- 92.906 +3 +5 Nb 41 2-8-18-12-1
- 95.94 +6 Mo 42 2-8-18-13-1
- [98] +4 +6 +7 Tc 43 2-8-18-13-2
- 101.07 +3 +6 +8 Ru 44 2-8-18-15-1
- 102.906 +3 Rh 45 2-8-18-16-1
- 106.42 +2 +4 Pd 46 2-8-18-18
- 107.868 +1 Ag 47 2-8-18-18-1
- 112.41 +2 Cd 48 2-8-18-18-2
- 114.82 +3 In 49 2-8-18-18-3
- 118.71 +2 +4 Sn 50 2-8-18-18-4
- 121.75 -3 +3 +5 Sb 51 2-8-18-18-5
- 127.60 -2 +4 +6 Te 52 2-8-18-18-6
- 126.905 -1 +1 +5 +7 I 53 2-8-18-18-7
- 131.29 0 +2 +4 +6 Xe 54 2-8-18-18-8

Period 6

- 132.91 +1 Cs 55 2-8-18-18-8-1
- 137.33 +2 Ba 56 2-8-18-18-8-2
- 138.906 +3 La 57 2-8-18-18-9-2
- 178.49 +4 Hf 72 -18-32-10-2
- 180.948 +5 Ta 73 2-8-18-32-11-2
- 183.85 +6 W 74 2-8-18-32-12-2
- 183.85 +4 +6 +7 Re 75 2-8-18-32-13-2
- 190.2 +3 +4 +6 +8 Os 76 2-8-18-32-14-2
- 192.22 +3 +4 Ir 77 -18-32-15-2
- 195.08 +2 +4 Pt 78 -18-32-17-1
- 196.967 +1 +3 Au 79 -18-32-18-1
- 200.59 +1 +2 Hg 80 -18-32-18-2
- 204.383 +1 +3 Tl 81 -18-32-18-3
- 207.2. +2 +4 Pb 82 -18-32-18-4
- 208.980 +3 +5 Bi 83 -18-32-18-5
- [209] +2 +4 Po 84 -18-32-18-6
- [210] -1 +1 +5 +7 At 85 -18-32-18-7
- [222] +2 +4 Rn 86 -18-32-18-8

Period 7

- [223] +1 Fr 87 -18-32-18-8-1
- 226.025 +2 Ra 88 -18-32-18-8-2
- 227.028 +3 Ac 89 -18-32-18-9-2
- [261] +3 Rf 104
- [262] +3 Db 105
- [262] Sg 106
- [272] Bh 107
- [277] Hs 108
- [276] Mt 109
- [281] Ds 110
- [280] Rg 111
- [285] Cn 112
- [284] Uut 113
- [289] Uuq 114
- [288] Uup 115
- [292] Uuh 116
- (?) Uus 117
- [294] Uuo 118

Lanthanoid Series

- 104.12 +3 Ce 58
- 140.908 +3 Pr 59
- 144.24 +3 Nd 60
- [145] Pm 61
- 150.36 +2 +3 Sm 62
- 151.96 +2 +3 Eu 63
- 157.25 +2 +3 Gd 64
- 158.925 +3 Tb 65
- 162.50 +3 Dy 66
- 164.930 +3 Ho 67
- 167.26 +3 Er 68
- 168.934 +3 Tm 69
- 173.04 +2 +3 Yb 70
- 174.967 +3 Lu 71

Actinoid Series

- 232.038 +4 Th 90
- 231.036 +4 +5 Pa 91
- 238.029 +3 +4 +5 +6 U 92
- 237.029 +3 +4 +5 +6 Np 93
- [244] +3 +4 +5 +6 Pu 94
- [243] +3 +4 +5 +6 Am 95
- [247] +3 Cm 96
- [247] +3 Bk 97
- [251] +3 Cf 98
- [252] +3 Es 99
- [257] +3 Fm 100
- [258] +3 Md 101
- [259] +3 No 102
- [260] +3 Lr 103

Rare Earth metals

Group Names and Characteristics   (also see table on page 23)

Group 1: Alkali metals
. Found in nature as compounds (not as free elements) due to high reactivity
. Are obtained from electrolytic reduction of fused salts (NaCl, KBr, etc.)
. Francium is the most reactive metal in Group 1, and of all metals
. Francium is also radioactive
. All alkali metals exist as solids at room temperature

Group 2: Alkaline Earth metals
. Found in nature as compounds (not as free elements) due to high reactivity.
. Are obtained from fused salt compounds ($MgCl_2$, $CaBr_2$, etc.)
. All alkaline earth metals exist as solids at room temperature

Group 3 – 12: Transition metals
. Properties of these elements vary widely
. They tend to form multiple oxidation numbers
. Most can lose electrons in two or more different sublevels of their atoms
. Their ions usually form colorful compounds
    Examples: **$CuCl_2$** – is a bluish color compound
                     $FeCl_2$ – is a reddish-orange color compound

Group 17: Halogens
. Exist as diatomic (two-atom) molecules (F_2 , Br_2..etc)
. The only group with elements in all three phases at STP
. Fluorine is the most reactive of the group, and of all nonmetals
. Halogens are obtained from fused salt compounds (NaF, NaCl..etc)
. Astatine (At) in this group is a metalloid

Group 18: Noble Gases
. Exist as monatomic (one-atom) molecules   (Ne, He, Kr, etc)
. They all have full and stable valence shells with 8 electrons (He is full with just 2 electrons)
. All are very stable and non-reactive (do not form many compounds)
. Argon (Ar) and Xenon (Xe) have been found to produce a few stable compounds with fluorine.
        Ex. **XeF_4** (xenon tetrafluoride)

Lesson 3: Periodic Trends

Introduction

Periodic trends refer to patterns of properties that exist as elements are considered from one end of the table to the other.

Trend in atomic number is a good example (and the most obvious) of a periodic trend found on the Periodic Table.

As elements are considered one after the other from:

Left to **Right** across a Period: Atomic number of the elements increases.

Bottom to **Top** up a Group: Atomic number of the elements decreases.

Many other trends exist on the Periodic Table even though they may not be so obvious.

In this lesson, you will learn of the following trends.

> Trends in atomic radius (size).
> Trends in metallic and nonmetallic properties.
> Trends in electronegativity and ionization energy.

Summary of Periodic Trends

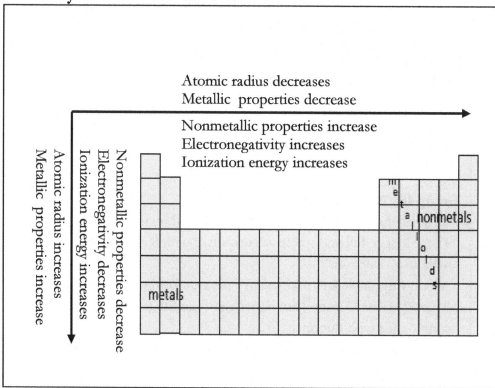

Trends in Atomic Radius

Atomic radius is defined as half the distance between two nuclei of the same atom when they are joined together.

Atomic radius measurement gives a good approximation of the size of each atom. The trend in atomic radius is as follows.

Top to Bottom down a Group:
Atomic size (radius) increases due to an increase in the number of *electron shells*.

H — One shell: Smallest radius

Li

Left to Right across a Period:
Atomic size (radius) decreases due to an increase in *nuclear charge*.

Na — Three shells: Largest radius

electron shells

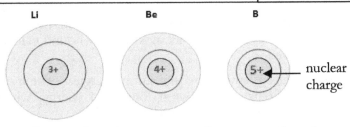

Li   Be   B

3+   4+   5+ — nuclear charge

Smallest nuclear charge   Greatest nuclear charge
Biggest radius (size)   Smallest radius (size)

Use Reference Table S to note and compare atomic radii of atoms.

Trends in Metallic and Nonmetallic Properties

Trends in properties and reactivity vary between metals and nonmetals. The bottom left corner contains the most reactive metals. ***Francium*** is the most reactive of all metals. The top right corner contains the most reactive nonmetals. ***Fluorine*** is the most reactive of all nonmetals.

Trends in metallic and nonmetallic properties and reactivity are summarized below.

Top to Bottom down a Group:
Metallic properties and reactivity increase *(ex. K is more reactive than Na)*
Nonmetallic properties and reactivity decrease *(ex. Br is less reactive than Cl)*

LEFT to Right across a Period:
Metallic properties and reactivity decrease. *(ex. Mg is less metallic than Na)*
Nonmetallic properties and reactivity increase. *(ex. Cl is more nonmetallic than S)*

Trends in Electronegativity and Ionization Energy

Electronegativity defines an atom's ability to attract (or gain) electrons from another atom during chemical bonding. The electronegativity value assigned to each element is relative to one another. The higher the electronegativity value, the more likely it is for the atom to attract (or gain) electrons and form a negative ion during bonding.

Fluorine (F) is assigned the highest electronegativity value of 4.0.

Francium (Fr) is assigned the lowest electronegativity value of 0.7 .

This means that of all the elements, fluorine has the greatest tendency to attract (or gain) electrons. Francium has the least ability or tendency to attract electrons during bonding.

Ionization energy refers to the amount of energy needed to remove an electron from an atom. The *first ionization energy* is the energy to remove the most loosely bound electron from an atom. Ionization energy measures the tendency of (how likely) an atom to lose electrons and form a positive ion. The lower the first ionization energy of an atom, the easier (the more likely) it is for that atom to lose its most loosely bound valence electron and form a positive ion.

Metals lose electrons because of their low ionization energies. The *alkali metals* in Group 1 generally have the lowest ionization energy, which allows them to lose their one valence electron most readily.

Nonmetals have a low tendency to lose electrons because of their high ionization energies. The *noble gases* in group 18 tend to have the highest ionization energy values. Since these elements already have a full valence shell of electrons, a high amount of energy is required to remove any electron from their atoms.

Trends in electronegativity and ionization energy are as follows.

Top to **Bottom** down a **Group**:
   Electronegativity (tendency to gain or attract electrons) decreases
         due to increase in atomic sizes.
         ex. S will attract electrons less readily than O because S is bigger than O

   Ionization energy (tendency to lose or give up electrons) decreases
         due to increase in atomic sizes.
         ex. S will lose electrons more readily than O because S is bigger than O

Left to **Right** across a **Period**:
   Electronegativity increases due to decrease in atomic sizes.
         ex. S will attract electrons more readily than P because S is smaller than P

   Ionization energy increases due to decrease in atomic sizes.
         ex. S will lose electrons less readily than P because S is smaller than P

Use Reference Table S to note and compare electronegativity and ionization energy values of the elements.

Practice Questions

Lesson 1: Arrangement of the Elements
Define the following terms and answer multiple choice questions below.

1. Periodic Law   2. Group   3. Period   4. Allotrope

5. The observed regularities in the properties of the elements are periodic functions of their
    1) Oxidation state   2) Atomic number   3) Atomic mass   4) Reactivity

6. Which of the following information cannot be found in the box of elements on the Periodic Table?
    1) Oxidation state   2) Atomic number   3) Atomic mass   4) Phase

7. In general, elements within each group of the Periodic Table share similar
    1) Chemical properties   3) Mass numbers
    2) Electron configurations   4) Number of occupied energy levels

8. Which list contains elements with the greatest variation in chemical properties?
    1) O, S and Se   2) N, P and As   3) Be, N, O   4) Ba, Sr and Ca

9. Which element has similar chemical reactivity to the element chlorine?
    1) Bromine   2) Sulfur   3) Argon   4) Calcium

10. Oxygen and sulfur can both form a bond with sodium with similar chemical formulas. The similarity in their formulas is due to
    1) Oxygen and sulfur having the same number of kernel electrons
    2) Oxygen and sulfur having the same number of valence electrons
    3) Oxygen and sulfur having the same number of protons
    4) Oxygen and sulfur having the same molecular structure

Lesson 2: Types of Elements and Properties
Define the following terms and answer multiple choice questions below.

11. Malleable   12. Luster   13. Brittleness   14. Ductile   15. Ionization energy
16. Electronegativity   17. Density   18. Atomic radius   19. Alkali metal
20. Alkaline earth metal   21. Transition element   22. Halogen   23. Noble gas

24. Solid nonmetal elements tend to be
    1) Malleable   2) Brittle   3) Ductile   4) Shiny

25. An element has luster as one of its physical properties. Which is true of this element?
    1) It is a gas   2) It is a metal   3) It is a nonmetal   4) It is a halogen

26. Which properties are characteristics of metallic elements?
    1) Low ionization energy and malleable   3) Brittleness and dullness
    2) Low heat conductivity and luster   4) Brittleness and ductile

27. Which physical characteristic of a solution indicates the presence of a transition element?
    1) Its effect on litmus   2) Its density   3) Its color   4) Its reactivity

28. Element X is a solid at STP. Element X could be a
    1) Metal   3) Metalloid
    2) Nonmetal   4) Metal, nonmetal, or metalloid

29. Which element is a metalloid?
    1) B   2) Al   3) Sn   4) Au

30. Which group contains only metallic elements?
    1) Group 2   2) Group 13   3) Group 14   4) Group 17

31. Which of these elements in Period 2 is likely to form a negative ion?
    1) Oxygen   2) Boron   3) Ne   4) Li

32. Which properties best describe the element silver?
    1) Malleable and low electrical conductivity
    2) Brittle and low electrical conductivity
    3) Malleable and high electrical conductivity
    4) Brittle and high electrical conductivity

33. Which set contains elements that are never found in nature in their atomic state?
    1) C and Na   2) K and S   3) Na and P   4) Na and K

34. A Period 2 element forms a compound with oxygen with a formula of Z_2O?
    Element Z could be
    1) Neon   2) Boron   3) Be   4) Li

35. Element L is in Period 3 of the Periodic Table. Which element is L if it forms
    a compound with bromine with the formula LBr_3?
    1) Na   2) Mg   3) Al   4) Cl

36. The elements potassium and cesium are both classified as
    1) Transition metals   2) Alkali metals   3) Halogens   4) Noble gases

Lesson 3: Periodic Trends

Answer the following multiple choice questions.

37. As the elements in Group 1 of the Periodic Table are considered in order of
    increasing atomic number, the atomic radius of each successive element increases.
    This is primarily due to an increase in the number of
    1) Neutrons in the nucleus   3) Valence electrons
    2) Unpaired electrons   4) Electron shells

38. When the elements within Group 16 are considered in order of increasing atomic
    number, the electronegativity value of successive elements
    1) Increases   2) Decreases   3) Remains the same

39. When the elements within a period on the Periodic Table are considered in order
    of increasing atomic number, the nonmetallic properties of successive elements
    1) Increases   2) Decreases   3) Remains the same

40. When elements within Group 16 are considered in order of decreasing atomic
    number , the first ionization energy of successive elements generally
    1) Increases   2) Decreases   3) Remains the same

41. As the halogens in Group 17 are considered in order from bottom to top , the number of valence electrons of successive elements generally
    1) Increases   2) Decreases   3) Remains the same

42. Which of these Group 14 elements has the smallest atomic radius?
    1) Lead   2) Tin   3) Silicon   4) Carbon

43. Which atom has a bigger atomic radius than an atom of sulfur?
    1) Oxygen   2) Phosphorus   3) Chlorine   4) Argon

44. According to the Periodic Table, which sequence correctly places the elements in? order of increasing atomic size?
    1) Na → Li → H → K   3) Te → Sb → Sn → In
    2) Ba → Sr → Mg → Ca   4) H → He → Li → Be

45. Which of these halogens is the most reactive on the Periodic Table?
    1) I   2) Br   3) Cl   4) F

46. Which of these elements has the most metallic properties ?
    1) Radium   2) Strontium   3) Magnesium   4) Beryllium

47. Which element has the least tendency to lose its valence electrons during bonding?
    1) Potassium   2) Selenium   3) Bromine   4) Calcium

48. Which element has the greatest tendency to attract electrons during bonding?
    1) Se   2) S   3) Te   4) O

49. Which sequence of elements is arranged in order of decreasing tendency to attract electrons during chemical bonding?
    1) Al, Si, P   2) Cs, Na, Li   3) I, Br, Cl   4) C, B, Be

50. Which of these Group 2 elements has the highest eletronegativity value?
    1) Be   2) Mg   3) Ca   4) Sr

Topic Mastery / Constructed Response

51. Explain why hydrogen is not considered to be a member of Group 1 alkali metals.

52. Element X has an atomic radius of 160 pm, and an electronegativity of 1.3. Using the reference tables, identify the elements that X could be. Using other properties on the table, how would you test to see which of these elements you identified is element X.

53. Explain why the chemical reactivity of Group 1 elements increases from top to bottom, while it decreases from top to bottom of Group 17 elements.

54. Mendeleev arranged the Periodic Table in order of increasing atomic masses. Locate iodine and tellurium on the table and note that they are not arranged by increasing mass, and yet Mendeleev placed iodine in Group 17 and tellurium in Group 16.

    a) What is the likely reason that he did not arrange them by increasing mass?

    b) Locate two other elements on the table that are *not* arranged by increasing mass.

Lesson 1: Historical Development of the Modern Atom

Introduction

The **atom** is the most basic unit of matter. Since atoms are very small and cannot be seen with the most sophisticated equipment, several scientists over hundreds of years have proposed different models of atoms to help explain the nature and behavior of matter.

In this lesson, you will learn about these historical scientists, their experiments and their proposed models of the atom.

Atomic Models

The **wave mechanical-model** is the current and the most widely accepted model of the atom. This current model of the atom is due to work and discoveries of many scientists over hundreds of years.

According to the wave-mechanical model:

. Each atom has a small dense positive nucleus

. Electrons are found outside the nucleus in regions called **orbitals**

. An **orbital** is the most probable location of finding an electron in an atom.

Below is a list of historical scientists and their proposed models of the atom.

Diagrams and descriptions of each model are also given below.

John Dalton	**J.J. Thomson**	**Ernest Rutherford**	**Niels Bohr**	**Many scientists**
(earliest)				(current)

Hard sphere model (Cannonball model)	*Plum pudding model*	*Empty space model (Nuclear model)*	*Bohr's model (Planetary model)*	*Wave mechanical (electron cloud)*
.No internal structure	.Electrons and positive charges disperse throughout the atom.	.Small dense positive nucleus . Electrons revolve around the nucleus	. Electrons in specific orbits . Orbits have fixed energy .Orbits create electron shells	.Electrons in orbitals . An orbital is the region of an atom where an electron is likely to be found

Historical Scientific Experiments

Cathode Ray experiment (J.J. Thomson):
Led to the discovery of electrons

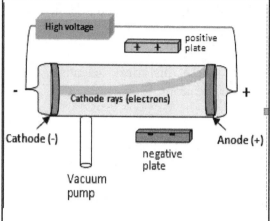

The set up
A tube with a metal disk at each end was set up to trace a beam from an electrical source. The metals were connected to an electrical source.
    Anode: The metal disk that is +.
    Cathode: The metal disk that is -

Results
A beam of light (ray) travels from the cathode end to the anode end of the tube. When electrically charged + and - plates were brought near the tube, the beam (ray) was deflected toward and attracted the positive plate. The beam was repelled by the negative plate.

Conclusions
The beam is composed of negatively charged particles. The term "electron" was later used to describe the negatively charged particles of an atom.

Gold Foil experiment (Rutherford)
Led to the discovery of the nucleus, and the proposed "empty space theory."

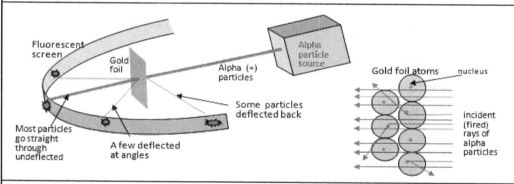

The setup:
Alpha particles (+α) were fired at gold foil. A fluorescent screen was set up around the foil to detect paths of the particles once they had hit the gold foil.

Result 1
Most of the alpha particles went straight through the gold foil undeflected.

Conclusion 1
An atom is mostly empty space (Empty Space Theory)

Result 2
A few of the particles were deflected back or hit the screen at angles.

Conclusion 2
The center of the atom is dense, positive, and very small.

Lesson 2: The Atom

Introduction

Although the atom is described as the smallest unit of matter, it is also composed of much smaller particles called **subatomic particles**. The three **subatomic particles** are: protons, electrons, and neutrons.

In this lesson, you will learn more about the modern atom and the subatomic particles. You will also learn the relationships between the subatomic particles, atomic number, and mass number of an atom.

Structure of the Atom

Atom

The atom is the basic unit of matter. All atoms (except a hydrogen atom with a mass of 1, ^1H) are composed of three subatomic particles: protons, electrons and neutrons.

. An atom is mostly empty space
. An atom has a small dense positive core (nucleus), and negative electron cloud surrounding the nucleus
. Elements are composed of atoms with the same atomic number
. Atoms of the same element are similar
. Atoms of different elements are different

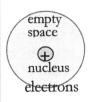

Nucleus

The nucleus is the center (core) of an atom.
. The nucleus contains protons (+) and neutrons (no charge)
. Overall charge of the nucleus is (+) due to the protons
. Compared to the entire atom, the nucleus is small and very dense.
. Most of an atom's mass is due to the mass of its nucleus

the nucleus

Protons

Protons are positively charged subatomic particles found in the nucleus of an atom.
. A proton has a mass of 1 atomic mass unit (amu) and a +1 charge
. A proton is about 1836 times more massive (heavier) than an electron
. Protons are located inside the nucleus
. The number of protons is the atomic # of the element
. All atoms of the same element must have the same number of protons
. The number of protons in the nucleus is also the **nuclear charge** of the element

Li nucleus

. Atomic #
. # of protons
. Nuclear Charge

Electrons

Electrons are negatively charged subatomic particles found in orbitals outside the nucleus of an atom.

. An electron has insignificant mass (zero) and -1 charge
. Mass is $1/1836^{th}$ that of a proton (or neutron)
. Electron arrangements in an atom determine chemical properties of the elements
. Number of electrons is always equal to the number of protons in a neutral atom

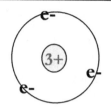

a Li atom is neutral because it contains **3+** protons and **3-** electrons

Neutrons

Neutrons are neutral (no charge) subatomic particles located inside the nucleus of an atom.

. A neutron has a mass of 1 amu and a zero charge
. A neutron has the same mass (1 amu) as a proton
. Neutrons are in the nucleus along with protons
. Atoms of the same element differ in their numbers of neutrons

The diagrams below show two different nuclei of Li

For this Li nucleus

Atomic # = **3**

Nucleons = **7** (3p + 4n)

Mass # = **7 amu**

Nucleons

Nucleons are particles in the nucleus of an atom (protons and neutrons)

. Nucleons account for the total mass of an atom
. The total number of nucleons in an atom is equal to the sum of protons *plus* neutrons

Atomic number

Atomic number identifies each element
. Atomic number is equal to the number of protons
. Elements are made of atoms with the same atomic number

For this Li nucleus

Atomic # = **3**

Nucleons = **8** (3p + 5n)

Mass # = **8 amu**

Mass number

Mass number identifies different isotopes of the same element.

. Atoms of the same element differ by their mass numbers
. The mass number is equal to the number of protons *plus* neutrons
. The mass number shows the total number of nucleons

Summary Table for Subatomic Particles

Subatomic Particle	Symbol	Mass	Charge	Location
Proton	$_{+1}^{1}p$	1	+1	Nucleus
Neutron	$_{0}^{1}n$	1	0	Nucleus
Electron	$_{-1}^{0}e$	0	-1	Orbital (outside the nucleus)

Summary of Relationships Between the Atomic Structures

Number of protons	= the atomic # of the element = electrons (for neutral atoms) = nuclear charge = nucleons − neutrons = mass # − neutrons
Number of electrons **(for neutral atoms)**	= protons = atomic number = nuclear charge = mass # − neutrons
Number of electrons **(for ions)**	= atomic number − charge of ion = protons − charge of ion = nuclear charge − charge of ion
Number of neutrons	= mass # − protons = mass # − atomic # = mass # − electrons (for neutral atoms) = nucleons − protons
Atomic number **(Nuclear charge)**	= protons = electrons (for neutral atoms) = mass # - neutrons
Mass number	= neutrons + protons = neutrons + electrons (for neutral atoms) = neutrons + nuclear charge = nucleons
Number of Nucleons	= mass # = neutrons + protons = neutrons + electrons (for neutral atoms) = neutrons + nuclear charge

Isotopes

Isotopes are atoms of the same element with the same number of protons but different numbers of neutrons.

For example: There are a few different atoms of element lithium. All atoms of lithium contain the same number of protons in their nucleus. The difference between these atoms is the number of neutrons. Since all lithium atoms have the same number of protons (3), they all have the same atomic number of 3. Since they have different number of neutrons, they each have a different mass number.

These different atoms of lithium are referred to as isotopes of lithium.

Isotopes of the same element must have:

. *Different* mass numbers (nucleons)	7	8
. *Same* atomic number	Li	Li
. *Same* number of protons		
. *Same* number of electrons	3	3
. *Same* chemical reactivity		
. *Different* numbers of neutrons	4 (mass# - protons) 5	

Isotope notations

Isotopes of an element have different mass numbers. Therefore, the mass number of an isotope is written next to the element's name (or symbol) to distinguish it from all the other isotopes of that element.

Summary of isotope notations for the two Li isotopes are shown below.

Element – mass number	*Lithium* – 7	*Lithium* – 8
Symbol – mass # notations:	*Li* – 7	*Li* – 8
Common isotope notations	$_3^7Li$	$_3^8Li$
Nuclear diagrams:	4 n / 3 p	5n / 3p

               SurvivingChem.com

Atomic Mass Unit

Atomic mass unit (amu): unit for measuring mass of atoms based on carbon – 12.

$$1 \text{ amu } = \quad ^1/_{12}\text{th the mass of } ^{12}\text{C}$$

Interpretation:

Hydrogen–**1** (**^{1}H**) has a mass that is $1/12$th the mass of ^{12}C

Lithium–**6** (**^{6}Li**) has a mass that is $6/12$th or half the mass of ^{12}C

Magnesium–**24** (^{24}Mg) has a mass that is $24/12$th or 2 times the mass of ^{12}C

Atomic Mass

Atomic mass of an element is the average mass of all the naturally occurring stable isotopes of that element. Natural samples of an element consist of a mix of two or more isotopes (different atoms). Usually, there is a lot of one isotope and very little of the others. **Atomic mass** of an element (given on the Periodic Table) is calculated from mass numbers and abundances (percentages) of the element's naturally occurring isotopes.

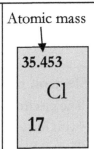

Atomic mass

35.453

Cl

17

Calculating atomic mass

Example 1: *A natural sample of chlorine contains 75% of ^{35}Cl and 25% of ^{37}Cl. Calculate the atomic mass of chlorine.*

change % to decimal x mass # = product   Add all products to get atomic mass

75% of ^{35}Cl   .75   x   35 = **26.25**

25 % of ^{37}Cl   .25   x   37 = **9.25**

$+ \} = $ **35.5 amu**

Example 2: *A sample of unknown element X contains the following isotopes: 80 % of ^{64}X, 15% of ^{65}X, and 5% of ^{66}X. What is the average atomic mass of element X?*

80 % of ^{64}X   .80   x   64 = **51.2**

15 % of ^{65}X   .15   x   65 = **9.75**

5 % of ^{66}X.   .05   x   66 = **3.3**

$+ + \} = $ **64.25 amu**

Lesson 3: Location and Arrangement of Electrons

Introduction

According to the wave-mechanical model of atoms, electrons are found in orbitals outside the nucleus. **Orbitals** describe the area (or region) outside the nucleus where an electron is likely to be found.

The orbital an electron occupies depends on the energy of the electron. While one electron of an atom may have enough energy to occupy an orbital far from the nucleus, another electron of that same atom may have just enough energy to occupy a region closer to the nucleus. The result is the formation of energy levels (or electron shells) around the nucleus of the atom.

The arrangement of electrons in atoms is complex. In this lesson, you will learn the basic and simplified arrangement of electrons in electron shells. You will also learn of electron transition (movement) from one level to another, and the production of a spectrum of colors (spectral lines).

Electron shells refer to the energy levels the electrons of an atom occupy.
. The electron shell (1st) closest to the nucleus always contains electrons with the least amount of energy
. The electron shell farthest from the nucleus contains electrons with the most amount of energy
. On the Periodic Table, the period (horizontal row) number indicates the total number of electron shells in the atoms of elements.

Electron configurations show the arrangement of electrons in an atom. Electron configurations can be found in the box of each element on the Periodic Table.

Bohr's (shell) diagram can be drawn to show electrons in the electron shells of an atom.

Periodic Table info for P

Bohr's (shell) diagram for P

Interpretation

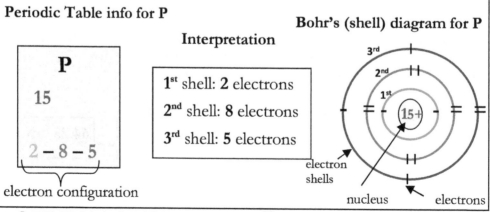

1st shell: **2** electrons

2nd shell: **8** electrons

3rd shell: **5** electrons

P

15

2 – 8 – 5

electron configuration

electron shells

nucleus   electrons

Maximum Number of Electrons

Each electron shell has a maximum number of electrons that can occupy that shell. A full understanding of this concept requires lessons on quantum numbers, which is briefly discussed on pages 46 – 47.

Maximum number of electrons

The maximum number of electrons in any electron shell can be determined using a very simple formula: $2n^2$ n represents the electron shell

For example: n = 1 means 1st shell, n= 3 means 3rd shell..etc

Maximum electrons in the 1st = $2(n^2)$ = $2(1^2)$ = 2 electrons
Maximum electrons in the 2nd = $2(n^2)$ = $2(2^2)$ = 8 electrons
Maximum electrons in the 3rd = $2(n^2)$ = $2(3^2)$ = 18 electrons

Completely and partially filled shells

An electron shell is completely filled if it has the maximum number of electrons according to the equation $2n^2$.
The electron configuration given on the Periodic Table for phosphorus is shown below. According to this configuration:

$2 - 8 - 5$ 1st shell of P is completely filled with electrons
2nd shell of P is completely filled with electrons
3rd shell of P is partially filled.

Valence electrons and Lewis electron-dot diagram

Valence electrons are electrons in the outermost electron shell of an atom. Valence shells of an atom are the last (outermost) shell that contains electrons. The number of valence electrons in an atom is always the last number in its electron configuration. Elements in the same group (vertical column) of the Periodic Table have the same number of valence electrons, therefore similar chemical reactivity.

A **Lewis electron-dot diagram** is a notation that shows the **symbol** of an atom and dots *equal* to the number of valence electrons. Lewis electron-dot diagrams can be drawn for neutral atoms, ions and compounds. In this topic, you'll learn to draw and recognize Lewis electron-dot diagrams for neutral atoms and ions. In topic 4, you'll learn to draw and recognize Lewis electron-dot diagrams for ionic and covalent compounds.

Valence e- for P

$2 - 8 - \underline{5}$

Phosphorus has **5 valence** electrons. Its valence shell is the 3rd shell.

electron-dot diagram for phosphorus

·P :

5 dots = 5 valence e-

Ground and Excited State Atoms

An atom is most stable when its electrons occupy the lowest available electron shells. When this is the case, the atom is said to be in the ground state. When one or more electrons of an atom occupy a higher energy level than they should, the atom is said to be in the excited state. Facts related to ground and excited state atoms are summarized below.

Ground state atom: When an atom is in the ground state: . The electron configuration is the same as on the Periodic Table . Electrons are filled in order from lowest to highest shell . Energy of the atom is at its lowest, and the atom is stable . An electron in a ground state atom must absorb energy to go from a lower level to a higher level . As an electron of a ground state atom absorbs energy and moves to the excited state, energy of the electron and of the atom increases	**P** **15** **2 − 8 − 5** **Ground state** configuration for phosphorous. Same as given on the Periodic Table
Excited state atom: When an atom is in the excited state: . The electron configuration is different from that of the Periodic Table for that atom . Energy of the atom is high, and the atom is unstable . An electron in an excited state atom must release energy to return from a high level to a lower level (ground state) . As an electron in the excited state atom releases energy to return to the ground state, energy of the electron and of the atom decreases . Spectra of colors (spectral lines) are produced when excited electrons release energy and return to the ground state **Quanta** are discrete (specific) amounts of energy absorbed or released by an electron to go from one level to another.	**2 − 8 − 4 − 1** **2 − 7 − 6** **1 − 8 − 6** **Possible excited state** configurations for phosphorus. Configurations are all different from the ground state, however, the total # of e- is the same and equal to the atomic number.

Spectral Lines

Spectral lines are bands of colors produced when excited electrons return from high (excited) to low (ground) state.

. Spectral lines are produced from energy released by excited electrons as they return to the ground state

.Spectral lines are viewed through a spectroscope

Spectral Lines

.Spectral lines are called "fingerprints' of the elements because each element has its own unique pattern (wavelength) of colors

Bright-line spectra charts show bands of colors at different wavelengths that are produced by elements.

Bright-line spectra for hydrogen, lithium, sodium and potassium are shown on the chart below. A spectrum for a mixture of unknown composition is also given. The bright-line spectrum of the mixture can be compared to those of H, Li, Na and K. Substances in the unknown can be identified by matching the lines in the unknown to the lines for H, Li, Na and K.

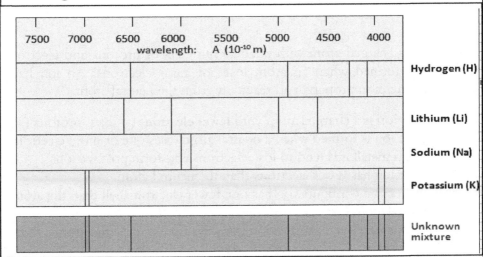

The unknown mixture contains potassium and hydrogen

Flame test

A flame test is a lab procedure in which compounds containing metallic ions are heated to produce unique flame colors. Flame color produced is due to the excited electrons in the metal ion as they return from high (excited) state to low (ground) state. Flame color produced can be used to identify which metal ion is in a compound. However, since two or more metallic ions can produce similar color flames, flame test results are not very reliable. A flame color can be further separated into unique bands of colors using a spectroscope.

Lesson 4: Neutral Atoms and Ions

Introduction

Most atoms (with the exception of the noble gases) are unstable because they have incomplete valence (outermost) electron shells. For this reason, most atoms need to lose, gain or share electrons to get a full valence shell and become more stable. A neutral atom may lose all its valence electrons to form a new valence shell that is completely filled. A neutral atom may also gain or share electrons to fill its valence shell.

An ion is formed when a neutral atom loses or gains electrons.
In this lesson, you will learn differences and similarities between neutral atoms and ions.

Neutral atom

A neutral atom has equal numbers of protons and electrons.
The electron configurations given on the Periodic Table are for neutral atoms of the elements in the ground state.

Ion

An ion is a charged atom with unequal numbers of protons and electrons. An ion is formed when an atom loses or gains electrons. An ion has a different chemical property and reactivity from the neutral atom.

A **positive ion** is a charged atom with **fewer electrons (-)** than protons (+).
. A positive ion is formed when a neutral atom loses one or more electrons
. Metals and metalloids tend to lose electrons and form positive ions
. A positive ion has fewer electrons than the neutral atom
. A +ion electron configuration has one fewer electron shell than the atom
. As a neutral atom loses electrons, its size decreases
. Ionic radius (size) of a positive ion is always smaller than the atomic radius

A **negative ion** is a charged atom with more electrons (-) than protons(+)
. A negative ion is formed when a neutral atom gains one or more electrons
. Nonmetals tend to gain electrons and form negative ions
. A negative ion has more electrons than its neutral atom
. A –ion electron configuration has the same # of electron shells as the atom
. As a neutral atom gains electrons, its size increases
. Ionic radius (size) of a negative ion is always larger than the atomic radius

> **Number of electrons in ion = Protons – charge of ion**
>
> **Charge of an ion = Atomic number – electrons**

Comparing Ions to Neutral Atoms

When electrons are lost or gained by a neutral atom, the ion formed will be different in many ways from the neutral atom. Number of electrons, electron configuration, properties, and size of the ion will all be different from the neutral atom. Below are diagrams and tables showing comparisons between atoms and ions.

Comparing a positive ion to the neutral atom

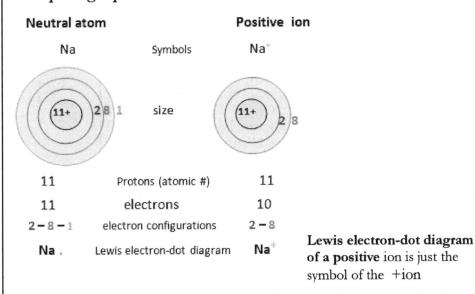

Neutral atom		Positive ion
Na	Symbols	Na⁺
	size	
11	Protons (atomic #)	11
11	electrons	10
2 − 8 − 1	electron configurations	2 − 8
Na ·	Lewis electron-dot diagram	Na⁺

Lewis electron-dot diagram of a positive ion is just the symbol of the +ion

Comparing a negative ion to the neutral atom

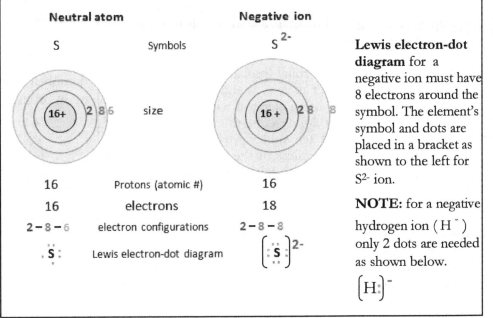

Neutral atom		Negative ion
S	Symbols	S²⁻
	size	
16	Protons (atomic #)	16
16	electrons	18
2 − 8 − 6	electron configurations	2 − 8 − 8
·S̈:	Lewis electron-dot diagram	[:S̈:]²⁻

Lewis electron-dot diagram for a negative ion must have 8 electrons around the symbol. The element's symbol and dots are placed in a bracket as shown to the left for S²⁻ ion.

NOTE: for a negative hydrogen ion (H⁻) only 2 dots are needed as shown below.

[H:]⁻

Lesson 5: Quantum Numbers and Electron Configurations

In lesson 3, you learned the basic arrangement of electrons (electron configuration) in an atom. A better understanding of electron configurations requires a brief lesson in quantum chemistry.

Quantum theory uses mathematical equations to describe location, as well as behavior of electrons in an atom. This theory uses a set of four quantum numbers to describe location of an electron in atoms.

First quantum number: Principal energy level (electron shell)

The first quantum number uses letters (K, L, M..) or numbers (1, 2, 3..) to designate the major energy level of an electron. For example, an electron with a principal quantum number of 2(L) is in the second energy level. On the Periodic Table, the period number of an element indicates how many principal energy levels are in the atoms of that element.

Second quantum number: Sublevel of an electron.

The second quantum number uses s, p, d, f... to indicate the sublevel of an electron within the principal energy level. The s sublevel is always the first sublevel in any principal energy level. The next sublevel is p. The number of sublevels in an atom is equal to the principal energy level number. For example, the 1st principal energy has 1 sublevel (1s) . The 3rd principal energy level has three sublevels (3s, 3p, and 3d). The difference between the sublevels is the shape of their orbitals. The s sublevel is described as having a spherical shape. The p sublevel is described as having a dumbbell shape. The shapes of d, f, g, and h sublevels are much too complex and will not be discussed here.

Third quantum number: Orbital (probable location)

The third quantum number uses x, y and z to describe the orbital (probable location) of an electron within the sublevels. For example: $2p_x$, $2p_y$, and $2p_z$ describe the three p orbitals of the second energy level. Each sublevel has a set number of orbitals. All s sublevels (regardless of the energy level) have 1 orbital. All p sublevels have 3 orbitals. The d sublevels have 5 orbitals.   Each orbital, regardless of the sublevel, can hold a maximum of two electrons.

Fourth quantum number: Spin of electron.

The fourth quantum number describes the spin direction of an electron in orbitals. An orbital with 2 electrons must have the electrons spinning in opposite directions to overcome like charge repulsion.

The principal
energy levels

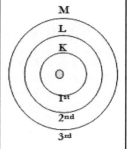

spherical shapes
of s orbitals

Size of an orbital
varies depending
on the principal
energy level

dumbbell shapes
of 2p orbitals

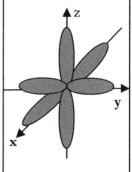

Summary of Principal Quantum Numbers

Principal energy level (n)	Number of sublevels	Types and available sublevels	Number of orbitals available	Maximum number of electrons in energy level ($2n^2$)
1	1	1s	1	2
2	2	2s	1	8
		2p	3	
3	3	3s	1	18
		3p	3	
		3d	5	
4	4	4s	1	32
		4p	3	
		4d	5	
		4f	7	

Note: Each orbital can hold a maximum of 2 electrons

Electron Configurations and Orbital Notations

Electron configurations show arrangement of electrons in the energy levels and sublevels. Electrons in a ground state atom must always have electrons in the lowest available levels. The order in which electrons must fill in the energy levels is given below:

> 1s 2s 2p   3s 3p   4s 3d 4p 5s 4d 5p ......
> lowest energy ——— increase energy ——————▶

Ground state for Fluorine

$$1s^2 2s^2 2p^5$$

Orbital notation shows distribution of electrons in the orbitals. When placing electrons in orbitals, keep the following in mind:
- No more than two electrons in an orbital
- Each orbital in p, d, f.. must have an electron before pairing
- Two electrons in an orbital must show opposite spins (↑↓)
- Valence e- are *only* the electrons in the s and p sublevels of the highest level

Excited state for Fluorine

$$1s^2 2s^2 2p^4 3s^1$$

Examples of configurations and orbital notations for four elements.

	H 1e-	He 2e-	N 7e -	Na 11e-
e- config.	$1s^1$	$1s^2$	$1s^2$ $2s^2$ $2p^3$	$1s^2$ $2s^2$ $2p^6$ $3s^1$
orbital notation	↑	↑↓	↑↓ ↑↓ ↑ ↑ ↑	↑↓ ↑↓ ↑↓ ↑↓ ↑↓ ↑
e- config	1	2	2 – 5	2 – 8 – 1
valence e-	1	2	5	1

Practice Questions

Lesson 1: Historical development of the Modern atom

Answer the multiple choice questions below.

1. According to the wave-mechanical model of the atom, electrons in the atom
   1) Are most likely to be found in an excited state
   2) Are located in orbitals outside the nucleus
   3) Travel in defined circles
   4) Have a positive charge

2. The modern model of the atom is based on the work of
   1) One scientist over a short period of time
   2) Many scientists over a short period of time
   3) One scientist over a long period of time
   4) Many scientists over a long period of time

3. Which conclusion is based on the "gold foil experiment" and the resulting model of the atom?
   1) An atom is mainly empty space, and the nucleus has a positive charge
   2) An atom is mainly empty space, and the nucleus has a negative charge
   3) An atom has hardly any empty space, and the nucleus has a positive charge
   4) An atom has hardly any empty space, and the nucleus has a negative charge

4. Which particles are found in the nucleus of an atom?
   1) Electrons, only
   2) Neutrons, only
   3) Protons and electrons
   4) Protons and neutrons

5. Which group of atomic models is listed in order from the earliest to most recent?
   1) Hard-sphere model, wave-mechanical model, electron-shell model
   2) Hard-sphere model, electron-shell model, wave mechanical model
   3) Electron-shell model, wave-mechanical model, hard-sphere model
   4) Electron-shell model, hard-sphere model, wave-mechanical model

Lesson 2: The Atom

Define the following terms and answer multiple choice questions below.

6. Nucleus   7. Neutron   8. Proton   9. Electron   10. Nucleons 11. Isotopes
12. Atomic number   13. Mass number   14. Atomic mass   15. Atomic mass unit

16. What is the charge and mass of an electron?
    1) Charge of +1 and a mass of 1 amu
    2) Charge of +1 and a mass of 1/1836 amu
    3) Charge of -1 and a mass of 1 amu
    4) Charge of -1 and a mass of 1/1836 amu

17. Which particle has approximately the same mass as a proton?
    1) Alpha   2) Beta   3) Electron   4) Neutron

18. The mass of an atom is due primarily to the
    1) Mass of protons plus the mass of electrons
    2) Mass of neutrons plus the mass of electrons
    3) Mass of protons plus the mass of positrons
    4) Mass of neutrons plus the mass of protons

19. The mass number of an element is always equal to the number of
    1) Protons plus electrons   3) Neutrons plus protons
    2) Protons plus positrons   4) Neutrons plus positrons

20. The atomic number of an element is always equal to the number of
    1) Protons   2) Positrons   3) Neutrons   4) Electrons

21. The number of neutrons in the nucleus of an atom can be determined by
    1) Adding the mass number to the atomic number of the atom
    2) Adding the mass number to the number of electrons of the atom
    3) Subtracting the atomic number from the mass number of the atom
    4) Subtracting the mass number from the atomic number of the atom

22. All isotopes of a given atom have
    1) The same mass number and the same atomic number
    2) The same mass number but different atomic numbers
    3) Different mass numbers but the same atomic number
    4) Different mass numbers and different atomic numbers

23. An atom contains 23 electrons, 21 protons, and 24 neutrons. What is the atomic number of this atom?
    1) 44   2) 23   3) 24   4) 21

24. An atom contains 83 protons, 80 electrons, and 126 neutrons. What is the mass number of this atom?
    1) 163   2) 209   3) 206   4) 46

25. A neutral atom with an atomic number of 9 and a mass number of 17 will also have
    1) 9 protons, 9 electrons, and 9 neutrons
    2) 9 protons, 9 electrons, and 8 neutrons
    3) 9 protons, 8 electrons, and 9 neutrons
    4) 9 protons, 8 electrons, and 8 neutrons

26. Which element could have a mass number of 86 atomic mass units and 49 neutrons in its nucleus?
    1) In   2) Rb   3) Rn   4) Au

27. Which pair of atoms are isotopes of the same element X?

    1) $^{226}_{91}$X and $^{226}_{90}$X   3) $^{226}_{90}$X and $^{227}_{91}$X

    2) $^{227}_{91}$X and $^{227}_{91}$X   4) $^{226}_{91}$X and $^{227}_{91}$X

28. Which pair of atoms do the nuclei contain the same number of neutrons?
    1) $^{7}_{3}$Li and $^{9}_{4}$Be   3) $^{40}_{19}$K and $^{41}_{19}$K

    2) $^{42}_{20}$Ca and $^{40}_{18}$Ar   4) $^{14}_{7}$N and $^{16}_{8}$O

29. What is the mass number in the nucleus of the symbol $^{40}_{18}$Ar ?

    1) 40   2) 22   3) 58   4) 18

30. What is the nuclear charge of the atom $^{227}_{91}X$?

    1) +91   2) +136   3) +227   4) +318

31. Which is true of the isotope symbol $^{9}_{4}Be$?

    1) It has 4 protons, 4 electrons, and 9 neutrons
    2) It has 9 protons , 9 electrons, and 4 neutrons
    3) It has 4 protons, 4 electrons, and 5 neutrons
    4) It has 9 protons, 4 electrons, and 5 neutrons

32. The nuclides ^{14}C and ^{14}N are similar in that they both have the same
    1) Mass number   3) Atomic Number
    2) Number of neutrons   4) Nuclear charge

33. Compared to an atom of $^{40}_{20}Ca$, an atom of $^{38}_{18}Ar$ has

    1) Greater nuclear charge   3) The same nuclear charge
    2) A greater number of neutrons   4) The same number of neutrons

34. In which isotope does the nucleus contain the greatest number of nucleons?
    1) $^{226}_{88}Ra$ 2) $^{224}_{87}Fr$ 3) $^{223}_{86}Rn$ 4) $^{210}_{85}At$

35. Which name is correct for the isotope symbol represented as $^{19}_{9}X$?

    1) Potassium – 19   2) Potassium - 9   3) Fluorine – 19   4) Fluorine – 9

36. Which diagram represents the nucleus of an atom $^{53}_{24}Cr$?

    1) (24 p / 53 n)   2) (53 p / 24 n)   3) (24 p / 29 n)   4) (29p / 24n)

Lesson 3: Arrangement of Electrons

Define the following terms and answer multiple choice questions below.

37. Orbital   38. Electron shell   39. Ground state   40. Excited state   41.Quanta
42. Spectral lines 43. Flame test 44. Valence electrons   45. Lewis electron-dot diagram

46. Compared to a sodium atom in the ground state, a sodium atom in the excited state must have
    1) A greater number of electrons   3) An electron with greater energy
    2) A smaller number of electrons   4) An electron with smaller energy

47. When an electron in an excited atom returns to a lower energy state, the energy emitted can result in the production of
    1) Alpha particles   2) Isotopes   3) Protons   4) Spectral lines

48. As an electron moves from a higher energy level to a lower energy level, the electron will
    1) Lose energy   2) Lose a proton   3) Gain energy   4) Gain a proton

49. How do the energy and the most probable location of an electron in the third shell of an atom compare to the energy and the most probable location of an electron in the first shell of the same atom?
   1) In the third shell, an electron has more energy and is closer to the nucleus
   2) In the third shell, an electron has more energy and is farther from the nucleus
   3) In the third shell, an electron has less energy and is closer to the nucleus
   4) In the third shell, an electron has less energy and is farther from the nucleus

50. In the configuration, $2 - 8 - 8 - 1$, which electron shell contains electrons with the most energy?
   1) 4th   2) 2nd   3) 8th   4) 1st

51. How many electrons are in the 3rd electron shell of a neutral strontium atom in the ground state?
   1) 2   2) 3   3) 8   4) 18

52. What is the total number of electrons in an atom with a configuration of $2 - 8 - 18 - 4 - 2$?
   1) 5   2) 34   3) 28   4) 2

53. An atom of which element has an incomplete third electron shell?
   1) Calcium   2) Bromine   3) Krypton   4) Silver

54. What is the ground state electron configuration of a neutral atom with 27 protons?
   1) $2 - 8 - 14 - 3$ 2) $2 - 8 - 15 - 2$ 3) $2 - 8 - 17$ 4) $2 - 8 - 8 - 8 - 1$

55. An atom has 16 protons and 16 electrons. Which is the electron configuration of this atom in the excited state?
   1) 2-18-8-4   2) 2-18-8-8-3-1   3) 2-8-6   4) 2-8-5-1

56. An electron in an atom of neon will gain the most energy when moving from
   1) 2nd to 3rd   2) 3rd to 2nd   3) 2nd to 4th   4) 4th to 2nd

57. Which electron transition will produce spectral lines?
   1) From 2nd to 1st shell   3) From 2nd to 3rd shell
   2) From 3rd to 5th shell   4) From 3rd to 4th shell

Lesson 4: Neutral Atoms and Ions
Define the following terms and answer multiple choice questions below.

58. Neutral atom   59. Ion   60. Positive ion   61. Negative ion

62. When an atom becomes a positive ion, the radius of the atom
   1) Remains the same   2) Increases   3) Decreases

63. Compared to a Be^{2+} ion, a Be^0 atom has
   1) More protons   3) Fewer protons
   2) More electrons   4) Fewer electrons

64. Compared to a negative ion, a neutral atom of the same element
   1) Is smaller because it has fewer electrons
   2) Is bigger because it has fewer electrons
   3) Is smaller because it has more electrons
   4) Is bigger because it has more electrons

65. Which changes occur as an atom becomes a positively charged ion?
    1) The atom gains electrons, and the number of protons increases
    2) The atom gains electrons, and the number of protons remains the same
    3) The atom loses electrons, and the number of protons decreases
    4) The atom loses electrons, and the number of protons remains the same

66. What is the total number of electrons in a Cr^{3+} ion?
    1) 3   2) 21   3) 24   4) 27

67. The total number of electrons in an F^- ion is
    1) 9   2) 8   3) 10   4) 17

68. The ion Mn^{4+} has
    1) 25 protons and 25 electrons   3) 25 protons and 21 electrons
    2) 25 protons and 4 electrons   4) 21 protons and 25 electrons

69. An atom has 16 protons, 17 neutrons and 18 electrons. What is the charge of this atom?
    1) +1   2) -1   3) +2   4) -2

70. An atom with a nuclear charge of +14 and an ionic charge of -4 has
    1) 14 protons and 18 electrons   3) 14 protons and 4 electrons
    2) 14 protons and 14 electrons   4) 4 protons and 14 electrons

71. The ionic configuration for a calcium ion is
    1) 2 – 8 – 8 – 2   2) 2 – 8 – 2   3) 2 – 8 – 8   4) 2 – 8 – 8 – 8

72. Which configuration is correct for a Br^- ion?
    1) 2 – 8 – 18 – 7   2) 2 – 8 – 18   3) 2 – 8 – 18 – 8   4) 2 – 18 – 8 – 8

73. The electron configuration 2 – 8 – 18 – 8 could represent which particle?
    1) Ca^{2+} 2) Ge^{4-} 3) Cl^- 4) Br^{5+}

Lesson 5: Quantum Numbers and Electron Configurations

74. What is the total number of occupied energy levels in an atom of neon in the ground state?
    1) 1   2) 2   3) 8   4) 18

75. What is the total number of sublevels in the third principal energy level of a tin atom?
    1) 8   2) 6   3) 3   4) 4

76. Which of the following sublevels has the highest energy?
    1) 2p   2) 3p   3) 3d   4) 4s

77. Which sublevel contains a total of 7 orbitals?
    1) s   2) p   3) d   4) f

78. What is the maximum number of electrons that can be found in a 3s orbital of a potassium atom?
    1) 1   2) 2   3) 8   4) 18

79. Which is the correct electron configuration of a magnesium atom in the ground state?
    1) $1s^2\, 2s^2\, 2p^6\, 3s^1\, 3p^1$
    2) $1s^2\, 2s^2\, 2p^6$
    3) $1s^2\, 2s^2\, 2p^6\, 3s^2$
    4) $1s^2\, 2s^2\, 2p^6\, 3s^2\, 3p^1$

80. Which electron configuration represents an atom of sodium in the ground state?
    1) $1s^2\, 2s^2\, 2p^6\, 3p^1$
    2) $1s^2\, 2s^2\, 2p^5\, 3s^1$
    3) $1s^2\, 2s^2\, 2p^6\, 3s^2\, 3p^6\, 4s^1$
    4) $1s^2\, 2s^2\, 2p^6\, 3s^1\, 4s^1$

81. An atom in the excited state can have an electron configuration of
    1) $1s^2\, 2p^1$ 2) $1s^2\, 2s^2$ 3) $1s^2\, 2s^2\, 2p^5$ 4) $1s^2\, 2s^2\, 2p^6$

82. What is the electron configuration of an Mn atom in the excited state?
    1) $1s^2\, 2s^2\, 2p^6\, 3s^2$
    2) $1s^2\, 2s^2\, 2p^6\, 3s^2\, 3p^6\, 3d^6\, 4s^1$
    3) $1s^2\, 2s^2\, 2p^6\, 3s^2\, 3p^6\, 3d^5 4s^2$
    4) $1s^2\, 2s^2\, 2p^6\, 3s^2\, 3p^6\, 3d^5$

83. Which atom in the ground state has only three electrons in the 3p sublevel?
    1) Phosphorus   2) Potassium   3) Argon   4) Aluminum

84. Which atom in the ground state has two half-filled orbitals?
    1) P   2) O   3) Li   4) Si

85. What is the total number of completely filled principal energy levels in an atom with a configuration of $1s^2\, 2s^2\, 2p^6\, 3s^2\, 3p^6\, 3d^{10}\, 4s^2\, 4p^1$?
    1) 1   2) 2   3) 3   4) 4

Topic Mastery / Constructed Response

86. When electrons move from the 4th energy level to the second energy level, they emit visible light. Explain why the light emitted when an electron makes this move in a sodium atom is a different color than the light emitted by an electron moving from the fourth to the second level of a hydrogen atom.

87. A natural sample of element X has the following composition: 80.0% of ^{70}X, 12.25% of ^{69}X, and 7.75% of ^{68}X. Calculate the atomic mass of element X .

Answer questions 88 and 89 based on the information below.
An atom has an atomic number of 9, a mass number of 19, and an electron configuration of $2 - 6 - 1$

88. Explain why the number of electrons in the second and third shells show that this atom is in an excited state.

89. Draw two Bohr's atomic diagrams: One for the atom in the excited state and the other for the atom when it is in the ground state. Show the correct number of particles in the nucleus and use "–" to represent the electrons.

90. Using quantum method (s, p, d..), write electron configurations and draw orbital notations for the following atoms and ions.

    atoms: C, Al, S, Ar, Ca, Se   ions: Li^+, Mg^{2+}, K^+, F^-, S^{2-}, As^{3-}

Additional Materials

Energy of a Hydrogen Atom

Energy of an electron is quantized, meaning it is specific for each energy level. The equation below can be used to calculate the energy, E_n, of an electron in a hydrogen atom if its principal energy level, n, is known.

$$E_n = \frac{-2.178 \times 10^{-18}}{n^2} \text{ Joules}$$

E_n = energy of the electron

n = principal energy level

Light, Wavelength and Frequency

Light is a form of electromagnetic radiation that travels at a **speed (c)** of 3.00×10^8 m/sec. Every electromagnetic radiation (different light colors) is emitted at a specific **wavelength** (λ). **Frequency (v)** of light, in Hertz, indicates the number of completed wave per second. The mathematical relationship between these three aspects of light is given in the equation below:

$$v = \frac{c}{\lambda}$$

Energy of Atoms, Frequency, Wavelength

When atoms absorb and release energy in the form of electromagnetic radiation during electron transition from one energy level to another, the energy change, ΔE (in Joules), can be calculated using the equation below.

$$\Delta E = hv = \frac{h\,c}{\lambda}$$

h = Planck's constant, 6.63×10^{-34} Joules · sec.
v = frequency of the radiation (1/sec or Hz)
λ = wavelength of the radiation (m)
c = speed of light, 3.00×10^8 m/sec

91. Calculate the energy of an electron of a hydrogen atom in these three shells.
    a) n = 1   b) n= 2   c) n = 3

92. Violet light has a wavelength of 4.10×10^{-12} m. What is its frequency?

93. A helium laser emits light with a wavelength of 633 nm. What is the frequency of the light?

94. Calculate the wavelength of radiation with a frequency of 8.0×10^{14} Hz.

95. Green light has a frequency of 6.01×10^{14} Hz. What is the wavelength?

96. Calculate the energy of a photon of radiation with a frequency of 8.5×10^{14} Hz.

97. Calculate the energy of a gamma ray photon whose frequency is 5.02×10^{20} Hz.

98. Calculate the energy of a photon of radiation with a wavelength of 6.4×10^{-7} m.

99. What is the energy of light whose wavelength is 4.06×10^{-11} m?

100. An FM radio station broadcasts at a frequency of 107.9 MHz. What is the wavelength of the radio signal?

Lesson 1: Stability and Energy in Bonding

Introduction

Chemical bonding is the simultaneous attraction of two positive nuclei to negative electrons. Chemical bonding is said to be the "glue" that holds particles (atoms, ions, molecules) together in matter. Since most atoms do not have full valence shells, they are unstable. For these atoms to attain full valence shells and be stable, they must bond with other atoms. When atoms bond, energy of the atoms decreases as they become more stable. (ex. Hydrogen)

In this lesson, you will learn about stability and energy in bonding.

Bonding and Stability

Atoms bond so they can attain full valence shells and become stable. The **octet rule** states that a stable valence shell configuration must have eight electrons. **NOTE:** Not every atom needs eight valence electrons to be stable.

. An atom can get a full and stable valence shell configuration by

A) **Transferring** or **Accepting electrons** (*during ionic bonding)*

or

B) **Sharing electrons** *(during covalent bonding)*

. The ground state electron configuration of a bonded atom is similar to that of the nearest noble gas (Group 18) atom.
(Remember that noble gases have full valence shells)

Electron configuration of atoms in a bond

In a bond between sodium and chlorine in the substance NaCl

Na (atomic # 11): closest noble gas is Ne (atomic #10).
In **NaCl**, **Na** is **Na$^+$** ion (10 electrons) . Its configuration is 2–8 , which is the same as that of Ne (2–8).

Cl (atomic # 17): closest noble gas is Ar (atomic # 18).
In NaCl, Cl is **Cl$^-$** ion (18 electrons) . Its configuration is 2–8–8 , which is the same as that of Ar (2–8–8).

Use the Periodic Table to figure out which noble gas (group 18 element) is the closest (by atomic #) to each element in a formula.

Bonding and Energy

All chemical substances contain certain amounts of potential energy.

Potential energy is stored in the bonds holding particles of substances together. The amount of potential energy depends on *composition and structure* of a substance.

Bond formation

Bond formation between two atoms is an exothermic process. Exothermic processes release heat energy. When two atoms come together to form a bond, heat energy is always released. Since energy is released, the energy of the atoms decreases. The atoms are now more stable than they were before bonding. As energy is released during bond formation:

. Potential energy of the atoms decreases

. Stability of the atoms increases

. Stability of the chemical system increases

A **bond formation equation** has energy released to the right of the equation.

$$H \ + \ Cl \ \longrightarrow \ H-Cl \ + \ \textbf{Energy}$$

A **Chemical bond formed** between H and Cl atoms. The bonded H and Cl atoms are more stable than the free H and Cl atoms on the left.

Bond breaking

Breaking of a bond in chemical substances is an endothermic process. Endothermic processes absorb heat energy. When a bond between atoms of a substance is to be broken, energy must be absorbed by the substance. Since energy is absorbed, the energy of the atoms increases. The atoms (separated) are now less stable than when they were bonded together. As energy is absorbed during bond breaking:

. Potential energy of the atoms increases

. Stability of the atoms decreases

. Stability of the chemical system decreases

A **bond breaking equation** has energy absorbed to the left of the equation.

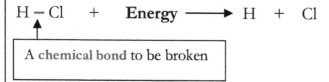

$$H-Cl \ + \ \textbf{Energy} \ \longrightarrow \ H \ + \ Cl$$

A **chemical bond** to be broken

Lesson 2: Types of Bonding and Substances

Introduction
Intramolecular forces describe bonds that hold atoms together to create molecules and compounds. Bonding between atoms is a result of atoms competing for electrons to get full valence shells.

Bonding between atoms can occur by two atoms sharing electrons to form covalent bonds, or by atoms transferring and accepting electrons to form ionic bonds.

In this lesson, you will learn about the different types of bonding between atoms.

Ionic Bonds and Ionic Compounds

Ionic bonds are forces holding charged particles together in ionic compounds. **Ionic bonds** are formed by the ***transfer of electron(s)*** from a metal to nonmetal. . The metal atom always loses (or transfers) electrons and becomes a positively (+) charged ion . The nonmetal atom always gains (or accepts) electrons and becomes a negatively (–) charged ion . Ionic bonds are formed by the electrostatic attraction between the +metal ion and the - nonmetal ion . Electronegativity difference between the nonmetal and metal atoms in ionic bonds is usually 1.7 or greater	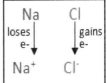 An **Ionic bond** is an electrostatic attraction between oppositely (+ and -) charged ions.
Ionic Compounds are formed by positively and negatively charged particles. There are two categories of ionic compounds.	
Ionic compounds containing just ionic bonds These compounds are composed of two different atoms. They are binary ionic compounds composed of a positively charged metal and a negatively charged nonmetal. Example formulas for this category are given on the right.	**NaCl** (sodium chloride) **K₂O** (potassium oxide)
Ionic compounds containing both ionic and covalent bonds These compounds usually have three or more different atoms because they typically contain polyatomic ions. Polyatomic ions (**See Table E**) are ions containing two or more nonmetal atoms with an excess charge. Bonding within all polyatomic ions is covalent. A compound of this category is generally formed by the electrostatic attraction (ionic bond) between a positive metal and a negative polyatomic ion. Note: NH_4^+ is a positive polyatomic ion.	**NaNO₃** (sodium nitrate) **(NH₄)₂O** ammonium oxide

Covalent Bonds and Molecular Substances

	nonmetal nonmetal
Covalent bonds are forces holding atoms of nonmetals together in covalent and molecular substances.	
. **Covalent bonding** occurs between two nonmetal atoms that are **sharing** electrons	$$H - Cl$$ ↑
. A single covalent bond contains two (1 pair of) shared e-	
. A double covalent bond contains four (2 pairs of) shared e-	A **Covalent bond** formed between H and Cl atoms.
. A triple covalent bond contains six (3 pairs of) shared e-	A (–) between two nonmetal atoms represents two (a pair of) shared electrons.
. Sharing in covalent bonds could be equal or unequal	
. Electronegativity difference between the two nonmetals in covalent bonds is usually less than **1.7**	
Polar and Nonpolar Covalent Bonds and Substances	
Polar covalent bonds are formed by unequal sharing of electrons between two different nonmetal atoms.	$$N - O$$ ↑ polar bond
. Sharing of electrons in a polar covalent bond is unequal	
. Polar covalent bonds are the most common bond between atoms of molecular substances.	
Nonpolar covalent bonds are formed by equal sharing of electrons between two of the same nonmetal atoms.	$$F - F$$ ↑ nonpolar bond
. Sharing of electrons in nonpolar covalent bonds is equal	
. Nonpolar bonds are commonly found in diatomic (two-atom) molecules	
Molecular compounds are substances containing molecules.	hydrogen bromide (HBr) $$H - Br$$
A **molecule** is a group of covalently bonded atoms.	
A molecular substance is classified as polar or nonpolar depending on the symmetry of its molecules.	ammonia (NH_3)
Polar molecular substances contain molecules that have asymmetrical structures. A molecule has an asymmetrical structure when charges are unevenly distributed within the molecule. A polar molecule is only formed by polar covalently bonded atoms (as in HBr and NH_3)	$$H - N - H$$ $$\vert$$ $$H$$
Nonpolar molecular substances contain molecules that have symmetrical structures. A molecule has a symmetrical structure when charges are evenly distributed within the molecule. Even charge distribution means that a molecule does not have net positive and negative poles. Nonpolar means no poles. A nonpolar molecule can be formed by nonpolar covalently bonded atoms (as in O_2) or by polar covalently bonded atoms (as in CH_4).	Oxygen (O_2) $$O = O$$ methane (CH_4) $$H$$ $$\vert$$ $$H - C - H$$ $$\vert$$ $$H$$

Other types of Covalent bonds

Coordinate Covalent Bonds

A coordinate covalent bond is formed when both shared electrons are provided by only one of the atoms in the bond.

. The bond is formed when H^+ (hydrogen ion), which does not have an electron, bonds with a molecule such as NH_3(ammonia) or H_2O (water)

. NH_3 and H_2O molecules have lone pairs of electrons that they can share with an H^+ (hydrogen ion, proton) that has no electron.

Two (all you need to know) **formulas containing coordinate covalent bonds:**

H_3O^+ (hydronium ion)   *forms from* H_2O (water) and H^+ (hydrogen ion)
NH_4^+ (ammonium ion)   *forms from* NH_3 (ammonia) and H^+ (hydrogen ion)

Network Covalent Bonds

A network covalent bond is formed between nonmetal atoms in network solid compounds. Compounds formed by network covalent bonding cannot exist as discrete individual molecules.

Example of network solid compounds.

C	SiO_2	SiC
(Diamond)	(Silicon dioxide)	(Silicon carbide)

Metallic Bonds

A metallic bond is a force that holds metal atoms together in metallic substances.
. Metallic bonding is described as "positive ions immersed in a sea of mobile valence electrons"
. Mobile electrons allow for high electrical conductivity in metals

Example of substances containing metallic bonds:
Ca (calcium)   **Au** (Gold)   **Fe** (iron)

(**NOTE** Substances containing metallic bonds are metallic elements)

Types of Substances and Properties

Below are example solids and their melting points for the four types of substances.

Note the differences in temperature at which each solid will melt at STP.

Type of substance	Molecular	Ionic	Metallic	Network Solid
Example solid:	Ice (H_2O)	Salt (NaCl)	Gold (Au)	Diamond (C)
Melting point	0°C	801°C	1065°C	3550°C

Summary Table: Types of Substances and Properties

Types of substance	Phase at room temperature	Physical Properties (characteristics)		
		Melting point	Conductivity	Solubility (in water)
Metallic	Solid (except Hg - liquid)	Very High	Good (High) (in Solid and Liquid phases) (due to mobile electrons)	NO (insoluble)
Ionic	Solid only	High	Good (High) (in Liquid and Aqueous phases) (due to mobile ions)	Yes (soluble)
Molecular	solid, liquid, gas	Low	Poor (low) (in all phases)	Yes (slightly soluble)
Network solid	Solid only	Extremely high	Very poor (in all phases)	NO (Insoluble)

Bond types: summary of facts and examples

Bond Type	Types of elements involved in bonding	Bond description	Electronega- tivity difference	Types of substances containing bond	Example formula containing bond
Metallic	metal atoms of the same element	positive ions in sea of electrons	--------------	metallic substances	Ag K
Ionic	Metal & nonmetal	transfer of electrons	1.7 or greater	ionic substances	NaCl Li$_2$O
Covalent	nonmetals only	sharing of electrons	less than 1.7	molecular and network solids	HCl
Polar covalent	Two different nonmetals	unequal sharing	greater than 0 but less than 1.7	polar and nonpolar molecular	H$_2$O CH$_4$
Nonpolar covalent	same nonmetal (or nonmetal atoms with the same electronegativity)	equal sharing of electrons	zero (0)	diatomic nonpolar molecular	H$_2$ O$_2$
Coordinate covalent	two different nonmetals	One atom provides both shared electrons	--------------	polyatomic ions	NH$_4^+$ H$_3$O$^+$
Network solid covalent	nonmetals only	No discrete particles	-------------	network solids	C , SiC, SiO$_2$

Lesson 3: Molecular Polarity and Intermolecular forces

Introduction

Bond polarity in a substance refers to the extent of the electrical (positive and negative) charges on the bonded atoms. Bond polarity depends largely on the electronegativity difference (ED) between two bonded atoms. The bigger the difference in electronegativity, the greater the ionic and polar characteristics of the bond. The smaller the difference in electronegativity values, the greater the covalent characteristics of the bond.

Molecular polarity refers to the extent of the overall positive and negative charges on a molecule. Molecular polarity of a substance depends largely on the electronegativity difference between the bonded atoms, as well as the symmetry of its structure.

Degree of Polarity

Comparing the degree of polarity between two or more substances can be done by determining and comparing the electronegativity difference (ED) of the bonded atoms. *Recall* that electronegativity measures an atom's ability to attract (pull) electrons from another atom during chemical bonding. Electronegativity values for the elements can be found on Reference Table S.

To calculate electronegativity difference between two atoms in a bond:

Step 1 : Use Table S to get electronegativity values for atoms in each formula

Step 2: Determine ED = High electronegativity – Low electronegativity

To determine which formula is most or least ionic or polar: Use information below.

Most ionic, Most polar, or Least covalent: Formula with **Highest ED**

Least ionic, Least polar, or Most covalent : Formula with **Lowest ED**

The note below shows you how to compare the degree of polarity between LiCl, KCl, and CsCl

ED for three formulas are calculated. Relative polarity are determined based on ED values.	**LiCl**	**KCl**	**CsCl**
	Cl = 3.2	Cl = 3.2	Cl = 3.2
	Li = 1.0	K = 0.8	Cs = 0.7
	ED 2.2	2.4	2.5
	(Lowest ED)		*(Highest ED)*
	LiCl : Least ionic		**CsCl** : Most ionic
	Least polar		Most polar
	Most covalent		Least covalent

Concepts	Explanations	Depends on	Types	Description	Examples
Bond polarity	Describes polarity (+ and − charges) of a covalent bond between two atoms	Depends largely on the type of atoms or their electronegativity difference	Polar bond	A bond that produces + and − ends on bonded atoms. Found between two different nonmetals	C — H P — Cl
			Nonpolar bond	A bond that does not produce + and − ends on the bonded atoms. Found between two of the same nonmetal atoms	H — H O = O
Molecular polarity	Describes the overall polarity (+ and − charges) of a molecule	Depends largely on the symmetry and charge distributions on a molecule	Polar molecule	Asymmetrical structure. Uneven + and − charge distributions	HF H — F H_2O
			Nonpolar molecule	Symmetrical structure. Even + and − charge distributions	Cl_2 Cl — Cl CH_4
Molecular symmetry	Describes the overall arrangement of atoms to make a molecule	Depends largely on the nature or type of atoms and the number of each atom of the molecule	Symmetrical molecules	Arrangement of atoms is evenly distributed	Br — Br H — C — H
			Asymmetrical molecules	Arrangement of atoms is unevenly distributed	H — Cl H — N — H
Molecular shapes	Describes structural shapes of molecules due to arrangements of its atoms	Depends on several factors including types of atoms, as well as shared and unshared electrons	Linear		H — Cl O = C = O
			Tetrahedral		Cl—C—Cl
			Angular		S (with H, H)
			Pyramidal		H — N — H

Intermolecular forces (IMF)

Intermolecular forces are forces that exist between molecules in molecular substances. Intermolecular forces hold molecules of molecular substances together in liquid and solid states. These forces exist in molecular substances because of the unequal charge distribution within molecules. Intermolecular forces are generally weaker than the intramolecular forces (bonding between atoms) of the substance.

Properties of substances that are due to Intermolecular Forces (IMF):

Melting point, boiling point and vapor pressure of a substance depends on the strength of its intermolecular forces.
The stronger the intermolecular forces of a substance:
. The higher the melting and boiling points of the substance

. The lower the vapor pressure of the substance.

Strength of intermolecular forces depends on the following three factors:
1. The polarity of the molecules
Polar substances generally have stronger IMF than nonpolar substances. Therefore, polar substances tend to have higher boiling points, higher melting points, and lower vapor pressures when compared to a nonpolar substances. Example comparison is shown below.

Molecular substances	*Relative strength of intermolecular force*	*Relative boiling point*
CH_4 (nonpolar)	Weaker	Lower (-161°C)
H_2O (polar)	Stronger	Higher (100°C)

2. Size of the molecules
The strength of intermolecular forces among similar nonpolar substances varies depending on the size of their molecules. In general, intermolecular forces (IMF) are stronger in a nonpolar substance with large molecular mass when compared to a similar substance of smaller molecular mass.

Relative comparisons of molecular size, IMF strength, and boiling points for three groups of similar substances are shown below.

Similar nonpolar substances			*Relative size of molecule*	*Relative IMF Strength*	*Relative Boiling point*
Halogens	*Noble gases*	*Hydrocarbons*			
F_2	He	CH_4	Smallest	Weakest	Lowest
Cl_2	Ne	C_2H_6			
Br_2	Ar	C_3H_8	Biggest	Strongest	Highest

3. Phase of a substance/distance between the molecules

The strength of intermolecular forces of a substance varies depending on the phase of the substance. In general, intermolecular forces are stronger between molecules of a substance in the solid phase. The force is weaker when the substance is in the gas phase. This is best observed among the halogens (Group 17 element).

Halogen	Phase at STP	Relative Strength of intermolecular forces
F_2 and Cl_2	Gas	Weakest
Br_2	Liquid	A little stronger
I_2	Solid	Strongest

At STP, iodine is a solid and fluorine is a gas because iodine has stronger intermolecular forces than fluorine.

Hydrogen Bonding

Hydrogen bonding is a type of intermolecular force that exists in certain polar substances. Among similar polar substances, the degree of polarity varies. Because of these differences in polarity, the strength of intermolecular forces also varies among similar polar substances.

Hydrogen bonding is a strong intermolecular force that exists in the following three polar substances:

         H_2O (water), **NH_3** (ammonia) and **HF** (hydrogen fluoride).

Hydrogen bonding exists in these substances because H in each formula is bonded to an atom (O, F, or N) of small radius and high electronegativity.

When H_2O is compared to a similar substance (such as H_2S), H_2O will always have stronger intermolecular forces (hydrogen bonding) than H_2S. As a result, the boiling point and the melting point of H_2O are higher than those of H_2S.

Bonding in water

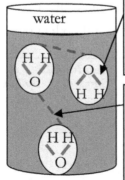

Intramolecular (polar covalent bonding)
. Holds O and H atoms to make water molecules
. Chemical properties (or reactions) of water require the breaking of this bond
. A stronger bond than the intermolecular forces

Intermolecular (hydrogen bonding)
. Holds the molecules together in solid and liquid phases
. Physical properties (such as vapor pressure, boiling and melting points) depend on the strength of this bond
. A weaker force than the intramolecular bond

Lesson 4: Valence electrons and Lewis electron-dot diagrams

Introduction

Valence electrons are electrons in the outermost electron shell of an atom. During ionic bonding, valence electrons are lost by a metal to form a positive ion, and are gained by a nonmetal to form a negative ion. During covalent bonding, nonmetal atoms share their valence electrons.

In this lesson, you will learn how to show different bond types using Lewis electron-dot diagrams.

Lewis Electron–dot Diagrams for Neutral atoms and Ions

A **Lewis electron- dot diagram** is a notation that shows the symbol of an atom and dots to represents valence electrons of the atom. Lewis electron-dot diagrams can be drawn for neutral atoms, ions and compounds.

Neutral atoms

A Lewis electron-dot diagram for a neutral atom is the symbol of the atom and dots equal to the number of its valence electrons. Examples are given below.

	e- configuration	valence electrons	dot diagram
Sodium atom (Na)	2 – 8 – 1	1	Na ·
Phosphorus atom (P)	2 – 8 – 5	5	·P:

Positive ions

A Lewis dot-diagram for a positive ion is just the symbol of the positive ion, which can be determined from the Periodic Table.

	e- configuration	valence electrons	dot diagram
Sodium ion (Na$^+$)	2 – 8	8	Na$^+$
Beryllium ion (Be^{2+})	2	2	Be^{2+}

Negative ions

A Lewis electron-dot diagram for a negative ion is the symbol of the ion and 8 dots around it. A bracket often surrounds the atom's symbol and the dots.

Note: A Lewis electron-dot diagram for a negative hydrogen ion (H-) will have just 2 dots as shown below . Hydrogen has only one occupied electron shell (the 1st), which has enough orbitals for just two electrons.

	e- configuration	valence electrons	dot diagram
Phosphide ion (P^{3-})	2 – 8 – 8	8	$\left[:P: \right]^{3-}$
Hydride ion (H$^-$)	2	2	$\left[H: \right]^-$

Note: Use the Periodic Table to get the correct ion formulas

Lewis Electron-dot Diagram for Ionic Compounds

Recall that ionic compounds are composed of positive (+) and negative (-) ions. *Also recall* that the positive ion is formed by a metal transferring (losing) its valence electrons to a nonmetal. The nonmetal accepts (gains) the electrons to become a negative ion.

Lewis electron-dot diagrams for ionic formulas must show the Lewis electron-dot symbols for both the positive and negative ions of the ionic compound.

A *correct* Lewis electron-dot diagram for a given ionic formula must show the following:

The *correct* symbol and charge of the positive ion in the formula.

The *correct* symbol and charge of the negative ion in the formula.

The *correct* number of each ion in the formula.

The *correct* number of dots around the negative ion of the formula.
A bracket should surround the dot diagram of the negative ion.

Below, Lewis electron-dot diagrams for three ionic compounds are given.

Name of compound	*Chemical formula*	*Electron-dot diagrams*
Sodium chloride	NaCl	$Na^+ \left[:\overset{..}{\underset{..}{Cl}}: \right]^-$
Calcium bromide	$CaBr_2$	$Ca^{2+}\ 2\ [:\overset{..}{\underset{..}{Br}}:]^-$
Potassium oxide	K_2O	$2K^+ \left[:\overset{..}{\underset{..}{O}}: \right]^{2-}$
		or
		$K^+ \left[:\overset{x\ .}{\underset{.\ x}{O}}: \right]^{2-} K^+$

Note: x represents the valence electrons transferred from the metal atom.

Note the importance of having the correct number of each ion.
Compounds are neutral, so the sum of the charges in a compound must equal zero.

In calcium bromide, 2 bromides (each a -1 ion) are needed to equalize the charge of 1 calcium ion (a +2 ion).

In potassium oxide, 2 potassium ions (each a +1 ion) are needed to equalize the charge of 1 oxide ion (a -2 ion).

Lewis Electron-dot Diagrams for Molecular Substances

Lewis electron-dot diagrams for covalently bonded atoms (molecules) must show the sharing of valence electrons by the nonmetal atoms. Each pair of electrons (2 electrons) shared between two atoms forms one (single) covalent bond (−). A correct Lewis electron-dot diagram for a molecular formula must have the following:

Correct symbols and number of the nonmetal atoms.
Correct number of shared electrons between the atoms.
Correct number of valence electrons around each atom.

Below are electron-dot diagrams for common polar and nonpolar substances.

Polar substances (note how these diagrams have asymmetrical shapes)

Molecular name	Molecular formula	Lewis electron-dot diagram

Hydrogen chloride — HCl

Water — H_2O

Ammonia — NH_3

Nonpolar substances (note how these diagrams have symmetrical shapes)

Molecular name	Molecular formula	Lewis electron-dot diagrams

Chlorine — Cl_2

Carbon dioxide — CO_2

Methane — CH_4

Carbon tetrachloride — CCl_4

Practice Questions

Lesson 1: Stability and Energy in Bonding

Answer the multiple choice questions below.

1. Chemical bonding is the simultaneous attraction of two nuclei to
    1) Protons   2) Neutrons   3) Electrons   4) Positron

2. When atoms bond, their stability
    1) Increases   2) Decreases   3) Remains the same

3. When atoms bond, the electron configuration of each atom in the bond resembles those of the nearest
    1) Noble gas   2) Halogen   3) Alkaline earth   4) Alkali

4. What type of energy is stored in the bonds of chemical substances?
    1) Kinetic energy   3) Activation energy
    2) Potential energy   4) Ionization energy

5. Stored energy in chemical bonds of substances depends on
    1) The composition of the chemical substances only
    2) The structure of the chemical substances only
    3) Both the composition and the structure of chemical substances
    4) Neither the composition nor the structure of chemical substances

6. As a bond is broken in a compound, the potential energy of the atoms generally
    1) Remains the same   2) Decreases   3) Increases

7. Bond formation between two atoms is generally
    1) Exothermic , which absorbs energy   3) Endothermic , which absorbs energy
    2) Exothermic, which releases energy   4) Endothermic, which releases energy

8. Which statement is true concerning the process taking place in the reaction?

$$AB \ + \ energy \ \rightarrow \ A \ + \ B$$
    1) A bond is broken and energy is absorbed
    2) A bond is formed and energy is absorbed
    3) A bond is broken and energy is released
    4) A bond is formed and energy is released

   Given the reaction:
$$H_2 \ + \ Cl_2 \ \rightarrow \ 2HCl$$
9. Which statement best describes the energy changes as bonds are formed and broken in this reaction?
    1) The breaking of Cl–Cl bonds absorbs energy
    2) The forming of H–Cl bonds absorbs energy
    3) The breaking of H–H bonds releases energy
    4) The forming of H–Cl bonds releases energy

10. When two fluorine atoms combine to produce a molecule of fluorine
    1) A bond will be formed, and energy will be absorbed
    2) A bond will be broken, and energy will be absorbed
    3) A bond will be formed, and energy will be released
    4) A bond will be broken, and energy will be released

Lesson 2: Types of Bonding and Substances

Define the following terms and answer the multiple choice questions below.

11. Intramolecular force   12. Ionic bond   13. Covalent bond   14. Polar covalent
15. Nonpolar covalent   16. Network solid covalent   17. Coordinate covalent
18. Metallic bond   19. Molecule   20. Polar substance   21. Nonpolar substance

22. When combining with a metallic atom, a nonmetallic atom tends to
    1) Lose electrons and form a negative ion   3) Gain electrons and form a negative ion
    2) Lose electrons and form a positive ion   4) Gain electrons and form a positive ion

23. When two atoms form an ionic bond, the electronegativity difference between these two atoms is generally
    1) Greater than 1.7   2) Exactly zero   3) Less than 1.7   4) Less than Zero

24. The sharing of electrons in covalent bonding
    1) Must always be equal   3) Is neither equal nor unequal
    2) Must always be unequal   4) Can be equal or unequal

25. The ability to conduct electricity in the solid state is a characteristic of metallic substances. This characteristic is best explained by the presence of
    1) Mobile neutrons   2) Mobile ions   3) Mobile protons   4) Mobile electrons

26. Which pair of elements forms a bond that is mostly ionic?
    1) $CaCl_2$ 2) CCl_4 3) HCl   4) PCl_5

27. Element X combines with rubidium to form an ionic bond. In which group of the Periodic Table could element X be found?
    1) Group 1   2) Group 2   3) Group 13   4) Group 16

28. Which compound contains atoms held together by covalent bonds?
    1) Sodium chloride   3) Aluminum oxide
    2) Calcium hydride   4) Nitrogen (II) oxide

29. Coordinate covalent bonding would be found in which species?
    1) Hydronium ion   3) Hydrogen ion
    2) Oxygen   4) Sodium chloride

30. Which electron configuration belongs to a substance whose atoms are held together by metallic bonds?
    1) 2 − 8 − 8   3) 1
    2) 2 − 8 − 18 − 18   4) 2 − 8 − 18 − 5

31. Which formula contains both ionic and covalent bonds?
    1) MgS   2) NaBr   3) $C_6H_{12}O_6$ 4) $MgSO_4$

32. Which best describes the bonding in Cl_2?
    1) Polar and covalent   3) Network sold and covalent
    2) Nonpolar and covalent   4) Coordinate and covalent

33. Bonding in ammonia is best described as
    1) Covalent   2) Ionic   3) Coordinate   4) Metallic

34. Two atoms with ground state electron configurations of $2 - 8 - 8 - 1$ and $2 - 8 - 6$ would most likely form a bond that is
    1) Covalent, because there will be a sharing of electrons
    2) Covalent, because there will be a transferring of electrons
    3) Ionic, because there will be a sharing of electrons
    4) Ionic, because there will be a transferring of electrons

35. Which two substances are covalent compounds?
    1) $C_6H_{12}O_6(s)$ and $KI(s)$
    2) $C_6H_{12}O_6(s)$ and $HCl(g)$
    3) $KI(s)$ and $NaCl(s)$
    4) $NaCl(s)$ and $HCl(g)$

36. Which formula represents an ionic compound?
    1) $FeCl_2$ 2) Fe 3) Cl_2 4) PCl_3

37. The table below contains properties of compounds A, B, C, and D.

Compound	Melting point	Conductivity	Solubility in water
A	High	Excellent (liquid)	soluble
B	High	Very poor (solid)	Insoluble
C	Low	Poor (solid)	Slightly soluble
D	High	Excellent (solid)	Insoluble

    Which list identifies the type of solid each compound represents?
    1) A – ionic, B – network , C – metallic, D – molecular
    2) A – network, B – ionic, C – molecular, D – metallic
    3) A – metallic, B – molecular, C – network, D – ionic
    4) A – ionic, B – network, C – molecular, D – metallic

38. A solid substance is found to have the following properties:

    • Non electrolytes   • Low solubility in water   • Low melting point
    Based on the above properties, the solid substance could be

    1) $I_2(s)$ 2) $Ag(s)$ 3) $NaCl(s)$ 4) $SiO_2(s)$

39. A solid substance has a high melting point and is a good conductor of electricity as a solid and as a liquid. This substance could be
    1) Calcium chloride   2) Carbon dioxide   3) Silver   4) Carbon

40. Which property is true of copper?
    1) It has a low melting point
    2) It is a non-conductor
    3) It has a high melting point
    4) It is soluble in water

41. Which substance at STP conducts electricity because the substance contains mobile electrons?
    1) $NaCl$ 2) S 3) Mg 4) H_2O

42. Which set of properties best describes $NH_4Cl(s)$?
    1) Low solubility in water and a poor conductor of electricity as aqueous
    2) Low solubility in water and a good conductor of electricity as aqueous
    3) High solubility in water and a poor conductor of electricity as aqueous
    4) High solubility in water and a good conductor of electricity as aqueous

Lesson 3: Molecular Polarity and Intermolecular Forces

Answer the multiple choice questions below.

43. Asymmetrical distribution of charge in a molecule usually results in the molecule being
    1) Polar
    2) Metallic
    3) Nonpolar
    4) Ionic

44. The bonding in nonpolar molecules usually results in the molecules having
    1) Asymmetrical shape with equal charge distribution
    2) Asymmetrical shape with unequal charge distribution
    3) Symmetrical shape with equal charge distribution
    4) Symmetrical shape with unequal charge distribution

45. The degree of polarity of molecular substances is mainly due to the
    1) Difference in number of bonds
    2) Difference in electronegativity
    3) Difference in number of protons
    4) Difference in shape

46. The relatively high boiling point of water is primarily due to the presence of
    1) Hydrogen bonds
    2) Covalent bonds
    3) Metallic bonds
    4) Network solid bonds

47. The formula of which substance represents a nonpolar molecule containing nonpolar bonds?
    1) CH_4 2) CO_2 3) H_2O 4) N_2

48. The formula of which substance represents a nonpolar molecule with polar covalent bonds?
    1) NH_3 2) Na   3) CH_4 4) Cl_2

49. The shape and bonding in hydrogen fluoride, HF, are best described as
    1) Symmetrical and polar
    2) Symmetrical and nonpolar
    3) Asymmetrical and polar
    4) Asymmetrical and nonpolar

50. The bonding in which compound has the least degree of ionic character?
    1) KBr   2) HF   3) MgO   4) PCl_3

51. Which structural formula represents a nonpolar symmetrical molecule?
    1) $Na - Cl$ 2) $O = C = O$ 3) $H - I$ 4)

52. Which diagram best represents a polar molecule?

    1) Br_2 2) HBr   3) CH_4 4) LiBr

53. Hydrogen bonding is strongest between the molecules of
    1) HCl(l)   2) HBr(l)   3) HI(l)   4) HF(l)

54. Which of the following compounds has the highest normal boiling point?
    1) $H_2O(l)$ 2) $H_2S(l)$ 3) $H_2Se(l)$ 4) $H_2Te(l)$

55. Which of the following substance has the lowest normal boiling point?
    1) C_5H_{10} 2) C_4H_8 3) C_3H_6 4) C_2H_4

Lesson 4: Lewis Electron-dot Diagrams in Bonding

Answer the multiple choice questions below.

56. In the Lewis electron-dot diagram H:Cl: , the dots represent
   1) Valence electrons of H only
   2) Valence electrons of Cl only
   3) Valence electrons for both H and C atom
   4) All the electrons found in H and C atoms

57. Which electron-dot symbol is correctly drawn for the atom it represents?
   1) Al·
   2) S·
   3) ·B·
   4) Li·

58. Which diagram correctly represents the electron-dot diagram for an oxygen ion?
   1) $\left[: O : \right]^{2-}$
   2) $\left[O : \right]^{2-}$
   3) $\left[: O : \right]^{2-}$
   4) $\left[: O : \right]^{2-}$

59. Which electron-dot formula represents ionic bonding between two atoms?
   1) $^{xx}_{x}$Br $^{x}_{xx}$ Br :
   2) H ^{x} Br :
   3) Na$^+$ $\left[^{x}_{xx} F ^{x}_{xx} \right]^{-}$
   4) H ^{x} F $^{xx}_{xx}$ ^{x}

60. Carbon dioxide is correctly represented by which Lewis electron-dot diagram?
   1) :O::C::O:
   2) :O::C::O:
   3) O::C::O
   4) :O::C::O:

61. Which electron-dot diagram is correct for barium fluoride ?
   1) Ba^{2+} 2$\left[: F : \right]^{2-}$
   2) $\left[: Ba : \right]^{2+}$ 2F –
   3) Ba^{2+} 2F –
   4) $\left[:Ba : \right]^{2+}$ 2$\left[: F : \right]^{-}$

Topic Mastery / Constructed Response

Draw Lewis electron dot diagrams for the following compounds.

62. Lithium fluoride
63. Aluminum Bromide
64. Magnesium oxide
65. Hydrogen (H_2)
66. Nitrogen (N_2)
67. Carbon tetrafluoride (CF_4)

68. Describe the bond polarity and molecular polarity of the molecule below:

```
     Cl
     |
Cl – C – Cl
     |
     Cl
```

Bond polarity:

Molecular polarity:

69. How would you compare the intermolecular forces and boiling point of H_2O to that of carbon tetrachloride, whose molecule is shown in #68.

Intermolecular forces:

Boiling point:

70. Draw a diagram to show hydrogen bonding between three hydrogen fluoride molecules. Use (------) to represent hydrogen bonding.

Lesson 1: Interpretation of Chemical Formulas

Introduction

Chemical formulas are used to represent the compositions of elements and compounds (pure substances). A chemical formula expresses the *qualitative* and *quantitative* compositions of a substance.

Qualitative information of a formula shows the types of atoms (or ions) that make up the substance.

Quantitative information of a formula shows how many of each atom (or ion) is in the formula. The number of each atom in a formula is shown with a subscript. A **subscript** in chemical formulas is the whole number written to the bottom right of each atom in a formula.

H_2SO_4

subscripts

Counting Atoms in Formulas

Qualitative and quantitative information of a formula can be determined by counting how many of each atom is in the formula. Three examples are given below.

Types of formulas	Example formula	# of each atom	Total # of atoms
Simple formula	H_2SO_4	2 **H** atoms 1 **S** atom 4 **O** atoms	**Three** different atoms. **7** total atoms
Formula with parentheses	$(NH_4)_2O$	2 **N** atoms (2 x 1) 8 **H** atoms (4 x2) 1 **O** atom	**Three** different atoms. **11 total atoms**
Formula of hydrates	$CuSO_4 \cdot 5H_2O$	1 **Cu** atom 1 **S** atom 9 **O** atoms (4 + 5) 10 **H** atoms (5 x 2)	**Four** different atoms. **21 total atoms**

Counting ratio of ions in formulas

Another way of expressing the qualitative and quantitative compositions of a substance is to determine the ratio of ions in the formula.

Type of formula	Example formula	Ions in formula	Ratio of ions
Binary ionic	$CaCl_2$ calcium chloride	Ca^{2+} Cl^- calcium ion chloride ion	$1\ Ca^{2+} : 2\ Cl^-$
Polyatomic formula (with parentheses)	$Al_2(SO_4)_3$ aluminum sulfate	Al^{3+} SO_4^{2-} aluminum ion sulfate ion	$2\ Al^{3+} : 3\ SO_4^{2-}$
polyatomic formula (without parentheses)	KNO_3 potassium nitrate	K^+ NO_3^- potassium ion nitrate ion	$1\ K^+ : 1\ NO_3^-$

Lesson 2: Types of Chemical Formulas

There are three types of chemical formulas that are used to show compositions of substances.

In this lesson, you will learn about molecular formulas, empirical formulas, and structural formulas.

Types of Formulas:

A **molecular formula** is a formula showing the true composition of a known substance.

A **structural formula** is a formula showing how atoms of a substance are bonded together.

An **empirical formula** is a formula in which the elements are in the smallest whole-number ratio.

Examples of the three formulas are shown below:

	ethane	water
Molecular	C_2H_6	H_2O

Structural

```
        H   H              O
        |   |             / \
    H – C – C – H        H   H
        |   |
        H   H
```

Empirical	CH_3	H_2O

C_2H_6 is reduced to CH_3 by dividing each subscript of the formula by **2** (Greatest Common Factor of 2 and 6)

$C_6H_{12}O_6$ can be reduced to CH_2O by dividing each subscript of the formula by **6** (Greatest Common Factor of 6,12, and 6)

Lesson 3 – Chemical Nomenclature

Introduction:

There are millions of known chemical substances, and many more are being discovered.

Chemical nomenclature refers to the systematic rules for naming and writing formulas of chemical substances. The International Union of Pure and Applied Chemistry (IUPAC) is an organization that makes recommendations as to how chemical substances are named.

In this lesson, you will learn how to apply IUPAC rules to writing formulas and names for compounds in different classes of *inorganic* compounds.

Chemical Formulas

A chemical formula is correctly written for a known substance when both the qualitative and quantitative information of the formula are both correct. This to say that:

. Element (or ion) symbols in a formula must all be correct for the substance.
. Subscripts of the elements (or ions) in a formula must be in the correct ratio. Correct subscripts in a formula allow the sum of charges in the formula to equal zero. All compound formulas must be neutral.

Steps to writing chemical formulas for ionic compounds

When the IUPAC name for an ionic compound is given, use the steps below to write its correct formula.

Step 1:   **Write** the correct ion symbols for the chemical name.

       Use the Periodic Table to get the correct ion symbol for an element.

       Use Table E to get the correct polyatomic ion symbol.

       Always put parentheses around polyatomic atoms. Ex. $(SO_4)^{2-}$

Step 2:   **Criss-cross** charge values so one becomes the subscript for the other.

Step 3:   **Clean up** formula after criss-crossing by:

       Reducing subscripts that are reducible to empirical form.

       For polyatomic ion compounds:
       Do not change subscripts of the polyatomic ion

       Remove parentheses if subscript outside parentheses is a 1

       Keep parentheses if subscript outside parentheses is greater than a 1

Steps shown above and on the next pages are to ensure that your final (correct) formula has the correct element symbols and correct subscripts for the compound name that is given. If you can write correct formulas without going through all these steps, you should do so.

Writing Formulas for Ionic Compounds

Binary ionic compounds have formulas that are composed of two different elements: a metal and a nonmetal. IUPAC names of binary compounds always end with –*ide*. Examples: Calcium brom*ide*, Aluminum sulf*ide*, and Zinc ox*ide*

Example 1: *Calcium bromide*   *Aluminum Sulfide*   *Zinc Oxide*

Step 1 Ca^{2+} Br^{1-} Al^{3+} S^{2-} Zn^{2+} O^{2-}

Step 2 Ca^{2+} Br^{1-} criss-crossing Al^{3+} S^{2-} Zn^{2+} O^{2-}
         charge values

     Ca_1 Br_2 Al_2 S_3 Zn_2 O_2

Step 3
(formulas)   **$CaBr_2$**   **Al_2S_3**   **ZnO**

Ionic Compounds Containing a Polyatomic Ion

Polyatomic ions are composed of two or more atoms with an excess charge. *Reference Table E lists some common polyatomic ions*. IUPAC names of polyatomic ions typically end with -*ate* or –*ite*. Examples of compounds containing a polyatomic ion are: sodium *nitrate*, calcium *sulfite*, and *ammonium* oxide.

Example 2: *Sodium Nitrate*   *Calcium Sulfite*   *Ammonium Oxide*

Step 1 Na^{+1} $(NO_3)^{1-}$ Ca^{2+} $(SO_3)^{2-}$ $(NH_4)^{1+}$ O^{2-}

Step 2 Na^{+1} $(NO_3)^{1-}$ Ca^{2+} $(SO_3)^{2-}$ $(NH_4)^{1+}$ O^{2-}

     Na_1 $(NO_3)_1$ Ca_2 $(SO_3)_2$ $(NH_4)_2$ O_1

Step 3
(formulas)   **$NaNO_3$**   **$CaSO_3$**   **$(NH_4)_2O$**

Ionic Compounds Containing an Atom with Multiple Oxidation #s.

The **stock system** nomenclature uses Roman numerals in parentheses to distinguish names of compounds produced by different positive oxidation states of an atom. Examples of Stock system naming and the interpretation of a Roman numeral in names are given below.

Iron **(II)** chloride   **(II)** indicates a compound of a +2 iron.

Iron **(III)** chloride   **(III)** indicates a compound of a +3 iron

Nitrogen **(IV)** oxide   **(IV)** indicates a compound of a +4 nitrogen

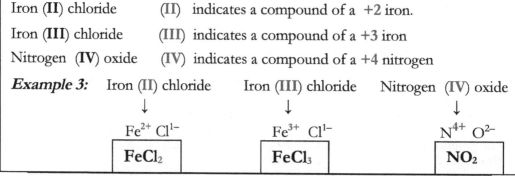

Example 3:   Iron (II) chloride   Iron (III) chloride   Nitrogen (IV) oxide

         ↓   ↓   ↓

     Fe^{2+} Cl^{1-} Fe^{3+} Cl^{1-} N^{4+} O^{2-}

     $FeCl_2$ **$FeCl_3$**   **NO_2**

Writing IUPAC Names for Ionic Compounds

The IUPAC name is correctly written for a given formula when all of the following are represented correctly.

· Atoms and/or ions in the formula are named correctly.

· Name ending , if necessary, is applied correctly.

· Roman numeral, if necessary, is correctly used.

Binary ionic compounds contain just two elements: a metal and nonmetal. *Examples* are $ZnCl_2$, CaO and Al_2N_3. IUPAC naming of binary compounds involves changing the nonmetal ending to *–ide*. The metal name is never changed.

Example 5: $ZnCl_2$ CaO Al_2N_3

Zinc Chlor*ine*   Calcium O*xygen*   Aluminum Nitr*ogen*

| Zinc Chlor*ide* | Calcium ox*ide* | Aluminum nitr*ide* |

Compounds containing a polyatomic ion generally contain three or more elements. Examples are $Mg_2(PO_4)_3$, NH_4NO_3 and NH_4Cl. When naming compounds containing a polyatomic ion, no change should be made to the name of the polyatomic ion (See Table E) or to the name of the metal.

Example 6: $Mg_2(PO_4)_3$ NH_4NO_3 NH_4Cl

| Magnesium phosphate | Ammonium nitrate | Ammonium chlor*ide* |

Compounds containing an element with multiple oxidation numbers must be named using the Stock System. In each of the three formulas below, the first element has multiple (+) oxidation numbers (See the Periodic Table to confirm). A Roman numeral (in parentheses) is used in naming to identify which positive charge of the element formed the compound.

Example 7: Sn F_4 N_2O $Fe_3(PO_4)_2$

| Tin (IV) fluor*ide* | Nitrogen (I) ox*ide* | Iron (II) phosphate |

In some formulas (like the three above) the *subscript* of the second symbol in each formula is used as the Roman Numeral (or the +charge) value in the ( ). In some formulas (like the two below), the *+charge value* must be determined mathematically by following steps given in the box to the left.

Example 8:

	CrN_2	$MnSO_4$
Assign (−) charge value.	Cr N_2^{3-}	Mn $(SO_4)^{2-}$
Multiply (−) charge by *subscript* to get total (−) in formula .	*2* x 3- = - 6	*1* x 2- = -2
Determine **total (+)** needed to make charges = 0	+6	+2
Use **+ charge** as **Roman numeral** in ( ) to name the formula·	Chromium (VI) nitr*ide*	Manganese (II) sulfate

Writing Formulas and Naming Covalent (Molecular) Substances

Molecular (covalent) compounds are composed only of nonmetal atoms. **Binary molecular** compounds, which contain two different nonmetals, are commonly named with IUPAC recommended prefixes. A **prefix** in a chemical name indicates how many of the nonmetal atom is in a given compound.

The table below lists prefixes for naming covalent compounds.

Number of atom	Prefix	Number of atom	Prefix
1	mono-	6	hexa-
2	di-	7	hepta-
3	tri-	8	octa-
4	tetra-	9	nona-
5	penta-	10	deca-

Writing formulas for covalent substances: Follow rules and examples below

. Prefixes are interpreted into subscripts for the elements.

. Absence of a prefix indicates that there is just one of that atom.

. No criss-crossing or reducing of formula into empirical form is necessary.

Example 9

Molecular name	Carbon *di*oxide	Carbon *mono*xide	*di*nitrogen *mono*xide
Interpretation	1 C 2 O	1 C 1 O	2 N 1 O
Formula	CO_2	CO	N_2O

Writing names for covalent substances: Follow rules and examples below.

. Subscripts are interpreted into prefixes for the elements

. No prefix is used when there is just one of the first nonmetal atom (see PCl_3)

. The "a" or "o" of a prefix is dropped if the addition of the prefix resulted in a name having two vowels next to each other (see N_2O_5)
   In N_2O_5, the *a* in *pentaoxide* is dropped, and the formula is correctly named *pentoxide*.

. Name ending for the second nonmetal atom must be changed to *-ide*

Example 10:

PCl_3	N_2O_5	H_2S
1 Phosphorus **3** Chlorine	**2** nitrogen **5** oxygen	**2** hydrogen **1** sulfur
Phosphorus *trichloride*	*di*nitrogen *pentoxide*	*di*hydrogen *monosulfide*

Lesson 4: Chemical Equations

Introduction
Equations show changes that are taking place in substances. There are three major types of changes, and each can be represented with an equation.

Chemical equations show changes in chemical compositions of one or more substances to other substances.	***Example equations*** $H_2(g) + O_2(g) \rightarrow H_2O(l)$
Physical equations show a change of a substance from one phase to a different form without changing its chemical composition.	$H_2O(s) \rightarrow H_2O(l)$
Nuclear equations show changes in the nucleus contents of one or more atoms to those of different atoms. In this lesson, you will learn only of chemical changes and equations.	$^{220}_{87}Fr \rightarrow \ ^{4}_{2}He + \ ^{216}_{85}At$

Interpreting Chemical Equations

A **chemical equation** uses symbols to show changes in chemical compositions of substances during a chemical change (reaction).
A **chemical reaction** is a means by which a chemical change occurs.

Reactants are the starting substances that will go through a chemical change. (Reactants are shown to the **LEFT** of the arrow in equations)

Products are the substances that remain after a change has occurred. (products are shown to the **RIGHT** of the arrow in equations)

A **coefficient** is a whole number in front of a substance to show the number of moles (how many) of that substance taking part in the reaction.

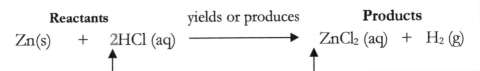

Reactants	**Products**
Coefficient of 2 : indicates that there are 2 moles of HCl	**Coefficient of 1:** Indicates that there is 1 mole of ZnCl₂.
Coefficient of 2 or more is always written in front of the substance in equations.	A coefficient of 1 is never written in front of the substance.

Types of Reactions

Four types of chemical reactions are defined and explained below. Diagrams and example equations representing each type of reaction are given to the right of each reaction.

Synthesis reactions always involve two or more substances as reactants. During a synthesis reaction, the reactants combine to form one product.

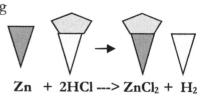

$$2H_2 + O_2 \rightarrow 2H_2O$$

Decomposition reactions always involve one single substance as a reactant. During decomposition, the reactant breaks down (or decomposes) into two or more products.

$$2H_2O \rightarrow 2H_2 + O_2$$

Single replacement reactions likely involve a compound and a free element as reactants. During a single replacement reaction, the free element replaces one of the elements in the compound. This reaction only occurs when the free element reactant is more reactive than the similar element in the compound it is replacing.

$$Zn + 2HCl \dashrightarrow ZnCl_2 + H_2$$

Double replacement reactions usually involve two compounds in aqueous phase. During a double replacement reaction, the ions of the compounds switch partners. This reaction is also called "metathesis."

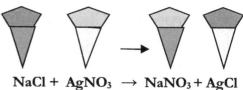

$$NaCl + AgNO_3 \rightarrow NaNO_3 + AgCl$$

Combustion reactions typically involve the burning of an organic substance in the presence of oxygen. Water and carbon dioxide are usually produced in combustion reactions.

$$CH_4 + 2O_2 \rightarrow CO_2 + H_2O$$

organic substance

Balanced Equations

Law of conservation states that during a chemical reaction:

. Neither atoms, mass, charge or energy are created nor destroyed.

A **balanced chemical** equation (shown below) is a way of showing conservation in chemical reactions.

Conservation of atoms

$$N_2 + 3H_2 \longrightarrow 2NH_3$$

2 N	2 N
6 H	6 H
atoms of reactants =	**atoms of products**
(before reaction)	(after reaction)

A balanced chemical equation contains the correct combinations of smallest whole-number coefficients that allow the number of atoms on both sides of the equation to be equal.

Conservation of Mass

During a chemical reaction, mass of substances before and after the reaction is the same.

In the equation below, note the mass of substances in the reaction:

$$3Fe + 2O_2 \rightarrow Fe_3O_4$$

$$20.9\ g + 8.0\ g = 28.9\ g \quad \textit{the total mass of Fe and } O_2 \textit{ is the same as the total mass of } Fe_3O_4$$

Balancing Equations

An equation is balanced when it contains the correct combination of smallest whole-number coefficients. Correct coefficients allow the number of each atom on both sides of an equation to be the same.

To balance an equation:

One or more coefficients in front of the substances must be changed in the equation.

The right combination of coefficients will make the number of atoms on both sides equal.

Suggestions to balancing equations

. Make a table to keep track of the number of atoms as coefficients are changed.

. Try balancing one atom at a time.

. Every time a coefficient is changed, RECOUNT and note the number of each atom affected by the change (be sure to count atoms correctly).

. Always change coefficients of free elements (ex. Na, Cl_2) last.

. Always put parentheses around polyatomic ions and count them as one unit.

. Be sure that your final coefficients are in smallest whole-number ratios.

Examples of Unbalanced and Balanced Equations

Unbalanced	$Li_3N \rightarrow Li + N_2$	
Balanced	$2Li_3N \rightarrow 6\,Li + N_2$	
Sum of coefficients =	$2 + 6 + 1 = 9$	
Unbalanced	$Ca(OH)_2 + H_3PO_4 \rightarrow Ca_3(PO_4)_2 + H_2O$	
Balanced	$3Ca(OH)_2 + 2H_3PO_4 \rightarrow Ca_3(PO_4)_2 + 6H_2O$	
Sum of coefficients =	$3 + 2 + 1 + 6 = 12$	
Unbalanced	$C_3H_4 + O_2 \rightarrow CO_2 + H_2O$	
Balanced	$C_3H_4 + 4O_2 \rightarrow 3CO_2 + 2H_2O$	
Sum of coefficients =	$1 + 4 + 3 + 2 = 10$	

Practice Questions

Lessons 1 and 2: Interpretation of Formulas and Types of Formulas

Define the following terms and answer multiple choice questions below

1. Chemical formula   2. Qualitative   3. Quantitative   4. Subscript
5. Molecular formula   6. Empirical formula   7. Binary compound

8. A chemical formula can be used to represent compositions of
   1) Elements, only
   2) Compounds, only
   3) Elements and compounds
   4) Compounds and mixtures

9. Which list includes only types of chemical formulas?
   1) Combustion, synthesis, and decomposition
   2) Empirical, molecular, and substitution
   3) Empirical, molecular, and structural
   4) Structural, combustion, and synthesis

10. A chemical formula is an expression of
    1) Qualitative composition, only
    2) Quantitative composition, only
    3) Both qualitative and quantitative composition
    4) Neither qualitative nor quantitative composition

11. A type of formula showing the simplest ratio in which atoms are combined is
    1) A molecular formula
    2) An empirical formula
    3) A structural formula
    4) A condensed formula

12. What is the total number of moles of sulfur atoms in 1 mole of $Fe_2(SO_4)_3$?
    1) 1   2) 12   3) 3   4) 4

13. What is the total number of nitrate ions found in the formula $NaNO_3$?
    1) 1   2) 2   3) 3   4) 4

14. In the compound, $Ca_3(PO_4)_2$, what is the total number of phosphate ions?
    1) 3   2) 2   3) 8   4) 4

15. How many atoms of oxygen are in the formula $Al(ClO_3)_3 \cdot 6H_2O$?
    1) 6   2) 9   3) 10   4) 15

16. What is the total number of atoms in the formula $CaSO_4$?
    1) 3   2) 4   3) 5   4) 6

17. What is the total number of atoms in one formula unit of $MgSO_4 \cdot 7H_2O$?
    1) 27   2) 13   3) 16   4) 20

18. What is the ratio of sodium ions to phosphate ions in the formula Na_3PO_4?
    1) 4 : 3   2) 3 : 4   3) 1 : 3   4) 3 : 1

19. In the compound Al_2O_3, the ratio of aluminum to oxygen is
    1) 2 grams of aluminum to 3 grams of oxygen
    2) 3 grams of aluminum to 2 grams of oxygen
    3) 2 moles of aluminum to 3 moles of oxygen
    4) 3 moles of aluminum to 2 moles of oxygen

20. An example of an empirical formula is
    1) C_4H_{10} 2) $C_6H_{12}O_6$ 3) $HC_2H_3O_2$ 4) CH_2O

21. Which represents both an empirical formula and a molecular formula?
    1) P_2O_5 2) N_2O_4 3) C_3H_6 4) $C_6H_{12}O_6$

22. What is the empirical formula of $C_{12}H_{22}O_{11}$?
    1) $C_{12}H_{22}O_{11}$ 2) $C_6H_{11}O_{11}$ 3) $C_3H_6O_3$ 4) $C_{22}H_{48}H_{22}$

23. The molecular formula of a compound is represented by X_3Y_6. What is the empirical formula of this compound?
    1) X_3Y 2) X_2Y 3) XY_2 4) XY_3

24. Which molecular formula is correctly paired with its empirical formula?
    1) CO_2 and CO 3) C_4H_4 and C_2H_2
    2) P_2O_4 and PO_2 4) P_4O_{10} and PO_5

25. The formula C_2H_4Br is an empirical formula for which structure?.

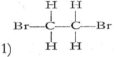
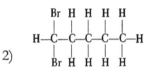

Lesson 3: Formula Writing and Naming

26. The correct formula for potassium oxide is
    1) PO_2 2) P_2O 3) KO_2 4) K_2O

27. Which is a correct formula for a compound with an IUPAC name of Nickel (III) hypochlorite?
    1) $NiCl_3$ 2) Ni_3ClO 3) $NiClO_3$ 4) $Ni(ClO)_3$

28. The correct formula for manganese (VII) oxide is
    1) Mg_7O_2 2) Mg_2O_7 3) Mn_2O_7 4) Mn_7O_2

29. Which formula is correct for ammonium carbonate?
    1) NH_4CO_3 2) $(NH_4)_2CO_3$ 3) $(NH_4)_3CO_3$ 4) $(NH_4)_3(CO)_3$

30. Which formula is correct for antimony (V) oxide?
    1) SbO_3 2) Sb_2O 3) Sb_2O_5 4) Sb_5O_2

31. Which formula correctly represents lead(II) thiosulfate?
    1) PbS_2O_3 2) $Pb_2S_4O_6$ 3) $Pb_2(S_2O_3)_2$ 4) $PbSO_3$

32. Which formula is correct for nitrogen (I) oxide?
    1) NO_2 2) N_2O 3) NO 4) N_4O_2

33. What is the IUPAC name for the compound with the formula of Ca_3P_2?
   1) Calcium phosphide
   2) Calcium (II) phosphide
   3) Calcium phosphate
   4) Calcium (II) phosphate

34. The compound with the formula of $Cu(ClO_2)_2$ is
   1) Copper (I) Chlorite
   2) Copper (II) chlorite
   3) Copper (I) chlorate
   4) Copper (II) chlorate

35. The correct name for $NaClO_4$ is sodium
   1) Chloride
   2) Chlorate
   3) Perchlorate
   4) chlorite

36 Which formula is correct for $V(NO_3)_2$?
   1) Vanadium (I) nitrate
   2) Vanadium(II) nitrate
   3) Vanadium (III) nitrate
   4) Vanadium (IV) nitrate

37. What is the correct IUPAC name for CoO?
   1) Copper (III) oxide
   2) Cobalt (III) oxide
   3) Copper (II) oxide
   4) Cobalt (II) oxide

38. Which of the following compounds is composed of just two elements?
   1) Lithium hydroxide
   2) Magnesium sulfate
   3) Aluminum oxide
   4) Ammonium chloride

Lesson 4: Chemical Equations
Define the following terms and answer multiple choice questions below.

39. Coefficient   40. Reactant   41. Product   42. Yield   43. Synthesis
44. Decomposition   45. Single replacement   46. Double replacement

47. What is conserved during chemical reactions?
   1) Energy, only
   2) Matter, only
   3) Both matter and energy
   4) Neither matter nor energy

48. If equations are balanced properly, both sides of the equation must have the same number of
   1) Atoms
   2) Coefficients
   3) Molecules
   4) Moles of molecules

49. Given a balanced chemical equation, it is always possible to determine
   1) Whether a reaction will or will not take place
   2) The conditions necessary for the reaction to take place
   3) The relative number of moles taking place in the reaction
   4) The physical state of the products and reactants

50. Which list is composed only of types of chemical reactions?
   1) Synthesis, decomposition, single replacement
   2) Synthesis, decomposition, freezing
   3) Decomposition, evaporation, and double replacement
   4) Decomposition, melting, combustion

51. Given the equation : C_3H_8 + $5O_2$ → $3CO_2$ + $4H_2O$
    This reaction represents
    1) Combustion   3) Single replacement
    2) Synthesis   4) Double replacement

52. The reaction: $N_2(g)$ + $3H_2(g)$ → $2NH_3(g)$ is best described as
    1) Synthesis   3) Single replacement
    2) Decomposition   4) Double replacement

53. Given the chemical equation : $2KClO_3(s)$ → $2KCl(s)$ + $3O_2(g$,
    What type of reaction is represented by the above equation?
    1) Combustion   3) Synthesis
    2) Neutralization   4) Decomposition

54. Which equation represents a double replacement reaction?
    1) $2Na$ + $2H_2O$ → $2NaOH$ + H_2
    2) $CaCO_3$ → CaO + CO_2
    3) $LiOH$ + HCl → $LiCl$ + H_2O
    4) CH_4 + $2O_2$ → CO_2 + $2H_2O$

55. Which of these equations is correctly balanced?
    1) $Fe(s)$ + $O_2(g)$ → $Fe_2O_3(s)$
    2) $Fe(s)$ + $O_2(g)$ → $2Fe_2O_3(s)$
    3) $2Fe(s)$ + $2O_2(g)$ → $Fe_2O_3(s)$
    4) $4Fe(s)$ + $3O_2(g)$ → $2Fe_2O_3(s)$

56. Which equation is correctly balanced?
    1) CaO + $2H_2O$ → $Ca(OH)_2$
    2) NH_3 + $2O_2$ → HNO_3 + H_2O
    3) $Ca(OH)_2$ + $2H_2PO_4$ → $Ca_3(PO_4)_2$ + $3H_2O$
    4) Cu + H_2SO_4 → $CuSO_4$ + H_2O + SO_2

57. When the equation   ___Na + ___H_2O → ___H_2 + ___$NaOH$

    is correctly balanced using the smallest whole number coefficients, what is the coefficient of H_2O ?
    1) 1   2) 2   3) 3   4) 4

58. Given the unbalanced equation: __C_5H_8 + __O_2 → __CO_2 + __H_2O

    When the equation is correctly balanced using the smallest whole-number coefficients, what is the coefficient of C_5H_8 ?
    1) 1   2) 5   3) 6   4) 10

59. When the equation   ___SiO_2 + ___C → ___SiC + ___CO

    is correctly balanced using the smallest whole-number coefficients, the sum of all coefficients is
    1) 6   2) 7   3) 8   4) 9

60. Given the unbalanced equation:
    __$Ca(OH)_2$ + __$(NH_4)_2SO_4$ → __$CaSO_4$ + __NH_3 + __H_2O

    What is the sum of all coefficients when the equation is correctly balanced using the smallest whole-number coefficients?
    1) 5   2) 7   3) 9   4) 11

Topic Mastery / Constructed Response

61. A compound is made up of iron and oxygen only. The ratio of iron ions to oxide ions is 2 : 3 in this compound. What is the IUPAC name for this compound?

62. Element X reacts with iron to form two different compounds with formulas FeX and Fe_2X_3. In which Group on the Periodic Table does element X belong?

63. What is the correct IUPAC name for the hydrate $NaNO_3 \cdot 4H_2O$?

Write the correct balanced equation for the following reactions.

64. Nickel and oxygen combining to form nickel(II) oxide.

65. Aluminum oxide decomposing to form aluminum and oxygen.

66. Chromium and lea (II) nitrate undergoing a single replacement reaction.

67. Potassium carbonate and barium sulfate undergoing a double replacement reaction.

Balance the equations below.

68. $C_2H_4O_2$ + PCl_3 $\rightarrow$ C_2H_3OCl + H_3PO_3

69. C_8H_{16} + O_2 $\rightarrow$ CO_2 + H_2O

Read the passage below and answer questions 70 to 72.

Scientists discovered, and have confirmed, that sulfur dioxide (SO_2) and nitrogen oxides (NO_x) are the primary causes of acid rain. In the US, about $^2/_3$ of all SO_2 comes from electric power generators that rely on burning fossil fuels like coal.

When sulfur dioxide reaches the atmosphere, it oxidizes to first form sulfur trioxide SO_3. It then becomes sulfuric acid as it joins with water in the air and falls back down to earth. Acid rain causes acidification of lakes and streams. In addition, acid rain accelerates the decay of building materials and paints, including irreplaceable buildings, statues, and sculptures that are part of our nation's cultural heritage.

70. Write a balanced chemical equation for the reaction between SO_2 and O_2 to form sulfur trioxide.

71. Write a balanced chemical equation for the reaction between water and sulfur trioxide to form sulfuric acid.

72. Buildings and statues are often made of limestone which is composed of calcium carbonate. Write the formula for calcium carbonate.

Lesson 1: Mole Calculations in Formulas

Introduction

A **mole** is a unit that describes a quantity of 6.02×10^{23}. A mole is, therefore, a unit of quantity in the same sense that a dozen refers to the quantity of 12.
The following are all units of quantities:

> **1 dozen** eggs   = **12** eggs
> **1 gross** of apples = **144** apples.
> **1 mole** of atoms   = **60200000000000000000000** atoms.

A mole is a very large unit of quantity that is only used to represent the amount of particles (atoms, molecules, ions, or electrons, etc) in chemical substances. The number, **60200000000000000000000**, is called **Avogadro's number**. It is always written in its scientific notation form: $\mathbf{6.02 \times 10^{23}}$.

Stoichiometry is the study and calculations of relative quantities of substances in chemical formulas (composition stoichiometry) and in chemical equations (reaction stoichiometry).
In this lesson, you will learn to interpret and calculate molar quantities in formulas.

Moles of Atoms in Formulas

The number of moles of an atom in a given formula can be determined by counting how many of that atom are in the formula, and then multiplying that by the number of moles of the formula.

moles of atom = Given moles x How many of the atom in the formula

Example 1
1 mole of HNO_3 can be represented as HNO_3. This formula consists of:

1	x	1 H	= **1** mole of H atoms
1	x	1 N	= **1** mole of N atoms
1	x	3 O	= **3** moles of O atoms

> Total moles of atoms in 1 mole of HNO_3 = **5** moles of atoms

Example 2
2 moles of HNO_3 can be represented as $2HNO_3$. This formula consists of:

2	x	1 H	= **2** moles of H atoms
2	x	1 N	= **2** moles of N atoms
2	x	3 O	= **6** moles of O atoms

> Total moles of atoms in 2 moles of HNO_3 = **10** moles of atoms

Example 3
0.5 mole of $Al_2(SO_4)_3$ can be represented as ½ $Al_2(SO_4)_3$. This consists of :

0.5	x	2 Al	= **1.0** mole of Al atoms
0.5	x	3 S	= **1.5** moles of S atoms
0.5	x	12 O	= **6.0** moles of O atoms

> Total moles of atoms in 0.5 mole of $Al_2(SO_4)_3$ = **8.5** moles of atoms

Molar Mass

The **molar mass** of a substance is the mass, in grams, of 1 mole of that substance. *Recall* that one mole of a substance contains 6.02×10^{23} particles (atoms, molecules, or ions) found in that substance.

For example, water is composed of water molecules. One mole of water contains 6.02×10^{23} (602000000000000000000000) molecules of water.

The molar mass of water, which is known to be 18 g, is the mass of 6.02×10^{23} molecules of water.

Below are the different variations of molar mass.

Atomic mass specifically refers to the average mass, in atomic mass units, of an element. Atomic mass of an element can be found on the Periodic Table.

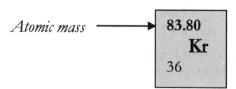

Atomic mass ⟶

83.80
Kr
36

Formula mass is commonly used when referring to the sum of the atomic masses of the elements in a formula.

Molecular mass is commonly used when referring to the mass of 1 mole of a molecular substance. Ex, H_2O, CO_2

Regardless of the formula, the mass of one mole of a substance is the sum of the masses of all the atoms in the formula.

Gram-formula mass = Mass of 1 mole of a substance (g/mol)

Gram-formula mass = Sum of all the atomic masses in the formula (g/mol)

There are different methods of calculating gram-formula mass. Two are shown below.

Example 4
What is the gram-formula mass of H_2O?

$2\,H + 1\,O$ ⟵ rounded atomic mass

$2(1) + 1(16)$ *setup*

Gram-formula Mass = $\boxed{18\ g/mol}$ *calculated result*

Example 5
What is the gram-formula mass of $(NH_4)_2SO_4$?

$2\,N + 8\,H + 1\,S + 4\,O$

$2(14) + 8(1) + 1(32) + 4(16)$ *setup*

Gram-formula mass = $\boxed{132\ g/mol}$ *calculated result*

Example 6

What is the gram-formula mass of $NaNO_3 \cdot 4H_2O$?

You can also use a table to setup

Atoms	Atomic Mass x	How Many	Total Mass
Na	23	1	23 g
N	14	1	14 g
H	1	8	8 g
O	16	7	112 g

Gram-formula mass = $\boxed{157\ g/mol}$

Mole - Mass Calculations in Formulas

The mass of one mole of a substance is the gram-formula mass of that substance. In other words, 6.02×10^{23} particles (one mole) of a given substance has a mass equal to the calculated gram-formula mass. What if there is more than one mole (more than 6.02×10^{23} particles of that substance)? It makes sense to think that a sample containing more than one mole of a substance (more than 6.02×10^{23} particles) will have a mass that is greater than the calculated gram-formula mass. Likewise, a sample containing less than one mole of a substance (fewer than 6.02×10^{23} particles) will have a mass that is less than the calculated gram-formula mass. The mathematical relationship between moles and mass is given by the equations below.

Table T equation

Mass = moles given x gram-formula mass	$$\textbf{Moles} = \frac{\textbf{Mass given}}{\textbf{Gram-formula mass}}$$

Examples problems 7 - 10

7. What is the mass of 3 moles of water, H_2O?

Mass = 3 x 18 = $\boxed{\textbf{54 g}}$

       setup   *calculated result*

8. What is the mass of 0.25 moles of water, H_2O?

Mass = 0.25 x 18 = $\boxed{\textbf{4.5g}}$

9. What is the mass of 4.5 moles of ammonium sulfate, $(NH_4)_2SO_4$?

Mass = 4.5 x 132 = $\boxed{\textbf{594 g}}$

10. What is the mass of 0.2 moles of ammonium sulfate,?

0.2 moles $(NH_4)_2SO_4$ x $\dfrac{132\,g}{1\ mole}$

Mass = $\boxed{\textbf{26.4 g (NH}_4\textbf{)}_2\textbf{SO}_4}$

Gram-formula masses of H_2O (**18 g**) and $(NH_4)_2SO_4$ (**132 g**) were calculated on pg 88.

Example problems 11 - 14

11. How many moles of H_2O are in 100 grams of the substance?

Moles = $\dfrac{100}{18}$ = $\boxed{\textbf{5.6 mol}}$

       setup   *calculated result*

12. How many moles of water are there in 3.1 g of the substance?

Moles = $\dfrac{3.1}{18}$ = $\boxed{\textbf{0.17 mol}}$

13. The total number of moles in 250 g of $(NH_4)_2SO_4$ is

Moles = $\dfrac{250}{132}$ = $\boxed{\textbf{1.9 mol}}$

14. What is the number of moles of ammonium sulfate containing 50 grams of the substance?

50 g $(NH_4)_2SO_4$ x $\dfrac{1\ mol}{132\,g}$

Moles = $\boxed{\textbf{0.38 mol (NH}_4\textbf{)}_2\textbf{SO}_4}$

Percent Composition

Percent composition by mass indicates the portion of a mass of a substance that is due to the mass of an individual element in a formula.

The percent composition equation is given on **Table T** as:

$$\% \text{ composition} = \frac{\text{Total mass of an element (part)}}{\text{Formula mass (whole)}} \times 100$$

Examples 15: What is the percent composition of each element in water, H_2O?

$$\% \text{ H} = \frac{2}{18} \times 100 = \boxed{11.1\,\%} \qquad \% \text{ O} = \frac{16}{18} \times 100 = \boxed{88.9\,\%}$$

setup   *calculated result*

Example 16: What is the percent composition of each element in $(NH_4)_2SO_4$?

$$\% \text{ N} = \frac{28}{132} \times 100 = \boxed{21.2\,\%} \qquad \% \text{ H} = \frac{8}{132} \times 100 = \boxed{6.0\,\%}$$

$$\% \text{ S} = \frac{32}{132} \times 100 = \boxed{24.2\,\%} \qquad \% \text{ O} = \frac{64}{132} \times 100 = \boxed{48.5\,\%}$$

Percent Composition of Hydrates

Hydrates are ionic compounds that contain water within their crystalline structures. An example of a hydrate is given below.

$CuSO_4 \cdot 5H_2O$ Copper (II) sulfate pentahydrate (**penta**hydrate means $5H_2O$). Gram-formula mass (mass of 1 mole) of a hydrate is due in part to the mass of the water. Percent by mass of water in a hydrate can be calculated in three steps as shown in the example below.

Example 17: What is the percent by mass of water in copper (II) sulfate pentahydrate ?

Step 1
Formula mass of hydrate, $CuSO_4 \cdot 5H_2O$ $1\,Cu + 1\,S + 10\,H + 9\,O$
$1(64) + 1(32) + 10(1) + 9(16) = \mathbf{250\ g}$

Step 2
Mass of water, $5H_2O$: $10H + 5O = 10(1) + 5(16) = \mathbf{90\ g}$ or $5(18) = \mathbf{90\ g}$

Step 3
$$\% \text{ H}_2\text{O} = \frac{\text{mass of H}_2\text{O}}{\text{formula mass of hydrate}} \times 100$$

$$\% \text{ H}_2\text{O} = \frac{90\text{ g}}{250\text{ g}} \times 100 = \boxed{36\,\%}$$

Percent Composition of Hydrates from Lab Data

A hydrate can be heated to remove its water (by evaporation) in a laboratory experiment.

An **anhydrous** solid remains after a hydrate is heated and the water is removed.

If the mass of a hydrate and of the anhydrous solid are known, the mass of water that was in the hydrate can be determined. From this mass, percent of water in the hydrate can be calculated.

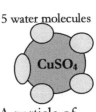

5 water molecules

CuSO₄

A particle of
$CuSO_4 \cdot 5H_2O$

hydrate

+ heat →

5 g

water (removed)

+

1.5 g

anhydrous

3.5 g

Example 18
What is the percent of water from the information above.

$$\% \text{ water} = \frac{\text{Mass of water}}{\text{Mass of hydrate}} \times 100 = \frac{1.5 \text{ g}}{5 \text{ g}} \times 100 = \boxed{\textbf{30 \%}}$$

Molecular formula from molecular mass and empirical formula.

A **molecular formula** of a substance shows the true composition of the substance. The molecular mass (mass of 1 mole) of water (18 grams) is calculated from its molecular formula.

The **empirical formula** of a substance shows atoms in a formula in their lowest ratio.

If the empirical formula and molecular mass of a substance are known, the molecular formula of the substance can be determined. See example below.

Example 19
A substance has a molecular mass of 116 g and an empirical formula of C_2H_5. What is the molecular formula of this substance?

Find **mass** of empirical formula = C_2H_5 = 2C + 5H = 2(1) + 5(1) = **29 g**

Find **number of units** of empirical formula = $\dfrac{\text{Molecular mass}}{\text{Empirical mass}} = \dfrac{116 \text{ g}}{29 \text{ g}} = 4$

Find Molecular formula = 4 (C_2H_5) = $\boxed{\textbf{C}_8\textbf{H}_{20}}$
(Multiply # of units by subscripts)

Moles – Avogadro's Number Calculations

As mentioned at the beginning of this topic, 1 mole of a substance contains 6.02×10^{23} particles

$$1 \text{ mole } = \; 6.02 \times 10^{23}$$

The math relationship between moles and # of molecules is given below.

# of particles = Given mole (6.02×10^{23})	**Moles = $\dfrac{\text{Given Particles}}{6.02 \times 10^{23}}$**

Example 20
How many molecules of water are there in **2** moles of the substance?
# of molecules = **2** (6.02×10^{23})

# of molecules = $\boxed{1.204 \times 10^{24}}$ molecules

Example 21
What is the number of gold atoms in **0.3** mol of gold?

$$0.3 \text{ mol } \times \; \frac{6.02 \times 10^{23} \text{ atoms}}{1 \text{ mol}}$$

$$\boxed{1.86 \times 10^{23}} \text{ atoms}$$

Example 22
How many moles of water contain 2.30×10^{24} molecules?

$$\text{moles} = \frac{2.30 \times 10^{24}}{6.02 \times 10^{23}} = \boxed{3.80} \text{ mol}$$

Example 23
The number of moles of gold containing 8.5×10^{22} atoms is

$$8.5 \times 10^{22} \text{ atoms } \times \; \frac{1 \text{ mol}}{6.02 \times 10^{23} \text{ atoms}}$$

$$\boxed{0.14} \text{ mol}$$

Molar volume : Mole – Volume Calculations

Molar volume describes the volume occupied by 1 mole of a gas at STP.

$$1 \text{ mole of gas } = \; 22.4 \text{ L}$$
(at STP)

The mathematical relationship between moles and volume are given below.

Volume = Given moles x 22.4 L	**moles = $\dfrac{\text{Given volume}}{22.4 \text{ L}}$**

Example 24
How much volume is occupied by 5 moles of O_2 gas at STP?

Volume = $5 \times 22.4 = \boxed{112 \text{ L}}$

Example 25
How much volume will 0.25 moles of hydrogen gas occupy at STP?

Volume = $0.25 \times 22.4 = \boxed{5.6 \text{ L}}$

Example 26
How many moles of CO_2 gas occupy 50.8L at STP?

setup $50.8 \text{ L } CO_2 \times \; \dfrac{1 \text{ mol } CO_2}{22.4 \text{ L } CO_2}$

calculated result $\boxed{2.27 \text{ mol } CO_2}$

Lesson 2: Mole Calculations in Equations

Introduction:

A balanced chemical equation shows substances that are reacting and are being produced, and also the mole proportions (or mole ratios) of the substances in the reaction. If mole ratios of reacting substances in a balanced equation are known, one can make any number of moles of the products by combining more or less of the reactants in the same proportion. A balanced chemical equation is like a recipe for making chemical substances.

In this lesson, you will learn how to interpret and solve problems that involve mole proportions in chemical equations.

Mole Ratios and Proportions in Equations

The coefficients in front of substances in a balanced equation indicate numbers of moles of the substances. From these coefficients, mole ratios of substances can be determined. as shown in the example below.

$$4NH_3 \ + \ 5O_2 \ \rightarrow \ 4NO \ + \ 6H_2O$$

> Mole ratio of NH_3 to O_2 is **4 : 5**
>
> Mole ratio of NH_3 to NO is **1 : 1**
> (reduced from 4 : 4)
>
> Mole ratio of NO to H_2O is **2 : 3**
> (reduced from 4 : 6)

Mole – Mole Calculations in Equations

An example of a mole – mole problem is given and solved below.

Example 27: Given the balanced equation below:
$$4NH_3 \ + \ 5O_2 \ \rightarrow 4NO \ + \ 6H_2O$$

How many **moles of NO** are produced when **12 moles** of O_2 is consumed?

Follow these steps to solve

re-write equation	$4NH_3 \ + \ 5O_2 \ \rightarrow \ \ 4NO \ + 6H_2O$
write info from *question* underneath the substances	*12* *x*
set up mole proportion	$\dfrac{5}{12} = \dfrac{4}{x}$ } *setup*
cross-multiply	$5x = 48$
solve for x	$x = \boxed{\textbf{9.6 mol of NO}}$ *calculated result*

Volume – Volume Calculations in Equations

An example of a volume - volume problem is given and solved below.

Example 28: Given the balanced equation below:

$$C_3H_8 \;+\; 5O_2 \;\rightarrow\; 3CO_2 \;+\; 4H_2O$$

How many liters of propane, **C_3H_8**, will react to produce 9 liters of **CO_2**?

re-write equation

write info from *question*
underneath the substances

$$1C_3H_8 \;+\; 5O_2 \;\rightarrow\; 3CO_2 + 4H_2O$$

$$x \qquad\qquad\qquad 9$$

set up mole-volume proportion

$$\frac{1}{x} \;=\; \frac{3}{9} \Bigg\} \; setup$$

cross-multiply

$$3x \qquad\qquad 9$$

solve for x

$$x \;=\; \boxed{3\,L} \quad calculated\ result$$

Mass-Mass Calculations in Equations

Note how the set up for volume – volume is the same as in mole-mole. Units (mole and Liter) can be mixed when setting up volume - volume problems.

An example of a mass – mass problem is given and solved below.

Example 29: *Given the balanced equation below:*

$$2\,KClO_3 \;\rightarrow\; 2\,KCl \;+\; 3\,O_2$$

How many grams of KCl are produced by decomposing 100 g of *KClO₃* ?

VERY IMPORTANT:

Mass proportion
should be set up as so.

Calculate masses :

$$2\,KClO_3 \;\rightarrow\; 2\,KCl + 3\,O_2$$

$$100\,g \qquad\qquad x$$

$$\frac{\text{Mass of 2KClO}_3}{100} \;=\; \frac{\text{Mass of 2KCl}}{x}$$

Mass of 2 KClO₃	Mass of 2 KCl
2 K 2(39) = 78 g	2K 2(39) = 78g
2 Cl 2 (35) = 70 g	2Cl 2(35) = 70 g
6 O 6(16) = 96 g	
244g	**148 g**

$$\frac{244}{100} \;=\; \frac{148}{x}$$

$$244\,x \;=\; 14800$$

$$x \;=\; \boxed{60.65\ g}$$

Units (mole and gram) can't be mixed when setting up mass to mass problems.

Practice Questions

Lesson 1: Mole Interpretations in Formulas
Define the following terms and answer multiple choice questions below.

1. Mole   2. Avogadro's number   3. Molar mass   4. Gram atomic mass
5. Gram-formula mass   6. Percent composition   7. Hydrate   8. Anhydrous

9. Which quantity best describes the formula "N_2"?
   1) 2 grams of atoms   3) 1 liter of atoms
   2) 2 moles of atoms   4) 1 mole of atoms

10. Which quantity of particles is correctly represented by the formula "CO_2" ?
    1) 1 mole of molecules   3) 1 mole of atoms
    2) 3 moles of molecules   4) 44 moles of atoms

11. In a sample of oxygen gas at STP, which represents the greatest number of molecules?
    1) One molecule   2) One liter   3) One gram   4) One mole

12. What is the total number of moles of hydrogen in 1 mole of $(NH_4)_2HPO_4$?
    1) 5   2) 7   3) 8   4) 9

13. How many moles of oxygen atoms are present in one mole of $CaSO_4 \cdot 3H_2O$?
    1) 7   2) 4   3) 3   4) 5

14. What is the total number of moles of atoms in 0.5 mole of formula $Na_2S_2O_3$?
    1) 7.0   2) 6.0   3) 14   4) 3.5

15. How many moles of hydrogen atoms are there in 2.5 moles of $(NH_4)_2CO_3 \cdot 5H_2O$?
    1) 8   2) 32.5   3) 45   4) 37.5

16. The gram-formula mass of $C_3H_5(OH)_3$ is
    1) 48 g/mol   2) 58 g /mol   3) 74 g/mol   4) 92 g/mol

17. What is the molar mass of $Ba(OH)_2 \cdot 8H_2O$?
    1) 452 g/mol   2) 187 g/mol   3) 242 g/mol   4) 315 g/mol

18. A student measured 56 grams of Fe_2O_3 for a laboratory experiment. How many moles of Fe_2O_3 does this mass represents?
    1) 1.00   2) 0.35   3) 0.50   4) 2.00

19. The number of moles of H_2SO_4 that weighs 245 grams is equal to
    1) 0.4 mole   2) 1 mole   3) 2.5 moles   4) 3 moles

20. How many moles are represented by 184 grams of $C_3H_5(OH)_3$?
    1) 1   2) 0.5   3) 1.5   4) 2

21. How many moles are represented by 286 grams of $Na_2CO_3 \cdot 10H_2O$?
    1) 0.2 mole   2) 0.5 mole   3) 1 mole   4) 2 moles

22. Which setup is correct for calculating the number of moles of $Al(ClO_3)_3 \cdot 6H_2O$ in 576 grams of the substance?
    1) 576 x 384   2) 6 x 576   3) $\dfrac{384}{576}$ 4) $\dfrac{576}{384}$

23. What is the total mass of 0.75 mole of Zn?
    1) 48 grams   2) 85 grams   3) 23 grams   4) 30 grams

24. What is the mass of 0.5 moles of O_2?
    1) 8 g   2) 64 g   3) 16 g   4) 32 g

25. What is the mass of 1 mole of $CaCO_3$?
    1) 20 g   2) 40 g   3) 80 g   4) 100 g

26. What is the total mass in grams of 3 moles of $Al_2(CrO_4)_3$?
    1) 134   2) 402   3) 1206   4) 1530

27. What is the mass of 0.3 moles of $Ca(C_2H_3O_2)_2$?
    1) 47g   2) 190 g   3) 950 g   4) 38 g

28. The total number of grams in 1.3 moles of $Na_2CO_3 \cdot 10H_2O$?
    1) 286   2) 372 g   3) 220 g   4) 429 g

29. What is the volume of 1.50 moles of an ideal gas at STP?
    1) 11.2 L   2) 22.4 L   3) 33.6 L   4) 44.8 L

30. What is the volume of 0.1 mole of O_2 gas at STP?
    1) 2.24 L   2) 4.48 L   3) 44.8 L   4) 0.2 L

31. Which substance will occupy a volume of 67.2 L at STP?
    1) 1.0 mole of He   3) 67.2 mole of Ne
    2) 3.0 mole of H_2 4) 0.5 mole of N_2

32. What is the total number of molecules in 0.25 mole of NO_2?
    1) 2.5×10^{23} 2) 24.08   3) 4.515×10^{23} 4) 1.5×10^{23}

33. What is the total number of atoms in 2.31 moles of sodium?
    1) 1.39×10^{24} 2) 2.31×10^{24} 3) 2.606   4) 1.39×10^{23}

34. What is the total number of moles represented by 9.0×10^{23} molecules of water?
    1) 1.0 mole   2) 1.5 moles   3) 3 moles   4) 0.67 moles

35. Which substance contains 2.0×10^{22} atoms?
    1) 3.3×10^{-2} moles of Li   3) 1.2×10^1 moles of Na
    2) 3.3×10^{-1} moles of Li   4) 1.2×10^2 moles of Na

36. What is the approximate percent by mass of hydrogen in the formula $C_3H_5(OH)_3$?
    1) 6.5 %   2) 4.8 %   3) 8.7 %   4) 3.6 %

37. Which setup is correct for calculating the percent by mass of carbon in the compound $HC_2H_3O_2$?
    1) $\frac{12}{60} \times 100$ 2) $\frac{60}{24} \times 100$ 3) $\frac{24}{60} \times 100$ 4) $\frac{60}{12} \times 100$

38. What is the approximate percent composition of $CaCO_3$?
    1) 48 % Ca, 12 % C and 40 % O   3) 40 % Ca, 48 % C, and 12 % O
    2) 12 % Ca, 48 % C, and 40 % O   4) 40 % Ca, 12 % C and 48 % O

39. Which formula has the least percent composition by mass of carbon?
    1) CH_4 2) C_2H_2 3) C_2H_6 4) C_3H_8

40. Which compound has the greatest composition of sulfur by mass?
    1) $Fe_2(SO_3)_3$ 2) $Fe_2(SO_4)_3$ 3) $FeSO_4$ 4) $FeSO_3$

41. What is the percent composition of water in the hydrate $Al(ClO_3)_3 \cdot 6H_2O$?
    1) 56 %   2) 28%   3) 1.6 %   4) 60 %

42. A 10.0 gram sample of a hydrate was heated until all water of hydration was driven off. The mass of the anhydrous product remaining was 8.00 grams. What is the percent of water in the hydrate?
    1) 12.5   2) 20.0   3) 25.0   4) 80.0

43. What is the molecular formula of a compound with a molecular mass of 78 g/mol and an empirical formula of CH?
    1) C_3H_3 2) C_4H_4 3) C_6H_6 4) C_4H_{10}

44. A compound has a molecular mass of 284 g and an empirical formula of P_2O_5. What is the molecular formula of this compound?
    1) P_4O_{10} 2) P_5O_2 3) P_2O_5 4) $P_{10}O_4$

45. A compound has an empirical formula of HCO_2 and a molar mass of 90 g/mole. What is the molecular formula of this compound?
    1) HCO   2) $H_2C_2O_4$ 3) $H_4C_4O_8$ 4) $H_6C_6O_{12}$

Lesson 2: Mole Interpretations in Equations
Answer the following multiple choice questions

46. Given the reaction $2C_2H_2(g) \ + \ 5O_2(g) \ \rightarrow \ 4CO_2(g) \ + \ 2H_2O(l)$

    What is the mole ratio of C_2H_2 to O_2 reacted?
    1) 4 : 5   2) 1 : 1   3) 5 : 2   4) 2 : 5

47. Given the reaction: $2C_2H_6 \ + \ 7O_2 \ \rightarrow \ 4CO_2 \ + \ 6H_2O$

    What is the mole ratio of CO_2 produced to moles of C_2H_6 consumed?
    1) 1 to 1   2) 2 to 1   3) 3 to 2   4) 7 to 2

48. Given the reaction: $3Cu \ + \ 8HNO_3 \ \rightarrow \ 3Cu(NO_3)_2 \ + \ 2NO \ + \ 4H_2O$

    The mole ratio of NO produced to HNO_3 reacted is
    1) 4 : 1   2) 2 : 3   3) 1 : 4   4) 2 : 3

49. In the reaction: $4NH_3 \ + \ 5O_2 \ \rightarrow \ 4NO \ + \ 6H_2O$

    What is the total number of moles of NO produced when 2 moles of O_2 is completely consumed?
    1) 2.0 moles   2) 2.4 moles   3) 1.6 moles   4) 8.0 moles

50. Given the reaction: $6CO_2 \ + \ 6H_2O \ \rightarrow \ C_6H_{12}O_6 \ + \ 6O$

    What is the total number of moles of water needed to make 1.75 moles of $C_6H_{12}O_6$?
    1) 10.5   2) 6   3) 7.5   4) 1.75

51. According to the reaction: $2SO_2\,(g)\quad+\quad O_2(g)\quad\rightarrow\quad 2SO_3(g)$

What is the total number of liters of $O_2(g)$ that will react completely with 89.6 liters of SO_2 at STP?
1) 1.0 L   2) 0.500 L   3) 22.4 L   4) 44.8 L

52. Given the reaction: $C_2H_4\quad+\quad 3O_2\quad\rightarrow\quad 2CO_2\quad+\quad 2H_2O$

How many liters of CO_2 are produced when 15 liters of O_2 are consumed?
1) 10 L   2) 15 L   3) 30 L   4) 45 L

53. Given the reaction: $4Al(s)\;+\;3O_2(g)\;\rightarrow\;2Al_2O_3(s)$

What is the minimum number of grams of O_2 gas required to produce 102 grams of Al_2O_3?
1) 32.0 g   2) 192 g   3) 96.0 g   4) 48.0 g

54. Given the balanced equation below:
$$3Cu\quad+\quad 8HNO_3\;\rightarrow\;3Cu(NO_3)_2\quad+\quad 2NO\;+\;4H_2O$$

The total number of grams of Cu needed to produce 188 grams of $Cu(NO_3)_2$ is
1) 64   2) 128   3) 32   4) 124

55. According to the reaction: $2C_2H_2\quad+\quad 5O_2\rightarrow 4CO_2\quad+\quad 2H_2O$

How many grams of CO_2 is produced from reacting 80 grams of C_2H_2?
1) 160 g   2) 271 g   3) 320 g   4) 176 g

Topic Mastery / Constructed Reponses

56. Which contains more particles, 8.0 g of helium gas or 10. g of neon gas? Explain.

57. The data below was collected from a laboratory procedure to determine percent of water in a hydrate.

Mass of evaporating dish + cover ....….... 26.0 g

Mass of hydrate + evaporating dish + cover ...... 31.0 g

Mass of anhydrous + evaporating dish + cover ... 28.9 g

What is the percent by mass of water in the hydrate?

58. What is the total number of moles of atoms in 0.5 moles of aluminum carbonate, $Al_2(CO_3)_3$?

59. Some years ago, pennies were made entirely of copper. These pennies have a mass of approximately 2.5 g. How many pennies are needed to make 2.5 moles of copper?

60. The equation for one of the reactions in the process of reducing iron ore to the metal is
$$Fe_2O_3(s)\;+\;3CO(g)\;\rightarrow\;2Fe(s)\;+\;3CO_2(g)$$

For a particular reaction, 454 g of iron (III) oxide reacts.

a) How many moles of iron (III) oxide reacts?

b) How many moles of carbon monoxide are needed to reduce this amount of iron (III) oxide?

c) What mass of CO is required to reduce the iron (III) oxide to iron metal?

Additional Materials

Density

Density (D) is the mass (m) per volume (V) ratio of a substance. Molecular density of a gas is equal to the ratio of the molar mass per molar volume of the gas at STP. Recall that at STP all gases have a molar volume of 22.4 L.

$$D = \frac{m}{V}$$

Example 30: What is the density of oxygen, O_2, at STP ?

$$D = \frac{\text{molar mass of } O_2}{\text{molar volume}} = \frac{32 \text{ g}}{22.4 \text{ L}} = \boxed{1.43 \ \frac{g}{L}}$$

Mixed Quantities in Formulas

Calculations that you learned in lesson 1 focus on solving formula problems in which moles of a substance are given or asked to be calculated. The example problems in this section show how to use the factor-label method to set up and solve formula related problems that involve mixed quantities.

Example 31: *What is the mass of a 100-liter sample of carbon dioxide, CO_2, at STP?*

Mass = volume given x mole/molar volume x formula mass

$$\textbf{Mass} = \quad 100 \text{ L} \quad \text{x} \quad \frac{1 \text{ mol}}{22.4 \text{ L}} \quad \text{x} \quad \frac{44 \text{ g}}{1 \text{ mol}} = \boxed{\textbf{196.4 g } CO_2}$$

Example 32: *How many molecules of HCl would be found in a 10-gram sample of HCl?*

# of molecules = mass given x mole/FM x # of molecules/mole

$$\textbf{# of molecules} = \quad 10 \textit{ g} \quad \text{x} \quad \frac{1 \text{ mol}}{36 \textit{ g}} \quad \text{x} \quad \frac{6.02 \times 10^{23} \textbf{ molecules}}{1 \textit{ mol}} = \boxed{\textbf{1.67} \times \textbf{10}^{23} \textbf{ molecules of HCl}}$$

Mixed Quantities in Equations

Calculations that you learned in lesson 2 focus on solving equation problems of the same quantity (ex. mole to mole or volume to volume). The example in this section shows how to use the factor-label method to set up and solve equation problems involving mixed quantities (In the example below: mass to volume)

Example 33: *Given the reaction;* $2C(s) + 3H_2(g) \rightarrow C_2H_6 (g)$.
How many liters of C_2H_6 (g) will be produced from reacting 36 g of C at STP?

Volume = mass given x gram-formula x mole ratio x volume/mole
mass of given in equation ratio

$$\textbf{Volume} = \quad 36 \textit{ g } C \quad \text{x} \quad \frac{1 \textit{ mol } C}{12 \textit{ g } C} \quad \text{x} \quad \frac{1 \textit{ mol } C_2H_6}{2 \textit{ mol } C} \quad \text{x} \quad \frac{22.4 \textbf{ L } C_2H_6}{1 \textit{ mol } C_2H_6} = \boxed{\textbf{33.6 L } C_2H_6}$$

Your factor-label setup should allow for the crossing out of all units (*in italics*) except for the one of the quantity you are solving for (**bolded**).

Limiting Reagent in a Reaction

A **limiting reagent** is the reactant in a reaction that is completely used up first. A reaction cannot proceed once the limiting reactant is used up, therefore the amount of products formed depends on the the amount of that reactant. An equation problem with quantities of two reactants given is usually a limiting reagent problem. The example below shows typical limiting reagent questions and their solutions. **Note.** Multiple steps are involved in solving limiting reagent problems

Example 1.   Given the balanced equation for the reaction:

$$2\,Cu(s)\ +\ S(s)\ \rightarrow\ Cu_2S(s)$$

a) What is the limiting reagent if 80.0 g of Cu reacts with 25 g of S?

Step 1: Determine moles of Cu and S given for the reaction.

moles of Cu given = 80.0 g x $\dfrac{1\text{ mol Cu}}{63.5\text{ g Cu}}$ = 1.26 mol Cu

moles of S given = 25.0 g x $\dfrac{1\text{ mole S}}{32.1\text{ g S}}$ = 0.779 mol S

NOTE: If moles of the reactants are given, skip this step.

Step 2: Use mole (coefficient) ratio in equation to determine how much of one reactant is really needed to react with the other

moles of S needed = 1.26 *mol Cu* x $\dfrac{1\text{ mole S}}{2\text{ }mol\text{ }Cu}$ = 0.630 mol S

moles of Cu needed = 0.779 *mol S* x $\dfrac{2\text{ mole Cu}}{1\text{ }mol\text{ }S}$ = 1.56 mol Cu

given   ratio   needed

NOTE: You only need to calculate one of these to determine the limiting reagent and excess reactant.

Step 3. Determine limiting reagent using comparisons between needed and given

More Cu (1.6 mol) is needed than given (1.3 mol): **Cu is Limiting Reagent**

More S (0.779 mol) is given than needed (0.63 mol): **S is reactant in excess**

b) What is the maximum number of grams of Cu_2S that can be produced?
Setup and solve using the number of moles of the limiting reagent, Cu.

mass of Cu_2S = 1.26 mol Cu x $\dfrac{1\text{ mole }Cu_2S}{2\text{ mol Cu}}$ x $\dfrac{159\text{ g }Cu_2S}{1\text{ mol }Cu_2S}$ = **100 g Cu_2S**

c) How many grams of the excess reactant will remain after the reaction is over?
Step 1: Sulfur is in excess: Calculate mass of sulfur actually reacted or needed.

mass of S reacted = 0.630 mol S x $\dfrac{32.1\text{ g S}}{1\text{ mol S}}$ = 20.2 g S

Step 2: **mass of S remaining** = mass S given – mass S reacted

mass of S remaining = 25 g – 20.2 g = **4.8 g S**

Practice Questions on Additional Materials

61. How many milliliters of a salt solution with a density of 1.8 g/mL are needed to provide 400. g of salt solution:
    1) 220 mL   2) 22 mL   3) 720 mL   4) 400 mL

62. Which gas has a density of of 2.05 grams per liter at STP?
    1) N_2O_5 2) NO_2 3) HF   4) HBr

63. Which gas sample contains a total of 3.0 x 10^{23} molecules?
    1) 71 g of Cl_2 3) 14 g of N_2
    2) 2.0 g of H_2 4) 38 g of F_2

64. Given the balanced equation: $4Fe + 4H_2O \rightarrow Fe_3O_4 + 4H_2$

    What is the total number of liters of H_2 produced at STP when 36 grams of H_2O is consumed?

    1) 22.4   2) 33.5   3) 44.8   4) 89.6

65. Given the reaction: $2C_2H_2(g) + 5O_2(g) \rightarrow 4CO_2(g) + 2H_2O(g)$

    What is the total number of grams of $O_2(g)$ needed to react with 0.50 moles of $C_2H_2(g)$

    1) 10. g   2) 40. g   3) 80. g   4) 160 g

66. A piece of metal was determined to have a volume of 245 cm^3 and a mass of 612 g. What is the density of the metal?

67. How many molecules of $C_2H_2(OH)_2$ are in 15 grams of the substance?

68. A sample of carbon dioxide gas contains 1.0 x 10^{22} molecules of the substance. What is the volume of this gas at STP?

69. Based on the equation : $Mg + 2HCl \rightarrow MgCl_2 + H_2$

    How many molecules of hydrogen will be produced if 10 grams of Mg is reacted?

70. Given the reaction: $2Al + 3Cl_2 \rightarrow 2AlCl_3$
    If 3.0 mol of aluminum and 5.3 mol of chlorine react:

    a) Identify the limiting reagent for the reaction.
    b) Calculate the number of moles of the product formed.
    c) How many moles of the excess reagent remain after the reaction?

71. Given the reaction: $4NH_3 + 5O_2 \rightarrow 4NO + 6H_2O$
    In an experiment, 3.25 g of NH_3 are allowed to react with 3.50 g of O_2 .
    a) Which reactant is the limiting reagent?
    b) How many grams of NO are formed?
    c) How much of the excess reactant remains after the reaction?

72. Consider the reaction: $3NH_4NO_3 + Na_3PO_4 \rightarrow (NH_4)_3PO_4 + 3NaNO_3$

    If 30 grams of ammonium nitrate and 50 grams of sodium phosphate are reacted:

    a) Which of the reagents is the limiting reagent?
    b) What is the maximum amount of each product that can be formed?
    c) How much of the other reagent is left over after the reaction is complete?

Lesson 1 : Properties of Aqueous Solutions

Introduction

Solutions are homogeneous mixtures. A homogeneous mixture is a type of mixture in which all of the components are evenly and uniformly mixed throughout the mixture. One good example of a solution is salt-water. Milk is also a homogeneous mixture (or solution). Although there are many different kinds of solutions, the discussion of solutions in this topic will focus on aqueous solutions only.

Aqueous solutions are solutions in which one of the substances in the mixture is **water (solvent)**.

In this lesson, you will learn about properties of aqueous solutions.

Components of Aqueous Solutions

Solute

A solute is the substance that is being dissolved in a solution.
A solute is always present in a smaller amount than the solvent. solute can be a solid, liquid or gas. Dissolving of a solute is a physical change.

LiCl(s)

solute

Solvent (Water)

A solvent is the substance in which the solute is dispersed.
A solvent is always present in a greater amount relative to the solute . In aqueous solutions the solvent is always water. In all solutions the solvent is usually a liquid.

$H_2O(l)$

solvent

Aqueous Solution

An aqueous solution is a mixture of a solvent (water) and solute.

The equation below shows the dissolving of a salt (solute) in water.

LiCl(aq)

$$\text{LiCl (s)} \quad + \quad \text{H}_2\text{O(l)} \quad \xrightarrow{\;dissolving\;} \quad \text{LiCl (aq)}$$

Solute	**solvent**	**mixture**
(s) solid	**(l)** liquid	**(aq)** aqueous

Solution

Dissolving (hydration) of a salt

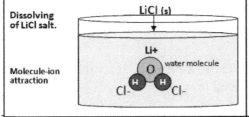

Dissolving of LiCl salt.

Molecule-ion attraction

LiCl (s)

Li+

water molecule

Cl-   Cl-

In LiCl solution:

Li+ (the + ion of the salt) attracts
O (the - end of a water molecule)

Cl- (the - ion of the salt) attracts
H (the + ends of a water molecule)

SurvivingChem.com

Properties of Solutions

A properly made solution will have the following characteristics:

. Solutions are homogenous mixtures.

. Solutions are generally clear.

. Solutions that are colorful likely contain an ion of a transition element

. Solutions are transparent and do not disperse light.

. Particles in a solution will not settle to the bottom of the container or separate into layers.

. Solute and solvent can be separated by boiling, evaporation or distillation processes.

Crystallization is a process of recovering a salt (solute) from a mixture by evaporating (or boiling) off the water. When a solution is boiled, particles of water will evaporate out of the mixture, leaving behind ions of the solute to re-crystallize.

Filtration *cannot* be used to separate the solute from the solvent of a mixture. Both the solute and solvent particles are generally smaller than holes of a filter paper. As a result, both solute and solvent will filter through during a filtration process.

Examples of Solutions

A chemical formula can only be used to represent pure substances such as elements and compounds. Aqueous solutions can be represented by symbols, not by chemical formulas. A symbol for an aqueous solution is not a chemical formula of that solution.

Examples below give names and symbols of some common solutions, as well as the solute of each solution.

Solution name	Solution symbol	Solute formula
Sodium chloride solution	$NaCl$ (aq)	$NaCl$ (s) or Na^+Cl^-
Potassium nitrate solution	KNO_3 (aq)	KNO_3 (s) or $K^+NO_3^-$
Sugar solution	$C_6H_{12}O_6$ (aq)	$C_6H_{12}O_6$ (s)
Carbon dioxide solution	CO_2 (aq)	CO_2 (g)
Ethanol (alcohol) solution	C_2H_5OH (aq)	C_2H_5OH (l)

NOTE: The aqueous symbol (aq) next to a formula of a substance always indicates that the substance is dissolved in water.

Lesson 2 : Solubility Factors

Introduction

Not every substance that is put in water will dissolve. Some substances dissolve very well, others very little, and some not at all. In addition, how well a given substance dissolves in water is affected by conditions such as temperature and/or pressure.

In this lesson, you'll learn about factors that affect how well substances dissolve in water. You will also learn how to determine which substance will dissolve and which will not dissolve in water.

Solubility

Solubility describes the extent to which a substance will dissolve in water at specific conditions.

Soluble means that a substance has HIGH solubility.

Soluble salts dissolve very well in water to produce a solution with high ion concentration.
Ex. NaCl (sodium chloride salt) is soluble in water.

Insoluble means that a substance has LOW solubility.

Insoluble salts dissolve very little in water to produce a solution with low ion concentration.
Ex. AgCl (silver chloride salt) is insoluble in water.

Miscibility describes the extent to which two liquids will mix.

Miscible refers to two liquids with HIGH miscibility. Two miscible liquids will mix evenly, and will not form layers.
Ex. Ethanol and water are miscible liquids.

Immiscible refers to two liquids with LOW miscibility. Two immiscible liquids will not mix evenly, and may separate into layers.
Ex. Oil and water are immiscible liquids.

Factors that Affect Solubility

The extent to which a solute dissolves in water depends largely on the following three factors: **Temperature, pressure, and nature of the solute.**

Temperature

The effect of temperature on solubility of a solute depends on if the solute is a solid or a gas.

Solid solutes: Ex: $NaNO_3(s)$, $KCl(s)$, or Sugar.

Solubility of a solid usually increases when the temperature of water increases. $NaNO_3(s)$, $KCl(s)$ and sugar dissolve better in hot water than in cold water.

Gaseous Solutes: Ex. $O_2(g)$, $CO_2(g)$, or nitrogen gas.

Solubility of a gas always increases when water temperature decreases. $O_2(g)$, $CO_2(g)$, and nitrogen gas dissolve better in cold water than in hot water.

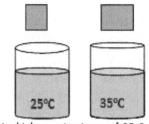

At a higher water temp of 35°C, a greater amount of the solid can be dissolved in water.

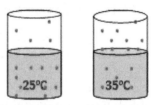

At a lower temperature of 25°C, the water contains more dissolved gas particles.

Pressure

For a given gaseous solute, the solubility of the solute changes with a change in pressure.

Gaseous solutes: Solubility of a gas increases when the pressure on the gas increases. $O_2(g)$ and $CO_2(g)$ will dissolve better in a high pressure system than in a low pressure system.

Solid solutes: Pressure has no effect on the solubility of solids in water. The amount of $NaNO_3(s)$ or $KCl(s)$ that dissolves in water will not be affected by a change in pressure.

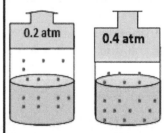

At a higher pressure of 0.4 atm, more gas particles are pushed into the water, and the water will contain more dissolved gas particles .

Nature of Solutes

 "Like dissolves like" is a saying that emphasizes the fact that polar solutes and ionic solutes dissolve better in polar solvents.

Ionic solutes (such as NaCl) dissolve well in water because they are alike in terms of polarity.

·Water is a polar substance with + and – ends
·Ionic substances are composed of + and – ions

Nonpolar solutes (such as I_2), which have no + and no – ends, do not dissolve very well in water.

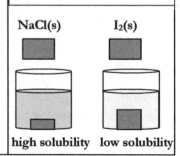

high solubility   low solubility

106

Soluble and Insoluble Salts

Solubility of an ionic solute depends on the nature of the ions it contains. **Solubility Guidelines (Table F)** below list ions that form soluble and insoluble compounds.

Solubility Guidelines (Table F)

Soluble ions   **Insoluble ions**

Ions That Form *Soluble* Compounds	Exceptions	Ions That Form *Insoluble* Compounds*	Exceptions
Group 1 ions (Li$^+$, Na$^+$, etc.)		carbonate (CO$_3$$^{2-}$)	when combined with Group 1 ions or ammonium (NH$_4$$^+$)
ammonium (NH$_4$$^+$)		chromate (CrO$_4$$^{2-}$)	when combined with Group 1 ions, Ca^{2+}, Mg^{2+}, or ammonium (NH$_4$$^+$)
nitrate (NO$_3$$^-$)			
acetate (C$_2$H$_3$O$_2$$^-$ or CH$_3$COO$^-$)		phosphate (PO$_4$$^{3-}$)	when combined with Group 1 ions or ammonium (NH$_4$$^+$)
hydrogen carbonate (HCO$_3$$^-$)		sulfide (S^{2-})	when combined with Group 1 ions or ammonium (NH$_4$$^+$)
chlorate (ClO$_3$$^-$)		hydroxide (OH$^-$)	when combined with Group 1 ions, Ca^{2+}, Ba^{2+}, Sr^{2+}, or ammonium (NH$_4$$^+$)
halides (Cl$^-$, Br$^-$, I$^-$)	when combined with Ag$^+$, Pb^{2+}, or Hg$_2$$^{2+}$		
sulfates (SO$_4$$^{2-}$)	when combined with Ag$^+$, Ca^{2+}, Sr^{2+}, Ba^{2+}, or Pb^{2+}	*compounds having very low solubility in H$_2$O	

Table F is used in explaining why compounds below are soluble or insoluble.

LiCl   *Soluble*
Li$^+$ ion (and all Group 1 ions) is listed on the soluble side.
Cl$^-$ ion, a halide ion, is also listed on the soluble side.
Neither ion is listed as an exception for the other.
Therefore, LiCl is a soluble compound.

AgSO$_4$ *Insoluble*
SO$_4$$^{2-}$ (sulfate ion) is listed on the soluble side with exceptions.
Ag$^+$ (silver ion) is listed as one of the exceptions for sulfate.
Therefore, AgSO$_4$ is an insoluble compound.

Barium hydroxide   *Soluble*
Hydroxide ion (OH$^-$) is listed on the insoluble side with exceptions.
Barium (Ba^{2+}) is listed as one of the exceptions for OH$^-$ ion.
Therefore barium hydroxide is a soluble compound

Magnesium sulfide   *Insoluble*
Sulfide ion (S^{2-}) is listed on the insoluble side with exceptions.
Magnesium ion (Mg^{2+}) is not listed as an exception for S^{2-} ion.
Therefore, magnesium sulfide is an insoluble compound.

Lesson 3: Descriptions of Solutions and Solubility Curves

Introduction

A solution can be described as saturated, unsaturated, supersaturated, dilute, or concentrated depending on four factors of the solution: **Type of solute, amount of the solute, amount and temperature of water.**

Since it is difficult to classify a solution just by looking at it, a Solubility Curve Table is often used to determine and describe types of solutions.

In this lesson, you will learn terms that are used to describe solutions. You will also learn how to use the Solubility Curve (Table G) to answer questions about a solution.

Descriptions of Solutions

Below are the different ways of describing a solution.

Saturated solution
A solution containing the maximum amount of the solute that can be dissolved at a given water temperature. In a saturated solution, equilibrium exists between dissolved and undissolved particles. If additional solute is added, it will settle to the bottom as crystals.

Unsaturated solution
A solution containing less than the maximum amount of the solute that can be dissolved at the given water temperature. An unsaturated solution can dissolve more solute.

Supersaturated solution
An unstable solution containing more than the maximum amount of the solute that can be dissolved at the given water temperature. A supersaturated solution is made by heating a saturated solution, adding more solute (which will dissolve at the new temperature) and then cooling down the solution.

Dilute solution
A solution containing a smaller amount of dissolved solute relative to the amount of water (solvent)

Concentrated solution
A solution containing a larger amount of dissolved solute relative to the amount of water (solvent).

Solubility Curves (Table G)

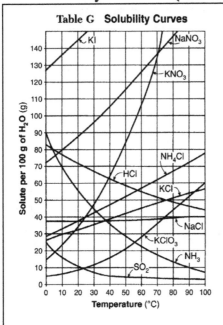

Table G Solubility Curves

The curves on Table G show changes in solubility of a few selected solid and gaseous solutes in 100 grams of water at different temperatures.

Note the following about the curves.

. *Solid solutes (ex. KCl)* have curves with positive slopes because the solubility of a solid increases as water temperature increases.

. *Gaseous solutes (ex. NH₃)* have curves with negative slopes because the solubility of a gas decreases as water temperature increases.

The notes that follow show how to use Table G to answer several questions about a solution.

Example 1: **Determining Amount of Solute to form a Saturated Solution**

Recall that a *saturated solution* contains the maximum amount of the solute that can be dissolved in a given amount of water at a specified temperature.

Step 1: Locate temperature on the x axis.

Step 2: Go up the temp line to intersect the curve for the given substance.

Step 3: Go left (from intersect point) to the y axis and read grams of solute.

Adjust saturated grams if amount of water is different from 100 g.

If amount of water is 200 grams: Double the grams of solute you determined.

If amount of water is 50 grams : Halve the grams of solute you determined

According to Table G, at 90°C In 100 g H_2O: **72 grams** of NH_4Cl will form a saturated solution.

In 50 g H_2O: 72 ÷ 2 = **36 g of NH_4Cl** will form a saturated solution.

In 300 g H_2O: 72 x 3 = **216 g of NH_4Cl** will form a saturated solution.

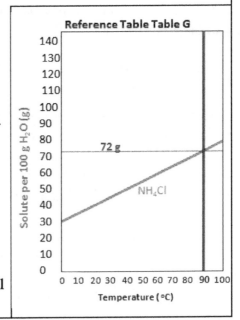

Reference Table Table G

Example 2: Determining Type of Solution from Table G

A solution is described as saturated, unsaturated, or supersaturated based on how much of the solute is in the solution, the amount of water, and the temperature of the water .

Using the **Solubility Curve Table G,** you can determine the type of solution by following the steps below.

To determine type of solution from Table G

Step 1: Locate temp of the solution. Go up the temperature line

Step 2: Stop when you've gone up as high as the solute amount in the solution

Step 3: Describe solution as

Supersaturated if you stop **above** the curve.(♦)
Saturated if you stop **on the curve** (x)
Unsaturated if you stop **below** the curve (•)

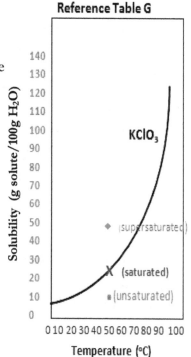

Reference Table G

According to the graph on the right.

In 100 grams of water at 50°C:

22 g of KClO₃ forms a *saturated solution.*

10 g of KClO₃ forms an *unsaturated solution.*

50 g of KClO₃ forms a *supersaturated solution.*

If the amount of water is 200 g at 50°C

44 g of KClO₃ will form a *saturated solution.*

20 g of KClO₃ will be an *unsaturated solution.*

50 g KClO₃ will still be a *supersaturated solution.*

A **concentrated solution** contains a large amount of solute relative to the amount of water.

A **dilute solution** contains a small amount of solute relative to the amount of water.

The solubility curve to the right shows four different solutions of KNO₃ at 10°C and 60°C in 100 g of H₂O. Each solution is described below.

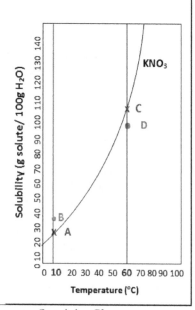

Solution A: Saturated and Dilute
Solution B: Supersaturated and Dilute
Solution C: Saturated and Concentrated
Solution D: Unsaturated and Concentrated

Adding solute to an unsaturated solution.

A solution that is unsaturated can dissolve more solute. How many more grams of a solute that should be added to bring an unsaturated solution to saturated can be determined as shown below.

. **Determine saturated grams** of the solute at the given temperature (use Table G)

. Note grams of the solute in question

. **Determining how much more solute to** add = Saturated grams - Grams in question

Example 3

An unsaturated solution of $KClO_3$ contains 10 grams of the salt in 100 g of H_2O at 50^0C. How many more grams are needed to make this a saturated solution ?

Saturated amount = **22g**

Grams in question = **10 g**

Amount needed = **22 – 10**

= **12g**

See top graph on last page

Re-crystallizing Salt (precipitate)

When a salt solution that is saturated at one temperature is cooled to a lower temperature, a smaller amount of the solute will be soluble. As a result, the ions of the solute will re-crystallize and precipitate (settle out) from solution. A **precipitate** is a solid that forms out of a solution. The amount of solute that precipitated (settled out) at the lower temperature can be determined as shown below.

 cooled to 60°C

A saturated solution of NH_4Cl at 90°C

Undissolved NH_4Cl precipitated at the lower temperature of 60°C.

Amount precipitated = **saturation - saturation**
higher temp   lower temp

Example 4

A saturated solution of KNO_3 solution at 60^oC is cooled to 10^oC. How much of the KNO_3 will precipitate?

Sat. grams at 60oC = 108 g

Sat grams at 10oC   = 22 g

Precipitated = 108 – 22 = **86g**

Example 5
Determining Most and Least Soluble Salts

Using the Solubility Curves (Table G) you can determine which solute is most or least soluble at any given temperature. The graph to the right marks the saturation points of four solutes at **60oC.**

Highest point: $NaNO_3$ is the **Most soluble** salt.
An $NaNO_3$ solution will be the **Most concentrated** and also the **Least dilute** at this temperature.

Lowest point: KCl is the **Least soluble** salt.
A KCl solution will be the **Least concentrated** and also the **Most dilute** at this temperature.

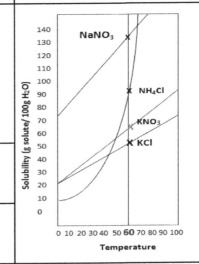

Lesson 4: Expressions of concentration of solutions

Introduction

Concentration of a solution indicates how much dissolved solute is in a given amount of the solution (or the solvent). In this lesson, you will learn two concentration expressions: Parts per million and Molarity.

Most questions dealing with concentration involve calculations. Equations for concentration calculations can be found on **Reference Table T**.

Parts Per Million

Parts per million (ppm) expresses the concentration of a solution in number of grams of solute that is in every one million parts of the solution.

The equation for calculating ppm concentration is given below (**See Table T**).

$$\text{Parts per million (ppm)} = \frac{\text{mass of solute}}{\text{mass of Solution}} \times 1\,000\,000$$

Example 6 *A solution of carbon dioxide contains 0.5 gram of the solute in 500 grams of the solution. What is the concentration in parts per million?*	$ppm = \dfrac{0.5}{500} \times 1000000$ *setup* $ppm = \boxed{1000 \text{ ppm}}$ *calculated result* 1000 ppm means that every one million parts of the solution contains 1000 grams of carbon dioxide solute.

Molarity

Molarity (M) expresses concentration of a solution in number of moles of solute per liter (volume) of the solution. Molarity of a solution can be calculated using the **Table T** equation below.

$$\text{Molarity} = \frac{\text{moles of solute}}{\text{Liter of solution}} \quad or \quad \text{Molarity} = \frac{\text{grams solute}}{\text{gram-formula mass of solute} \times \text{Liters}}$$

Example 7	**Example 8**
What is the concentration of a solution that contains 1.4 moles of solute in 2 L of the solution?	*A 0.5 L solution of NaOH contains 20 grams of NaOH. What is the concentration of this solution.*
$\text{Molarity} = \dfrac{1.4}{2} = \boxed{\textbf{0.7 M or 0.7 mol/L}}$ *setup calculated result*	$\text{Molarity} = \dfrac{20}{40 \times 0.5} = \boxed{\textbf{1 M}}$ *setup calculated result*

Lesson 5 : Boiling and Vapor pressure

A **vapor** is the gas form of a substance that is normally a liquid at STP. For example, water is normally a liquid. **Water vapor** is the evaporated molecules of water in the gas phase.
Vapor pressure is the pressure exerted by evaporated particles of a liquid on the surface of the liquid.

. Vapor pressure varies depending on the temperature of the liquid.

. The higher the temperature of a liquid, the higher its vapor pressure.

. Different substances have different vapor pressure at a given temperature.

Table H shows the relationship between temperature and vapor pressure of liquids.

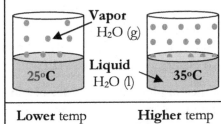

Vapor H_2O (g)

Liquid H_2O (l)

25°C   35°C

Lower temp	**Higher** temp
Less vapor	**More** vapor
Lower vapor pressure	**Higher** vapor pressure

Boiling and Pressure

Boiling is a rapid phase change of a liquid to the vapor phase. A liquid will boil when the vapor pressure of the liquid is equal to the atmospheric pressure. The **boiling point** is the temperature at which the vapor pressure of a liquid equals the atmospheric pressure. Normal atmospheric pressure is 101.3 kPa or 1 atm. The **normal boiling point** of a liquid is the temperature of the liquid that will create a vapor pressure of 101.3 kPa or 1 atm. Use Table H to determine boiling points at different pressures.

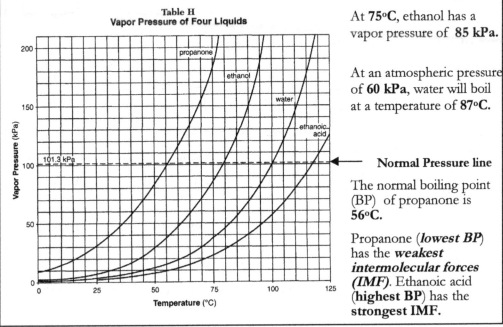

Table H
Vapor Pressure of Four Liquids

At **75°C**, ethanol has a vapor pressure of **85 kPa.**

At an atmospheric pressure of **60 kPa**, water will boil at a temperature of **87°C.**

Normal Pressure line

The normal boiling point (BP) of propanone is **56°C.**

Propanone (*lowest BP*) has the *weakest intermolecular forces (IMF)*. Ethanoic acid (**highest BP**) has the **strongest IMF.**

Lesson 6 : Effect of Solute on the Physical Properties of Water.

When a solute is dissolved in water to make a solution, physical properties of the solution will be different from those of water.

In this lesson, you will learn about changes in physical properties of water when a solute is added to water to make a solution.

Properties of Water.

Physical properties of pure water are listed below:

. Boiling point (BP) at 100°C
. Freezing point (FP) at 0°C
. Vapor pressure (VP) of 101.3 kPa (at 100°C)
. No electrical conductivity (EC)

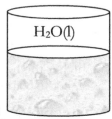

Pure water:
No dissolved particles

Changes to physical properties of water.

When a solute is dissolved in water to make a solution:

. The number of particles in water is increased (↑)

  As a result:

. Boiling Point of the water is elevated   ↑BP
. Freezing Point of the water is depressed   ↓FP
. Vapor pressure of the water is lowered   ↓VP
. Electrical conductivity of the water is increased ↑EC

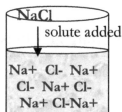

NaCl solution:
Contains dissolved particles

Concentration Effect

The higher the molarity concentration, the higher the BP and the lower the FP of the solution.

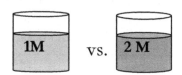

Lower FP
Higher BP

Type of Solute (# of dissolved particles)

Molecular solutes do not dissolve to produce ions. All molecular solutes produce *one* dissolved particle. Molecular solutes have the least effect on BP and FP.

Ionic solutes are capable of producing *two or more* dissolved ions (particles) in solution.

The **more dissolved ions** an ionic solute produces, the bigger its effect on BP and FP.

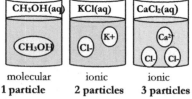

molecular	ionic	ionic
1 particle	**2 particles**	**3 particles**

Highest VP		**Lowest VP**
Highest FP		**Lowest FP**
Lowest BP		**Highest BP**
Lowest EC		**Highest EC**

Therefore:

A 1.0 M KCl (2 ions ionic) solution elevates BP and depresses FP of water better than a 1.0 M CH₃OH (1 particle molecular) solution.

But a 1.0 M CaCl₂ (3 ions ionic) solution will affect BP and FP better than the 1.0 M KCl (2 ions ionic) solution.

Practice Questions

Lesson 1 : Properties of Aqueous Solutions
Define the following terms and answer multiple choice questions below.

1. Aqueous solution   2. Homogeneous mixture   3. Solute   4. Solvent
5. Crystallization   6. Filtration   7. Hydration of ions

8. In a true solution, the dissolved particles
   1) Are visible to the eyes
   2) Will settle out on standing
   3) Are always solids
   4) Cannot be removed by filtration

9. One similarity between all solutions and compounds is that both
   1) Are always heterogeneous
   2) Are always homogeneous
   3) Have a definite ratio of composition
   4) Are composed of two or more substances

10. When sample X is passed through a filter paper, a white residue, Y, remains on
    the paper and a clear liquid, Z, passes through. When Z is vaporized, another
    white residue remains. Sample X is best classified as
    1) An element
    2) A compound
    3) A heterogeneous mixture
    4) A homogeneous mixture

11. An aqueous solution of copper sulfate is poured into a filter paper cone. What
    passes through the filter paper?
    1) Only the solvent
    2) Only the solute
    3) Both solvent and solute
    4) Neither the solvent nor solute

12. A small amount of $CaSO_4$ is dissolved in H_2O to make a solution. In this solution,
    1) $CaSO_4$ is the solute
    2) $CaSO_4$ is the solvent
    3) H_2O is the solute
    4) H_2O is the precipitate

13. In an aqueous solution of ammonium chloride, the solute is
    1) NH_4^+ only   2) Cl^- only   3) NH_4^+ and Cl^- 4) H_2O

14. What happens when $KI(s)$ is dissolved in water?
    1) I^- ions are attracted to the oxygen atoms of water
    2) K^+ ions are attracted to the oxygen atoms of water
    3) K^+ ions are attracted to the hydrogen atoms of water
    4) No attractions are involved; the crystal just falls apart

15. Which diagram best illustrates the molecule-ion attractions that occur when
    $NaBr(s)$ is added to water?
    1)

    3)

    2) [diagram]   4) [diagram]

Lesson 2 : Solubility Factors
Define the following terms and answer multiple choice questions below.

16. Solubility 17. Soluble 18. Insoluble 19. Miscibility 20. Miscible 21. Immiscible

22. The solubility of a salt in a given volume of water depends largely on the
    1) Surface area of the salt crystals
    2) Temperature of the water
    3) Rate at which the salt and water are stirred
    4) Pressure on the surface of the water

23. As the temperature of water increases, the solubility of all gases
    1) Decreases, and the solubility of all solids increases
    2) Increases, and the solubility of all solids decreases
    3) Decreases, and the solubility of all solids also decreases
    4) Increases, and the solubility of all solids also increases

24. A change in pressure has the greatest effect on the solubility of a solution that contains a
    1) Solid in a liquid   3) Liquid in a liquid
    2) Gas in a liquid   4) Liquid in a solid

25. As water temperature increases, the solubility of which substance will increase?
    1) Nitrogen   2) Sodium chloride   3) Oxygen   4) Carbon dioxide

26. A decrease in water temperature will increase the solubility of
    1) $C_6H_{12}O_6$(s)   2) NH_3(g)   3) KCl (s)   4) Br_2 (l)

27. Which substance increases its solubility in water when the water temperature is changed from 30°C to 50°C?
    1) $NaNO_3$ 2) NH_3 3) Cl_2 4) CH_4

28. At standard pressure, water at which temperature will contain the most dissolved NH_4Cl particles?
    1) 5°C   2) 10°C   3) 15°C   4) 20°C

29. Under which conditions would carbon dioxide be most soluble in water?
    1) 10°C and 1 atm   3) 10°C and 2 atm
    2) 20°C and 1 atm   4) 20°C and 2 atm

30. According to Table F, which of these compounds is soluble in water?
    1) $SrSO_4$ 2) $BaSO_4$ 3) $ZnCO_3$ 4) Na_2CO_3

31. Which of these compounds will be the best electrolyte?
    1) $Ba_3(PO_4)_2$ 2) $BaCO_3$ 3) $BaCl_2$ 4) $Ba(NO_3)_2$

32. Based on Reference Table F, which of these substances is insoluble?
    1) NH_4Cl 2) $PbCl_2$ 3) NaCl   4) $CaCl_2$

33. At STP, which aqueous solution will contain the least amount of dissolved ions?
    1) $NaNO_3$ 2) Na_2SO_4 3) $Pb(NO_3)_3$ 4) $PbSO_4$

34. Which of these salts is soluble in water?
    1) Lithium phosphate   3) Magnesium sulfide
    2) Lead (II) phosphate   4) Silver sulfide

Lesson 3: Descriptions of Solutions and Solubility Curves.
Define the following terms and answer multiple choice questions below.

35. Saturated   36. Supersaturated   37. Unsaturated   38. Concentrated   39. Dilute

40. According to Reference Table G, approximately how many grams of HCl are needed to saturate 100 grams of H_2O at 50°C?
    1) 50   2) 116   3) 58   4) 42

41. What is the amount of $NaNO_3$ needed to saturate 50 grams of water that is at 10°C?
    1) 80 grams   2) 100 grams   3) 40 grams   4) 50 grams

42. How many grams of KCl must be dissolved in 200 g of H_2O to make a saturated solution at 60°C?
    1) 30 g   2) 45 g   3) 56 g   4) 90 g

43. According to Reference Table G, which solution is a saturated solution at 30°C?
    1) 12 g of $KClO_3$ in 100 g of water   3) 30 g of NaCl in 100 g of water
    2) 12 g of $KClO_3$ in 200 g of water   4) 30 g of NaCl in 200 g of water

44. An unsaturated solution of $NaNO_3$ contains 70 g of $NaNO_3$ dissolved in 100 g of water at 20°C. How many more grams of $NaNO_3$ are needed to make this a saturated solution?
    1) 70 g   2) 95 g   3) 30 g   4) 18 g

45. A student dissolved 40 grams of NaCl in 80 grams of water that is at 90°C. To make this a saturated solution, the student must add to the solution
    1) 10 g of NaCl   2) 10 g of H_2O 3) 20 g of NaCl   4) 20 g of H_2O

46. When the temperature of a saturated solution of $KClO_3$ that is made with 100 g of H_2O is cooled from 25°C to 10°C, some salt crystals reformed at the bottom of the beaker. How many grams of the $KClO_3$ salt are at the bottom of the beaker?
    1) 5 g   2) 10 g   3) 15 g   4) 20 g

47. A test tube contains a saturated solution of KNO_3 that was prepared with 100 grams of H_2O at 60°C. If the test tube is cooled to 30°C, what will be found at the bottom of the test tube?
    1) 30 g of KNO_3 2) 30 g of H_2O 3) 57 g of KNO_3 4) 57 g of H_2O

48. A solution containing 10 grams of NH_3 in 100 grams of water at 90°C is classified as
    1) Supersaturated   2) Saturated   3) Unsaturated

49. A solution of KCl contains 90 grams of the solute in 200 grams of water at 60°C. This solution can be best classified as
    1) Unsaturated   2) Supersaturated 3) Saturated

50. Based on Reference Table G, a solution of SO_2 that contains 15 grams of the solute dissolved in 100 g of H_2O at 10°C is best described as
    1) Saturated and dilute   3) Unsaturated and concentrated
    2) Saturated and concentrated   4) Supersaturated and concentrated

51. Which of these saturated solution is the most dilute at 20°C?
    1) KI (aq)   2) KCl (aq)   3) $NaNO_3$ (aq)   4) NaCl (aq)

52. According to Table G, which of these substances is most soluble at 60°C?
    1) NaCl   2) KCl   3) $KClO_3$ 4) NH_4Cl

Lesson 4: Expression of Concentration of Solutions
Answer the multiple choice questions below.

53. Which unit can be used to express solution concentration?
    1) J/mol   2) L/mol   3) mol/L   4) mol/s

54. What is the concentration of a solution of 10.0 moles of copper (II) nitrate dissolved in 5.00 liters of the solution?
    1) 0.50 M   2) 5.00 M   3) 10.0 M   4) 2.00 M

55. A 0.25 liter potassium chloride solution contains 0.75 mole of KCl. What is the concentration of this solution?
    1) 0.33 M   2) 0.75 M   3) 3.0 M   4) 6.0 M

56. A solution of NaCl contains 1.8 moles of the solute in 600 mL of solution. What is the concentration of the solution?
    1) 3 M   2) 0.003 M   3) 333 M   4) 0. 05 M

57. What is the molarity of a solution that contains 40 grams of NaOH in 0.50 liter of solution?
    1) 1.0 M   2) 0.5 M   3) 0.25 M   4) 2.0 M

58. What is the concentration of a solution of KNO_3 that contains 50.5 g of KNO_3 in 2.00 liters of solution?
    1) 25.25 M   2) 2.00 M   3) 0.500 M   4) 0.25 M

59. How many moles of KNO_3 are required to make 0.50 L of a 2 M solution of KNO_3?
    1) 1.0   2) 2.0   3) 0.50   4) 4.0

60. What is the total number of moles of solute in 2230 mL of a 3.0 M NaOH solution?
    1) 6.7 moles   2) 3.0 moles   3) 1.5 moles   4) 0.743 moles

61. How many liters of a 0.5 M sodium hydroxide solution would contain 1 mole of the solute?
    1) 0.5 L   2) 1.0 L   3) 2.0 L   4) 4.0 L

62. A 500 gram oxygen solution contains .05 grams of dissolved oxygen. The concentration of this solution expressed in parts per million is closest to
    1) 1.0 x 10^4 ppm   3) 1.0 x 10^{-4} ppm
    2) 1.0 x 10^2 ppm   4) 2.5 x 10^7 ppm

63. What is the concentration in parts per million of a solution containing 20 grams of $C_6H_{12}O_6$ in 80.0 grams of H_2O?
    1) 2.50 x 10^5 ppm   3) 4.00 x 10^6 ppm
    2) 2.00 x 10^5 ppm   4) 5.00 x 10^6 ppm

64. How many grams of KNO_3 must be dissolved in water to make 100 grams of a 250 ppm solution?
    1) 2.5 x 10^{-1} g   3) 2.5 x 10^{-4} g
    2) 2.5 x 10^{-2} g   4) 2.5 x 10^{-3} g

65. How many grams of NaCl must be dissolved in water to make 2000 grams of a 100 ppm solution?
    1) 2 g   2) 0.05 g   3) 0.2 g   4) 0.5 g

Lesson 5:   Vapor Pressure

66. As water in a sealed container is cooled from 20°C to 10°C, its vapor pressure
    1) Decreases   2) Increases   3) Remains the same

67. When the vapor pressure of a liquid equals the atmospheric pressure, the liquid will
    1) Freeze   2) Melt   3) Boil   4) Condense

68. According to Reference Table H, what is the vapor pressure of propanone at 50°C?
    1) 101.3 kPa   2) 33 KPa   3) 50 kPa   4) 82 kPa

69. A sample of a pure liquid is boiling at a temperature of 150°C. The atmospheric
    pressure is 65 kPa. The vapor pressure of the liquid is
    1) 10 kPa   2) 65 kPa   3) 150 kPa   4) 101.3 kPa

70. According to Reference Table H, which sample has the highest vapor pressure?
    1) Water at 70°C   3) Propanone at 65°C
    2) Ethanol at 75°C   4) Ethanoic acid at 110°C

71. The normal boiling point of ethanol is closest to
    1) 80°C   2) 100°C   3) 200°C   4) 90°C

Lesson 6: Effect of Solutes on Properties of Water

72. As a solute is added to a solvent, what happens to the freezing point and the boiling
    point of the solution?
    1) The freezing point decreases and the boiling point decreases
    2) The freezing point decreases and the boiling point increases
    3) The freezing point increases and the boiling point decreases
    4) The freezing point increases and the boiling point increases

73. As water is added to a 0.10 M NaCl solution, the conductivity of the solution
    1) Decreases because the concentration of the ions decreases
    2) Decreases because the concentration of the ions remains the same
    3) Increases because the concentration of the ions decreases
    4) Increases because the concentration of the ions remains the same

74. Which 1 M solution will produce the greatest increase on the boiling point of water?
    1) CH_3OH (aq)   2) $C_2H_4(OH)_2$(aq)   3) $CuCl_2$ (aq)   4) $C_6H_{12}O_6$ (aq)

75. Which 0.1 M solution has the highest boiling point?
    1) NaCl (aq)   2) $MgCl_2$ (aq)   3) LiCl (aq)   4) CsCl (aq)

76. Which 1 M solution has the lowest boiling point?
    1) KNO_3 (aq)   2) K_2SO_4 (aq)   3) $Ca(OH)_2$ (aq)   4) $C_6H_{12}O_6$ (aq)

77. Which concentration of NaOH has the lowest freezing temperature?
    1) 2.0 M   2) 1.5 M   3) 1.0 M   4) 0.1 M

78. Which solution will boil at the highest temperature?
    1) 2 M Na_2SO_4 2) 1 M Na_2SO_4 3) 2 M $NaNO_3$ 4) 1 M $NaNO_3$

Topic Mastery / Constructed Response

79. 5 g of iron filings and 20 g of KCl salt were mixed together in a beaker containing 100 g of H_2O. The mixture was shaken until all of the salt was dissolved. Choose and describe different methods that can be used to separate and collect each of the three substances.

80. Describe how to prepare 500 mL of a 4.0 M NaOH(aq) solution.

81. 100 g of water contains 2.137 g of N_2O_3(g). Calculate *both* the molarity and parts per million concentrations of the resulting solution.

82. 100 g of H_2O at 40°C contains 80 g of KNO_3(s). Use the solubility curve (Table G) to describe two specific ways that this solution can be made saturated.

Answer questions 83 and 84 based on the information from the table below.

Consider the following data of solubility of Na_2SO_4 (s)

Temperature (°C)	0	20	50	100
Solubility (g/100 g H_2O)	4.76	62	50.	41

83. What is the relationship between the temperature and the amount of dissolved materials?

84. Given the nature of Na_2SO_4(s), what is unusual about the data given on the table?

85. Substance X is a molecular substance that is soluble in water. It costs $.90/ton. Substance Y is an ionic substance that costs $1.00/ton. Both have the same environmental impacts, are easy to handle, and are nontoxic. Using your knowledge of chemistry, which would be more cost effective to melt snow on roads? Explain or show work to justify your answer.

Acids, Bases and Salts

Properties of Acids and Bases: Summary of characteristics

Acids and bases have sets of properties that are used to identify them. Below is a summary of these properties. In the next few lessons, you will learn more about these characteristics of acids and bases.

Acids	Bases
similarities	
1) Are electrolytes	1) Are electrolytes
2) Change color of indicators	2) Change color of indicators
3) React with bases in a neutralization reaction to produce water and a salt	3) React with acids in a neutralization reaction to produce water and a salt
differences	
4) Produce H^+ as the only positive ion	4) Produce OH^- as the only negative ion
5) Contain more H^+ than OH^-	5) Contain more OH^- than H^+
6) When added to water, increase H^+ ion concentration of the water	6) When added to water, decrease H^+ ion concentration of the water
7) When added to water, decrease OH^- ion concentration of the water	7) When added to water, increase OH^- ion concentration of the water
8) When added to water, decrease pH	8) When added to water, increase pH
9) Have pH values less than 7	9) Have pH values greater than 7
10) Turn litmus red	10) Turn litmus blue
11) Have no effect on phenolphthalein (stays colorless)	11) Turn phenolphthalein, which is colorless, to pink
12) Taste sour	12) Taste bitter and feel slippery
13) React with certain metals to produce salt and hydrogen gas	

Neutral substances

1) pH value of 7
2) Have equal amount of H^+ and OH^- ions

Lesson 1: Defining Acids and Bases

Introduction

What is an acid? What is a base? These questions cannot be answered with just one simple definition. Acids and bases can be defined by different theories and characteristics.

In this lesson, you will learn how acids and bases are defined by theories and other characteristics. As you study this lesson, pay attention to similarities and differences between acids and bases.

Arrhenius Theory of Acids and Bases.

Arrhenius acids (See Table K) are substances that can produce H^+ (hydrogen ion, proton) as the only positive ion in solutions. Properties of acids (listed on the summary table) are due to properties of H^+ ions they produced. H^+ ions produced by Arrhenius acids usually combine with H_2O to become H_3O^+ .

$$H^+ \quad + \quad H_2O \longrightarrow H_3O^+$$

(hydronium ion)

(H^+ and H_3O^+ are synonymous with each other)

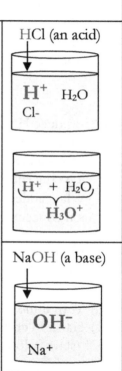

Arrhenius Bases (See Table L) are substances that can produce OH^- (hydroxide ion) as the only negative ion in solutions. Properties of bases (listed on the summary table) are due to properties of OH^- ions they produced. Most bases are ionic compounds.

Alternate (a different) Theory of Acids and Bases

Brönsted-Lowry Theory is an alternate theory that defines acids and bases by their ability to donate or accept a proton (H^+ or hydrogen ion) in certain reactions.

Bronsted-Lowry acids are substances that can *donate a proton* (H^+ or hydrogen ion) during a reaction.

Bronsted-Lowry bases are substances that can *accept a proton* (H^+ or hydrogen ion) during a reaction.

$$H_2O \quad + \quad NH_3 \leftrightarrow NH_4^+ \quad + \quad OH^-$$

acid   base   acid   base

SurvivingChem.com

pH Values of Acids and Bases

pH is a measure of the hydrogen ion (H^+) or the hydronium ion (H_3O^+) concentration of a solution. A typical pH scale ranges in value from $0 - 14$. Acids and bases can be defined by their pH values.

Acids are substances with pH values *less* than 7.

Neutral substances have pH values *equal* to 7.

Bases are substances with pH values *greater* than 7.

	Acid	Neutral	Base
pH scale	0 ------------------------------	7 ------------------------------	14
	strong weak	weak	strong
	HCl HNO₃ CH₃COOH	H₂O NH₃	KOH NaOH

Acid-Base Indicators (Table M)

Acid – Base indicators are substances that can change color in the presence of an acid or a base. Acids and bases can be defined by the changes they cause on indicators.

Phenolphthalein is a colorless acid-base indicator.
Acids have *no effect* on phenolphthalein (it stays colorless).

Bases are substances that change colorless phenolphthalein to *pink*.
Phenolphthalein is a good indicator to test for the presence of a base.

Litmus papers come in a variety of colors. When wet with an acidic or a basic solution, they will change color.
Acids are substances that will change color of litmus paper to *red*.

Bases are substances that will change color of litmus paper to *blue*.

Other common indicators are listed on Table M of the Reference Table

Indicator	Approximate pH Range for Color Change	Color Change
methyl orange	3.1–4.4	red to yellow
bromthymol blue	6.0–7.6	yellow to blue
phenolphthalein	8–9	colorless to pink
litmus	4.5–8.3	red to blue
bromcresol green	3.8–5.4	yellow to blue
thymol blue	8.0–9.6	yellow to blue

Reading Table M:

Methyl orange will be :
Red in pH below 3.1
Yellow in pH above 4.4

Thymol blue will be:
Yellow in pH below 8.0
Blue in pH above 9.6

Relative Ion concentration of Acids and Bases

Any solution made with water contains both H^+ and OH^- ions. A solution can be defined as acidic or basic depending on the relative amount of H^+ and OH^- in the solution.

Acidic solutions contain *more* (higher concentration of) H^+ ions than OH^- ion.
The stronger the acid, the greater the H^+ ion concentration in comparison to OH^- ions concentration.
Example: HCl(aq) (hydrochloric acid solution) contains more H^+ ions than OH^- ions.

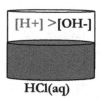

[H+] >[OH-]

HCl(aq)

Neutral solutions and pure water contain *equal* amounts of H^+ and OH^-.
Example: NaCl (a neutral salt solution) and pure water contain equal concentrations of H^+ and OH^- ions

[H+]=[OH-]

H₂O(l)

Basic solutions contain *more* (higher concentration of) OH^- ions than H^+ ions.
The stronger the base, the greater the OH^- ion concentration in comparison to H^+ ion concentration.
Examples: NaOH(aq) (sodium hydroxide solution) contains more OH^- ions than H^+ ions

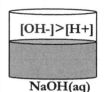

[OH-]>[H+]

NaOH(aq)

The math relationship between pH and H^+ ion concentration is shown below.

$$pH = -\log [H^+]$$ or $$[H^+] = 10^{-pH}$$

When the $[H^+]$ or $[H_3O^+]$ of a solution is given in the form of: $1 \times 10^{-x} M$

pH value of the solution = x

Examples

H_3O^+ concentration	pH value	Type of solution
1.0×10^{-2} M	2	Acidic
1.0×10^{-8} M	8	Basic

Based on the mathematical relationship of pH to $[H^+]$, a solution with a pH of 3 has a higher concentration of H^+ ions than a solution with a pH of 4.

. As H^+ ion concentration of a solution increases, pH of the solution decrease.
. The lower the pH, the more H^+ ions in a solution.

1 value difference in pH = 10 times (fold) difference in $[H^+]$

A solution of pH 3 has 10 times more H^+ than a solution of pH 4.

As a solution changes from pH 3 to pH 5, $[H^+]$ decreases 100 fold (times).

Difference in $[H^+]$ of two solutions = $10^{(\text{difference in pH})}$

Lesson 2: Reactions of Acids and Bases

Introduction

Acids and bases undergo chemical reactions with other substances and with each other.

In this lesson, you will learn about reactions of acids with metals, and reactions of acids and bases with each other.

Reaction of an Acid with a Metal

Acids react with certain metals to produce **hydrogen gas** and a **salt**. The reaction between an acid and a metal is a single replacement reaction.

General equation: Metal + Acid   → Salt   + Hydrogen gas

Example equation 1: Zn + $2HCl$ → $ZnCl_2$ + H_2

Example equation 2: Mg + $2HNO_3$ → $Mg(NO_3)_2$ + H_2

Since the reaction is single replacement, the salt is formed by the metal replacing hydrogen of the acid. In the equation:

$$2Li + 2HBr \longrightarrow 2LiBr + H_2$$

(metal)   (acid)   **(salt)**   (hydrogen gas)

Li (metal) replaces **H** of **HBr** (acid) to form LiBr (salt). The displaced H atoms from acid form H_2 gas. LiBr is a correct formula for lithium bromide.

NOTE: Be sure the salt formula is correct. (Review formula writing in Topic 5)

Which metals will react with acids?

Not every metal will react with acids to produce hydrogen gas and a salt.	Most active **Li**	H₂ gas produced
Reference Table J shows the activity series of metals. This table is used to predict which metal-acid reaction will occur spontaneously.	↓	
Metals above H₂ (Li to Pb) *will react* with an acid to produce H_2.	Pb **H₂** Cu Au	No reaction
Metals below H₂ (Cu to Ag) *will not react* with any acid .	Least active **Ag**	

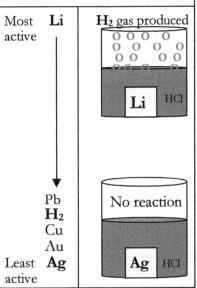

Neutralization Reactions

Neutralization is a reaction between an acid and a base to produce **water** and a **salt**. A neutralization reaction is a double replacement reaction. During a neutralization reaction, equal moles of H^+ (of an acid) and OH^- (of a base) combine to neutralize each other.

General equation: Acid + Base   →   Water + Salt

Example equation: HCl + NaOH   → H_2O + NaCl

(hydrochloric acid) (Sodium hydroxide) (water) (sodium chloride)

Net ionic equation: H^+ + OH^- → H_2O

The formula of the **salt** that is formed in a neutralization reaction can be determined by replacing the H of the acid with the metal (or NH_4) of the base. In the equation below:

$$H_2SO_4 + LiOH → HOH + Li_2SO_4$$

(acid)   (base)   (water)   (salt)

Note how **H** of H_2SO_4 is replaced by **Li** to form Li_2SO_4 salt.

Titration

Titration is a lab process used for determining the concentration of an unknown solution by reacting it with a solution of known concentration. A titration process usually involves an acid and a base (acid – base titration). During an acid – base titration lab, a base (usually from a buret) is slowly added to an acid (usually in a flask). When moles of H^+ and OH^- are equal, neutralization has occurred, and the **endpoint** of the titration is reached. Phenolphthalein (a base indicator) is usually added to the acid beaker to indicate the endpoint. Titration is stopped when the solution in the beaker has a faint pink color. This indicates that all the acid in the beaker has been neutralized, and the solution in the beaker is slightly basic.

If any three of the following information about a titration process are known:

. Volume of the acid (V_A) or base (V_B)
. Concentration of the acid (M_A) or the base (M_B)

you can calculate for the unknown in the titration process using the *Reference Table T* titration equation below.

$$\boxed{M_A \times V_A = M_B \times V_B}$$

For acids with 2 or more H^+ (H_2SO_4) or bases with 2 or more OH- , ($Ca(OH)_2$,), use equation:

$\boxed{\text{# of } H^+ \times M_A \times V_A = \text{# of OH- } \times M_B \times V_B}$

Example 1: 30 mL of 0.6 M HCl solution is neutralized with 90 mL NaOH solution. What is the concentration of the base?

$M_A \times V_A = M_B \times V_B$

0 .6 (30) = M_B (90) *setup*

$\boxed{0.2\ M}$ = M_B *result*

Example 2: 40 mL of 1.5 M NaOH solution was used to titrate 10 mL of a H_2SO_4 solution. What is the acid concentration?

$(2)(M_A)(10) = 1(1.5)(40)$ *setup*

M_A = $\boxed{3\ M}$ *result*

Lesson 3: Salts and Electrolytes

One property that acids, bases and salts share is their ability to conduct electricity in aqueous solutions. Acids, bases and salts are considered electrolytes. In this lesson you will learn about substances that are electrolytes and how electrolytes conduct electricity.

Salts

Salts are ionic compounds composed of a positive ion (other than H^+) and a negative ion (other than OH^-).

. A salt is one of the products of acid-base neutralization reactions.

. Salts are electrolytes (conduct electricity when dissolved in water).

. Soluble salts are better electrolytes than insoluble salts.

Recall that Table F can be used to determine soluble and insoluble salts. Formulas and names of some common salts are given below.

NaBr	*CaSO₄*	*NH₄Cl*
sodium bromide	*calcium sulfate*	*ammonium chloride*
metal -nonmetal	*metal - polyatomic ion*	*NH₄ - nonmetal*

Electrolytes

Electrolytes are substances that can conduct electricity when dissolved in water.

. Electrolytes dissolve in water to produce a solution with positive (+) and negative (-) ions.

. Electrolytes conduct electricity because the mobile ions in the solution allow for a complete circuit.

. Acids (Table K), bases (Table L) and salts are electrolytes.

Nonelectrolytes are substances that do not produce ions when dissolved, therefore do not conduct electricity in solutions. Organic substances (other than organic acids) are typically nonelectrolytes. Organic substances are discussed in Topic 10.

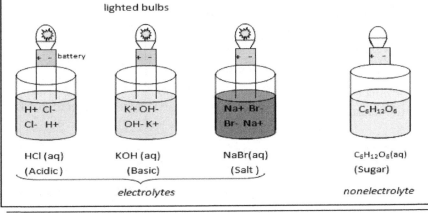

Lesson 4: Acid Names and Formulas

An acid can be classified as organic or inorganic. Inorganic acids can further be classified as binary or ternary acids.

Chemical Formulas of Acids

Inorganic acids

Chemical formulas of inorganic acids usually start with H, follow by a nonmetal or a negative polyatomic ion.

Binary acid formulas are composed of just two nonmetal atoms: hydrogen atom and another nonmetal atom.

Examples of binary acids: HCl   hydrochloric acid

                               H_2S hydrosulfuric acid

Ternary acid formulas are composed of three atoms: hydrogen atom and a polyatomic ion (Table E)

Examples of ternary acids: : HNO_3 nitric acid

                             H_2SO_3 sulfurous acid

Organic acids

Chemical formulas of organic acids usually end with *–COOH*.

Examples of organic acids: CH_3COOH ethanoic (acetic) acid

                          HCOOH   methanoic acid

Chemical Names of Inorganic Acids

Chemical names of acids vary depending on if an acid is a binary, ternary, or an organic acid.

Binary acids have names that begin with **hydro-** and end with **–ic.** Names of binary acids are formed by dropping the *–gen* of hydrogen and modifying the nonmetal ending to *–ic.*

   Ex.   Hydro*gen* chlor*ide*   Hydro*gen* sul*fide*

        Hydrochlor*ic* acid   Hydrosulfur*ic* acid

Ternary acids have names that reflect only the name of the polyatomic ion (See Table E).

H_2SO_4
ion: sulf**ate**
acid : sulfur**ic** acid

If an acid formula contains a polyatomic ion ending with **–ate**, the name ending of the acid is **–ic.**

If an acid formula contains a polyatomic ion ending with **–ite**, the name ending of the acid is **–ous.**

H_2SO_3
ion: sulf**ite**
acid: sulfur**ous** acid

Practice Questions

Lesson 1: Defining Acids and Bases

Define the following terms and answer multiple choice questions below

1. Arrhenius acid   2. Arrhenius base   3. Hydrogen ion   4. Hydronium ion
5. Hydroxide ion   6. Alternate acid theory   7. Alternate base theory
8. Acidity   9. Alkalinity   10. Indicator   11. pH

12. Which ion is produced by all Arrhenius acids as the only positive ion in solutions?
    1) OH^+ 2) NH_4^+ 3) SO_4^{2+} 4) H_3O^+

13. Which ion is produce by a base when it is dissolved in water?
    1) Hydroxide ion   3) Ammonium ion
    2) Hydrogen ion   4) Hydronium ion

14. What are the relative ion concentrations of a basic solution?
    1) More OH^- ions than H^+ ions
    2) H^+ ions but no OH^- ions
    3) Fewer OH^- ions than H^+ ions
    4) Equal number of H^+ ions and OH^- ions

15. As a solution becomes more basic, the H^+ ion concentration in the solution
    1) Increases   2) Decreases   3) Remains the same

16. As a solution of a base is added to an acidic solution, the pH of the solution
    1) Increases   2) Decreases   3) Remains the same

17. According to an alternate theory, a base in an acid-base reaction is any species that can
    1) Donate a proton   3) Accept a proton
    2) Donate an electron   4) Accept an electron

18. According to an "alternate theory" of acids and bases, H_2O will act as a base in a reaction if it
    1) Donates OH^- to another species in the reaction
    2) Donates H^+ to another species in the reaction
    3) Accepts OH^- from another species in the reaction
    4) Accepts H^+ from another species in the reaction

19. A solution of a base in the presence of phenolphthalein will
    1) Turn pink   2) Turn red   3) Turn blue   4) Stay colorless

20. Which property do acids and bases have in common?
    1) Both contain an equal number of OH^- ions   3) Both turn litmus red
    2) Both contain an equal number of H^+ ions   4) Both are electrolytes

21. When a solution of an acid is tested with pH paper, the result will be a pH
    1) Above 7, and the solution will conduct electricity
    2) Above 7, and the solution will not conduct electricity
    3) Below 7, and the solution will conduct electricity
    4) Below 7, and the solution will not conduct electricity

22. According to the Arrhenius theory, which list of compounds includes only acids?
    1) HNO_3, H_2SO_4, and $C_6H_{12}O_6$
    2) LiOH, HNO_3, and CH_3OH
    3) H_2PO_4, HCO_3, and NH_4Cl
    4) HF, H_2CO_3, and HNO_3

23. According to the Arrhenius theory, which list of compounds includes only bases?
    1) KOH, $Ca(OH)_2$, and CH_3OH
    2) $Mg(OH)_2$, NaOH, and LiOH
    3) LiOH, $Ca(OH)_2$, and $C_2H_4(OH)_2$
    4) NaOH, $Ca(OH)_2$, and CH_3COOH

24. A solution of LiOH is classified as
    1) An Arrhenius base, with a pH below 7
    2) An Arrhenius base, with a pH above 7
    3) An Arrhenius acid, with a pH below 7
    4) An Arrhenius acid, with a pH above 7

25. Both HNO_3 (aq) and CH_3COOH (aq) can be classified as
    1) Acids that turn blue litmus red
    2) Acids that turns red litmus blue
    3) Bases that turn blue litmus red
    4) Bases that turn red litmus blue

26. In an aqueous solution of NH_3, phenolphthalein is
    1) Pink because the NH_3 solution contains a greater amount of H^+ than OH^-
    2) Pink because the NH_3 solution contains a greater amount of OH^- than H^+
    3) Colorless because the NH_3 solution contains a greater amount of H^+ than OH^-
    4) Colorless because the NH_3 solution contains a greater amount of OH^- than H^+

27. Which pH of a solution indicates the strongest base?
    1) 6   2) 7   3) 8   4) 9

28. Which indicates a pH of an acidic solution?
    1) 4   2) 7   3) 9   4) 14

29. An aqueous solution turns litmus red. The pH of the solution could be
    1) 14   2) 11   3) 8   4) 5

30. An aqueous solution with a pH of 8 turns litmus
    1) Blue, and methyl orange will be red
    2) Blue, and methyl orange will be yellow
    3) Red, and methyl orange will be red
    4) Red, and methyl orange will be yellow

31. As NH_4OH is added to an HCl solution, the pH of the solution
    1) Decreases as the OH^- ion concentration increases
    2) Decreases as the OH^- ion concentration decreases
    3) Increases as the OH^- ion concentration increases
    4) Increases as the OH^- ion concentration decreases

32. As a solution changes from a pH of 4 to a pH of 1, there is a
    1) 1000 fold increase in H^+ ions
    2) 1000 fold decrease in H^+ ions
    3) 3 fold increase in H^+ ions
    4) 3 fold decrease in H^+ ions

33. A solution with a H_3O^+ concentration of 1.0×10^{-11} M will be
    1) Basic with a pH of 11
    2) Basic with a pH of 3
    3) Acidic with a pH of 11
    4) Acidic with a pH of 3

34. A solution with an H^+ concentration of 1.0×10^{-5} moles/L is
    1) Acidic because it contains more H^+ than OH^-
    2) Basic because it contains more H^+ than OH^-
    3) Acidic because it contains more OH^- than H^+
    4) Basic because it contains more OH^- than H^+

Lesson 2: Reactions of Acids and Bases

35. What type of reaction occurs when equal moles of an acid and a base react?
    1) Single replacement   2) Combustion   3) Neutralization 4) Hydrolysis

36. Which substances are produced in reactions between an acid and a base?
    1) Water and a salt   3) A salt and hydrogen gas
    2) Water and hydrogen gas   4) A sugar and a salt

37. According to Reference Table J, which metal will react with hydrochloric acid to produce hydrogen gas?
    1) Ag   2) Hg   3) Cu   4) Ni

38. According to Reference Table J, which reaction will not occur under at STP?
    1) $Sn(s)$ + $2\,HCl\,(aq)$ $\rightarrow$ $H_2\,(g)$ + $SnCl_2\,(aq)$
    2) $Cu\,(s)$ + $2\,HCl\,(aq)$ $\rightarrow$ $H_2\,(g)$ + $CuCl_2\,(aq)$
    3) $Ba(s)$ + $2\,HCl\,(aq)$ $\rightarrow$ $H_2\,(g)$ + $BaCl_2\,(aq)$
    4) $Pb\,(s)$ + $2\,HCl\,(aq)$ $\rightarrow$ $H_2\,(g)$ + $PbCl_2\,(aq)$

39. Which balanced equation represents a neutralization reaction?
    1) Mg + $NiCl_2$ $\rightarrow$ $MgCl_2$ + Ni
    2) $2KClO_3$ $\rightarrow$ $2\,KCl$ + $3O_2$
    3) $BaCl_2$ + $Cu(NO_3)_2$ $\rightarrow$ $Ba(NO_3)_2$ + $CuCl_2$
    4) H_2SO_4 + $2LiOH$ $\rightarrow$ Li_2SO_4 + $2H_2O$

40. Which equation is showing a neutralization reaction?
    1) $H^+\,(aq)$ + $OH^-\,(aq)$ $\rightarrow$ $H_2O\,(l)$
    2) $Ag^+\,(aq)$ + $I^-\,(aq)$ $\rightarrow$ $AgI\,(s)$
    3) $Zn\,(s)$ + $Cu^{2+}\,(aq)$ $\rightarrow$ $Zn^{2+}\,(aq)$ + $Cu(s)$
    4) $2H_2\,(g)$ + $O_2\,(g)$ $\rightarrow$ $2H_2O\,(l)$

41. In the neutralization reaction:
    $HC_2H_3O_2 + NH_4OH$ $\rightarrow$ $NH_4C_2H_3O_2 + H_2O$, the salt is

    1) NH_4OH 2) $HC_2H_3O_2$ 3) $NH_4C_2H_3O_2$ 4) H_2O

42. Which two substances can react to produce H_2O and a salt with the formula K_3PO_4?
    1) KOH and H_3PO_4 3) K_3P and H_2O
    2) K_2O and H_3PO_4 4) KOH and H_2O

43. What is the name of the salt from a reaction of calcium hydroxide with sulfuric acid?
    1) Calcium thiosulfate   3) Calcium sulfide
    2) Calcium sulfate   4) Calcium sulfite

44. In a titration experiment, 20 mL of 1.0 M HCl neutralized 10 mL of NaOH solution of unknown concentration. What was the concentration of the base?
    1) 2.5 M   2) 2.0 M   3) 1.5 M   4) 0.50 M

45. If 100 mL of 0.75 M HNO_3 is required to exactly neutralize 50 mL of NaOH, what is the concentration of the base?
    1) 0.25 M   2) 0.75 M   3) 1.0 M   4) 1. 5M

46. How many milliliters of 1.5 M H_2SO_4 are needed to neutralize a 35 mL sample of a 1.5 M KOH solution?
    1) 17.5 mL   2) 35 mL   3) 52.5 mL   4) 3.0 mL

Lesson 3. Salts and Electrolytes

47. Which list of compounds includes only salts?
    1) HNO_3, $NaNO_3$, and $Ca(NO_3)_2$ 3) C_2H_5OH, CH_3COOH, and $CaCl_2$
    2) CH_3OH, $NaOH$, and $NaCl$ 4) $Ba(NO_3)_2$, Na_2SO_4, and $MgCl_2$

48. A substance that conducts electrical current when dissolved in water is called
    1) An isotope   2) A catalyst   3) A metalloid   4) An electrolyte

49. A water solution conducts electrical current because the solution contains mobile
    1) Atoms   2) Ions   3) Molecules   4) Electrons

50. Which list contains types of substances that are electrolytes?
    1) Soluble salts, sugar, and acids   3) Soluble salts, acids and bases
    2) Soluble salts, alcohols, and bases   4) Acids, bases, and alcohols

51. Which 0.1 M solution contains electrolytes?
    1) $C_6H_{12}O_6$ (aq)   3) CH_3COOH (aq)
    2) CH_3OH (aq)   4) CH_3OCH_3 (aq)

52. Which compound is classified as an electrolyte?
    1) H_2O 2) $C_{12}H_{22}O_{11}$ 3) CH_3OH 4) $Ca(OH)_2$

53. An example of a nonelectrolyte is
    1) $C_6H_{12}O_6$ (aq)   2) K_2SO_4 (aq)   3) $NaCl$ (aq)   4) HCl (aq)

54. According to Reference Table F, which salt solution would be the best electrolyte?
    1) $AgCl$(aq)   2) $PbCl_2$(aq)   3) NH_4Cl (aq)   4) $HgCl_2$(aq)

Topic Mastery / Constructed Response

55. A blue solution containing an acid-base indicator was tested with a pH meter and found to have a pH of 5.5. Which indicator on Table M was in the solution?

56. In a titration, 3.00 M NaOH(aq) was added to an Erlenmeyer flask containing 25.00 millimeters of H_2SO_4 (aq) and three drops of phenolphthalein until one drop of NaOH(aq) turned the solution a light-pink color. The following data were collected by a student performing this titration.

    Initial NaOH(aq) buret reading: 14.45 milliliters
    Final NaOH(aq) buret reading: 32.66 milliliters

    a) Show set up and the calculated result for the concentration of the acid.

    b) Write a balanced equation for the neutralization reaction that occurs.

57. What are the names for these acids: H_2Te HI $HClO$ $H_2C_2O_4$ HNO_2

Answer questions 58 through 60 based on the information below.
Some carbonated beverages are made by forcing carbon dioxide gas into a beverage solution. When a bottle of one kind of carbonated beverage is first opened, the beverage has a pH value of 3.

58. State, in terms of the pH scale, why this beverage is classified as acidic.

59. Using Table M, identify one indicator that is yellow in a solution that has the same pH value as this beverage.

60. After the beverage bottle is left open for several hours, the hydronium ion concentration in the beverage solution decreases to 1/1000 of the original concentration. Determine the new pH of the beverage solution.

Additional Materials

Hydrolysis

Hydrolysis is a process by which a salt reacts with water to produce a solution that is either acidic, basic, or neutral.

$$\text{Salt} + \text{water} \rightarrow \text{Acid} + \text{Base}$$

One way to tell the type of solution that will form from a hydrolysis reaction is to note the strength of the acid and base produced as shown below.

NH_4Br +	H_2O	$\rightarrow$	HBr +	NH_4OH
salt	water		**strong acid**	weak base

A solution of **NH_4Br** will be **acidic**

Na_2CO_3 +	$2H_2O$	$\rightarrow$	H_2CO_3 +	$NaOH$
salt	water		weak acid	**strong base**

A solution of **Na_2CO_3** will be **basic**

KCl +	H_2O	$\rightarrow$	HCl +	KOH
salt	water		**strong acid**	**strong base**

A solution of **KCl** will be **neutral**

Strong acids include: HI, HBr, HCl, HNO_3, H_2SO_4, $HClO_3$ and $HClO_4$
These acids completely dissociate (ionize) in water to produce large $[H^+]$.
All other acids are considered weak acids.

Strong bases include: $LiOH$, $NaOH$, KOH, $RbOH$, $CsOH$, $Ca(OH)_2$, and $Ba(OH)_2$.
These bases completely dissociate (ionize) in water to produce large $[OH^-]$.
All other bases are considered weak bases.

Conjugate Acid-Base Pairs

In some acid-base reactions protons (H^+) are donated and accepted by species in the reactions.

Bronsted-Lowry acids are species that donate protons.
Bronsted-Lowry bases are species that accept protons.

When Bronsted-Lowry acids and bases react conjugate species are produced as shown below.

H_2S +	H_2O	$\leftrightarrow$	H_3O^+ +	HS^-
acid	*base*		*conjugate acid*	*conjugate base*

In the above reaction:
H_2S is an acid because it donates (gives up) an H^+ and becomes **HS^- (a base)**
H_2O is a base because it accepts the H^+ and becomes **H_3O^+ (an acid)**

Two conjugate **acid - base** pairs can be determined from the equation.

conjugate pair 1: H_2S and HS^-

conjugate pair 2 H_3O^+ and H_2O

Note: Each conjugate acid-base pair contains similar species that differ only by one H^+. The acid in each pair contains one more H^+ than the base.

Ionization Constant of Water

Water is composed of H^+ and OH^- ions. Any sample of pure water contains equal concentrations of both ions.

$[H^+] = [OH^-] = 1.0 \times 10^{-7}$ M in pure water.

Ionization constant of water, K_w, is 1.0×10^{-14}. This value is equal to the product of the concentrations of H^+ and OH^- ions as shown below.

$\mathbf{K_w} = [H^+] \times [OH^-] = [1.0 \times 10^{-7}] \times [1.0 \times 10^{-7}] = \mathbf{1.0 \times 10^{-14}}$

Relating H^+, OH^-, pH and pOH

The same relationship shown above for water also exists in acidic and basic solutions. However, unlike water:

    Acidic solutions have a higher concentration of H^+ than OH^-.
    Basic solutions have a higher concentration of OH^- than H^+.

If the concentration of one of the ions in a solution is known, you can calculate the concentration of the other ion using the relationship:

$$\boxed{[H^+] \times [OH^-] = 1.0 \times 10^{-14}}$$ H_3O^+ is sometimes used in place of H^+

The relationships between the ions and pH and pOH are as follows:

$$\boxed{\begin{array}{l} \text{pH} = -\log[H^+] \\ \text{pOH} = -\log[OH^-] \\ \text{pH} + \text{pOH} = 14 \end{array}}$$

Example 3	*Example 4*
A solution has $[H^+]$ of 1.0×10^{-5} M.	A solution has $[OH^-]$ of 1.7×10^{-3} M
a) Calculate the [OH-] of the solution.	*a) Calculate the $[H_3O^+]$ of the solution*
$[OH-] = \dfrac{1.0 \times 10^{-14}}{1.0 \times 10^{-5}} = \mathbf{1.0 \times 10^{-9}}$	$[H_3O^+] = \dfrac{1.0 \times 10^{-14}}{1.7 \times 10^{-3}} = \mathbf{5.88 \times 10^{-12}}$ **M**
b) Calculate the pH of the solution	*b) Calculate the pH of the solution*
$\mathbf{pH} = -\log[H^+] = -\log[1.0 \times 10^{-5}] = \mathbf{5}$	$\mathbf{pH} = -\log[5.88 \times 10^{-12}] = \mathbf{11.23}$
c) Calculate the pOH of the solution	*c) Calculate the pOH of the solution*
$\mathbf{pOH} = 14 - \text{pH} = 14 - 5 = \mathbf{9}$	$\mathbf{pOH} = -\log[1.7 \times 10^{-3}] = \mathbf{2.77}$

Practice Questions on Additional Materials

61. In the reaction: $H_2PO_4^- + H_2O \leftrightarrow H_3PO_4 + OH^-$
which pair represents an acid and its conjugate base?
   1) H_2O and $H_2PO_4^-$ 3) H_3PO_4 and OH^-
   2) H_2O and H_3PO_4 4) H_3PO_4 and $H_2PO_4^-$

62. Given the reaction: $HSO_4^- + H_2O \leftrightarrow H_3O^+ + SO_4^{2-}$
Which is a correct conjugate acid-base pair?
   1) HSO_4^- and SO_4^{2-} 3) SO_4^{2-} and H_3O^+
   2) HSO_4^- and H_2O 4) SO_4^{2-} and H_2O

63. What is the conjugate base of NH_3?
   1) NH_4^+ 2) NH_2^- 3) NO_3^- 4) NO_2^-

64. Hydrolysis of which salt will produce an acidic solution?
   1) $NaC_2H_3O_2$ 2) Li_2CO_3 3) NH_4NO_3 4) K_3PO_4

65. Hydrolysis of which salt will produce a solution with a pH close to 11.
   1) $NaNO_3$ 2) K_3PO_4 3) $(NH_4)_2SO_4$ 4) $NaCl$

66. The $[OH^-]$ of a solution is 1.0×10^{-6} M. At 298 K and 1 atm, the product of $[H_3O^+]$ $[OH^-]$ is
   1) 1.0×10^{-2} 2) 1.0×10^{-6} 3) 1.0×10^{-8} 4) 1.0×10^{-14}

67. A solution with a H^+ concentration of 1.0×10^{-12} M will also have a OH^- concentration of
   1) 1.0×10^{-12} M   2) 1.0×10^{-14} M   3) 1.0×10^{-26} M   4) 1.0×10^{-2} M

68. What is the pH of a solution with a hydroxide concentration of 1.0×10^{-10} ?
   1) 10   2) 4   3) 14   4) 1

69. Below, H^+ concentrations of three different solutions are given.
Determine pH, $[OH^-]$, and pOH of each solution.

                    pH $[OH^-]$ pOH

    a) 1.0×10^{-12} M H^+

    b) 2.0×10^{-12} M H^+

    c) 3.76×10^{-4} M H^+

70. Below, pH values of three different solutions are given.
Determine $[H_3O^+]$, $[OH^-]$, and pOH of each solution.

                    $[H_3O^+]$ $[OH^-]$ pOH

    a) pH $= 3$

    b) pH $= 5.9$

    c) pH $= 9.8$

Lesson 1 : Kinetics

Introduction

Kinetics is the study of rates and mechanisms of chemical reactions.
A **rate** is the speed at which a reaction is taking place.
A **mechanism** is a series of reactions that lead to final products of a reaction.

In this lesson, you will learn about the rate of chemical reactions and factors that can affect rate.

Rate of Reaction

Rate of a reaction is the speed at which a chemical reaction or a physical change occurs.

Collision theory states that for a chemical reaction to occur between reactants, there *must be effective collisions* between the reacting particles.

Effective collisions occur when reacting particles collide with *sufficient (right amount of) kinetic energy* and at a *proper orientation (angle)* .

. Rate of a reaction depends on frequency of (how often) effective collisions occur between particles.

. Any factor that can change the frequency of effective collisions between reacting particles will change the rate of that reaction.

For example: Any change made to a chemical reaction that increases frequency of effective collisions between the reacting particles will cause the rate of the reaction to increase.

The diagram below shows the difference between effective and ineffective collisions.

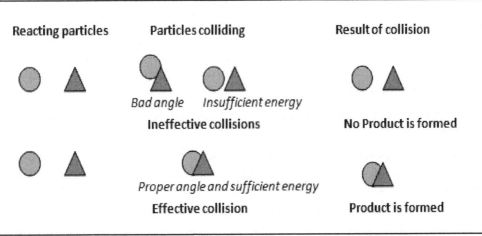

Reacting particles	Particles colliding	Result of collision
	Bad angle *Insufficient energy*	
	Ineffective collisions	**No Product is formed**
	Proper angle and sufficient energy	
	Effective collision	**Product is formed**

Activation Energy and Catalyst

Activation energy is the energy needed to start a chemical reaction.

All chemical reactions, both endothermic and exothermic, require some amount of activation energy. Any factor that can change the amount of activation energy for a reaction will change the rate of that reaction.

A **catalyst** is any substance that can increase the speed (rate) of a reaction by lowering the activation energy for that reaction. A catalyst in a reaction provides an alternate (lower activation energy) pathway for a reaction to occur faster.

Below is a list of factors that increase rate, and reasons for the rate increase.

Factors that increase reaction rate	Why rate increases
Increasing concentration of reactants	↑ number of reacting particles ↑ frequency of effective collisions between the reacting particles
Increasing temperature of reactants	↑ kinetic energy of particles ↑ frequency of effective collisions
Increasing pressure on the reaction	↓ volume of gaseous reactants ↑ concentration of reactants ↑ frequency of effective collisions
Increasing surface area of reacting solid	↑ or exposes more area for reactions to occur ↑ frequency of effective collisions
Least surface area Most surface area	
Addition of a catalyst to a reaction	↓ lowers activation energy. Provides alternate pathway for a reaction to occur faster

Nature of Reactants:

Reactions of ionic solutions are very fast (almost instantaneous) because no bond breaking is required.

Reactions of molecular substances are slow because the reactions require breaking of strong covalent bonds. High activation energy is usually required for reactions involving molecular substances.

Some metals, because of their nature, react faster than others in solutions.

Lesson 2: Energy and Chemical Reactions

Introduction

Every chemical substance contains some amount of energy that is stored within the bonds of the substance. During chemical reactions, substances absorb and release energy as bonds are broken and formed, respectively.

In this lesson, you will learn the relationship between energy and chemical (or physical) changes.

Energy and Reactions:

Potential energy is stored energy in chemical substances. The amount of potential energy in a substance depends on its *structure* and *composition*.

Potential Energy of reactants is the amount of energy stored in the bonds of the reactants. *Recall* that reactants are substances that are present at the start of a chemical reaction.

Potential Energy of products is the amount of energy stored in the bonds of the products. *Recall* that products are substances that remain at the end of a chemical reaction.

Heat of reaction (ΔH) is the overall energy absorbed or released during a reaction. ΔH of a reaction is the difference between the potential energy of the products and of the reactants.

$$\Delta H \;=\; \text{Energy of products} \;-\; \text{Energy of reactants}$$

Heat of reaction (ΔH) can be negative or positive.

Negative heat of reaction (- ΔH) means that:

. The products of a reaction have *less energy* than the reactants

. The reaction is exothermic (releases heat)

Positive heat of reaction (+ΔH) means that:

. The products of a reaction *have more* energy than the reactants

. The reaction is endothermic (absorbs heat)

Exothermic and Endothermic Reactions

Some chemical reactions absorb energy, while others release energy. Reactions that release energy are exothermic. Reactions that absorb energy are endothermic. Since most chemical and physical processes occur in some form of a liquid (water or aqueous) environment, measuring temperature of the liquid before and after a reaction is usually one way to tell if a reaction is exothermic or endothermic. If heat was released during a reaction, the temperature of the liquid will be higher after the reaction. If heat was absorbed during a reaction, the temperature of the liquid will be lower after the reaction.

Exothermic Reactions and Energy

Exothermic reactions occur when products formed from a reaction contain less energy than the reactants. Since the products have less energy than the reactants, the reactants lost (or released) energy during the chemical change. When heat energy is released to the surrounding area where the reaction is occurring, the temperature of the surroundings will go up (or increase).
Heat of reaction, ΔH, is always negative ($-\Delta H$) for all exothermic reactions.

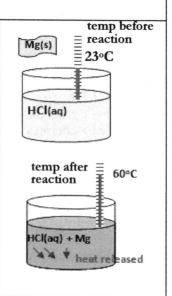

Example equation of an exothermic reaction:

$$Mg + 2\,HCl \longrightarrow MgCl_2 + H_2 + \textbf{Energy}$$

Endothermic Reactions and Energy

Endothermic reactions occur when products formed from the reaction contain more energy than the reactants. Since the products have more energy than the reactants, the reactants gained (or absorbed) energy during the chemical change. When heat energy is absorbed from the surrounding area where the reaction is occurring, the temperature of the surroundings will go down (or decrease).
Heat of reaction, ΔH, is always positive ($+\Delta H$) for all endothermic reactions.

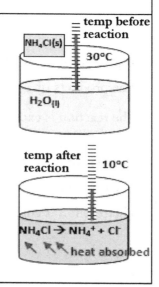

Example equation of an endothermic reaction:

$$NH_4Cl(s) + \textbf{Energy} \longrightarrow NH_4^+(aq) + Cl^-(aq)$$

140

Heats of Reaction (Reference Table I)

Reference Table I (below) lists equations for selected physical and chemical changes and their ΔH (heat of reaction) values.

NOTE the following about the Table.
Some equations have $-\Delta H$, and some have $+\Delta H$.

Table I
Heats of Reaction at 101.3 kPa and 298 K

Reaction	ΔH (kJ)*
$CH_4(g) + 2O_2(g) \longrightarrow CO_2(g) + 2H_2O(\ell)$	–890.4
$C_3H_8(g) + 5O_2(g) \longrightarrow 3CO_2(g) + 4H_2O(\ell)$	–2219.2
$2C_8H_{18}(\ell) + 25O_2(g) \longrightarrow 16CO_2(g) + 18H_2O(\ell)$	–10943
$2CH_3OH(\ell) + 3O_2(g) \longrightarrow 2CO_2(g) + 4H_2O(\ell)$	–1452
$C_2H_5OH(\ell) + 3O_2(g) \longrightarrow 2CO_2(g) + 3H_2O(\ell)$	–1367
$C_6H_{12}O_6(s) + 6O_2(g) \longrightarrow 6CO_2(g) + 6H_2O(\ell)$	–2804
$2CO(g) + O_2(g) \longrightarrow 2CO_2(g)$	–566.0
$C(s) + O_2(g) \longrightarrow CO_2(g)$	–393.5
$4Al(s) + 3O_2(g) \longrightarrow 2Al_2O_3(s)$	–3351
$N_2(g) + O_2(g) \longrightarrow 2NO(g)$	+182.6
$N_2(g) + 2O_2(g) \longrightarrow 2NO_2(g)$	+66.4
$2H_2(g) + O_2(g) \longrightarrow 2H_2O(g)$	–483.6
$2H_2(g) + O_2(g) \longrightarrow 2H_2O(\ell)$	–571.6
$N_2(g) + 3H_2(g) \longrightarrow 2NH_3(g)$	–91.8
$2C(s) + 3H_2(g) \longrightarrow C_2H_6(g)$	–84.0
$2C(s) + 2H_2(g) \longrightarrow C_2H_4(g)$	+52.4
$2C(s) + H_2(g) \longrightarrow C_2H_2(g)$	+227.4
$H_2(g) + I_2(g) \longrightarrow 2HI(g)$	+53.0
$KNO_3(s) \xrightarrow{H_2O} K^+(aq) + NO_3^-(aq)$	+34.89
$NaOH(s) \xrightarrow{H_2O} Na^+(aq) + OH^-(aq)$	–44.51
$NH_4Cl(s) \xrightarrow{H_2O} NH_4^+(aq) + Cl^-(aq)$	+14.78
$NH_4NO_3(s) \xrightarrow{H_2O} NH_4^+(aq) + NO_3^-(aq)$	+25.69
$NaCl(s) \xrightarrow{H_2O} Na^+(aq) + Cl^-(aq)$	+3.88
$LiBr(s) \xrightarrow{H_2O} Li^+(aq) + Br^-(aq)$	–48.83
$H^+(aq) + OH^-(aq) \longrightarrow H_2O(\ell)$	–55.8

*Minus sign indicates an exothermic reaction.

Equation with $-\Delta H$ (exothermic)

$2C(s) + 3H_2(g) \rightarrow C_2H_6(g)$
$\Delta H = -84$ kJ.

According to the equation and ΔH:

The formation of 1 mole of C_2H_6 (ethane) releases 84 kJ (kilojoules) of heat energy.

The formation of 2 moles of C_2H_6 will release 2(84 kJ) or 168 kJ of heat energy.

The product of this reaction has less energy than the reactants.

Equation with $+\Delta H$ (endothermic)

$NH_4Cl_{(s)} \rightarrow NH_4^+{}_{(aq)} + Cl^-{}_{(aq)}$
$\Delta H = +14.78$ kJ

According to the equation and ΔH:

The dissolving of **1** mole of NH_4Cl (ammonium chloride) absorbs 14.78 kJ of heat energy.

The dissolving of 0.5 mole of NH_4Cl will absorb 0.5 (14.78 kJ) or 7.39 kJ of heat energy.

The products of this process have more energy than the reactant.

Exothermic and Endothermic: Summary Table

Process	Potential Energy of Reactants	Potential Energy of Products	Energy Change	Temperature of Surrounding	Heat of reaction (ΔH)
Exothermic	Higher	Lower	Released	Increases	Negative ($-\Delta H$)
Endothermic	Lower	Higher	Absorbed	Decreases	Positive ($+\Delta H$)

Potential energy diagrams

Potential energy diagrams show changes in heat energy of substances over a course of a reaction. To understand potential energy diagrams, it is important to review components of a chemical reaction. These components are represented on all potential energy diagrams.

Consider this equation:

$$A + B_2 \longrightarrow ABB \longrightarrow AB + B$$

Reactants   *Activated*   *Products*
                           complex

Note the following three substances about the equation:

Reactants (A and B_2) are substances that are present at the beginning of the reaction.

Products (AB and B) are substances formed at the end of the reaction.

An **activated complex** (ABB) is a high energy intermediate substance that is formed during the reaction. Because of its high energy, an activated complex is very unstable and will always break down or rearrange to form more stable *products*. An activated complex is not usually shown in a reaction equation. However, for a potential energy diagram to be accurately drawn for any reaction, an activated complex must be represented on the diagram.

Exothermic Diagram (see above equation)

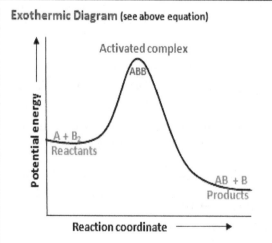

Endothermic Diagram

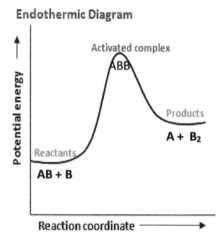

Since this is exothermic, note how the products are at a lower energy state than the reactants.

Since this is endothermic, note how the products are at a higher energy state than the reactants

Energy Measurements on Potential Energy Diagrams

The potential energy diagrams below show the important energy measurements. The left diagram shows measurements for a reaction that is uncatalyzed. The right diagram shows energy measurements for the same reaction with a catalyst added. Recall that a catalyst speeds up a reaction by lowering the activation energy. Note how certain energy measurements for the reaction are changed (lowered) with a catalyst.

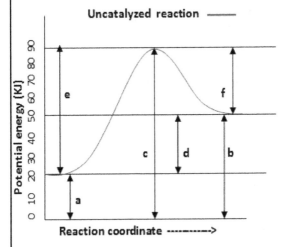

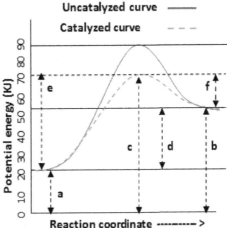

NOTE the following about each diagram:
The y axis is potential energy. The x axis is the reaction coordinate (or progress of reaction). Each curve shows the potential energy of substances that are present at different times over the course of a reaction (starting with reactants, ending with products).

Potential energy measurements of three substances are shown with arrows a, b and c.
These arrows are always drawn from the bottom of the diagram:

(a) Potential energy of the reactants   (no change with catalyst)

(b) Potential energy of the products   (no change with catalyst)

(c) Potential energy of the activated complex   (lower with catalyst)

Differences of two potential energies are shown with arrows d, e and f.
These arrows are always drawn between two energies of the diagram.

(d) Heat of reaction, ΔH (b $-$ a)   (no change with catalyst)

(e) Activation energy for forward reaction (c $-$ a)   (lower with catalyst)

(f) Activation energy for reverse reaction (c $-$ b)   (lower with catalyst)

Lesson 3: Entropy

Introduction

During chemical and physical changes, particles of a substance rearrange from one state to another. Particles can become more or less organized depending on the type of change the substance has gone through during the change.

In this lesson, you will learn about entropy, which describes organization of a system.

Entropy

Entropy is a measure of randomness or disorder of a system.

In chemistry, a system refers to any chemical or physical process that is taking place. Entropy of chemical and physical systems is relative, meaning that randomness or disorder of one system can only be described when compared to another system.

. Entropy increases from solid to liquid to gas.

. Entropy decreases from gas to liquid to solid.

. As temperature increases, so does the entropy of the system.

. As pressure increases, entropy of the system decreases.

. Entropy of free elements is higher than entropy of compounds.

. A chemical reaction is more likely to occur if the change will lead to substances with higher entropy (and lower energy, $-\Delta H$).

Change in Entropy Diagrams

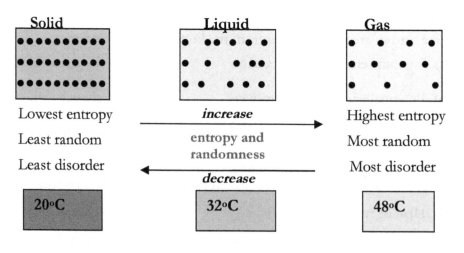

Solid	Liquid	Gas
Lowest entropy	*increase*	Highest entropy
Least random	entropy and randomness	Most random
Least disorder	*decrease*	Most disorder
20°C	32°C	48°C

Lesson 4: Equilibrium

Introduction

Equilibrium refers to a state of balance between two opposing processes taking place at the same time (simultaneously) and at equal rates. One example of two opposing processes is the freezing of water to ice, and the melting of the ice back to water. In this lesson, you will learn about physical and chemical equilibrium.

Equilibrium

Equilibrium can only occur in a system in which changes that are taking place are *reversible*. Equilibrium can only occur in a *closed system*. A closed system is a system in which nothing is allowed in or out.

Example of a reversible equilibrium equation:

$$N_2 \; + \; O_2 \; \overset{\text{Forward}}{\underset{\text{Reverse}}{\rightleftharpoons}} \; 2NO$$

At equilibrium:

. *Rates* of forward and reverse reactions are *equal*

. *Concentrations* (or amounts) of substances remain *constant*.

An equation showing a reversible process at equilibrium always contains a double ended arrow.

$\leftrightarrow$

or

$\rightleftharpoons$

Physical Equilibrium

Phase and solution equilibrium are examples of physical equilibrium.

A **phase equilibrium** occurs in a CLOSED system in which phase changes are occurring. Examples of phase equilibrium are given below.

Solid/Liquid equilibrium

Example: *Ice/water equilibrium* occurs at **0°C or 273 K** (at 1 atm pressure)

$$H_2O(s) \; \overset{\text{melting}}{\underset{\text{freezing}}{\rightleftharpoons}} \; H_2O(l).$$

Rates of melting and freezing are equal.
Amounts of ice and water stay constant

Liquid/Gas (vapor) equilibrium

Example: *Water/Steam equilibrium* occurs at **100°C or 373 K** (at 1 atm pressure)

$$H_2O(l) \; \overset{\text{evaporation}}{\underset{\text{condensation}}{\rightleftharpoons}} \; H_2O(g)$$

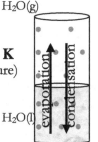

Rate of evaporation equals rate of condensation.
Amounts of water and vapor stay constant

Solution Equilibrium

Solution equilibrium occurs in a CLOSED system in which a substance is dissolving in a liquid.

Solid in liquid equilibrium: In a saturated solution

. Equilibrium exists between dissolved and undissolved particles.

$$NaCl(s) \underset{crystallizing}{\overset{dissolving}{\rightleftharpoons}} Na^+(aq) \quad + \quad Cl^-(aq)$$

. *Rate* of dissolving of solid is equal to rate of crystallization of ions

. *Amount*s of solid and ions remain *constant* in the solution.

Gas in liquid equilibrium: In a gaseous solution

. Equilibrium exists between dissolved gas in the liquid and
   undissolved gas above the liquid.

$$CO_2(g) \underset{undissolving}{\overset{dissolving}{\rightleftharpoons}} CO_2(aq)$$

. *Rate* of dissolving equals rate of undissolving of the gas.
. *Amount*s of undissolved gas (above liquid) and dissolved
   gas (in liquid) remain *constant*.

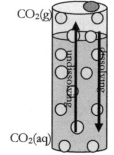

$CO_2(g)$

$CO_2(aq)$

a closed
soda can

Chemical Equilibrium

Chemical equilibrium only occurs in closed and reversible reactions. A state of balance exists between forward and reverse rates in reversible chemical processes at equilibrium.

Forward reaction

$$N_2(g) \quad + \quad 3H_2(g) \quad \rightleftharpoons \quad 2NH_3(g)$$

Reverse reaction

At equilibrium:

Rates of forward and reverse reactions are *equal*

Concentrations of N_2, H_2, and NH_3 remain *constant* (remain the same).

A **Stress** is any change that is made to a reaction at equilibrium. Increasing or decreasing concentration, temperature, or pressure are examples of a stresses on an equilibrium reaction. Questions on chemical equilibrium often involve determining changes to a reaction when a stress is introduced or determining a stress that will cause a specified change to a given reaction.

Le Chatelier's Principle

Le Chatelier's Principle states that when a stress is introduced into a reaction at equilibrium, the reaction will change by speeding up in one direction and slowing down in the other direction to bring back (re-establish) a new equilibrium state. Notes below explain how a reaction will change in response to the stress given. (see pg 149 for explanations of arrows).

Change in Concentration

Given the equilibrium reaction:

$$N_2 + 3H_2 \rightleftharpoons 2NH_3$$

Stress: Increase in concentration of N_2:

Results of stress (changes to reaction to re-establish a new equilibrium point)

a) Rate of forward increases
b) Rate of reverse decreases
c) Concentration of H_2 decreases
d) Concentration of NH_3 increases
e) Shift of reaction is to the RIGHT (reaction always shifts to the same direction as the rate increase)

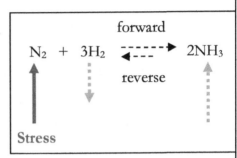

Given the equilibrium reaction:

$$X + WY \rightleftharpoons XY + W$$

Stress: Decrease in [WY]

Results of stress (changes to reaction)

a) Rate of forward decreases
b) Rate of reverse increases
c) [XY] and [W] decrease
d) [X] increases
e) Shift in reaction to the LEFT

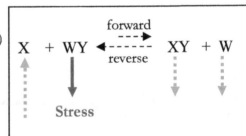

Changing Concentration by Common-Ion Effect

Many substances dissolve (ionize) in solution to produce a common ion. In the example below, KNO_3 and KCl have a common ion, K^+.

Given the equilibrium reaction:

$$KNO_3 (s) \rightleftharpoons K^+(aq) + NO_3^- (aq)$$

Stress: Addition of KCl ($\uparrow K^+$)

Results of stress (changes to reaction)

a) Rate of forward decreases
b) Rate of reverse increase
c) Concentration of NO_3^- decreases
d) Concentration of KNO_3 increases
e) Shift of reaction to the LEFT

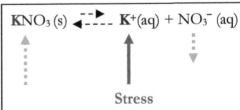

$[K^+]$ increases (stress) because K^+ is the common ion in KNO_3 and KCl.

Change in Temperature

Increasing temperature (adding heat) favors endothermic reactions.

Given the equilibrium equation: $HI + heat \rightleftharpoons H_2 + I_2$

Stress: Adding heat (↑ temperature)

Results of stress

a) Rate of forward increases
b) Rate of reverse decreases
c) [HI] decreases
d) [H₂] and [I₂] increase
e) Shift of reaction to the RIGHT

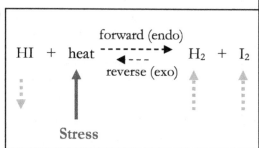

Decreasing temperature (removing heat) favors exothermic reactions.

Given the equilibrium equation: $A + B \rightleftharpoons AB + 40 \text{ kJ}$

Stress: Removing heat (↓ temp)

Results of stress

a) Rate of forward increases
b) Rate of reverse decreases
c) [AB] increases
d) [A] and [B] decrease
e) Shift of reaction to the RIGHT

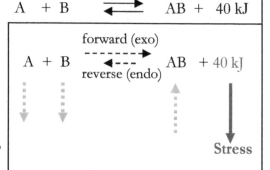

Change in Pressure (by Changing Volume)

When an equilibrium question deals with change in pressure, the number of moles of *gases only* on both sides of the equation must be considered.

Stress: Increasing pressure favors production of substances on the side with the smaller number of moles of gas.

Given the equilibrium reaction: $CH_{4(g)} + H_2O_{(g)} \rightleftharpoons 3H_{2\,(g)} + CO_{(g)}$

moles of gas   1 + 1   3 + 1
total number of moles   2 moles   4 moles

Results of increasing pressure

a) Rate of forward decreases
b) Rate of reverse increases
c) [CH₄] and [H₂O] increase
d) [H₂] and [CO] decrease
e) Shift of reaction to the LEFT

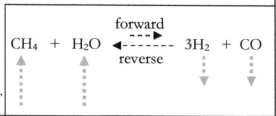

In reactions in which the total moles of gases on both sides of the equation are equal, a change in pressure has no effect on equilibrium (no shift).

Addition of a Catalyst

When a catalyst is added to a reaction at equilibrium:

. Rates of both the forward and reverse reactions increase (speed up) equally

   As a result:

. There will be no change on the equilibrium concentrations

. There will be no shift in either direction of the reaction

Notes on Le Chatelier's Principle

When studying notes on equilibrium from the last two pages, note the following:

. A stress is given

. General changes to rate, concentration, and shift are listed as *a* through *e*

. Example equation is given to the right of the stress

. A **Stress** is indicated with a solid arrow up ↑ to indicate an increase or with a solid arrow down ↓ to indicate a decrease.

. Results or changes to the reaction due to the stress given are indicated with dotted arrows

   An "upward" dotted arrow indicates an increase in concentration

   A "downward" dotted arrow indicates a decrease in concentration

   A "longer" dotted arrow indicates an increase in rate in that direction

   A "shorter" dotted arrow indicates a decrease in rate in that direction

Practice Questions

Lesson 1: Kinetics

Define the following terms and answer multiple choice questions below.

1. Kinetics   2. Rate   3.Mechanism   4. Collision theory   5. Effective collision
6. Catalyst   7. Activation energy

8. In order for any chemical reaction to occur, there must always be
   1) A bond that breaks in a reactant particle
   2) A reacting particle with a high charge
   3) Effective collisions between reacting particles
   4) A catalyst

9. Two particles collide with proper orientation. The collisions will be effective if the particles have
   1) High activation energy   3) Sufficient potential energy
   2) High electronegativity   4) Sufficient kinetic energy

10. Which conditions will increase the rate of a chemical reaction?
    1) Decreased temperature and decreased concentration
    2) Decreased temperature and increased concentration
    3) Increased temperature and decreased concentration
    4) Increased temperature and increased concentration

11. Increasing temperature speeds up a reaction by increasing
    1) The effectiveness of collisions, only
    2) The frequency of collisions, only
    3) Both the effectiveness and the frequency of the collisions
    4) Neither the effectiveness nor the frequency of the collisions

12. When a catalyst is added to a reaction, the reaction rate is increased because the catalyst
    1) Increases activation energy
    2) Decreases activation energy
    3) Increases potential energy of the reactants
    4) Decreases potential energy of the reactants

13. Given the reaction: $Mg(s) + 2HNO_3(aq) \rightarrow Mg(NO_3)_2(aq) + H_2(g)$
    At which temperature will the reaction occur at the greatest rate?
    1) 10°C   2) 30°C   3) 50°C   4) 70°C

14. Given the reaction
    $$CuSO_4(s) \rightarrow Cu^{2+}(aq) + SO_4^{2-}(aq)$$
    The $CuSO_4(s)$ dissolves more rapidly when it is powdered because the increase in surface area allows for
    1) Increased exposure of solute to solvent   3) Increased solute solubility
    2) Decreased exposure of solute to solvent   4) Decreased solute solubility

15. Based on the nature of the reactants in each equation, which reaction at 25°C will occur at the fastest rate?
    1) $KI(aq) + AgNO_3(aq) \rightarrow AgI(s) + KNO_3(aq)$
    2) $C(s) + O_2(g) \rightarrow CO(g)$
    3) $2SO_2(g) + O_2(g) \rightarrow 2SO_3(g)$
    4) $NH_3(g) + HCl(g) \rightarrow NH_4Cl(s)$

Lesson 2: Energy and Chemical Reactions

Answer the following multiple choice questions

16. Which best describes all endothermic reactions?
    1) They always release heat   3) They always occur spontaneously
    2) They always absorb heat   4) They never occur spontaneously

17. In which type of reaction is the energy of reactants always greater than the energy of products?
    1) Exothermic   2) Endothermic   3) Neutralization   4) Redox

18. Activation energy is needed for reactions that are
    1) Exothermic, only   3) Both exothermic and endothermic
    2) Endothermic, only   4) Neither exothermic nor endothermic

19. The heat of reaction (ΔH) is equal to
    1) Heat of products $-$ Heat of reactants   3) Heat of products $\times$ Heat of reactants
    2) Heat of products $+$ Heat of reactants   4) Heat of products $\div$ Heat of reactants

20. Which statement correctly describes heats of reaction for endothermic reactions?
    1) ΔH is negative because heat is absorbed
    2) ΔH is negative because heat is released
    3) ΔH is positive because heat is absorbed
    4) ΔH is positive because heat is released

21. When a substance is dissolved in water, the temperature of the water increases. This process is best described as
    1) Endothermic, with a release of energy
    2) Endothermic, with an absorption of energy
    3) Exothermic, with a release of energy
    4) Exothermic, with an absorption of energy

22. Solid X and solid Y were dissolved in separate 100 mL beakers of water. The water temperatures were recorded as shown in the table below.

	Salt X	Salt Y
Initial water temperature	40.3°C	40.3°C
Final water temperature	34.5°C	46.1°C

Which statement is the best conclusion from the above information?
    1) The dissolving of only Salt X was exothermic
    2) The dissolving of only Salt Y was endothermic
    3) The dissolving of both Salt X and Salt Y was exothermic
    4) The dissolving of Salt X was endothermic and the dissolving of Salt Y was exothermic

23. Salt A and salt B were each dissolved in separate beakers of water at 21°C. The temperature of salt A solution decreased, and the temperature of salt B solution increased.
    Based on these results, which conclusion is correct?
    1) The water gained energy from both salt A and salt B
    2) The water lost energy to salt A and gained energy from salt B
    3) The water lost energy to both salt A and salt B
    4) The water gained energy from salt A and lost energy to salt B

24. Given the reaction: I   +   I   → I_2 +   energy
    This reaction has
    1) +ΔH because the products have less energy than the reactants
    2) +ΔH because the products have more energy than the reactants
    3) - ΔH because the products have less energy than the reactants
    4) - ΔH because the products have more energy than the reactants

25. Given the equation: $2H_2O(l)$ +   energy   → $2 H_2(g)$ + $O_2(g)$
    Which statement is true concerning the potential energy of the products and of the
    reactants?
    1) The products have less energy than the reactants, and ΔH will be negative
    2) The products have more energy than the reactants, and ΔH will be positive
    3) The products have less energy than the reactants, and ΔH will be positive
    4) The products have more energy than the reactants, and ΔH will be negative

26. Given the reaction: X_2 + $2Y_2$ → $2XY_2$ +   10 kJ

    The formation of 2 moles of XY_2
    1) Releases 10 kJ of heat because the reaction is exothermic
    2) Releases 10 kJ of heat because the reaction is endothermic
    3) Absorbs 10 kJ of heat because the reaction is exothermic
    4) Absorbs 10 kJ of heat because the reaction is endothermic

27. Given the reaction: $N_2(g)$ + $3H_2(g)$ → $2NH_3(g)$ + 91.8 kJ

    What is the heat of reaction, ΔH, for the formation of 4 moles of $NH_3(g)$
    1) -91.8 kJ   2) +91.8 kJ   3) -183.6 kJ   4) +183.6 kJ

28. In the reaction: $CO(g)$ + $O_2(g)$ → $2CO_2(g)$ +   566 kJ
    Which is true of the heat of formation of $CO_2(g)$?
    1) ΔH = + 283 kJ /mole   3) ΔH = + 566 kJ /mole
    2) ΔH = - 283 kJ /mole   4) ΔH = - 566 kJ /mole

29. According to Reference Table I, which substance is formed by a reaction that
    absorbs heat energy?
    1) HI(g)   2) $H_2O(l)$ 3) $NH_3(g)$ 4) $H_2O(g)$

30. The dissolving of which salt is accompanied by the release of heat?
    1) Ammonium chloride   3) Potassium nitrate
    2) Lithium bromide   4) Ammonium nitrate

31. In which reaction, according to Reference Table I, do the products have a lower
    energy content than the reactants?
    1) $2C(s)$ + $3H_2(g)$ → $C_2H_6(g)$ 3) $N_2(g)$ + $O_2(g)$ → $2NO(g)$
    2) $2C(s)$ + $H_2(g)$ → $C_2H_2(g)$ 4) $N_2(g)$ + $2O_2(g)$ → $2NO_2(g)$

32. According to Table I, when 1 mole of $H_2O(g)$ is formed from its elements,
    1) 484 kJ of heat is absorbed   3) 242 kJ of heat is absorbed
    2) 484 kJ of heat is released   4) 242 kJ of heat is released

33. According to Reference Table I, what is ΔH for the formation of 0.5 mole of HI(g)
    from its elements?
    1) +26.5 kJ /mole   3) +53.0 kJ /mole
    2) +13.25 kJ /mole   4) +106.0 kJ /mole

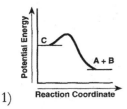

34. Given the reaction: A   +   B →   C   +   energy
    Which diagram below best represents the potential energy change for this reaction?

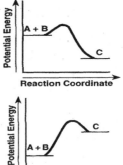

1)   3)

2)   4)

Answer questions 35 through 37 based on the diagram below.

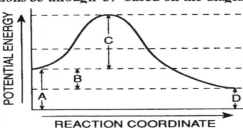

35. Activation energy for the forward reaction is represented by which arrow ?
    1) A   2) B   3) C   4) D

36. Which measurement correctly represents the heat content of the products?
    1) A   2) B   3) C   4) D

37. ΔH of this reaction is measured by which arrow?
    1) A   2) B   3) C   4) D

38. A diagram below shows the energy curve for catalyzed and uncatalyzed reactions.

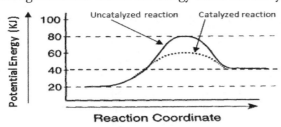

Which statement correctly describes the potential energy changes that occur in
the forward uncatalyzed reaction?
1) The activation energy is 40 kJ and ΔH is +20 kJ
2) The activation energy is 40 kJ and ΔH is - 20 kJ
3) The activation energy is 60 kJ and ΔH is +20 kJ
4) The activation energy is 60 kJ and ΔH is - 20 kJ

Answer questions 39 and 40 based on the diagram below.

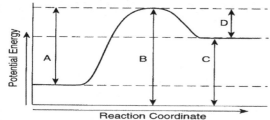

39. Energy of the activated complex is measured by which arrow in the above diagram?
    1) A   2) B   3) C   4) D

40. Which arrow represents the activation energy for the reverse reaction?
    1) A   2) B   3) C   4) D

Lesson 3: Entropy

Answer the following multiple choice questions.

41. Entropy measures which of the following about a chemical system?
    1) Activation energy of the system   3) Energy change of the system
    2) Intermolecular forces of the system   4) Disorder of the system

42. As a system becomes less random, its entropy
    1) Decreases   2) Increases   3) Remains the same

43. In which phase would particles of a substance be least random?
    1) Solid   2) Liquid   3) Gas   4) Aqueous

44. A system is most likely to undergo a reaction if the system after the reaction has
    1) Lower energy and lower entropy   3) Higher energy and higher entropy
    2) Lower energy and higher entropy   4) Higher energy and lower entropy

45. Which process is accompanied by a decrease in entropy?
    1) Evaporation of water   3) Melting of ice
    2) Condensing of steam   4) Sublimation of ice

46. At STP, which of the substances has the greatest degree of randomness?
    1) $H_2O(s)$ 2) $H_2O(l)$ 3) $N_2(l)$ 4) $N_2(g)$

47. A sample of water at which temperature would have molecules with the greatest degree of entropy?
    1) $O_2(g)$ at 35°C   3) $O_2(g)$ at 320 K
    2) $CO(g)$ at 50°C   4) $CO(g)$ at 280 K

48. Substance X is heated from one temperature to another. Which change in temperature of substance X is accompanied by a decrease in entropy of its particles?
    1) -10°C to -20°C   3) -10°C to -5°C
    2) 15°C to 20°C   4) 10°C to 15°C

49. In which chemical change would there be a change from a state of higher entropy to a state of lower entropy?
    1) $X_2(g) + Y_2(g) \rightarrow 2XY(g)$ 3) $A(s) + B(l) \rightarrow AB(aq)$
    2) $X_2(g) + Y_2(g) \rightarrow 2XY(l)$ 4) $A(l) + B(s) \rightarrow AB(g)$

Lesson 4: Equilibrium
Answer the following multiple choice questions.

50. A chemical reaction has reached equilibrium when
    1) The forward and reverse reactions are occurring at equal rates
    2) The forward and reversible reactions are occurring at different rates
    3) The concentrations of the substances are equal
    4) The concentrations of the reactants have been used up

51. Given the phase change equation: $H_2O(g) \leftrightarrow H_2O(l)$
    At 1 atm, at what temperature would equilibrium be reached?
    1) 273 K   2) 0 K   3) 373 K   4) 298 K

52. Solution equilibrium always exists in a solution that is
    1) Unsaturated   2) Saturated   3) Concentrated   4) Dilute

53. A sample of water in a sealed flask at 298 K is in equilibrium with its vapor. This is an example of
    1) Chemical equilibrium   3) Solution equilibrium
    2) Energy equilibrium   4) Phase equilibrium

54. In the reaction: $Pb(NO_3)_2(s) \leftrightarrow Pb^{2+}(aq) + 2NO_3^-(aq)$
    At equilibrium,
    1) The rate of dissolving of the salt and the rate of crystallization of ions is constant
    2) The concentrations of $Pb(NO_3)_2$ (aq) , $Pb^{2+}(aq)$, and $NO_3^-(aq)$ are constant
    3) The rate of dissolving of the salt is slower than the rate of crystallization of ions
    4) The concentration of Pb^{2+} is the same as the concentration of $Pb(NO_3)_2(s)$

55. Which description applies to a system in a sealed flask that is half full of water?
    1) Only evaporation occurs, but it eventually stops
    2) Only condensation occurs, but it eventually stops
    3) Neither evaporation nor condensation occurs
    4) Both evaporation and condensation occur

56. When more heat is added to an equilibrium reaction, the reaction will
    1) Shift in the direction of the exothermic reaction, and increase its rate
    2) Shift in the direction of the exothermic reaction, and decrease its rate
    3) Shift in the direction of the endothermic reaction, and increase its rate
    4) Shift in the direction of the endothermic reaction, and decrease its rate

57. Which change will have the least effect on concentration of substances in an equilibrium reaction?
    1) Adding a catalyst to the reaction   3) Increasing temperature of the reaction
    2) Increasing pressure on the reaction   4) Increasing concentration of the reactants

58. Given the reaction at equilibrium: $N_2(g) + 3H_2(g) \leftrightarrow 2NH_3(g)$

    Increasing the concentration of $N_2(g)$ will cause
    1) An increase in the concentration of $H_2(g)$
    2) An increase in the rate of the reverse reaction
    3) A decrease in the concentration of $H_2(g)$
    4) A decrease in the rate of the forward reaction

59. Given the equilibrium reaction: $N_2O_4(g) + 58.1 kJ \leftrightarrow 2NO_2(g)$
    If the concentration of $NO_2(g)$ is increased
    1) The rate of the forward reaction will increase, and equilibrium will shift right
    2) The rate of the forward reaction will increase, and equilibrium will shift left
    3) The rate of the reverse reaction will increase, and equilibrium will shift right
    4) The rate of the reverse reaction will increase, and equilibrium will shift left

60. Given the system at equilibrium: $2NH_3(g) + 92\,kJ \leftrightarrow N_2(g) + 3H_2(g)$
   Which statement is true of this reaction if the temperature is decreased?
   1) The equilibrium will shift left, and the concentration of $NH_3(g)$ will increase
   2) The equilibrium will shift right, and the concentration of H_2 will increase
   3) The forward reaction will increase, and the concentration of $H_2(g)$ will increase
   4) The forward reaction will decrease, and the concentration of NH_3 will decrease

61. Given the reaction at equilibrium: $2CO(g) + O_2(g) \leftrightarrow 2CO_2(g)$
   If pressure is increased on this reaction, the rate of the forward reaction will
   1) Decrease, and the concentration of CO_2 will also decrease
   2) Decrease, and the concentration of CO_2 will increase
   3) Increase, and the concentration of CO_2 will decrease
   4) Increase, and the concentration of CO_2 will also increase

62. The reaction below is at equilibrium
   $$2Cl_2(g) + 2H_2O(g) + 31.2\,kJ \leftrightarrow 4HCl(g) + O_2(g)$$
   Which stress will cause the rate of the reverse reaction to increase?
   1) Increase in temperature   3) Decrease in $HCl(g)$ concentration
   2) Increase in $Cl_2(g)$ concentration   4) Decrease in $H_2O(g)$ concentration

63. Given the equilibrium reaction below:
   $$SO_2(g) + NO_2(g) \leftrightarrow SO_3(g) + NO(g) + heat$$
   Which stress will NOT shift the equilibrium point of this reaction?
   1) Increasing pressure   3) Decreasing heat
   2) Increasing $SO_2(g)$ concentration   4) Decreasing $NO(g)$ concentration

Topic Mastery / Constructed Response

64. Using information provided on Table I, calculate the ΔH value for the combustion of 3.8 moles of C_8H_{18}:

65. Prepare a potential energy diagram to represent the following reaction:
   $B(s) + C(aq) \rightarrow D(aq) + 25\,kJ$. The heat of activation is 15 kJ.

66. Consider the following equation: $X_2(g) + 2Y_2(g) \leftrightarrow 2XY_2(g) + heat$

   What are two changes that would cause this reaction to shift to the left?

Answer questions 67 and 68 based on the information below.
   Pressure is increased on the equilibrium reaction below.

   $$2SO_2(g) + O_2(g) \leftrightarrow 2SO_3(g) + heat$$

67. Explain, using collision theory, why the concentration of O_2 would decrease.

68. What effect would the increased pressure have on the rate of the reverse reaction?

Additional Materials

Equilibrium Expression

The **equilibrium expression** shows the mathematical relationship between the reactants and products of a system at equilibrium. The equilibrium expression of a system is given as a fraction of the concentrations, [ ], of the products to reactants. Each concentration in the expression is raised to a power that is equal to the coefficient of the substance in the balanced equation. Solid and liquid substances are excluded from all equilibrium expressions. For any given reaction at a specified temperature the equilibrium expression results in a constant value called the *equilibrium constant, K_{eq}*.

In general:

$$K_{eq} = \frac{[Products]}{[Reactants]}$$

Variations of K_{eq}

Solubility Product Constant, K_{sp}
- expresses how well a salt dissolves
- the larger the K_{sp}, the more soluble the salt in water

$$K_{sp} = [product\ ions]$$

Acid Dissociation Constant, K_a
- expresses how well an acid ionizes
- the larger the K_a value, the stronger the acid, the more it ionizes in water

$$K_a = \frac{[H^+]\,[Base\ ion\ -]}{[Acid]}$$

Base Dissociation Constant, K_b
- expresses how well a base ionizes
- the larger the K_b value, the stronger the base, the more it ionizes in water

$$K_b = \frac{[Base\ ion\ ^+]\,[OH^-]}{[Base]}$$

Example 1

$$N_2\,(g)\ +\ 3\,H_2\,(g)\ \leftrightarrow\ 2\,NH_3\,(g)$$

$$K_{eq} = \frac{[NH_3]^2}{[N_2]\,[H_2]^3}$$

Example 2:

$$K_2SO_4\,(s)\ \leftrightarrow\ 2\,K^+(aq) + SO_4^{2-}\,(aq)$$

$$K_{sp} = [K^+]^2\,[SO_4^{2-}]$$ **Note:** $K_2SO_4(s)$ is not included in the expression

Example 3

$$HCl(aq)\ +\ H_2O(l)\ \leftrightarrow\ H^+(aq)\ +\ Cl^-(aq)$$

$$K_a = \frac{[H^+]\,[Cl^-]}{[HCl]}$$ **Note:** $H_2O(l)$ is not included in the expression

Example 4

$$Ca(OH)_2\,(aq)\ \leftrightarrow\ Ca^{2+}(aq)\ +\ 2\,OH^-(aq)$$

$$K_b = \frac{[Ca^{2+}]\,[OH^-]^2}{[Ca(OH)_2]}$$

A lot can be learned about a reaction at a particular temperature from its K_{eq} value.

$K_{eq} > 1$ indicates a reaction with a higher concentration of the products than the reactants. Therefore, the forward reaction is favored.

$K_{eq} < 1$ indicates a reaction with a higher concentration of the reactants than the products. Therefore, the reverse reaction is favored.

Additional Materials

Spontaneous and Nonspontaneous Reactions.

Earlier in the topic you learned about exothermic and endothermic reactions, as well as entropy.

Exothermic reactions released energy, and have $-\Delta H$ values (lower enthalpy).

Endothermic reactions absorbed energy, and have $+\Delta H$ values (high enthalpy).

Entropy change, ΔS, describes a change in randomness or disorder of a system.

Reactions that become more disorder (ex. solid $\rightarrow$ gas) have $+\Delta S$.

Reactions that become less disorder (ex. liquid $\rightarrow$ solid) have $-\Delta S$.

Spontaneous reactions are reactions that will occur under a specific set of conditions. Spontaneous reactions occur if the direction of the reaction leads to:

. **Lower Enthalpy** (less energy) products. This favors exothermic reactions.
. **Greater Entropy** (more random or less organized) products

Systems in the universe tend to proceed spontaneously in the direction of lower enthalpy and greater entropy.

Nonspontaneous reactions are the exact opposite.

Gibbs Free Energy

Gibbs Free Energy is the amount of energy available to do work. The equation for Gibbs Free Energy Change, ΔG, relates temperature (T), enthalpy change (ΔH), and entropy change (ΔS) of a reaction.

$$\Delta G = \Delta H - T\Delta S$$

The sign of ΔG determines if a reaction is spontaneous , nonspontaneous, or at equilibrium.

  $-\Delta G$ indicates a spontaneous reaction

  $+\Delta G$ indicates a nonspontaneous reaction

  $\Delta G = 0$ indicates a reaction at equilibrium

The table to the right shows different combinations of ΔH, ΔS, and T that will lead to a reaction with $-\Delta G$ or $+\Delta G$.

ΔH	ΔS	T	ΔG
-	+	Low	-
		High	-
+	-	Low	+
		High	+
+	+	Low	+
		High	-
-	-	Low	-
		High	+

Practice Questions on Additional

69. Which is the correct equilibrium expression for the reaction?

$$4NH_3(g) + 5O_2(g) \leftrightarrow 4NO(g) + 6H_2O(g)$$

1) $K_{eq} = \dfrac{[NH_3]^4 [O_2]^5}{[NO]^4 [H_2O]^6}$

3) $K_{eq} = \dfrac{[NO]^4 [H_2O]^6}{[NH_3]^4 [O_2]^5}$

2) $K_{eq} = \dfrac{[4NH_3] [5O_2]}{[4NO] [6H_2O]}$

4) $K_{eq} = \dfrac{[4NO] [6H_2O]}{[4NH_3] [5O_2]}$

70. What is the correct equilibrium expression for the reaction below?

$$Ca_3(PO_4)_2(s) \leftrightarrow 3Ca^{2+}(aq) + 2PO_4^{3-} (aq)$$

1) $K_{sp} = [Ca^{2+}]^3 [PO_4^{3-}]^2$

3) $K_{sp} = [3Ca^{2+}] [2PO_4^{3-}]$

2) $K_{sp} = [Ca^{2+}]^3 + [PO_4^{3-}]^2$

4) $K_{sp} = [3Ca^{2+}] + [2PO_4^{3-}]$

71. Which equation is used to determine the free energy change of chemical reaction?

1) $\Delta G = \Delta H - \Delta S$

3) $\Delta G = \Delta H - T\Delta S$

2) $\Delta G = \Delta H + \Delta S$

4) $\Delta G = \Delta H + T\Delta S$

72. A chemical reaction will always be spontaneous if the reaction has a negative

1) ΔS

3) ΔT

2) ΔG

4) ΔH

73. When the free energy change of a reaction is zero, the reaction is
   1) at equilibrium
   2) absorbing heat

3) spontaneous
4) nonspontaneous

Write equilibrium expressions for the reactions given in number 74 through 77.

74. $X_2(g) + 2Y_2(g) \leftrightarrow 2XY_2(g)$

75. $Pb(NO_3)_2(s) \leftrightarrow Pb^{2+}(aq) + 2NO_3^-(aq)$

76. $2Cl_2(g) + 2H_2O(l) \leftrightarrow 4HCl(aq) + O_2(g)$

77. $W(g) + 3X(g) \leftrightarrow 2Y(g) + 3Z(g)$

Write equilibrium expressions for the dissociation of:

78. $H_2CO_3(aq)$

79. $NH_4OH(aq)$

80. $H_2O(l)$

Lesson 1: Properties of organic compounds

Introduction

Organic compounds are compounds of carbon. Bonding properties of a carbon atom make it possible for carbon to bond with another carbon and with other nonmetals to form an enormous number of organic compounds that can range from one to several hundred atoms in length. Properties of organic compounds are due, in part, to chemical properties of a carbon atom.

In this lesson, you will learn about general properties of carbon and organic compounds.

Properties of Organic Compounds

Bonding properties of carbon atoms.

A carbon atom has four (4) valence electrons and must form 4 covalent bonds.

$$. \overset{\displaystyle .}{\underset{\displaystyle .}{C}} . \qquad -\overset{|}{\underset{|}{C}}- \qquad -\overset{|}{\underset{|}{C}}-\overset{|}{\underset{|}{C}}- \qquad -\overset{|}{C}=\overset{|}{C}- \qquad -C\equiv C-$$

electron-dot diagram for a carbon atom

All correctly drawn structures for organic compounds must have each C atom with exactly four bonds as shown above.

. Two carbon atoms can form a single (–) , double (=) or triple (≡) covalent bond

. Carbon atoms can join together to form a straight chain, branched, or ring-like structure

$$-C-C-C-C- \qquad \overset{\displaystyle CH_3}{\overset{|}{-C-C-C-C-}}$$

straight chain   branched   ring (cyclic)

. Carbon bonds easily with other nonmetals such as H, O, N and the halogens

Properties of organic compounds

General properties of organic compounds are listed below.

. They are molecular (covalent) substances.

. Bonding between atoms is covalent.

. Molecules are held together by weak intermolecular forces (IMF).

. Low melting point, low boiling point, and high vapor pressure due to weak IMF.

. Solids decompose easily under heat.

. Most are nonelectrolytes (except organic acids, which are weak electrolytes).

. Reactions are slow due to strong covalent bonding between atoms.

. Solubility varies depending on if the compound is polar (soluble) or nonpolar (insoluble).

These properties vary within a class and between classes of organic compounds.

Names of Organic Compounds:

The IUPAC (International Union of Pure and Applied Chemistry) name of an organic compound has systematic components that reveal much about the compound.

The **prefix** (beginning root) of a name indicates the number of carbon atoms. (See Reference Table P below)

The **suffix** (ending root) of a name indicates the class that the substance belongs. (See Table below and also reference Table Q and R).

Numbers in a name indicate positions of side chains, multiple bonds, or functional groups.

di- or **tri-** in a name indicates the presence of two or three of the same side chain or functional group.

Organic Prefixes (Table P)   **Name endings : See Tables Q and R**

# of carbon atom	Prefix
1	meth
2	eth
3	prop
4	but
5	pent
6	hex
7	hept
8	oct
9	non
10	dec

Class of compound	Name ending
Alkanes	- ane
Alkenes	- ene
Alkynes	-yne
Alcohols	-ol
Ethers	-yl
Aldehydes	-al
Ketones	-one
Organic acids	-oic
Esters	-oate
Amines	-amine
Amides	-amide

Halides are named with *halogen* prefixes: Ex. *Chloro*butane

Three IUPAC names of organic substances are given below. The components of their names are explained under each substance. Understanding these names will help you understand names, formulas, and structures to several organic compounds given as examples as each class is explained in the next few sections of this topic.

Prop*ane*

prop- : a 3 C-atom compound

- ane : *a compound of alkane*

2-Pentan*ol*

pent- : a 5 C-atom compound

-ol : *a compound of alcohol*

2 : *-OH functional group on carbon number 2*

2,3-*dimethyl*, **1**-butene

but-: 4 C atoms in main chain

-ene : *a compound of an alkene*

1: *double bond in 1st bond position*

2,3-*dimethyl*: 2 methyl side chains on carbons 2 and 3

Lesson 2: Classes of Organic Compounds

Homologous series are groups of related organic compounds in which each member of the class differs from the next member by a set number of atoms. Compounds belonging to the same homologous series always share the same general formula, same molecular name ending, and similar molecular structure.

In this lesson, you will learn about hydrocarbon compounds and functional group compounds.

Hydrocarbons

Hydrocarbons are classes of organic compounds that are composed of just two elements: Hydrogen (H) and carbon (C)

Bonding between carbon atoms in a hydrocarbon molecule could be single, double or triple covalent. Depending on the bond type found between the carbon atoms, a hydrocarbon can be classified as saturated or unsaturated.

Saturated hydrocarbons (Alkanes)

Saturated hydrocarbons are hydrocarbons in which the bonds between the carbon atoms are all single covalent bonds. A **single covalent** bond is formed between two C atoms when each atom contributes one (1) electron. Since each C atom contributes one electron, a single covalent bond is formed by 1 pair of (2 total) electrons
Alkanes are classified as saturated hydrocarbons.

$C \cdot \cdot C$	$C - C$
2 e-	a single
1 e- pair	bond

Unsaturated hydrocarbons (Alkenes and Alkynes)
Unsaturated hydrocarbons are hydrocarbons that contain one multiple (double or a triple) covalent bond between any two adjacent C atoms.

A **double covalent** bond is formed between two adjacent carbon atoms when each C atom contributes two (2) electrons. Since each C atom contributes two electrons, a double covalent bond contains 2 pairs of electrons (4 total electrons.)
Alkenes are unsaturated hydrocarbons with a double bond.

$C : : C$	$C = C$
4 e-	a double
2 e- pairs	bond

A **triple covalent bond** is formed between two adjacent carbon atoms when each C atom contributes three (3) electrons. Since each C atom contributes three electrons, a triple covalent bond contains 3 pairs of electrons (6 total electrons).
Alkynes are unsaturated hydrocarbons with a triple bond.

$C \vdots \vdots C$	$C \equiv C$
6 e-	a triple
3 e- pairs	bond

Alkanes

Alkanes are saturated hydrocarbons in which all members share the following characteristics:

Examples

General formula: C_nH_{2n+2} CH_4 C_3H_8

Bonding type: **Single bonds**

$$H-\underset{\underset{H}{|}}{\overset{\overset{H}{|}}{C}}-H \qquad H-\underset{\underset{H}{|}}{\overset{\overset{H}{|}}{C}}-\underset{\underset{H}{|}}{\overset{\overset{H}{|}}{C}}-\underset{\underset{H}{|}}{\overset{\overset{H}{|}}{C}}-H$$

IUPAC name ending: *-ane*   Meth*ane*   Prop*ane*

Alkenes

Alkenes are unsaturated hydrocarbons in which all members share the following characteristics:

Examples

General formula: C_nH_{2n} C_2H_4 C_4H_8

Bonding type: **One double bond**

$$\underset{\underset{H}{|}}{\overset{\overset{H}{|}}{C}}=\underset{\underset{H}{|}}{\overset{\overset{H}{|}}{C}} \qquad \underset{\underset{H}{|}}{\overset{\overset{H}{|}}{C}}=\underset{\underset{H}{|}}{\overset{\overset{H}{|}}{C}}-\underset{\underset{H}{|}}{\overset{\overset{H}{|}}{C}}-\underset{\underset{H}{|}}{\overset{\overset{H}{|}}{C}}-H$$

IUPAC name ending: *-ene*   Eth*ene*   1-But*ene*

Alkynes

Alkynes are unsaturated hydrocarbons in which all members share the following characteristics:

General formula: C_nH_{2n-2} C_2H_2 C_4H_6

Bonding type: **One triple bond**

$$H-C \equiv C-H \qquad H-\underset{\underset{H}{|}}{\overset{\overset{H}{|}}{C}}-C \equiv C-H$$

IUPAC name ending: *-yne*   Eth*yne*   Prop*yne*

Use Reference **Table Q** to learn more about alkanes, alkenes, and alkynes.

Functional Group Compounds

A **functional group** is an atom (other than hydrogen) or a group of atoms that replace one or more hydrogen atoms of a hydrocarbon compound. The element commonly found in most functional groups is oxygen (O). Nitrogen (N) and halogens (F, Cl, Br, or I) are also found in functional groups. Classes of functional group compounds include:

Halides, alcohols, ethers, aldehydes, ketones, organic acids, esters, amines and amides. Each class is briefly discussed below.

Use **Reference Table R** to help you answer questions related to functional group compounds.

Halides

Halides (aka halocarbons) are classes of organic compounds in which the functional group is one or more halogen atoms (F, Cl, Br, or I). Recall that halogens are elements in Group 17.

Functional group	General formula:	Naming:
- Halogen	$R - X$	halogen prefix

Condensed formula	$CH_3CH_2\mathbf{F}$	$CH_3\mathbf{CHBr}CH_2CH_3$
Structural formula	H H | | H – C – C – H | | H **F**	H H H H | | | | H – C – **C** – C – C – H | | | | H **Br** H H
IUPAC Molecular name:	Fluoroethane	2-bromobutane

Alcohols

Alcohols are classes of organic compounds with hydroxyl (-OH) as the functional group. There are a few different types of alcohols.

NOTE: Hydroxyl (-OH) is different than the hydroxide (OH⁻) found in aqueous solutions.

Functional group	General formula:	Name ending:
-OH (hydroxyl)	$R - OH$	-ol

Condensed formula	CH_5CH_2OH	$CH_3\mathbf{CH(OH)}CH_2CH_3$
Structural formula	H H | | H – C – **C** – OH | | H H	H OH H H | | | | H – C – **C** – C – C – H | | | | H H H H
IUPAC Molecular name:	Ethanol	2-butanol

Types of Alcohols

Monohydroxy alcohols are alcohols with one -OH group

Types of monohydroxy alcohols:

Primary alcohols are alcohols in which the **C** atom with the -OH is bonded to one other C atom.
  Ex. 1-propanol

$$-C-C-C-$$
$$\quad|$$
$$\quad OH \quad \textbf{1-propanol}$$

Secondary alcohols are alcohols in which the **C** atom with the -OH is bonded to two other C atoms.
  Ex. 2 - propanol

$$-C-C-C-$$
$$\quad\ \ |$$
$$\quad\ \ OH$$
$$\qquad \textbf{2-propanol}$$

Tertiary alcohols are alcohols in which the **C** atom with the -OH is bonded to three other C atoms.
   Ex. 2-methyl,2-propanol

$$\qquad C$$
$$\qquad |$$
$$-C-C-C-C-$$
$$\quad\ \ |$$
$$\quad\ \ OH$$
$$\quad \textbf{2-methyl,2-butanol}$$

Dihydroxy alcohols are alcohols with two -OH groups
  Ex. 1,3-propanediol

$$HO-C-C-C-OH$$
$$\textbf{1,3-propanediol}$$

Trihydroxy alcohols are alcohols with three -OH groups
  Ex. 1,2,3-propanetriol (glycerol)

$$-C-C-C-$$
$$\ |\ \ \ |\ \ \ |$$
$$OH\ OH\ OH$$
$$\textbf{1,2,3-propanetriol (glycerol)}$$

Ethers

Ethers are classes of organic compounds containing the functional group **–O–**

Functional group:	General formula:	Naming:
– O –	**R – O – R'**	Name must include prefixes for the two hydrocarbon chains

Condensed formula	CH_3OCH_3	$CH_3CH_2OCH_3$
Structural formula	$H-C-O-C-H$ (with H's) *methyl methyl*	$H-C-C-O-C-H$ (with H's) *ethyl methyl*
IUPAC Molecular name:	methyl methyl ether (dimethyl ether)	methyl ethyl ether *(the shorter chain is always named first)*

Aldehydes

Aldehydes are classes of organic compounds with the following characteristics.

Functional group:	General formula	Name ending:
O $\parallel$ $-C-H$ or $-CHO$	O $\parallel$ $R-CHO$ or $R-C-H$	-al

Condensed formula	HCHO	O $\parallel$ $CH_3CH_2 C - H$
Structural formula	O $\parallel$ $H - C - H$	$\begin{array}{ccc} H & H & O \\ \mid & \mid & \parallel \\ H-C-C-C-H \\ \mid & \mid \\ H & H \end{array}$
IUPAC Molecular name: (common name)	Methanal (formaldehyde)	Propanal

Ketones

Ketones are classes of organic compounds with the following characteristics.

Functional group	General formula:	Name ending:
O $\parallel$ $-C-$	O $\parallel$ $R-C-R'$	-one

Condensed formula	CH_3COCH_3	$CH_3CH_2CH_2COCH_3$
Structural formula	$\begin{array}{ccc} H & O & H \\ \mid & \parallel & \mid \\ H-C-C-C-H \\ \mid & & \mid \\ H & & H \end{array}$	$\begin{array}{ccccc} H & H & H & O & H \\ \mid & \mid & \mid & \parallel & \mid \\ H-C-C-C-C-C-H \\ \mid & \mid & \mid & & \mid \\ H & H & H & & H \end{array}$
IUPAC Molecular name: (common name)	Propanone (Acetone)	2 – Pentanone

Amines, amides and amino acids

CH_3NH_2 (methanamine)

Amines are groups of organic compounds with functional group $\quad -N- \atop \mid$

$\begin{array}{cc} H & H \\ \mid & \mid \\ H-C-N-H \\ \mid \\ H \end{array}$

Amides are groups of organic compounds with functional group $-C-NH \atop \parallel \atop O$

CH_3CONH_2 (ethanamide)

Amino acids are groups of organic compounds with functional groups $-C-COOH \atop \mid \atop NH_2$

$\begin{array}{ccc} H & O & H \\ \mid & \parallel & \mid \\ H-C-C-NH \\ \mid \\ H \end{array}$

Organic Acids

Organic acids are compounds with the following characteristics.		
Functional group	**General formula:**	**Name ending:**
O ‖ - C – OH	O ‖ R – C – OH or R–COOH	-oic

Condensed formula	HCOOH	CH₃COOH
Structural formula	O ‖ H – C – OH	H O | ‖ H – C – C – OH | H
IUPAC Molecular name: (common name)	Methanoic acid	Ethanoic acid (Acetic acid, Vinegar)

Organic acids ionize (are soluble) in water to produce + and - ions.
Organic acids are weak electrolytes, therefore can conduct electricity.
Organic acids will change litmus to red, and phenolphthalein will be colorless.

Esters

Esters are organic compounds with the following characteristics.		
Functional group	**General formula**	**Name ending**
O ‖ – C – O –	O ‖ R – C – O – R' or R-COO-R'	-oate

Condensed formula	CH₃COOCH₃	CH₃CH₂COOCH₂CH₃
Structural formula	H O H | ‖ | H – C – C – O – C – H | | H H ⌣eth- ⌣methyl	H H O H H | | ‖ | | H–C–C–C–O–C–C–H | | | | H H H H ⌣prop- ⌣ethyl
IUPAC Molecular name: (common name)	Methyl ethanoate (methyl acetate)	Ethyl propanoate

Ester compounds are generally responsible for characteristic smells of fruits and flowers, as well as scents of colognes and perfumes.

Esters can be synthesized (made) by reacting an organic acid with an alcohol.

The smells of bananas and strawberries are due in parts to compounds of esters.

Summary Table: Functional Group Compounds

Class of compound	Functional group	How functional group attaches to hydrocarbon chain (R)	Example formula
1. Halide	-Halogen	R-Halogen	$CH_3CH_2CH_2Br$
2. Alcohol	-OH	R-OH	$CH_3CH_2CH_2OH$
3. Ether	-O-	R-O-R'	$CH_3OCH_2CH_3$
4. Aldehyde	$\overset{\overset{O}{\|\|}}{-C-H}$	$\overset{\overset{O}{\|\|}}{R-C-H}$	$CH_3CH_2\overset{\overset{O}{\|\|}}{C}-H$
5. Ketone	$\overset{\overset{O}{\|\|}}{-C-}$	$\overset{\overset{O}{\|\|}}{R-C-R}$	$CH_3\overset{\overset{O}{\|\|}}{C}CH_2CH_2CH_3$
6. Organic Acid	$\overset{\overset{O}{\|\|}}{-C-OH}$	$\overset{\overset{O}{\|\|}}{R-C-OH}$	$CH_3CH_2\overset{\overset{O}{\|\|}}{C}-OH$
7. Ester	$\overset{\overset{O}{\|\|}}{-C-O}$	$\overset{\overset{O}{\|\|}}{R-C-O-R'}$	$CH_3CH_2\overset{\overset{O}{\|\|}}{C}OCH_3$

Lesson 3: Isomers

Isomers are organic compounds with the same molecular formula but different structural formulas. Compounds that are isomers are similar in that they have: same molecular formula, same number of atoms, same percent composition, and same number of bonds. Isomers are different in that they have different structures and different properties.

Only hydrocarbon compounds with four or more C atoms have isomers. As the number of C atoms increases, the number of possible isomers also increases.

Examples of isomers from different classes of compounds are given below.

Alkane isomers usually have different arrangements of the carbon chain so the structures would have one or more side chains (alkyl groups).

IUPAC names	pentane	2,2– dimethyl propane
Structural formula	H H H H H | | | | | H –C–C–C–C–C–H | | | | | H H H H H	H CH₃ H | | | H– C – **C** – C –H | | | H CH₃ H
Condensed formula	$CH_3CH_2CH_2CH_2CH_3$	$CH_3(CH_3)C(CH_3)CH_3$
Molecular formula	C_5H_{12}	C_5H_{12}

Alkene and alkyne isomers typically have the multiple (double or triple) bonds placed between different carbon atoms in the structure.

IUPAC names	1-butene	2-butene
Structural formula	H H | | H –C=C–C–C–H | | | | H H H H	H H | | H–C–C=C–C–H | | | | H H H H
Condensed formula	$CH_2CHCH_2CH_3$	$CH_3CHCHCH_3$
Molecular formula	C_4H_8	C_4H_8

IUPAC names	1-pentyne	2-pentyne
Structural formula	H H H | | | H –C–C–C–C≡C–H | | | H H H	H H H | | | H–C–C–C≡C–C–H | | | H H H
Condensed formula	$CH_3CH_2CH_2CCH$	$CH_3CH_2CCCH_3$
Molecular formula	C_5H_8	C_5H_8

Isomers of functional group compounds usually have the functional group attached to different carbon atoms. In some cases, a compound from one functional group may be an isomer of a compound from a different functional group class.

Halide isomers	1-bromopropane $\begin{array}{ccc} H & H & H \\ | & | & | \\ H-C-C-C-H \\ | & | & | \\ Br & H & H \end{array}$ $CH_2BrCH_2CH_3$ C_3H_7Br	2-bromopropane $\begin{array}{ccc} H & H & H \\ | & | & | \\ H-C-C-C-H \\ | & | & | \\ H & Br & H \end{array}$ $CH_3CHBrCH_3$ C_3H_7Br
Alcohol isomers	1-butanol $\begin{array}{cccc} H & H & H & H \\ | & | & | & | \\ H-C-C-C-C-OH \\ | & | & | & | \\ H & H & H & H \end{array}$ $CH_3CH_2CH_2CH_2OH$ C_4H_9OH	2-butanol $\begin{array}{cccc} H & H & H & H \\ | & | & | & | \\ H-C-C-C-C-H \\ | & | & | & | \\ H & H & OH & H \end{array}$ $CH_3CH_2CH(OH)CH_3$ C_4H_9OH
Ether and alcohol isomers	methyl methyl ether (dimethyl ether) $\begin{array}{cc} H & H \\ | & | \\ H-C-O-C-H \\ | & | \\ H & H \end{array}$ $CH_3 \, O \, CH_3$ C_2H_6O	Ethanol $\begin{array}{cc} H & H \\ | & | \\ H-C-C-OH \\ | & | \\ H & H \end{array}$ CH_3CH_2OH C_2H_6O
Ketone and aldehyde isomers	propanone $\begin{array}{ccc} H & O & H \\ | & || & | \\ H-C-C-C-H \\ | & & | \\ H & & H \end{array}$ $CH_3 \, COCH_3$ C_3H_6O	propanal $\begin{array}{ccc} H & H & O \\ | & | & || \\ H-C-C-C-H \\ | & | \\ H & H \end{array}$ CH_3CH_2CHO C_3H_6O
Ester isomers	methyl propanoate $CH_3CH_2COOCH_3$	ethyl ethanoate (ethyl acetate) $CH_3COOCH_2CH_3$

Lesson 4: Organic Reactions

Introduction

There are many kinds of organic reactions. An organic compound can react with other organic compounds or with inorganic compounds to form a wide range of organic products. Organic reactions are generally slower than reactions of inorganic compounds. This is due to the fact that organic reactions typically involve the breaking of strong covalent bonds within the organic molecules.

In this lesson, you'll learn about the different types of organic reactions.

Organic Reactions: Summary Table

Reactions	Reactants		Products	
1. Substitution	Alkane (saturated)	Halogen	1 – Halide (one halogen)	Acid (inorganic)
2. Addition				
Hydrogenation	Alkene (unsaturated)	Hydrogen	Alkane	
Halogenation	Alkene	Halogen	1,2 – Halide (a-two halogen halide)	
3. Saponification	Fat	Base	1,2,3-propanetriol (glycerol)	Soap
4. Fermentation	$C_6H_{12}O_6$ (sugar)		C_2H_5OH (ethanol)	CO_2
5. Combustion	Hydrocarbon	O_2	Carbon dioxide	Water
6. Esterification	Organic Acid	Alcohol	Ester	Water
7. Polymerization				
Condensation Polymerization	Alcohol (monomers)	Alcohol	Ether (a polymer)	Water
Additional Polymerization	$n(CH_2=CH_2)$ (ethene monomers)		$(-CH_2-CH_2-)_n$ (polyethylene polymer)	
8. Cracking	$C_{14}H_{30}$ (large long chain)		C_7H_{16} (small shorter chains)	C_7H_{14}

The notes below give example equations for organic reactions summarized on the previous page. Pay attention to how products of each reaction are formed from the reactants. You are often asked to predict a reactant or a product of a reaction.

Substitution: replacing hydrogen atom with a halogen

Alkane	+	Halogen	→	Halide	+	Acid

C_3H_8 + F_2 ⟶ C_3H_7F + **HF**

Propane   Fluorine   Fluoropropane   Hydrogen fluoride

Addition: Hydrogenation: adding hydrogen to a double bond

Alkene	+	Hydrogen	→	Alkane

C_3H_6 + H_2 ⟶ C_3H_8

Propene   hydrogen   Propane

Addition: Halogenation: adding halogens to a double bond

Alkene	+	Halogen	→	Halide

C_3H_6 + Br_2 ⟶ $C_3H_6Br_2$

Propene   Bromine   1,2-dibromopropane

Esterification: making an ester

Organic acid	+	Alcohol	→	Ester	+	Water

CH_3COOH + $HOCH_2CH_2CH_3$ ⟶ $CH_3COOCH_2CH_2CH_3$ + H_2O

ethanoic acid   propanol   propyl ethanoate   HOH

Condensation Polymerization: Joining small molecules by removing water

Monomer   +   Monomer $\longrightarrow$ Polymer   +   water

(alcohol monomers)   (ether polymer)

CH_3OH + $HOCH_2CH_3$ $\longrightarrow$ $CH_3OCH_2CH_3$ + H_2O

$$\underset{\text{Methanol}}{\overset{\displaystyle H \atop |}{\underset{\displaystyle | \atop H}{H-C-OH}}} + \underset{\text{Ethanol}}{\overset{\displaystyle H \; H \atop |\;\;|}{\underset{\displaystyle |\;\;| \atop H \; H}{HO-C-C-H}}} \longrightarrow \underset{\text{Methyl \; Ethyl \; ether}}{\overset{\displaystyle H \;\;\; H \; H \atop |\;\;\;\;\;|\;\;|}{\underset{\displaystyle |\;\;\;\;\;|\;\;| \atop H \;\;\; H \; H}{H-C-O-C-C-H}}} + \underset{\text{water}}{HOH}$$

Addition Polymerization: Joining small unsaturated molecules together

$n(-CH_2=CH_2)$ $\longrightarrow$ $(-CH_2-CH_2-)_n$

monomers   polymer

n represent several repeated units of the monomer.

Fermentation: Alcohol making process

Sugar   ethanol (an alcohol)   carbon dioxide

$C_6H_{12}O_6$ $\longrightarrow$ $2C_2H_5OH$ + CO_2

$$\overset{\displaystyle H \; H \atop |\;\;|}{\underset{\displaystyle |\;\;| \atop H \; H}{H-C-C-OH}}$$

Saponification: Soap making process

Fat   +   Base $\longrightarrow$ Soap   +   Glycerol

$$\overset{\displaystyle H \;\;\;\;\; H \;\;\;\;\; H \atop |\;\;\;\;\;\;\;\;|\;\;\;\;\;\;\;\;|}{\underset{\displaystyle |\;\;\;\;\;\;\;\;|\;\;\;\;\;\;\;\;| \atop OH \;\;\; OH \;\;\; OH}{H-C-C-C-H}}$$

1,2,3-propanetriol
(Glycerol, an alcohol)

Combustion: Burning of an organic substance

Organic compound   +   Oxygen $\longrightarrow$ Carbon dioxide   +   water

$2C_8H_{18}$ + $25O_2$ $\longrightarrow$ $16CO_2$ + $18H_2O$

Octane (car fuel)

Practice Questions

Lesson 1: Properties of Organic Compounds

Answer the following multiple choice questions.

1. Which type of bonds and solids are characteristics of organic compounds?
   1) Ionic bonds and ionic solids
   2) Ionic bonds and molecular solids
   3) Covalent bonds and ionic solids
   4) Covalent bonds and molecular solids

2. In general, which property do organic compounds share?
   1) High melting points
   2) High electrical conductivity
   3) High solubility in water
   4) Slow reaction rate

3. Which best explains why there are more organic compounds than inorganic compounds?
   1) The carbon atom readily forms covalent bonds with other carbon atoms
   2) The carbon atom readily forms ionic bonds with other carbon atoms
   3) The carbon atom readily combines with oxygen
   4) The carbon atom readily dissolves in water

4. A carbon atom in any organic compound can form a total of
   1) 1 covalent bond
   2) 2 covalent bonds
   3) 3 covalent bonds
   4) 4 covalent bonds

5. The four single bonds of a carbon atom are directed in space toward the corner of a
   1) Regular tetrahedron
   2) Regular octahedron
   3) Square plane
   4) Trigonal bipyramid

6. A compound that is classified as organic must contain the element
   1) Carbon
   2) Nitrogen
   3) Oxygen
   4) Hydrogen

7. A student investigated samples of four different substances in the solid phase. The table is a record of the behaviors observed (marked with an X) when each solid was tested.

Characteristic Tested	Substance A	Substance B	Substance C	Substance D
High Melting Point	X		X	
Low Melting Point		X		X
Soluble in Water	X			X
Insoluble in Water		X	X	
Decomposed under High Heat		X		
Stable under High Heat	X		X	X
Electrolyte	X			X
Nonelectrolyte		X	X	

Which substance has characteristics most like those of an organic compound?

1) A
2) B
3) C
4) D

Lesson 2: Classes of Organic Compounds

Answer the following multiple choice questions.

8. A series of hydrocarbons in which each member of a group differs from the preceding member by one carbon is called
   1) A periodic series
   2) A homologous series
   3) An actinide series
   4) A lanthanide series

9. Which list of compounds contains only hydrocarbons?
   1) Alkanes, alcohols, aldehydes
   2) Alkanes, alkenes, and alkynes
   3) Alkanes, alkenes, and halides
   4) Alkynes, amines, and alcohols

10. The number of electrons needed to form a single covalent bond between two adjacent carbon atoms in a saturated hydrocarbon is
    1) 1
    2) 2
    3) 3
    4) 4

11. Which series of hydrocarbons contain unsaturated molecules, only?
    1) Alkane and benzene series
    2) Alkyl and alkene series
    3) Alkene and alkyne series
    4) Alkane and alkyne series

12. As the compounds in the alkene series are considered in order of increasing number of carbons, the ratio of carbon atoms to hydrogen atoms
    1) Increases
    2) Decreases
    3) Remains the same

13. How many pairs of electrons are found between two atoms in a triple bond?
    1) 4
    2) 3
    3) 8
    4) 6

14. Which formula correctly represents the general formula for all alkene molecules?
    1) C_nH_{2n}
    2) C_nH_{2n+2}
    3) C_nH_{2n-2}
    4) C_nH_{2n+6}

15. An alcohol contains one –OH group that is bonded to an end carbon in a hydrocarbon chain. This alcohol should be classified as a
    1) Secondary alcohol
    2) Primary alcohol
    3) Trihydroxy alcohol
    4) Dihydroxy alcohol

16. Which IUPAC name ending is common for the class of organic compound called aldehydes?
    1) –yl
    2) –al
    3) –ol
    4) –one

17. Which is true of organic acids?
    1) They are nonelectrolytes
    2) They are weak electrolytes
    3) They turn litmus blue
    4) They turn phenolphthalein pink

18. The minimum number of carbon atoms a ketone may contain is
    1) 1
    2) 2
    3) 3
    4) 4

19. The sweet smells of fruits are likely due to compounds of
    1) Alkanes
    2) Ethers
    3) Organic acids
    4) Esters

20. Which group can be found in a molecule of an aldehyde?
    1) –OH
    2) – Cl
    3) –CHO
    4) – COOH

21. Which compound is a hydrocarbon?
     1) Pentanone   2) Pentyne   3) Butanal   4) Hexanol

22. Which compound is a saturated hydrocarbon?
     1) Chlorohexane   2) Hexanol   3) Hexene   4) Hexane

23. Which compound would have a triple bond between two adjacent carbon atoms?
     1) 1, 3- dimethyl butane   2) 3-octyne   3) 2-methyl propane   4) 2 –pentene

24. Which hydrocarbon is a member of the organic compound class with the general
     formula C_nH_{2n-2}?
     1) Heptane   2) Benzene   3) Propyne   4) Butene

25. The structure of which compound contains the functional group $-C-O-C-$?
     1) Dimethyl ether   2) Propanone   3) Methyl Butanoate   4) Ethanoic acid

26. The structure of which organic compound contains elements N and O?
     1) 1-butanamide   2) Butanamine   3) Methyl butanoate   4) Butanal

27. Which compound has the formula C_6H_{10}?
     1) Hexane   2) Hexene   3) Hexyne   4) Hexanal

28. The molecular formula $CH_3CH_2CHCl_2$ represents which compound?
     1) 2-chloropropane   3) Dichloropropane
     2) 3-chloropropane   4) Dichloropropene

29. Which compound has the formula CH_3CH_2COOH ?
     1) Propanoic acid   2) Propanal   3) 2-propanol   4) 2-propanone

30. The IUPAC name of a compound with the formula CH_3CH_2CHO is
     1) Propanoic acid   2) Propanone   3) Propanol   4) Propanal

31. The compound represented by the formula $CH_3COCH_2CH_3$ is
     1) 2-Butanone   3) Dimethyl ether
     2) 2-butanol   4) Methyl ethanoate

32. The compound $CH_3CH_2COOCH_3$ is an example of
     1) An ether   2) An alcohol   3) An ester   4) An acid

33. Which compound has the structural formula shown below?

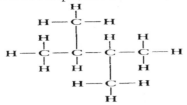

     1) Hexane
     2) 2,3-dimethyl butane
     3) 2,2-dimethyl hexane
     4) Ethyl butane

34. What is the correct IUPAC name for the molecule below.

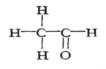

     1) Ethanal   3) Ethanol
     2) Ethene   4) Ethanoic acid

35. Which two formulas represent unsaturated hydrocarbons?
    1) C_2H_2 and C_2H_6 3) C_2H_6 and C_3H_8
    2) C_2H_2 and C_2H_4 4) C_3H_4 and C_4H_{10}

36. What is the correct formula for butyne?
    1) C_4H_{10} 2) C_4H_4 3) C_4H_6 4) C_4H_{10}

37. Chloropropane is correctly represented by which chemical formula?
    1) C_3H_5Cl 2) C_3H_6Cl 3) C_3H_7Cl 4) C_3H_8Cl

38. The condensed formula that represents methyl propanoate is
    1) $CH_3CH_2COOCH_3$ 2) CH_3CH_2CHO 3) CH_3COOH 4) CH_3CHO

39. Which best represents propanoic acid?
    1) C_2H_5COOH 2) C_3H_7COOH 3) C_2H_5CHO 4) C_3H_7CHO

40. The correct formula for dimethyl ether is
    1) CH_3COOCH_3 2) CH_3OCH_3 3) CH_3CH_3OH 4) CH_3COCH_3

41. Which structural formula represents a molecule of 2- butyne?

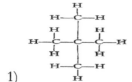

    1)   2)   3)   4)

42. Which structure represents a compound with an IUPAC name of 2-propanol?

    1)   2)   3)   4)

43. The correct structure for 3-pentanone is

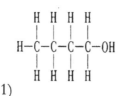

    1)   3)

    2)   4)

Lesson 3. Isomers

Answer the following multiple choice questions.

44. Two isomers must have the same

   1) Percent composition
   2) Arrangement of atoms
   3) Physical properties
   4) Chemical properties

45. What is the minimum number of carbon atoms a hydrocarbon must have in other to have an isomer?
   1) 1   2) 2   3) 3   4) 4

46. Which hydrocarbon has the least number of isomers?
   1) C_5H_8 2) C_4H_6 3) C_6H_{10} 4) C_7H_{12}

47. Which compound is an isomer of butanoic acid, $CH_3CH_2CH_2COOH$?
   1) $CH_3CH_2CH_2CH_2OH$ 3) $CH_3CH_2CH_2CH_2COOH$
   2) $CH_3CH_2COOCH_3$ 4) $CH_3CH_2OCH_3$

48. Which IUPAC name is an isomer of 3-hexene?
   1) 2-methyl hexene   2) 2-hexene   3) 3-heptene   4) 2-heptyne

49. Which structure is an isomer of dimethyl ether?

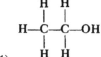

1)

2)

3)

4)

Lesson 4. Organic Reactions

Define the following terms and answer multiple choice questions below.

50. Substitution   51. Addition   52. Fermentation   53. Saponification
54. Combustion   55. Esterification   56. Polymerization
57. Addition polymerization   58. Condensation polymerization

59. Carbon dioxide and water are two products formed from which organic reaction?
   1) Combustion   3) Fermentation
   2) Esterification   4) Saponification

60. Unsaturated hydrocarbons can become saturated through which organic reaction?
   1) Esterification   2) Fermentation   3) Addition   4) Substitution

61. An alcohol and an organic acid are combined to form water and a compound with a pleasant odor. This reaction is an example of
   1) Esterification   2) Fermentation   3) Polymerization 4) Saponification

62. A compound of which formula is likely formed from an addition reaction?
   1) C_2H_6 2) C_2H_5OH 3) $C_2H_4Cl_2$ 4) CH_3OCH_3

63. Which compound is likely formed from a substitution reaction
   1) C_4H_6 2) $C_4H_8Br_2$ 3) C_4H_9Br 4) C_4H_8

64. Which organic product is likely to form from addition polymerization of alkene monomers?
   1) Glycerol   3) Dichloromethane
   2) Polyethylene   4) Ethanol

65. A structure of which organic compound likely formed from a reaction between an organic acid and alcohol?

   1)
   $$H-\overset{\overset{\displaystyle H}{|}}{\underset{\underset{\displaystyle H}{|}}{C}}-\overset{\overset{\displaystyle O}{\|}}{C}-O-\overset{\overset{\displaystyle H}{|}}{\underset{\underset{\displaystyle H}{|}}{C}}-H$$

   2)
   $$H-\overset{\overset{\displaystyle H}{|}}{\underset{\underset{\displaystyle H}{|}}{C}}-O-\overset{\overset{\displaystyle H}{|}}{\underset{\underset{\displaystyle H}{|}}{C}}-H$$

   3)
   $$H-\overset{\overset{\displaystyle H}{|}}{\underset{\underset{\displaystyle H}{|}}{C}}-\overset{\overset{\displaystyle OH}{|}}{\underset{\underset{\displaystyle H}{|}}{C}}-\overset{\overset{\displaystyle OH}{|}}{\underset{\underset{\displaystyle H}{|}}{C}}-H$$

   4)
   $$H-\overset{\overset{\displaystyle H}{|}}{\underset{\underset{\displaystyle Cl}{|}}{C}}-\overset{\overset{\displaystyle H}{|}}{\underset{\underset{\displaystyle Cl}{|}}{C}}-H$$

66. The reaction below
   $$CH_3COOH \quad + \quad CH_3OH \quad \rightarrow \quad CH_3COOCH_3 \quad + \quad H_2O$$
   is best classified as
   1) Esterification   3) Combustion
   2) Polymerization   4) Saponification

67. Given an organic reaction below:
   $$C_5H_{12} \quad + \quad Cl_2 \quad \rightarrow \quad C_5H_{11}Cl \quad + \quad HCl$$
   This reaction can be best classified as
   1) Addition   3) Polymerization
   2) Substitution   4) Hydrogenation

68. Which organic reaction is represented by the equation below?

$$\underset{H}{\overset{H}{\diagup}}C = C\underset{\diagdown H}{\overset{\diagup H}{}} \quad + \quad Br_2 \quad \rightarrow \quad H - \overset{\overset{\displaystyle H}{|}}{\underset{\underset{\displaystyle Br}{|}}{C}} - \overset{\overset{\displaystyle H}{|}}{\underset{\underset{\displaystyle Br}{|}}{C}} - H$$

   1) Fermentation   3) Addition
   2) Combustion   4) Substitution

69. Given the equation: $C_2H_6 \quad + \quad F_2 \quad \rightarrow \quad X \quad + \quad HF$
   What is the name of compound X produced?
   1) Ethene   3) 1,2-difluoroethane
   2) Flouroethane   4) Fluoropropane

Topic Mastery / Constructed Response

Draw structures for the following substances.

70. 3-octyne   71. 3-methyl, 2-pentene   72. 1,2-dichlobutane

73. 3-hexanol   74. Butyl butanoate   75. 2,2,4-trimethyl-3,5-heptanediol

76. Draw and name three structural isomers of C_8H_{18}

Base your answers to questions 77 to 79 on the formulas below.

Given the formulas: C_2H_5COOH and C_3H_7OH.

77. Draw structures for the two formulas.

78. Write an equation to show a reaction between the two substances.

79. What is the name of the organic product that forms from the reaction?

Answer questions 80 through 81 based on the information below.
A thiol is very similar to an alcohol, but a thiol has a sulfur atom instead of an oxygen atom in the functional group. One of the compounds in a skunk's spray is 2-butene-1-thiol. The formula of this compound is shown below.

$$\begin{array}{ccccc} H & H & & H & H \\ | & | & & | & | \\ H - C - C & = & C - & C - H \\ | & & & & | \\ SH & & & & H \end{array}$$

80. Explain, in terms of electron configuration, why oxygen and sulfur atoms form compounds with similar molecular structures.

81. Explain, in terms of composition, why this compound is a thiol.

Answer questions 82 through 85 based on the information and reaction below.

The hydrocarbon 2–methylpropane reacts with iodine as represented by the balanced equation below. At standard pressure, the boiling point of 2–methylpropane is lower than the boiling point of 2–iodo–2–methylpropane.

2-methylpropane   2-iodo-2-methylpropane

82. To which class of organic compounds does this organic product belong?

83. Explain, in terms of bonding, why the hydrocarbon 2-methylpropane is saturated.

84. Explain the difference in the boiling points of 2-methylpropane and 2-iodo-2-methylpropane in terms of both molecular polarity and intermolecular forces.

Molecular polarity:

Intermolecular forces:

Lesson 1 : Oxidation Numbers

Introduction

Most chemical reactions involve the losing and gaining of electrons by substances in the reaction. **Oxidation** is a **loss** of electrons by a substance in a reaction. **Reduction** is a **gain** of electrons by a substance in a reaction. **Redox** reactions are reactions in which **Red**uction and **Ox**idation are occurring at the same time (simultaneously). Atoms that gain or lose electrons undergo changes in their oxidation states.

In this lesson you will learn about oxidation numbers, which are important in determining which substance has lost and which has gained electrons during redox reactions.

Oxidation Numbers

An **oxidation number** is the charge an atom has (or appears to have) when it has lost or gained electrons. Rules for assigning oxidation numbers to elements in formulas are given on the next page.

An oxidation number of an atom can be 0, negative (-) or positive (+).

For example:.

The atom K or K^0 has an oxidation number of **0.**

The ion O^{2-} has an oxidation number of **-2.**

The ion Al^{3+} has an oxidation number of **+3.**

In all compounds, the sum of all oxidation numbers must equal **zero.**

In polyatomic ions (Table E), the sum of all oxidation numbers must equal the **charge** of the ion.

In the compound Na_2SO_4 , the sum of oxidation numbers of Na, S and O is Zero (0).

In the polyatomic ion CO_3^{2-} , the sum of oxidation numbers of C and O is equal to -2.

Determining Oxidation Numbers

Example 1: What is the oxidation number of **S** in the compound Na_2SO_4?

Note: The sum of charges must be equal to *Zero (0).*

Na = +1 charge: 2 Na = +2 total positive charge

O = -2 charge: 4 O = -8 total negative charge

S oxidation # must be a **+6** for all charges to equal *0*   *(+2 − 8 +6 = 0)*

Example 2: What is the oxidation number of **C** in the polyatomic ion CO_3^{2-} ?

Note: The sum of charges must be equal to *-2.*

O = -2 charge: 3 O = - 6 total negative charges

C oxidation # must be a **+4** for all charges to equal *-2*   *(-6 +4 = -2)*

Oxidation Number Rules

Oxidation numbers for the elements can be found in the box of each element on the Periodic Table. In redox equations, oxidation numbers are assigned to elements to keep track of electrons lost and gained. When assigning oxidation numbers to the elements in formulas and equations, it must be done according to arbitrary rules. These rules are summarized on the table below.

Table of Rules for Assigning Oxidation Numbers

Category of element	Common oxidation states	Example formulas		
Free element	0	Na	Zn	O_2 Cl_2
Simple ion	Charge on the ion	Na^+	Zn^{2+}	O^{2-} Cl^-
Group 1 element In **ALL** compounds	+1 (see Periodic Table)	**NaCl**	Li_2O	
Group 2 element In **ALL** compounds	+2 (see Periodic Table)	$MgCl_2$	CaO	
Hydrogen In **most** compounds In **metal hydride** compounds	+1 (see Periodic Table) -1	HCl LiH	H_2O CaH_2	H_2SO_4
Oxygen In **most** compounds In **OF_2** (a compound with **fluorine**) In **Peroxide** compounds	-2 (see Periodic Table) +2 -1	H_2O OF_2 H_2O_2	CO_2 N_2O_2	$HClO_3$
Group 17 halogen In **MOST** compounds	-1 (see Periodic Table)	**NaCl**	MgBr	CaI_2
In compounds in which a halogen is between other elements or is a first element.	+ (see Periodic Table) The correct + value can be determined mathematically	$NaBrO_3$	ClO_3	

In the hypothetical equation below, oxidation numbers are assigned to the elements using rules stated above.

$$\overset{0}{O_2} + \overset{+2}{Ca^{2+}} + \overset{+1\ -1}{NaH} + \overset{+2}{CaBr_2} \longrightarrow \overset{+1}{H_2O} + \overset{+5\ -2}{NaBrO_3} + \overset{-1}{CaBr_2}$$

Free element

Simple ion

Group 1 element in a compound

Hydrogen in metal hydride

Group 2 element in a compound

Hydrogen in a compound

Halogen between other elements

Oxygen in a compound

Halogen in a compound

Lesson 2: Oxidation and Reduction (redox) Reactions

Introduction

Redox reactions involve the simultaneous loss (oxidation) and gain (reduction) of electrons.
In this lesson, you will learn more about redox reactions, as well as oxidation and reduction.

Redox Reactions

All single replacement reactions are redox reactions. Most synthesis and decomposition reactions are redox reactions. Examples of these types of reaction are shown below. They are also covered in Topic 5.

Synthesis: $\qquad N_2 + O_2 \rightarrow 2NO$

Decomposition: $\quad 2H_2O \rightarrow 2H2O + O_2$

Single replacement: $Cu + 2AgNO_3 \rightarrow Cu(NO_3) + 2Ag$

Simplified redox: $\quad Cu + 2Ag^+ \rightarrow Cu^{2+} + 2Ag$

> **These and similar equations represent redox because:**
> .Two elements in each equation show change in oxidation number
>
> .Therefore, electrons are lost and gained

Non-redox reactions: All double replacement are *not* redox reactions. Examples of non redox reactions are given below.

Double replacement: $KI + AgNO_3 \rightarrow AgI + KNO_3$

Ions combining: $\quad Na^+ + Cl^- \rightarrow NaCl$

Ionization: $\qquad H_2O \rightarrow H^+ + OH^-$

> **These and similar equations are NOT redox because:**
> . None of the elements in the equations is showing a change in oxidation #.
> . Therefore, electrons are neither lost nor gained

Oxidation and Reduction

Redox reactions involve oxidation and reduction.

Oxidation:
Loss of Electrons is Oxidation **(LEO).**
An **oxidized substance** is the substance or ion that is losing (or transferring) its electrons. The oxidized substance is also the *reducing agent* because it will cause another substance in the reaction to gain electrons. Oxidation number of an oxidized substance always increases (becomes more positive) because the substance loses negative particles (electrons).

Reduction:
Gain of Electrons is Reduction **(GER).**
A **reduced substance** is the substance or ion that is gaining (or accepting) electrons. The reduced substance is also the *oxidizing agent* because it will cause another substance in the reaction to lose electrons. Oxidation number of a reduced substance always decreases (becomes more negative) because the substance gains negative particles (electrons).

Half-reactions

A **half-reaction** equation shows either the oxidation or reduction portion of a redox reaction. A correct half-reaction must show conservation of atoms, mass, and charge.

Consider the redox reaction below:

$$2Na + Cl_2 \rightarrow 2NaCl$$

Oxidation half-reactions show the loss of electrons by a substance in the redox reaction. In the above redox reaction, sodium is the species that is losing electrons. Electrons lost are always shown on the right side of the half-reaction equation as represented below.

$$2Na^0 \rightarrow 2Na^+ + 2e^- \quad \text{oxidation half-reaction}$$

Reduction-half-reactions show the gain of electrons by a substance in the redox reaction. In the above redox reaction, chlorine is the species that is gaining electrons. Electrons gained are always shown on the left side of the half-reaction equation as represented below.

$$Cl_2^0 + 2e^- \rightarrow 2Cl^- \quad \text{reduction half-reaction}$$

Note: Both half-reaction equations demonstrate conservation of mass, charge and atoms. This is to say that all half-reaction equations must be balanced.

Interpreting Half-reaction Equations

Half-reaction equations provide information about changes that substances are going through in a redox reaction. Below, two different half-reaction equations are given. One has electrons on the left and one has electrons on the right. Each half-reaction equation is interpreted by describing changes the substance is going through.

Reduction half-reaction *Equation with electrons on the LEFT*	Oxidation half-reaction *Equation with electrons on the RIGHT*
$C^0 + 4e^- \rightarrow C^{4-}$	$Sb^{3+} \rightarrow Sb^{5+} + 2e^-$
C^0 atom gains 4 electrons to become C^{4-}	Sb^{3+} loses 2 electrons to become Sb^{5+}
C^0 oxidation # decreases from 0 to -4	Sb^{3+} oxidation # increases from +3 to +5
C^0 is the reduced substance, and also the oxidizing agent.	Sb^{3+} is the oxidized substance, and also the reducing agent.
Number of electrons gained (4) is the difference between the two oxidation #'s. $0 - (-4) = 4 e^-$	Number of electrons lost (2) is the difference between the two oxidation #'s: $+5 - +3 = 2e^-$

Interpreting Oxidation Number Changes

Oxidation number changes can be used to determine if oxidation or reduction has occurred.

Oxidation or loss of electrons:

An increase in oxidation number represents oxidation.

$0 \longrightarrow +1$

This change indicates 1 e- lost.

$+3 \longrightarrow +5$

This change indicates 2 e- lost

Reduction or gain of electrons:

A decrease in oxidation number represents reduction.

$0 \longrightarrow -4$

This change indicates 4 e- gained

$+4 \longrightarrow +2$

This change indicates 2 e- gained

of electrons gained or lost = difference between two oxidation #s.

Making a scale like the one on the right can also help you determine the number of electrons gained or lost?

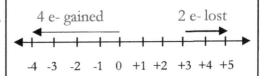

4 e- gained   2 e- lost

-4 -3 -2 -1   0 +1 +2 +3 +4 +5

Redox Equations:

Redox equations can be given in different forms as shown below.:

Redox equation 1 $Mg^0 + Al^{3+} \longrightarrow Mg^{2+} + Al^0$

Redox equation 2 $Ca + H_2SO_4 \longrightarrow CaSO_4 + H_2$

Note the difference between the equations. Equation 1 has oxidation numbers clearly noted for the elements. For equation 2, oxidation numbers must first be assigned to the elements before changes in oxidation numbers can be considered and used to answer questions.

For any redox equation that is given, you should be able to answer these questions:

1. What is the oxidation number change of a substance?
2. Which substance is oxidized (or lost electrons)?
3. Which substance is reduced (or gained electrons) ?
4. Which substance is the reducing agent?
5. Which substance is the oxidizing agent?
6. How many electrons are lost or gained?
7. What is the correct oxidation half-reaction?
8. What is the correct reduction half-reaction?

To answer most of these questions correctly, oxidation numbers must be correctly assigned, and the changes in oxidation numbers correctly considered.

Interpreting Redox Reaction Equations

The two equations given on the last page are interpreted below:

NOTE: When determining oxidized and reduced substances in a reaction, consider the following about the equation given.

Oxidized substance: The substance *left* of the arrow with the *smaller charge*

Reduced substance: The substance *left* of the arrow with the *greater charge*

$$3Mg^0 \quad + \quad 2Al^{3+} \quad \longrightarrow \quad 3Mg^{2+} \quad + \quad 2Al^0$$

Mg^0 has a *smaller* charge than Al^{3+}. Therefore: Mg^0 is oxidized Mg^0 loses (2) electrons Mg^0 is also the reducing agent Mg^0 oxidation number increases from 0 to +2 *Oxidation half-reaction:* $Mg^0 \;\rightarrow\; Mg^{2+} \;+\; 2e\text{-}$	Al^{3+} has a *larger* charge than Mg^0 Therefore: Al^{3+} is reduced Al^{3+} gains (3) electrons Al^{3+} is also the oxidizing agent Al^{3+} oxidation number decreases from +3 to 0 *Reduction half-reaction:* $Al^{3+} \;+\; 3e\text{-} \;\rightarrow\; Al^0$	Substances (Mg^{2+} and Al^0) to the RIGHT of the arrow in redox equations are the results of substances on the LEFT losing and gaining electrons. Therefore, these substances on the RIGHT are neither oxidized nor reduced, and they can never be the oxidizing nor reducing agents.

Note: For the equation below, oxidation numbers are ***correctly assigned*** (according to the rules) to elements before it can be interpreted.

$$Ca \quad + \quad H_2SO_4 \quad \longrightarrow \quad CaSO_4 \quad + \quad H_2$$

$$\overset{0}{Ca} \quad + \quad \overset{+1\;+6\;-2}{H_2SO_4} \quad \longrightarrow \quad \overset{+2\;+6\;-2}{CaSO_4} \quad + \quad \overset{0}{H_2}$$

Ca^0 has a *smaller* charge than H^{+1}. Therefore: Ca^0 is oxidized Ca^0 loses (2) electrons Ca^0 is also the reducing agent Ca^0 oxidation number increases from 0 to +2 *Oxidation half-reaction:* $Ca^0 \;\rightarrow\; Ca^{2+} \;+\; 2e\text{-}$	H^+ has a *greater* charge than Ca^0. Therefore: H^+ is reduced H^+ gains (1) electron H^+ is also the oxidizing agent H^+ oxidation number decreases from +1 to 0 *Reduction half-reaction:* $2H^+ \;+\; 2e\text{-} \;\rightarrow\; H_2^{\,0}$	Substances (Ca^{2+} and $H_2^{\,0}$) to the RIGHT of the arrow in redox equations are the results of substances on the LEFT losing and gaining electrons. Therefore, these substances on the RIGHT are neither oxidized nor reduced, and they can never be the oxidizing nor reducing agents.

Also, note that the oxidation numbers of S and O did not change. Therefore, S and O are neither oxidized nor reduced .

Lesson 3: Electrochemistry

Introduction

Electrochemistry is the study of relationships between redox chemical reactions and electrical energy. *Recall* from lesson 1 that redox reactions involve the loss and gain of electrons. When a substance in a redox reaction is oxidized, the electrons that are lost go to and are gained by the substance that is reduced. If a redox reaction system is set up so that there are paths for the electrons and ions to flow, electrical current can be produced.

A **battery** is a good example of a system that is set up to produce electrical energy from a redox reaction.

In Topic 9 you learned how exothermic chemical reactions release energy, and endothermic reactions absorb energy.

In this lesson of topic 11, you will learn how certain redox chemical reactions can produce or release electrical energy, while other redox reactions require the use of electrical energy for a reaction to occur.

Electrochemical Cells

An **electrochemical cell** is any device in which chemical energy can be converted to electrical energy or electrical energy to chemical energy. The two types of electrochemical cells are discussed below and on the next few pages.

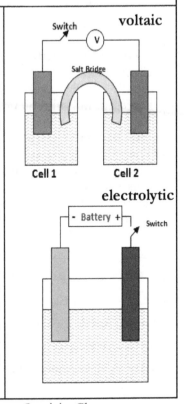

A **voltaic cell** is an electrochemical cell in which a spontaneous redox reaction occurs to produce electrical energy. In voltaic cells, chemical energy is converted to electrical energy. Reactions in voltaic cells are spontaneous and exothermic. Oxidation and reduction occur in two separate cells. A salt bridge connects the two half cells and provides a path for ions to flow. A **battery** is a type of voltaic cell.

An **electrolytic cell** is an electrochemical cell in which electrical energy is used to force a nonspontaneous redox reaction to occur. In electrolytic cells, electrical energy from an external energy source (such as a battery) is converted to chemical energy. Reactions in electrolytic cells are nonspontaneous and endothermic. Both oxidation and reduction occur in one (the same) cell.

Electrolytic reduction, electroplating of metals, and electrolysis of water use electrolytic cell processes.

Anode, Cathode, Wire, and Salt bridge

Oxidation and reduction reactions that occur in electrochemical cells take place at specific sites called electrodes.

Electrodes are sites on electrochemical cells where oxidation and reduction take place. The anode and cathode are the two electrodes on all electrochemical cells. The anode and cathode on electrochemical cells are usually labeled with − (negative) and +(positive) signs. The type of electrochemical cell determines which electrode is positive and which electrode is negative.

Anode: Oxidation
The anode is the electrode where oxidation occurs in both voltaic and electrolytic cells. The anode, therefore, is the site on any electrochemical cell where *electrons are lost*.

Signs for anode on voltaic and electrolytic cells:

> Voltaic cells − Anode is **N**egative (−)
> Electrolytic cells − Anode is **P**ositive (+)

Cathode: Reduction
The cathode is the electrode where reduction occurs in both voltaic and electrolytic cells. The cathode, therefore, is the site on any electrochemical cell where *electrons are gained*.

Signs for cathode on voltaic and electrolytic cells:

> Voltaic cells − Cathode is **P**ositive (+)
>
> Electrolytic cells − Cathode is **N**egative (−)

External conduit (wire): Permits flow of electrons
Electrons lost at the anode flow to the cathode via the external conduit, which is usually any electrical wire that connects the two electrodes. The external conduit is present in both voltaic and electrolytic cells.

Salt bridge: Permits flow of ions.
The salt bridge is any porous substance that connects solutions in the two half-cells of a voltaic cell. Positive and negative ions flow (migrate) between the two cells via the salt bridge. The flow of ions is necessary to keep the two half-cells neutral, and for appropriate functioning of a voltaic cell. The salt bridge is not present in electrolytic cells.

Use these codes to help you remember some key information:

LEO : Loss of **E**lectrons is **O**xidation   **GER**: Gain of Electrons is **R**eduction.

An Ox: **An**ode is for **Ox**idation   **Red Cat**: **Red**uction is at **Cat**hode

APE: **A**node is **P**ositive in **E**lectrolytic   **VCP**: **V**oltaic **C**athode is **P**ositive

VAN: **V**oltaic **A**node is **N**egative   **CEN**: **C**athode in **E**lectrolytic is **N**egative

Voltaic Cell Diagram

Below is a diagram representing a voltaic cell. Note the different components of the cell diagram. An equation representing the reaction taking place in this cell is given at the bottom of the diagram.

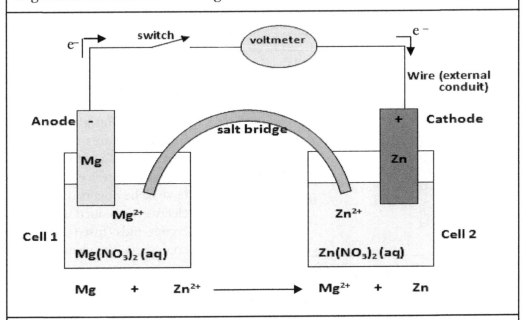

Answering questions about voltaic cells: Study the information below to help you determine answers to questions relating to any voltaic cell.

To determine:	Look for in the diagram:	In above diagram
1. The oxidized substance The reducing agent The substance that loses e⁻	The more active of the two metals. On Table J, the metal closer to the top	Mg
2. The reduced substance The oxidizing agent The substance that gains e⁻	The ion of the less active of the metals. On Table J, the ion of the metal closer to the bottom	Zn^{2+}
3. The anode (oxidation site) The positive electrode The electrode losing mass	The more active of the two metals. On Table J, the metal closer to the top	Mg
4. The cathode (reduction site) The negative electrode The electrode gaining mass	The less active of the two metals. On Table J, the metal closer to the bottom.	Zn
5. The oxidation equation Equation showing loss of e⁻	The more active metal $\rightarrow$ its ion $+$ e⁻ $Mg \rightarrow Mg^2 + 2e^-$	
6. The reduction equation Equation showing gain of e	The ion of the less active metal $+ e^- \rightarrow$ its metal $Zn^{2+} + 2e^- \rightarrow Zn$	

Electrolytic Reduction Cell Diagram

Electrolytic Reduction is a reaction by which a very reactive element is obtained from a fused salt compound. (ex. NaBr is a fused salt). In electrolytic reduction, an ion of the element is reduced (gains electrons) to form the element. The diagram below shows electrolytic reduction of a sodium ion (Na^+) to elemental sodium (Na).

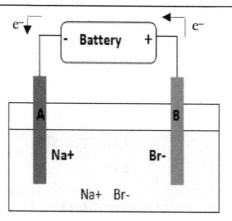

$2NaBr(l)$ + electricity $\rightarrow$ $2Na(s)$ + $Br_2(g)$

Equation showing the non-spontaneous redox reaction that is taking place in this cell.

Group 1 and **Group 2** metals, as well as **fluorine,** are very reactive elements. These elements are not found in nature in their free states because of their high reactivity. These elements have to be obtained through electrolytic reduction of compounds (fused salts) containing the element.

Answering questions about electrolytic reduction:

Study the information below to help you determine answers to questions relating to any electrolytic reduction cell.

To determine:	Look for in the diagram:	In above diagram
1. The oxidized substance The reducing agent The substance that loses e^-	The nonmetal negative (–) ion:	Br^-
2. The reduced substance The oxidizing agent The substance that gains e^-	The metal positive (+) ion	Na^+
3. The anode (oxidation site) The electrode losing mass	The metal connected to the +end of the battery (positive electrode)	**Metal B**
4. The cathode (reduction site) The electrode gaining mass	The metal connected to the – end of the battery (negative electrode)	**Metal A**
5. The oxidation equation Equation showing loss of e^-	The nonmetal –ion $\rightarrow$ nonmetal element + e^- $2Br^- \rightarrow Br_2 + 2e^-$	
6. The reduction equation Equation showing gain of e^-	The metal +ion + $e^- \rightarrow$ metal atom $Na^+ + e^- \rightarrow Na$	

Electroplating Cell Diagram

Electroplating is a process by which a thin layer of a metal is coated onto a surface of another object. In electroplating processes, the ion of a metal element is reduced, and the metal element that is produced is coated onto a surface of another object. The diagram below shows the electroplating of gold onto a surface of a spoon.

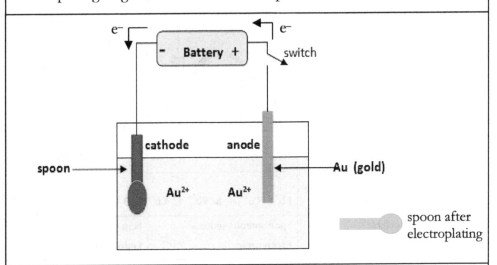

Answering questions about electroplating cells:

Study the information below to help you determine answers to questions relating to any electroplating cell.

To determine:	Look for in the diagram:	In above diagram:
1. The oxidized substance The substance that loses e⁻	The metal connected to the +end of the battery.	**Au**
2. The reduced substance The substance that gains e⁻	The ion of the metallic element	**Au²⁺**
3. The anode (oxidation site) The positive electrode The electrode that loses mass	The metal connected to the +end of the battery.	**Au**
4. The cathode (reduction site) The negative electrode The electrode that gains mass	The object connected to the end of the battery	**Spoon**
5. The oxidation equation Equation showing loss of e⁻	The metal element → the metal ion + e⁻ **Au → Au²⁺ + 2e⁻**	
6. The reduction equation Equation showing gain of e⁻	The metal ion + e⁻ → the metal element **Au²⁺ + 2e⁻ → Au**	

Summary and comparisons of the two electrochemical cells

Below is a summary of voltaic and electrolytic cells. Use this table for a quick review and comparisons of the two electrochemical cells.

		Voltaic	Electrolytic
	Diagrams		
D i f f e r e n c e s	Example redox equation	$Pb + Cu^{2+} \rightarrow Pb^{2+} + Cu$	$H_2O + electricity \rightarrow H_2 + O_2$
	Type of reaction	Spontaneous redox Exothermic	Non-spontaneous redox Endothermic
	Energy conversion	Chemical to electrical energy	Electrical to chemical energy
	Anode (site for oxidation)	Negative (-) electrode	Positive (+) electrode
	Cathode (site for reduction)	Positive (+) electrode	Negative (-) electrode
	Half-Reactions occur in	Two separate cells	One cell
	Salt bridge present?	Yes (connects the two cells) (permits the flow of ions)	No
	Usages and examples	Battery	Electroplating Electrolytic reduction Electrolysis
S i m i l a r i t i e s	Oxidation (losing of electrons) at	Anode (-) (loses mass)	Anode (+) (loses mass)
	Reduction (gaining of electrons) at	Cathode (+) (gains mass)	Cathode (-) (gains mass)
	Direction of Electron flow (through the wire)	Anode to Cathode	Anode to Cathode

Lesson 4: Spontaneous Reactions

A **spontaneous reaction** is a reaction that will take place (occur) under specific sets of conditions. The **Activity Series on Table J** can be used to predict if a reaction is spontaneous or nonspontaneous.

Spontaneous reactions occur when:
The free element reactant is more reactive than a similar element in the compound reactant.

Spontaneous reaction 1

$$Zn \quad + \quad Fe\,Cl_2 \quad \rightarrow \quad ZnCl_2 \ + \ Fe$$
$$\downarrow \qquad\qquad \downarrow$$
free element   *similar element*
reactant   in a compound

According to the equation, Zn replaces Fe to form $ZnCl_2$.
The reaction is *spontaneous* because Zn is more reactive (higher up on Table J) than Fe.

Spontaneous reaction 2

$$Cl_2 \quad + \quad Sn\,Br_2 \quad \rightarrow \quad SnCl_2 \ + \ Br_2$$
$$\downarrow \qquad\qquad \downarrow$$
free element   *similar element*
reactant   in a compound

According to the equation, Cl replaces Br to form $SnCl_2$.
The reaction is *spontaneous* because Cl is more reactive (higher up on Table J) than Br.

Nonspontaneous reaction

$$Pb \quad + \quad Ni\,Cl_2 \quad \rightarrow \quad PbCl_2 \ + \ Ni$$
$$\downarrow \qquad\qquad \downarrow$$
free element   *similar element*
reactant   in a compound

According to the equation, Pb replaces Ni to form $PbCl_2$. The reaction is *nonspontaneous* (will not occur on its own) because Pb is less active (lower down on Table J) than Ni.

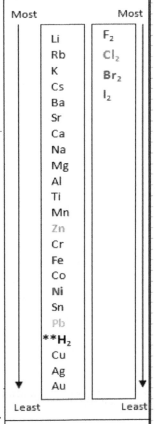

**Reference Table J
Activity Series**

Most	Most
Li	F_2
Rb	Cl_2
K	Br_2
Cs	I_2
Ba	
Sr	
Ca	
Na	
Mg	
Al	
Ti	
Mn	
Zn	
Cr	
Fe	
Co	
Ni	
Sn	
Pb	
**H₂	
Cu	
Ag	
Au	
Least	Least

** Activity series based on Hydrogen standard

Some elements are more easily oxidized, others are more easily reduced.

Metals
Most easily oxidized: Metal closest to top of Table J (Li)

Most easily reduced: Ion of metal closest to bottom (Au^+)

An element on the top will cause an ion of an element below it to reduce. For example, Ca will cause Na^+ to reduce to Na .
An ion of an element on the bottom will cause any element above it to oxidize. For example, Na^+ will cause Ca to oxidize to Ca^{2+}.

Nonmetals
Most easily oxidized: Ion of the nonmetal closest to bottom (I-)

Most easily reduced: Nonmetal closest to top (F_2)

Practice Questions

Lesson 1: Oxidation Numbers

Answer the following multiple choice questions

1. The sum of all oxidation numbers of atoms in a chemical formula must equal
   1) -1　　　　　　 2) 0　　　　　　 3) 1　　　　　　 4) 2

2. What is the oxidation number of oxygen in ozone, O_3,
   1) +1　　　　　　 2) 0　　　　　　 3) -2　　　　　　 4) -6

3. The oxidation number of hydrogen in BeH_2 is
   1) +1　　　　　　 2) -1　　　　　　 3) 0　　　　　　 4) +2

4. What is the oxidation number of calcium in CaH_2?
   1) 0　　　　　　 2) +1　　　　　　 3) +2　　　　　　 4) -2

5. What is the oxidation number of Pt in K_2PtCl_6?
   1) -4　　　　　　 2) +4　　　　　　 3) -2　　　　　　 4) +2

6. What are the two oxidation states of nitrogen in the compound NH_4NO_3?
   1) -3 and +5　　 2) -3 and -5　　 3) +3 and +5　　 4) +3 and -5

7. Below, two compounds of chlorine are given:
   Compound A:　Cl_2O　　　　Compound B: $HClO$
   Which is true of the oxidation number of chlorine in compounds A and B?
   1) Chlorine's oxidation number is +2 in A, but +1 in B
   2) Chlorine's oxidation number is +1 in A, but +2 in B
   3) Chlorine's oxidation number is +2 in both A and B
   4) Chlorine's oxidation number is +1 in both A and B

8. The oxidation number of phosphorus in a phosphate ion, PO_4^{3-} is
   1) +5　　　　　　 2) -3　　　　　　 3) +3　　　　　　 4) +8

9. What is the oxidation number of Cr in the polyatomic ion, $Cr_2O_7^{2-}$?
   1) +7　　　　　　 2) +6　　　　　　 3) -2　　　　　　 4) +2

10. In the ion O_2^{2-} , what is the oxidation number of O?
    1) 0　　　　　　 2) +1　　　　　　 3) -2　　　　　　 4) -1

11. Oxygen has an oxidation number of -2 in
    1) O_2　　　　　 2) NO_2　　　　 3) Na_2O_2　　　 4) OF_2

12. In which compound does chlorine have an oxidation number of +5?
    1) $HClO_4$　　　 2) $HClO$　　　 3) $HClO_2$　　　 4) $HClO_3$

13. In which substance does bromine have an oxidation number of +3?
    1) $KBrO$　　　 2) $KBrO_3$　　　 3) $KBrO_2$　　　 4) $KBrO_4$

14. Sulfur has an oxidation number of +6 in which two formulas?
    1) SO_3 and SO_4^{2-} 　　　　　　　 3) SO_2 and SO_4^{2-}
    2) H_2SO_4 and SO_2 　　　　　　　 4) HSO_4^- and $S_2O_3^{2-}$

Lesson 2: Oxidation and Reduction

Define the following terms and answer multiple choice questions below.

15. Redox   16. Oxidation   17. Reduction   18. Oxidized substance
19. Reduced substance   20. Oxidizing agent   21. Reducing agent
22. Oxidation number   23. Half-reaction

24. Oxidation in a redox reaction involves a
   1) Gain of protons   3) Gain of electrons
   2) Loss of protons   4) Loss of electrons

25. The oxidation number of oxidized substances in redox reactions always
   1) Decreases   2) Increases   3) Remains the same

26. A reduced substance in oxidation and reduction reactions
   1) Gains electrons and has a decrease in oxidation number
   2) Gains electrons and has an increase in oxidation number
   3) Loses electrons and has a decrease in oxidation number
   4) Loses electrons and has an increase in oxidation number

27. An oxidizing agent is a species in a redox reaction that is
   1) Reduced because it has lost electrons
   2) Reduced because it has gained electrons
   3) Oxidized because it has lost electrons
   4) Oxidized because it has gained electrons

28. Which is true of a reducing agent in oxidation-reduction reactions?
   1) A reducing agent loses electrons, and is oxidized
   2) A reducing agent loses electrons, and is reduced
   3) A reducing agent gains electrons, and is oxidized
   4) A reducing agent gains electrons, and is reduced

29. Which equation is a redox reaction?
   1) $Mg + H_2SO_4 \rightarrow MgSO_4 + H_2$
   2) $Mg(OH)_2 + H_2SO_4 \rightarrow MgSO_4 + H_2O$
   3) $Mg^{2+} + 2OH^- \longrightarrow Mg(OH)_2$
   4) $MgCl_2 + 6H_2O \rightarrow MgCl_2 \cdot 6H_2O$

30. Which equation represents an oxidation – reduction reaction?
   1) $SO_2 + H_2O \rightarrow H_2SO_3$
   2) $SO_3^{2-} + 2H^+ \rightarrow H_2SO_4$
   3) $O_2 + 2H_2 \rightarrow 2H_2O$
   4) $OH^- + H^+ \rightarrow H_2O$

31. Given the four equations below.
   I: $AgNO_3 + NaCl \rightarrow AgCl + NaNO_3$
   II: $Cl_2 + H_2O \rightarrow HClO + HCl$
   III: $CuO + CO \rightarrow CO_2 + Cu$
   IV: $LiOH + HCl \rightarrow LiCl + H_2O$

   Which two equations represent redox reactions?
   1) I and II   2) II and III   3) III and I   4) IV and II

32. Which change in oxidation number represents reduction?
    1) $+1 \rightarrow +2$ 3) $+2 \rightarrow +4$
    2) $0 \rightarrow -1$ 4) $-1 \rightarrow 0$

33. Which of the following oxidation number changes represents oxidation?
    1) 0 to +1   3) 0 to -1
    2) -2 to -3   4) +1 to 0

34. Which oxidation number change indicates the most number of electrons gained by a species in a redox reaction?
    1) +3 to -1   3) 0 to +4
    2) +6 to +3   4) +3 to +7

35. Which change occurs when an Sn^{2+} ion is oxidized to Sn^{4+}?
    1) Two electrons are lost   3) Two protons are lost
    2) Two electrons are gained   4) Two protons are gained

36. Which change occurs when N^{3+} is changed to an N atom?
    1) Three neutrons are lost   3) Three protons are gained
    2) Three electrons are lost   4) Three electrons are gained

37. Which half-reaction correctly shows reduction?
    1) $Sn^{2+} \rightarrow Sn^{4+} + 2e^-$ 3) $Sn^{2+} + 2e^- \rightarrow Sn^0$
    2) $Sn^{2+} \rightarrow Sn^0 + 2e^-$ 4) $Sn^{2+} + 2e^- \rightarrow Sn^{4+}$

38. Which half-reaction correctly represents oxidation?
    1) $Ag + e^- \rightarrow Ag^-$ 3) $Au^{3+} + 3e^- \rightarrow Au$
    2) $Ag \rightarrow Ag^+ + e^-$ 4) $Au^{3+} \rightarrow Au + 3e^-$

39. Which half-reaction correctly represents a reduction reaction?
    1) $Li^0 + e^- \rightarrow Li^+$ 3) $Br_2^0 + 2e^- \rightarrow 2Br^-$
    2) $Na^0 + e^- \rightarrow Na^+$ 4) $Cl_2^0 + e^- \rightarrow 2Cl^-$

40. In the half-reaction equation: $Ca \rightarrow Ca^{2+} + 2e^-$
    Which is true of the calcium atom?
    1) It is oxidized by gaining 2 electrons   3) It is reduced by gaining 2 electrons
    2) It is oxidized by losing 2 electrons   4) It is reduced by losing 2 electrons

41. In the half-reaction equation: $P + 3e^- \rightarrow P^{3-}$
    the phosphorus atom is
    1) Oxidized, and becomes the oxidizing agent
    2) Reduced, and becomes the reducing agent
    3) Oxidized, and becomes the reducing agent
    4) Reduced, and becomes the oxidizing agent

42. In the reaction: $H_2 + 2Fe^{3+} \rightarrow 2H^+ + 2Fe^{2+}$
    Which species is gaining electrons?
    1) Fe^{+2} 2) H^+ 3) Fe^{3+} 4) H_2

43. Consider the redox reaction: $Ni + Sn^{4+} \rightarrow Ni^{2+} + Sn^{2+}$
    the species oxidized is
    1) Sn^{4+} 2) Sn^{2+} 3) Ni^{2+} 4) Ni

44. Consider the equation. $Zn(s) + Cu^{2+}(aq) \rightarrow Zn^{2+}(aq) + Cu(s)$
The reducing agent is
1) $Cu^{2+}(aq)$ 2) $Zn(s)$ 3) $Cu(s)$ 4) $Zn^{2+}(aq)$

45. Given the redox reaction: $Fe + 2AgCl \rightarrow 2Ag + FeCl_2$
The species oxidized is
1) Fe^{3+} 2) Fe^0 3) Cl^- 4) Ag^+

46. Given the oxidation-reduction reaction:
$$2H_2O + 2Na \rightarrow 2NaOH + H_2$$
Which substance is reduced?
1) H_2 2) O^{2-} 3) H^+ 4) Na

47. Given the oxidation-reduction reaction below:
$$4HCl + MnO_2 \rightarrow MnCl_2 + 2H_2O + Cl_2$$
Which species in this reaction is gaining electrons?
1) H^+ 2) Cl^- 3) Mn^{4+} 4) Mn^{2+}

48. Given the reaction: $Pb + 2Ag^+ \rightarrow Pb^{2+} + 2Ag$
The lead atom is
1) Reduced, and its oxidation number changes from 0 to +2
2) Reduced, and its oxidation number changes from +2 to 0
3) Oxidized, and its oxidation number changes from +2 to 0
4) Oxidized, and its oxidation number changes from 0 to +2

49. In the reaction: $Mg + ZnCl_2 \rightarrow MgCl_2 + Zn$
Which is true of the magnesium?
1) It is oxidized by losing electrons   3) It is reduced by losing electrons
2) It is oxidized by gaining electrons   4) It is reduced by gaining electrons

50. Given the oxidation-reduction reaction:
$$Co(s) + PbCl_2(aq) \rightarrow CoCl_2(aq) + Pb(s)$$
Which statement correctly describes the oxidation and reduction that occur?
1) $Co(s)$ is oxidized and $Cl^-(aq)$ is reduced
2) $Co(s)$ is oxidized and $Pb^{2+}(aq)$ is reduced
3) $Co(s)$ is reduced and $Cl^-(aq)$ is oxidized
4) $Co(s)$ is reduced and $Pb^{2+}(aq)$ is oxidized

51. Consider the redox reaction: $Mn^0 + O_2 \rightarrow Mn^{4+} + 2O^{2-}$
Which half-reaction is correct for the reduction that occurs?
1) $O_2 \rightarrow 2O^{2-} + 4e^-$ 3) $Mn^0 + 4e^- \rightarrow Mn^{4+}$
2) $O_2 + 4e^- \rightarrow 2O^{2-}$ 4) $Mn^0 \rightarrow Mn^{4+} + 4e^-$

52. Given the following reaction: $Mg + 2HBr \rightarrow MgBr_2 + H_2$
Which equation correctly represents the oxidation that occurs?
1) $2H^+ \rightarrow H_2 + 2e^-$ 3) $2H^+ + 2e^- \rightarrow H_2$
2) $Mg^0 \rightarrow Mg^{2+} + 2e^-$ 4) $Mg^0 + 2e^- \rightarrow Mg^{2+}$

53. In the oxidation-reduction reaction: $2H_2O \rightarrow 2H_2 + O_2$
Which half-reaction equation is correct for the reduction that occurs?
1) $2H^+ + 2e^- \rightarrow H_2$ 3) $2O^{2-} + 2e^- \rightarrow O_2$
2) $2H_2 + 2e^- \rightarrow 2H^+$ 4) $O_2 + 2e^- \rightarrow 2O^{2-}$

Lesson 3: Electrochemistry

Define the following terms and answer the multiple choice questions below.

54. Electrochemical cell   55. Electrode   56. Anode   57. Cathode
58. Voltaic cell   59. Electrolytic cell   60. Electroplating   61. Electrolytic reduction
62. Electrolysis   63. Salt Bridge   64. Battery

65. What kind of reaction occurs in operating an electrolytic cell?
    1) Non-spontaneous oxidation-reduction   3) Non-spontaneous oxidation, only
    2) Spontaneous oxidation-reduction   4) Spontaneous reduction, only

66. Which is true of a voltaic cell but not of an electrolytic cell?
    1) Voltaic cells are used in electroplating
    2) Voltaic cells use an external energy source
    3) Voltaic cells involve redox reactions
    4) Voltaic cells contains a salt bridge

67. Which is true of the cathode in all electrochemical cells?
    1) The cathode is the site for oxidation
    2) The cathode is the site for reduction
    3) The cathode is the site for both oxidation and reduction
    4) The cathode is the site where protons are lost and gained

68. An electrochemical cell setup consists of two half cells connected by an external conductor and a salt bridge. The function of the salt bridge is to
    1) Block a path for the flow of electrons
    2) Block a path for the flow of ions
    3) Provide a path for the flow of electrons
    4) Provide a path for the flow of ions

69. In both the voltaic and the electrolytic cell, the anode is the electrode at which
    1) Reduction occurs and electrons are lost
    2) Reduction occurs and electrons are gained
    3) Oxidation occurs and electrons are lost
    4) Oxidation occurs and electrons are gained

70. In an electrolytic cell, the positive electrode is the
    1) Anode, at which reduction occurs   3) Cathode, at which reduction occurs
    2) Anode, at which oxidation occurs   4) Cathode, at which oxidation occurs

71. Given the reaction
    $$2H_2O(l)   +   electricity   \rightarrow   2H_2(g)   +   O_2(g)$$
    This reaction can be best be described as
    1) Redox and nonspontaneous   3) Non-redox and spontaneous
    2) Redox and spontaneous   4) Non-redox and nonspontaneous

72. Given the reaction:
    $$Mg(s)   +   FeSO_4(aq)   \rightarrow   Fe(s)   +   MgSO_4(aq)$$
    The reaction would most likely occur in
    1) A voltaic cell, and will produce energy
    2) An electrolytic cell, and will produce energy
    3) A voltaic cell, and will absorb energy
    4) An electrolytic cell, and will absorb energy

Answer questions 73 – 76 based on the diagram below:

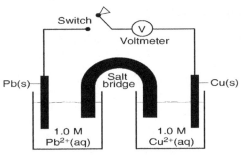

$$Pb(s) + Cu^{2+}(aq) \longrightarrow Pb^{2+}(aq) + Cu(s)$$

73. When the switch is
    closed, the species
    oxidized is

    1) $Cu^{2+}(aq)$

    2) $Pb^{2+}(aq)$

    3) $Pb(s)$

    4) $Cu(s)$

74. The anode in this electrochemical cell is the
    1) Cu atom, which is the positive electrode
    2) Pb atom, which is the positive electrode
    3) Cu atom, which is the negative electrode
    4) Pb atom, which is the negative electrode

75. The salt bridge in the electrochemical diagram will connect
    1) Pb atoms to Cu atoms   3) Pb^{2+} ions to Cu atoms
    2) Pb^{2+} ions to Cu^{2+} ions   4) Cu^{2+} ions to Pb atoms

76. Which correctly shows the half-reaction that occurs at the anode of this cell?
    1) $Pb^{2+} \rightarrow Pb + 2e^-$ 3) $Cu^{2+} + 2e^- \rightarrow Cu$
    2) $Pb \rightarrow Pb^{2+} + 2e^-$ 4) $Cu + 2e^- \rightarrow Cu^{2+}$

Answer questions 77 - 80 based on the diagram below.

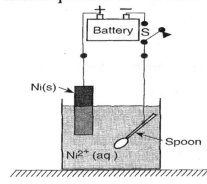

77. In this cell diagram, which is reduced?
    1) Ni atom   3) Ni^{2+} ions
    2) The battery   4) The spoon

78. Which statement best describes the
    spoon in this diagram?
    1) It acts as the anode, and is negative
    2) It acts as the cathode, and is negative
    3) It acts as the anode, and is positive
    4) It acts as the cathode, and is positive

79. Which statement correctly describes what occurs in this cell when the switch is
    closed?
    1) The Ni(s) will be oxidized, and the spoon will lose mass
    2) The Ni(s) will be oxidized, and the spoon will gain mass
    3) The Ni(s) will be reduced, and the spoon will lose mass
    4) The Ni(s) will be reduced, and the spoon will gain mass

80. The flow of electrons in this cell will be from
    1) Ni to Ni^{2+} 2) Ni^{2+} to Ni   3) Ni to spoon   4) Spoon to Ni

Lesson 4: Spontaneous Reactions and the Activity Series

Answer the following multiple choice questions.

81. Based on Reference Table J, which metal is most easily oxidized?
    1) Ni   2) Zn   3) Cr   4) Co

82. Based on Reference Table J, which ion is most easily reduced?
    1) Sr^{2+} 2) Ba^{2+} 3) Ca^{2+} 4) Mg^{2+}

83. Which metal will reduce Zn^{2+} to Zn?
    1) Mn   2) Cr   3) H_2 4) Ag

84. Which metal, according to Table J, will react spontaneously with Al^{3+}?
    1) Co(s)   2) Cr(s)   3) Cu(s)   4) Ca(s)

85. According to information from Reference Table J, which redox reaction occurs spontaneously?
    1) $Cu(s)$ + $2H^+(aq)$ $\rightarrow$ $Cu^{2+}(aq)$ + $H_2(g)$
    2) $Mg(s)$ + $2H^+(aq)$ $\rightarrow$ $Mg^{2+}(aq)$ + $H_2(g)$
    3) $2Ag(s)$ + $2H^+(aq)$ $\rightarrow$ $2Ag^+(aq)$ + $H_2(g)$
    4) $2Au(s)$ + $2H^+(aq)$ $\rightarrow$ $2Au^+(aq)$ + $H_2(g)$

86. Based on Reference Table J, which redox reaction will occur spontaneously?
    1) Br_2 + $2KI$ $\rightarrow$ $2KBr$ + I_2
    2) I_2 + $2KCl$ $\rightarrow$ $2KI$ + Cl_2
    3) Cl_2 + $2KF$ $\rightarrow$ $2KCl$ + F_2
    4) I_2 + $2KBr$ $\rightarrow$ $2KI$ + Br_2

Topic Mastery / Constructed Response

87. What is the oxidation number of O in the formula $Al(OH)_3$?

88. Complete the equation: $2N^{3-}$ $\rightarrow$ N_2^0 +   _____

89. Complete the equation: _____   + $4e-$ $\rightarrow$ Cr^{2+}

90. Write oxidation and reduction equations for the following redox reaction.

    $$3Zn^0 \;\; + \;\; 2Al^{3+} \;\; \rightarrow \;\; 3Zn^{2+} \;\; + \;\; 2Al^0$$

91. You are given an electrochemical cell in which you do not know the identity of the metals that comprise the anode and cathode. The cell is producing electricity spontaneously. What observations of the cathode and anode could you make so that you could correctly label them as cathode and anode?

92. Complete the diagram to the right by drawing all components necessary for the cell to operate when the switch is closed.

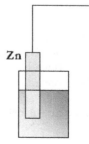
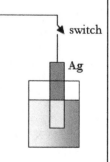

Additional Materials

Reduction Potentials and Calculation of Cell Potentials

In voltaic cells, electrons flow from the anode (oxidation-half cell) to cathode (reduction-half cell) as a redox reaction occurs. It is the flow of electrons that generates the electrical potential energy in voltaic cells. A voltmeter placed between the anode and cathode of a voltaic cell will measure the electrical potential difference, ***voltage***, resulting from the two half-reactions of the cell.

Every half-reaction has a known potential, E^0, associated with it. The Standard Reduction Potential Table on the next page shows some common reduction half-reactions and their standard potentials, E^0. Each reduction potential on the table is given in comparison to a hydrogen cell, which has E^0 of 0.00 V at standard conditions (1 M solution, 1 atm, 298 K). For any cell, voltaic or electrolytic, E^0 's for the two half-reactions occurring in the cell can be added to get the net reaction potential of the cell, E^0_{cell} .

Reading E^0 Values from the Table

Reduction Potential (E^0 value as written) $Cu^{2+} + 2e- \rightarrow$ Cu $E^0_{red} = +0.34\,V$

Oxidation Potential (E^0 sign is reversed) $Cu \rightarrow Cu^{2+} + 2e-$ $E^0_{oxi} = -0.34\,V$

Comparing Species on the Table

A species on the left of the table will cause any species on the right and above it to be oxidized   *Example:* Cu^{2+} will cause Zn to be oxidized to Zn^{2+}

A species on the right of the table will cause any species on the left and below it to be reduced.   *Example:*   Zn will cause Cu^{2+} to be reduced to Cu

Comparing Half-reactions on the Table

Given any two half-reactions:

The *half-reaction with the highest E^0* value will proceed forward as *reduction*

The *half-reaction with the lowest E^0* value will proceed in reverse as *oxidation*.

Calculating the Net Cell Reaction Potential, E^0_{cell}.

$$E^0_{cell} = E^0_{oxidation} + E^0_{reduction}$$

Example 3: Calculate the net cell potential for: $Zn + Cu^{2+} \rightarrow Zn^{2+} + Cu$

Step 1: Note the two half-reactions and their E^{0}'s :

Reduction-half $Cu^{2+} + 2e^- \rightarrow Cu$ $E^0_{reduction} = +0.34\,V$

Oxidation-half $Zn \rightarrow Zn^{2+} + 2e^-$ $E^0_{oxidation} = +0.76\,V$ (note: the sign is changed)

Step 2: Calculate the net cell potential, E^0_{cell}, by adding the two potentials

$E^0_{cell} = E^0_{oxidation} + E^0_{reduction}$

$E^0_{cell} = 0.76\,V + 0.34\,V = \boxed{+1.10V}$ *(Note:* Never multiply E^0 by a coefficient)

Interpreting the Net Cell Reaction Potential, E^0_{cell}

$+E^0_{cell}$: redox reaction is spontaneous   (*Example 3 reaction is spontaneous*)

$- E^0_{cell}$: redox reaction is nonspontaneous

if $E^0_{cell} = 0.00\,V$, the reaction in the cell is at equilibrium

Redox and Electrochemistry

Table of Standard Reduction Potentials
in 1 M water solution at 298 K and 1 atm

Least easily reduced

Most easily oxidized

Increase Strength of Oxidizing Agent

Increase Strength of Reducing Agent

Cathode (Reduction) Half-Reaction	Standard Potential E° (volts, V)
$Li^+(aq)\ +\ e^-\ \rightarrow\ Li(s)$	-3.04
$K^+(aq)\ +\ e^-\ \rightarrow\ K(s)$	-2.92
$Ca^{2+}(aq)\ +\ 2e^-\ \rightarrow\ Ca(s)$	-2.76
$Na^+(aq)\ +\ e^-\ \rightarrow\ Na(s)$	-2.71
$Mg^{2+}(aq)\ +\ 2e^-\ \rightarrow\ Mg(s)$	-2.37
$Ac^{3+}(aq)\ +\ 3e^-\ \rightarrow\ Ac(s)$	-2.20
$Be^{2+}(aq)\ +\ 2e^-\ \rightarrow\ Be(s)$	-1.85
$Al^{3+}(aq)\ +\ 3e^-\ \rightarrow\ Al(s)$	-1.66
$Zn^{2+}(aq)\ +\ 2e^-\ \rightarrow\ Zn(s)$	-0.76
$Cr^{3+}(aq)\ +\ 3e^-\ \rightarrow\ Cr(s)$	-0.74
$Fe^{2+}(aq)\ +\ 2e^-\ \rightarrow\ Fe(s)$	-0.41
$Cd^{2+}(aq)\ +\ 2e^-\ \rightarrow\ Cd(s)$	-0.40
$Co^{2+}(aq\ +\ 2e^-\ \rightarrow\ Co(s)$	-0.28
$Ni^{2+}(aq)\ +\ 2e^-\ \rightarrow\ Ni(s)$	-0.23
$Sn^{2+}(aq)\ +\ 2e^-\ \rightarrow\ Sn(s)$	-0.14
$Pb^{2+}(aq)\ +\ 2e^-\ \rightarrow\ Pb(s)$	-0.13
$Fe^{3+}(aq)\ +\ 3e^-\ \rightarrow\ Fe(s)$	-0.04
$2H^+(aq)\ +\ 2e^-\ \rightarrow\ H_2(g)$	0.00
$Sn^{4+}(aq)\ +\ 2e^-\ \rightarrow\ Sn^{2+}(aq)$	0.15
$Cu^{2+}(aq)\ +\ e^-\ \rightarrow\ Cu^+(aq)$	0.16
$Bi^{3+}(aq)\ +\ 3e^-\ \rightarrow\ Bi(s)$	0.31
$Cu^{2+}(aq)\ +\ 2e^-\ \rightarrow\ Cu(s)$	0.34
$Cu^+(aq)\ +\ e^-\ \rightarrow\ Cu(s)$	0.52
$I_2(s)\ +\ 2e^-\ \rightarrow\ 2I^-(aq)$	0.54
$Fe^{3+}(aq)\ +\ e^-\ \rightarrow\ Fe^{2+}(aq)$	0.77
$Hg_2^{2+}(aq)\ +\ 2e^-\ \rightarrow\ 2Hg(l)$	0.80
$Ag^+(aq)\ +\ e^-\ \rightarrow\ Ag(s)$	0.80
$Hg^{2+}(aq)\ +\ 2e^-\ \rightarrow\ Hg(l)$	0.85
$2Hg^{2+}(aq)\ +\ 2e^-\ \rightarrow\ Hg_2^{2+}(aq)$	0.90
$Br_2(l)\ +\ 2e^-\ \rightarrow\ 2Br^-(aq)$	1.07
$Cl_2(g)\ +\ 2e^-\ \rightarrow\ 2Cl^-(aq)$	1.36
$Ce^{4+}(aq)\ +\ e^-\ \rightarrow\ Ce^{3+}(aq)$	1.44
$Au^{3+}(aq)\ +\ 3e^-\ \rightarrow\ Au(s)$	1.52
$Co^{3+}(aq\ +\ e^-\ \rightarrow\ Co^{2+}(aq)$	1.82
$F_2(g)\ +\ 2e^-\ \rightarrow\ 2F^-(aq)$	2.87

Most easily reduced

Least easily oxidized

NOTE: This table can be in reverse, with F_2 on the top and Li^+ on the bottom.

 SurvivingChem.com

Practice Questions on Additional Materials

Use the Table of Standard Reduction Potential to answer questions 93 to 100.

93. What is the standard electrode potential, E^0, for the oxidation of gold to gold (III) ion?
   1) +1.52 V   2) 0.80 V   3) -0.80 V   4) -1.52 V

94. Which ion can be both an oxidizing agent and a reducing agent?
   1) Sn^{2+} 2) Fe^{3+} 3) Al^{3+} 4) Cu^{2+}

95. Which half-cell has a lower electrode potential than the standard hydrogen cell?
   1) $Au^{3+} + 3e- \rightarrow Au$ 3) $Cu^+ + e- \rightarrow Cu$
   2) $Hg^{2+} + 2e- \rightarrow Hg$ 4) $Pb^{2+} + 2e- \rightarrow Pb$

96. Given the redox reaction : $Mg(s) + 2Ag^+(aq) \rightarrow Mg^{2+}(aq) + 2Ag(s)$
   What is the cell voltage, E^0_{cell}, for the overall reaction?
   1) +1.57 V   2) +2.37 V   3) +3.17 V   4) +3.97 V

97. Given the reaction: $Zn(s) + Br_2(l) \rightarrow Zn^{2+}(aq) + 2Br-(aq)$.
   What is the net cell potential, E^0_{cell}, for the overall reaction?
   1) +0.76 V   2) -1.09 V   3) +1.83 V   4) 0.00 V

98. Given the reaction: $2NaCl(l) \rightarrow 2Na(l) + Cl_2(g)$
   What is the net cell potential, E^0_{cell}, for the overall reaction?
   1) - 4.07 V   2) +4.07 V   3) +0.35 V   4) - 0.35 V

99. Which overall reaction in a chemical cell has the highest net potential, E^0_{cell}?
   1) $Zn(s) + 2H^+ \rightarrow Zn^{2+} + H_2(g)$ 3) $Mg(s) + 2H^+ \rightarrow Mg^{2+} + H_2(g)$
   2) $Ni(s) + 2H^+ \rightarrow Ni^{2+} + H_2(g)$ 4) $Sn(s) + 2H^+ \rightarrow Sn^{2+} + H_2(g)$

100. A chemical cell is composed of two separate beakers connected by a salt bridge.

   In Beaker 1: A piece of $Ag(s)$ is placed in a 1.0 M $AgNO_3$ (aq) solution.

   In Beaker 2: A piece of $Fe(s)$ is placed in a 1.0 M $Fe(NO_3)_2$(aq) solution

   a) Which electrode of the cell is the anode? Which is the cathode?

   b) Write the overall balanced redox equation for the reaction that will occur in the cell.

   c) Write the balanced oxidation-half and reduction-half reactions that will occur.

   d) Calculate the net cell potential, E^0_{cell}, for the overall reaction that will occur.

   d) Indicate if the reaction will be spontaneous or nonspontaneous.

Lesson 1: Nuclear Transmutations

Introduction

Nuclear chemistry is the study of changes that occur in the nucleus of atoms. The nucleus of atoms contains protons and neutrons. The number of protons determines the identity (atomic number) of the atom. The number of neutrons determines the mass number of the atom. Any change to the nucleus of an atom likely involves

The nucleus of
Nitrogen – 16

9 neutrons
7 protons

changing the number of protons and/or neutrons. Any change to the nucleus of an atom will always change that atom to a different atom.

Transmutation is the changing (converting) of one atom to another by way of nuclear changes.

In this lesson, you will learn about the different types of nuclear changes, and ways of representing them by nuclear equations.

Nuclear Equations

Nuclear equations are used to show changes taking place during nuclear reactions. Three types of equations are shown below. NOTE the clear difference between the nuclear equation to chemical and physical change equations.

Nuclear change equation: $\quad {}^{90}_{38}Sr \longrightarrow {}^{86}_{36}Rn + {}^{4}_{2}He$

Chemical change equation: $\quad 2KClO_3(s) \longrightarrow 2KCl(s) + 3O_2(g)$

Physical change equation: $\quad CO_2(s) \longrightarrow CO_2(g)$

Nuclear Stability

Most nuclei are stable (do not undergo spontaneous decay) in their natural state. A few of the elements have no stable nuclei at all. *The ratio of neutrons to protons* in the nucleus determines stability of a nucleus.

. Nuclei of elements with equal amounts of neutrons and protons (ratio of 1 : 1) are generally stable and will not undergo radioactive decay

. All radioactive nuclei have more neutron than proton

. *All nuclei of elements with atomic number 83 and above* are unstable because of their high neutron to proton ratios. As a result, all elements with atomic number higher than 82 are naturally radioactive.

For example, Francium (#87) has no stable isotopes.

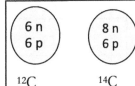

6 n
6 p

8 n
6 p

¹²C $\quad$ ¹⁴C

stable $\quad$ unstable

A carbon-14 nucleus contains two extra neutrons that make it unstable and radioactive.

Nuclear Chemistry Particles and Radiations

During nuclear transmutations and radioactivity, particles are absorbed and/or released by the nucleus. The change (or transmutation) depends on the type of particles absorbed and/or released.

Particles and radiations most commonly involved in nuclear changes are given below.

Alpha particles are similar to helium nuclei. They have mass of 4 and charge of +2.

Beta particles are produced when neutrons are converted to protons. A beta particle is similar to a high-speed electron. Beta particles have a mass of 0 and charge of -1.

Positrons are produced when protons are converted to neutrons. They have a mass of 0 and charge of +1.

Gamma rays (radiations) are similar to high energy x-rays. They have a mass of 0 and charge of 0.

Neutrons are found in the nucleus of atoms. They have a mass of 1 and charge of 0.

More information about nuclear particles is listed on the table below **and on Reference Table O.**

An **accelerator** is a device that moves charged particles to a high speed. Only charged particles (alpha, beta, and positron) can be accelerated.

Penetrating power refers to the strength of a particle to go through another object. See diagram below.

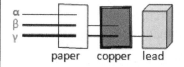

Summary Table of Common Nuclear Particles and Radiations

Nuclear Particle	Symbol	Mass	Charge	Penetrating power	Able to be accelerated
Alpha	$^{4}_{2}He$, α	4 amu	+2	Low (weakest)	Yes
Beta	$^{0}_{-1}e$, β^{-}	0 amu	-1	Medium	Yes
Positron	$^{0}_{+1}e$, β^{+}	0 amu	+1	Medium	Yes
Gamma	$^{0}_{0}\gamma$	0 amu	0	High (strongest)	No
Neutron	$^{1}_{0}n$	1 amu	0	------	No

Note: On Reference Table O, you can find name, notation, and symbol of each particle

Separation of Nuclear Particles

An **electric or magnetic field** can be used to separate particles and radiations that are released from a radioactive source during nuclear decay.

An electric field contains two charged plates; a positive and negative charged plate as shown below. Note the path of each radiation relative to the charged plates.

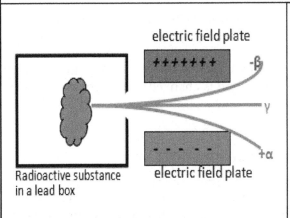

electric field plate

electric field plate

Radioactive substance in a lead box

As the particles are released

. **Negative (-)** particles will attract (are deflected) toward the positive plates (**+**) of the electric field.

. **Particles with no charge** will be unaffected (not deflected) by the electric field, and will go straight.

. **Positive (+)** particles will attract (are deflected) toward the negative plates (-) of the electric field.

Radioisotopes and Decay Modes

Decay mode refers to the type of radiation that a radioisotope will release as it decays. *Reference Table N* lists selected radioisotopes and their decay modes.

A **radioisotope** is any radioactive isotope of an element. A radioisotope can be described as one of the following depending on its decay mode:

An **alpha emitter** is a radioisotope that decays by releasing an alpha particle. Radioisotopes with atomic number 83 and above tend to be alpha emitters.

  Ex. Francium – 220 and uranium – 238 are alpha emitters.

A **beta emitter** is a radioisotope that decays by releasing a beta particle.

  Ex. Cobalt – 60 and strontium – 90 are beta emitters .

A **positron emitter** is a radioisotope that decays by releasing a positron.

  Ex. Iron – 53 and neon – 19 are positron emitters.

Radioisotopes of small atomic numbers tend to be beta and positron emitters.

Types of Transmutations

Transmutation is the changing (converting) of one atom to a different atom. Transmutation can be natural or artificial.

Natural transmutation occurs when a single unstable radioactive nucleus spontaneously changes by decaying (breaking down).

. Alpha decay, beta decay, and positron emission are all types of natural transmutation

Artificial transmutation occurs when a stable nonradioactive nucleus is hit (bombarded) with a high speed particle and is changed to an unstable nucleus.

Alpha Decay: a natural transmutation

Alpha decay occurs when a radioactive nucleus spontaneously breaks down to emit an alpha particle. The alpha decay equation below shows the decay of uranium-238, an alpha emitter.

$$\underset{92}{\overset{238}{}}U \longrightarrow \underset{2}{\overset{4}{}}He + \underset{90}{\overset{234}{}}Th$$

alpha emitter   alpha particle   new atom
(radioactive atom)   emitted

When a radioactive nucleus emits an alpha particle, atomic information such as atomic number and mass number of the new element can be compared to those of the radioactive atom. The comparison for the above equation is given on the table below.

	Radioactive atom $\underset{92}{\overset{238}{}}U$	New atom formed $\underset{90}{\overset{234}{}}Th$
Mass number	238	234 (decreases by 4)
Number of protons (atomic #)	92	90 (decreases by 2)
Number of neutrons (mass # - atomic #)	146	144 (decreases by 2)

Beta Decay: a natural transmutation

Beta decay occurs when a radioactive nucleus converts a neutron to a proton and an electron. The electron is then released from the nucleus. The beta decay equation below shows the decay of carbon-14, a beta emitter.

$$^{14}_{6}C \longrightarrow \, ^{0}_{-1}e \; + \; ^{14}_{7}N$$

beta emitter   beta particle   new atom
(radioactive atom)   emitted

When a radioactive nucleus emits a beta particle, atomic information such as atomic number and mass number of the new atom can be compared to those of the radioactive atom. The comparison for the above equation is given on the table below.

	Radioactive atom $^{14}_{6}C$	New atom formed $^{14}_{7}N$
Mass number	14	14 (stays the same)
Number of protons (atomic #)	6	7 (increases by 1)
Number of neutrons (mass # - atomic #)	8	7 (decreases by 1)

Positron Emission: a natural transmutation

A **positron emission** occurs when a radioactive nucleus converts a proton to a neutron and a positron. The positron is then released from the nucleus.

$$^{37}_{20}Ca \longrightarrow \, ^{0}_{+1}e \; + \; ^{37}_{19}K$$

positron emitter   positron emitted   new atom

When a radioactive nucleus emits a positron, atomic information such as atomic number and mass number of the new atom can be compared to those of the radioactive atom. The comparison for the above equation is given on the table below.

	Radioactive atom $^{37}_{20}Ca$	New atom formed $^{37}_{19}K$
Mass number	37	37 (stays the same)
Number of protons (atomic #)	20	19 (decreases by 1)
Number of neutrons (mass # - atomic #)	17	18 (increases by 1)

Artificial Transmutation

Artificial transmutation occurs when a stable nonradioactive nucleus is bombarded (hit) with a high speed particle and is changed (transmuted) into a different atom..

Example of artificial transmutation equation:

$$\underset{2}{^{4}}\text{He} \quad + \quad \underset{4}{^{9}}\text{Be} \quad \longrightarrow \quad \underset{6}{^{12}}\text{C} \quad + \quad \underset{0}{^{1}}\text{n}$$

| *accelerated high speed particle* | *stable and non-radioactive* | *unstable radioisotope* | *neutron released* |

The unstable radioisotope can decay through alpha, beta or positron emission.

Lesson 2: Nuclear Energy

During certain nuclear processes, it is known that the mass of the new atom (product) is slightly less than that of the reactants. The result of this is called the **mass defect.** The relationship between the missing mass and the tremendous amounts of energy produced from nuclear reactions is given by this well known equation:

$E = mc^2$ Where **E** is energy produced

m is the mass defect (missing mass)

c is the speed of light

According to the above equation, it can be concluded that during a nuclear reaction:

Energy is converted from mass (or mass is converted to energy).

Energy released is extremely high in comparison to that of ordinary chemical reactions.

Fission and **fusion** reactions are two types of nuclear reactions that can produce such high amounts of energy.

In this lesson, you will learn more about fission and fusion nuclear reactions.

Fission: a nuclear energy reaction

Fission is a nuclear reaction in which a large nucleus is split into smaller nuclei.

The diagram and the equation below are showing a nuclear fission reaction. In the reaction, a neutron hits a uranium nucleus, causing it to break into two smaller nuclei fragments. Three neutrons and a tremendous amount of energy and radiation are also produced.

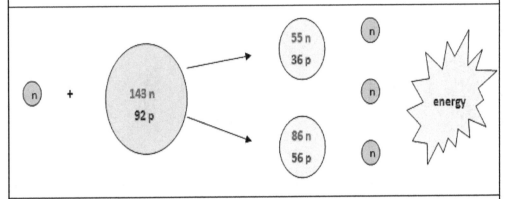

$$\underset{0}{^{1}}n \ + \ \underset{92}{^{235}}U \longrightarrow \ \underset{36}{^{91}}Kr \ + \ \underset{56}{^{142}}Ba \ + \ 3\underset{0}{^{1}}n$$

| slow-moving neutron | large fissionable (splittable) nucleus | Two smaller nuclei fragments | neutrons released | energy and radiation |

The outline below summarizes key points about fission reactions.

· A large fissionable (splittable) nucleus absorbs slow moving neutrons
   The large nucleus is split into smaller fragments, with release of more neutrons.

· Tons of nuclear energy is released. Energy is converted from mass
   Energy released is less than that of fusion reactions.

· In nuclear power plants, the fission process is well controlled.
   Energy produced is used to produce electricity

· In nuclear bombs, the fission process is uncontrolled
   Energy and radiations released are used to cause destruction

· Nuclear waste is also produced
   Nuclear wastes are dangerous and pose serious health and environmental problems.

   Nuclear wastes must be stored and disposed of properly.

Fusion: a nuclear energy reaction

Fusion is a nuclear reaction in which small nuclei are joined (fused) to create a larger nucleus. Only small atoms like those of hydrogen and helium can be fused (joined) in a nuclear fusion reaction.

The diagram and equation below are showing a nuclear fusion reaction. In the reaction, two small hydrogen nuclei join (fuse) to produce a larger helium nucleus. A tremendous amount of energy is also produced.

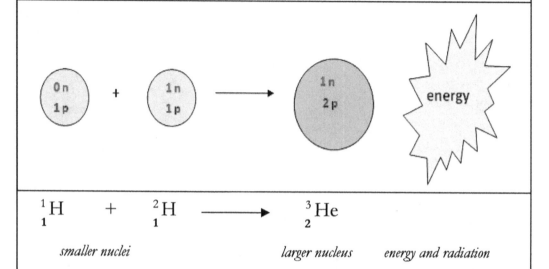

$$^{1}_{1}\text{H} \quad + \quad ^{2}_{1}\text{H} \quad \longrightarrow \quad ^{3}_{2}\text{He}$$

smaller nuclei   *larger nucleus*   *energy and radiation*

The outline below summarizes key points about fusion reactions.

· Two small nuclei are brought together under extremely high temperature and pressure.
　　The two nuclei are fused (joined) to create a slightly larger nucleus.

· Tons of nuclear energy is released. Energy is converted from mass
　　Energy released is much greater than that of fission reaction.

· Fusion produces no nuclear waste, unlike fission.

· Energy from the sun is due to fusion reactions that occur in the core of the sun.

· High temperature and high pressure are required for a fusion reaction to occur.
　　High temperature and pressure are necessary to overcome the repelling force of the two positive nuclei that are to be fused.

　　Recall that the nucleus is positively charged. In fusion, two positive nuclei must be brought (joined) together. Opposites attract, *but* similar charges repel. Therefore, extremely high temperature and pressure are needed to make two positively charged nuclei join together in a fusion reaction.

Nuclear Equations: Summary Table

Below is a summary of the five types of nuclear processes discussed in the last few pages.

Use this table for quick studying and for comparing the five nuclear reactions.

Nuclear process and equation	Mass number *after decay*	Protons (atomic number) *after decay*	Neutrons *after decay*
Alpha decay (natural transmutation) $^{226}_{88}\text{Ra} \rightarrow \ ^{222}_{86}\text{Rn} + \ ^{4}_{2}\text{He}$	$\downarrow 4$	$\downarrow 2$	$\downarrow 2$
Beta decay (natural transmutation) $^{14}_{6}\text{C} \rightarrow \ ^{14}_{7}\text{N} + \ ^{0}_{-1}\text{e}$	same	$\uparrow 1$	$\downarrow 1$
Positron emission (natural transmutation) $^{226}_{88}\text{Ra} \rightarrow \ ^{226}_{87}\text{Fr} + \ ^{0}_{+1}\text{e}$	same	$\downarrow 1$	$\uparrow 1$
Artificial Transmutation $^{40}_{18}\text{Ar} + \ ^{1}_{1}\text{H} \rightarrow \ ^{40}_{19}\text{K} + \ ^{1}_{0}\text{n}$	Bombarding nucleus with high speed particles		
Fission (nuclear energy) $^{235}_{92}\text{U} + \ ^{1}_{0}\text{n} \rightarrow \ ^{142}_{56}\text{Ba} + \ ^{91}_{36}\text{Kr} + \ 3^{1}_{0}\text{n}$	Nucleus splits into smaller nuclei. Mass is converted to energy. More energy then chemical reaction *Problems:* Produces dangerous radioactive wastes.		
Fusion (nuclear energy) $^{2}_{1}\text{H} + \ ^{2}_{1}\text{H} \rightarrow \ ^{4}_{2}\text{He} + \text{energy}$	Nuclei join to make a larger nucleus. Mass is converted to energy. Energy is more than that of fission. Produces no radioactive waste. *Problems:* High energy and High pressure to overcome repelling nuclei		

Balanced Nuclear Equations

A nuclear equation is balanced when the **top #s (mass #s) and bottom #s (charges)** are equal on both sides of the equation.	$$_{86}^{222}\text{Rn} \rightarrow {}_{2}^{4}\text{He} + {}_{84}^{218}\text{Po}$$
On the right is an incomplete equation in which X represents an unknown particle that must be determined.	$$X + {}_{-1}^{0}e \rightarrow {}_{17}^{37}\text{Cl}$$
X can be determined by using a little math.	Top # for X must be **37** Bottom # for X must be **18** **Note:** bottom # is atomic #. Use **Periodic Table** to locate element's symbol for # **18.** X is $_{18}^{37}\text{Ar}$

Writing balanced nuclear equations

Below are steps for writing balanced nuclear equations for two radioisotopes from Table N.

Note: This is generally done by piecing together information from Reference Tables N, O, and the Periodic Table.

Study the steps below to learn how to do the same for any radioisotope whose decay mode is known.

Write nuclear equations for the decay of plutonium-239 and iodine-131.

Step 1: Write	*Step 2: Write*	*Step 3 : Determine missing*
Nuclide symbol	→ Decay mode symbol	+ Top #, bottom #, and atom's symbol
(Use Table N)	(Use Table N and O)	(numbers must make for a balanced equation)

$$_{94}^{239}\text{Pu} \rightarrow {}_{2}^{4}\text{He} + {}_{92}^{235}\text{U}$$

$$_{53}^{131}\text{I} \rightarrow {}_{-1}^{0}e + {}_{54}^{131}\text{Xe}$$

Lesson 3: Half-life

Introduction

Half-life is the length of time it takes for a radioactive substance to decay to half its original mass. During a radioactive decay, the radioisotope is converted to a different substance. Over time, less and less of the radioactive substance remains, while more of the new substance is formed. At a certain time in the decay process, exactly half of the original mass (or atoms) of the radioactive substance will remain unchanged. The time (seconds, minutes, hours, or years) it takes the substance to decay to half its original mass is the half-life of the substance.

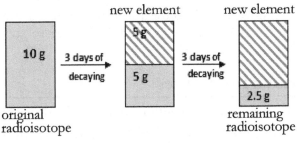

This diagram shows a 10-gram sample of a radioisotope decaying to 5 grams after 3 days, and to 2.5 grams in another 3 days.

. The half-life of the radioisotope is 3 days.

. The number of half-life periods (how many times it halved) is 2.

. Decaying of a radioisotope is at a constant rate, therefore, half-life of a radioisotope is constant

. Temperature, pressure, and amount do not change the half-life of a radioisotope

. The total length of time is 6 days.

Table N
Selected Radioisotopes

Nuclide	Half-Life	Decay Mode	Nuclide Name
^{198}Au	2.69 d	β^-	gold-198
^{14}C	5730 y	β^-	carbon-14
^{37}Ca	175 ms	β^+	calcium-37
^{60}Co	5.26 y	β^-	cobalt-60
^{137}Cs	30.23 y	β^-	cesium-137
^{53}Fe	8.51 min	β^+	iron-53
^{220}Fr	27.5 s	α	francium-220
^{3}H	12.26 y	β^-	hydrogen-3
^{131}I	8.07 d	β^-	iodine-131
^{37}K	1.23 s	β^+	potassium-37
^{42}K	12.4 h	β^-	potassium-42
^{85}Kr	10.76 y	β^-	krypton-85
^{16}N	7.2 s	β^-	nitrogen-16
^{19}Ne	17.2 s	β^+	neon-19
^{32}P	14.3 d	β^-	phosphorus-32
^{239}Pu	2.44×10^4 y	α	plutonium-239
^{226}Ra	1600 y	α	radium-226
^{222}Rn	3.82 d	α	radon-222
^{90}Sr	28.1 y	β^-	strontium-90
^{99}Tc	2.13×10^5 y	β^-	technetium-99
^{232}Th	1.4×10^{10} y	α	thorium-232
^{233}U	1.62×10^5 y	α	uranium-233
^{235}U	7.1×10^8 y	α	uranium-235
^{238}U	4.51×10^9 y	α	uranium-238

ms = milliseconds; s = seconds; min = minutes;
h = hours; d = days; y = years

Reference Table N lists selected radioisotopes and their half-life and decay mode.

When comparing the decay process of radioisotopes, keep the following in mind:

Decays to greatest extent
- Shortest half-life

Decays to least extent
- Longest half-life

Smallest remaining % :
- Shortest half-life
- Smallest mass

Greatest remaining % :
- Longest half-life
- Greatest mass

Number of Half-life Periods

Solving half-life problems quickly, easily and correctly depends on your understanding of the half-life concept. Most half-life problems can be solved with little or no set up if you have a clear understanding of the concept. When solving any half-life problem, the one key piece of information that must be known is the number of half-life periods.

Half-life period is the number of times a radioactive sample decays in half.

Below, you are shown how to determine the number of half-life periods if it is not given in a question. In the next few pages, you are shown how to solve other half-life related problems. As you study these problems, note that the number of half-life periods (given or determined) is needed in order to solve each problem.

Number of half-life periods from times

When the half-life (**T**) of a radioisotope and the length of time (**t**) of a decay are known, the number of half-life periods (**n**) can be calculated using the equation below.

$$n = \frac{t}{T}$$

Example 1:
The radioisotope C-14 (half-life of 5715 years) decays for 22860 years. What is the number of half-life periods?

$$n = \frac{22860}{5715} = \boxed{\textbf{4 half-life periods}}$$

Number of half-life periods from masses

If the original mass (**OM**) and remaining mass (**RM**) of a decaying radisotope are known, the number of half-life periods (**n**) can be determined using one of several methods. One of these methods is shown below.

From original mass to remaining mass:

Halve (divide by 2) the original mass as many times as needed to get to the remaining mass.

From remaining mass to original mass:

Reverse the above process by doubling (multiply by 2) the remaining mass as many times as needed to get to the original mass.

Example 2

In how many half-life periods would a 60g sample of a radioisotope decay to 7.5g?

$$\underset{\textbf{OM}}{\textbf{60}} \;\rightarrow\; 30 \;\rightarrow\; 15 \;\rightarrow\; \underset{\textbf{RM}}{\textbf{7.5g}}$$

3 arrows = $\boxed{\textbf{3 half-life periods (n).}}$

Note: Equations for solving half-life problems are not given on the reference tables.

Length of Time

Length of time (t) of a decaying process is the total time it takes for a radioisotope sample to decay from one mass to another.

From half-life (T) and number of half-life periods (n), length of time (t) can be calculated with equation below.

t = T x n	***Example 3:*** *What is the total number of years it takes for a sample of C-14 (half-life of 5715 years) to undergo 6 half-life periods ?* t = 5715 x 6 = **34,290 yrs**

From masses, length of time can be calculated in two steps as shown:
 	
1st: Find **n** from OM and RM as shown on the last page.
 	
2nd: Calculate t using above equation.
	Example 4; *How long will it take for a sample of C-14 to decay from 12 g to 3 g?*
	
	Find n: 12 g → 6 → 3 g
	     n = 2 (2 arrows)
	
	Find **t** = T x n
	     t = 5715 x 2 = **11,430 yrs**

Half-life

Half-life (T) of a radioisotope can be determined if it is not listed on Table N.

From length of time (t) and number of half-life periods (n)

$T = \dfrac{t}{n}$	***Example 5:*** *Radioisotope X takes 60 years to undergo 4 half-life periods. What is the half-life of X?* $T = \dfrac{60}{4} = $ **15 yrs**

From masses, half-life (T) of time can be calculated in two steps as shown:
  1st : Find **n** from masses as shown on last page.
  2nd : Calculate T using above equation

Original mass and Remaining mass

When the number of half-life periods (n) of a decaying process is known (given or calculated), the original or the remaining masses can be determined.

To determine original mass: *Double* remaining mass as many times as **n**.

To determine remaining mass: *Halve* original mass as many times as **n**.

Fraction Remaining

Fraction remaining expresses the remaining mass of a radioisotope in terms of ratio.

From number of half-life periods (n), fraction remaining can be calculated using the equation below:

Fraction Remaining $= \dfrac{1}{2^n}$	**Example 6:** *What fraction of a sample of C-14 remains unchanged after 3 half-life periods?* Fraction $= \dfrac{1}{2^3} = \dfrac{1}{2 \times 2 \times 2} = \boxed{\dfrac{1}{8}}$

From half-life (T) and length of time (t), use Reference Table T equation below to calculate fraction remaining.

Fraction Remaining $= \dfrac{1}{(2)^{t/T}}$ $t/T = n$	**Example 7:** *What fraction of iodine-131 (half-life of 8.021 days) will remain unchanged after 32 days ?* Fraction $= \dfrac{1}{(2)^{32/8.021}} = \dfrac{1}{2^4} = \boxed{\dfrac{1}{16}}$

Half-life Data and Graphs

The decaying process of a radioisotope can be represented on a data table and graph. Examples of such representations are given below.

Time (days)	Mass of radioisotope sample remaining (g)
0	160
4	120
8	80 (half original mass)
12	60
16	40
20	30
24	20
28	15
32	10

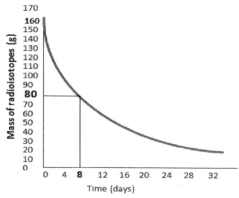

The half-life of the radioisotope is 8 days.
This is the number of days half (80 g) of the original (160 g) is unchanged.

The radioisotope is likely iodine-131.
According to Reference Table N, the half-life of I-131 is 8.021 days

Common uses (benefits) of selected radioisotope tracers

Some radioisotopes listed on Reference Table N have common uses in areas such as medicine, research, and geological (rocks) and archeological (fossil) dating.

A **tracer** is a radioisotope that is used to follow the path of a chemical reaction.

Radioisotope tracers in medical treatments and diagnoses must have short half-lives and be quickly eliminated from the body.

Radioisotopes for dating usually have very long half-lives.

The Table below gives a list of radioisotopes and their common applications.

Radioisotope name	Radioisotope symbol	Common application (benefits)	Field of application
Iodine-131	^{131}I	Thyroid disorder diagnosis and treatments	Medical
Technetium-99	^{99}Tc	Cancer tumor diagnosis	Medical
Cobalt-60	^{60}Co	Cancer treatments	Medical
Iron-56	^{56}Fe	Blood disorder treatments	Medical
Carbon-14 *(alone)*	^{14}C	Tracer for chemical reactions	Research
Carbon-14 *with* **Carbon-12**	^{14}C ^{12}C	Fossil dating	Archeological dating
Uranium – 238 *with* **Lead - 206**	^{238}U ^{206}Pb	Rock dating	Geological dating

Radioactive wastes and radiations (problems)

Radiations and wastes produced from nuclear reactors are very dangerous to life on earth. Prolonged and high dose exposures to radiation can cause serious health issues and sometimes death.

. *Radiation* from nuclear power plants must be well contained to protect humans and other living things.

. *Nuclear wastes* are equally dangerous because they are highly radioactive

. *Nuclear wastes* have to be stored in safe areas to protect the public from being exposed to them.

Solid Wastes (Highly radioactive): Sr-90   Cs-137

Gaseous Wastes: Rn-222   Kr-85   N-16

Practice Questions

Lesson 1: Nuclear transmutations

Define the following terms and answer multiple choice questions below.
1. Transmutation   2. Natural transmutation   3. Artificial transmutation
4. Alpha particle   5. Beta particle   6. Positron   7. Gamma ray
8. Accelerator   9. Alpha decay   10. Beta decay   11. Positron emission

12. Which process converts an atom from one element to another when the
     nucleus of an atom is bombarded with high-energy particles?
     1) Artificial transmutation   3)) Natural transmutation
     2) Addition polymerization   4) Condensation polymerization

13. Spontaneous decay of certain elements in nature occurs because these elements
     have
     1) Disproportionate ratios of electrons to protons
     2) Disproportionate ratios of neutrons to protons
     3) High reactivity with oxygen
     4) Low reactivity with oxygen

14. An electron has a charge identical to that of
     1) A positron   2) A beta particle 3) An alpha particle   4) A proton

15. Which list is showing the particles arranged in order of increasing penetrating
     power?
     1) Gamma → Beta → Alpha   3) Alpha → Beta → Gamma
     2) Beta → Gamma → Alpha   4) Gamma →   Alpha → Beta

16. Which nuclear emission moving through an electric field would be attracted
     toward a positive electrode?
     1) Proton   2) Gamma radiation   3) Beta Particle   4) Alpha particle

17. When an alpha particle is emitted by an atom, the atomic number of the atom
     1) Increases by 2   3) Increases by 4
     2) Decreases by 2   4) Decreases by 4

18. As a radioactive isotope emits a positron, the atomic number of the atom
     1) Decreases   2) Increases   3) Remains the same

19. Which nuclear radiation is similar to high energy X-rays?
     1) Beta   2) Alpha   3) Gamma   4) Neutron

20. Alpha particles and beta particles differ in
     1) Mass only   3) Both mass and charge
     2) Charge only   4) Neither mass and charge

21. In which list can all particles be accelerated by an electric field?
     1) Alpha, beta, and neutrons   3) Alpha, protons, and neutrons
     2) Alpha, beta, and protons   4) Beta, protons, and neutrons

22. Which notation of a radioisotope is correctly paired with the notation of its emission particle?

   1) $^{37}_{19}K$ and $^{0}_{-1}e$

   2) $^{16}_{7}N$ and $^{1}_{1}p$

   3) $^{222}_{86}Rn$ and $^{4}_{2}He$

   4) $^{99}_{43}Tc$ and $^{0}_{+1}e$

23 According to Reference Table N, the radioactive decay of which isotope will emit a particle with a charge of a +1?

   1) Phosphorus-32   2) Cobalt-60   3) Thorium-232   4) Iron-53

24. A nuclear change resulting in a release of an alpha particle is shown in which equation?

   1) $^{252}_{98}Cf \rightarrow ^{248}_{96}Cm + ^{4}_{2}He$

   2) $^{19}_{10}Ne \rightarrow ^{19}_{11}Na + ^{0}_{-1}e$

   3) $^{220}_{87}Fr + ^{4}_{2}He \rightarrow ^{224}_{89}Ac$

   4) $^{228}_{89}Ac \rightarrow ^{228}_{88}Ra + ^{1}_{1}p$

25. Artificial transmutation is represented by which nuclear equation?

   1) $^{238}_{92}U + ^{4}_{2}He \rightarrow ^{241}_{94}Pu + ^{1}_{0}n$

   2) $^{235}_{92}U + ^{1}_{0}n \rightarrow ^{87}_{35}Br + ^{146}_{57}La + 3 ^{1}_{0}n$

   3) $^{210}_{84}Po + \rightarrow ^{206}_{82}Pb + ^{4}_{2}He$

   4) $^{2}_{1}H + ^{1}_{1}H \rightarrow ^{3}_{2}He$

26. Which transmutation resulted in the emission of a beta particle?

   1) $^{210}_{84}Po \rightarrow ^{206}_{82}Pb + X$

   2) $^{206}_{81}Ti \rightarrow ^{206}_{82}Pb + X$

   3) $^{53}_{26}Fe \rightarrow ^{53}_{25}Mn + X$

   4) $^{32}_{16}S + ^{1}_{0}n \rightarrow ^{32}_{15}P + X$

27. Given the nuclear reaction

$$^{60}_{27}Co \rightarrow ^{0}_{-1}e + ^{60}_{28}Ni$$

   The reaction is an example of
   1) Fission
   2) Natural transmutation
   3) Fusion
   4) Artificial transmutation

28. Given the nuclear equation below

$$^{121}_{53}I \rightarrow X + ^{121}_{52}Te$$

   The reaction is best described as
   1) Beta decay
   2) Artificial transmutation
   3) Positron emission
   4) Alpha decay

29. In the nuclear equation:

$$^{234}_{91}Pa \rightarrow X + ^{0}_{-1}e$$

   Which particle is represented by the X ?

   1) $^{234}_{92}U$ 2) $^{234}_{93}Np$ 3) $^{235}_{92}U$ 4) $^{235}_{93}Np$

Lesson 2: Nuclear Energy

Answer the following multiple choice questions.

30. Which best describes what occurs in a fusion reaction?
    1) Light nuclei join to form heavier nuclei   3) Energy is converted to mass
    2) Heavy nuclei split into lighter nuclei   4) Electrons are converted to energy

31. The amount of energy released from a fission reaction is much greater than the energy from a chemical reaction because in a fission reaction
    1) Energy is converted to mass   3) Mass is converted to energy
    2) Ionic bonds are broken   4) Covalent bonds are broken

32. Which conditions are required for a fusion reaction to take place?
    1) Low pressure and low temperature
    2) Low pressure and high temperature
    3) High pressure and low temperature
    4) High pressure and high temperature

33. Which statement explains why fusion reactions are difficult to start?
    1) Positive nuclei attract each other   3) Negative nuclei attract each other
    2) Positive nuclei repel each other   4) Negative nuclei repel each other

34. A nuclear fission reaction and a nuclear fusion reaction are similar because both reactions
    1) Form heavy nuclides from light nuclides
    2) Release a large amount of energy
    3) Form light nuclides from heavy nuclides
    4) Absorb a large amount of energy

35. One benefit of nuclear fission is
    1) Nuclear reaction meltdowns   3) Biological exposure
    2) Storage of waste materials   4) Production of energy

36. Which equation represents nuclear fusion?
    1) $^2_1H + {}^3_1H \rightarrow {}^4_2He + {}^1_0n$

    2) $^{226}_{88}Ra \rightarrow {}^{222}_{84}Rn + {}^4_2He$

    3) $^{238}_{92}U + {}^1_0n \rightarrow {}^{239}_{93}Np + {}^{0}_{-1}e$

    4) $^7_3Li + {}^1_1p \rightarrow {}^8_4Be$

37. Fission is represented by which nuclear equation?
    1) $^{238}_{92}U + {}^4_2He \rightarrow {}^{241}_{94}Pu + {}^1_0n$

    2) $^{235}_{92}U + {}^1_0n \rightarrow {}^{87}_{35}Br + {}^{146}_{57}La + 3{}^1_0n$

    3) $^{14}_7N + {}^1_0n \rightarrow {}^{14}_6C + {}^1_1H$

    4) $^2_1H + {}^2_1H \rightarrow {}^3_2He + {}^1_0n$

Lesson 3: Half-life

Answer the following multiple choice questions.

38. As the temperature of a radioisotope increases, its half-life
    1) Increases   2) Decreases   3) Remains the same

39. The course of a chemical reaction can be traced by using a
    1) Polar molecule   3) Stable isotope
    2) Diatomic molecule   4) Radioisotope

40. A radioisotope is called a tracer when it is used to
    1) Determine the age of animal skeletal remains
    2) Kill cancerous tissue
    3) Determine the course of a chemical reaction
    4) Kill bacteria in food

41. Which procedure is based on the half-life of a radioisotope?
    1) Accelerating to increase kinetic energy
    2) Dating to determine age
    3) Counting to determine a level of radioactivity
    4) Radiating to kill cancer cells

42. Diagnostic injections of radioisotopes used in medicine normally have
    1) Short half-lives and are quickly eliminated from the body
    2) Short half-lives and are slowly eliminated from the body
    3) Long half-lives and are quickly eliminated from the body
    4) Long half-lives and are slowly eliminated from the body

43. What is the half life of potassium – 42?
    1) 1.23 s   2) 12.36 h   3) 14.28 days   4) 27.4 s

44. Which radioisotope has a half-life that is more than 1 minute?
    1) K – 37   2) K – 42   3) Ca – 37   4) Ne - 19

45. Compared to uranium – 238, uranium – 235 has a
    1) Shorter half-life and the same decay mode
    2) Shorter half-life and a different decay mode
    3) Longer half-life and the same decay mode
    4) Longer half-life and a different decay mode

46. The half life of radioisotope X is 30 days. In how many days will X undergo 3 half –life periods?
    1) 3 days   2) 90 days   3) 10 days   4) 33 days?

47. How many days are required for a 200 gram sample of Radon-222 to decay to 50.0 grams?
    1) 1.912   2) 3.823   3) 7.646   4) 11.464

48. Which set up is correct for calculating the total length of time it takes for a 50 g sample of iodine-131 to decay to 3.125 g?
    1) 8 x 3.125   2) 8 ÷ 3.125   3) 8 x 4   4) 8 ÷ 4

49. What is the half-life of a radioisotope that undergoes 2 half-life periods in 180 ms?
    1) 90 ms   2) 360 ms   3) 2 ms   4) 180 ms

50. What is the half-life of ^{25}Na if 1.00 grams of a 16.00 gram sample of ^{25}Na remains unchanged after 237 seconds?
    1) 47.4 s   2) 59.3 s   3) 79.0 s   4) 118 s

51. What amount of a 48 g sample of K-37 will remain after 5 half-life periods?
    1) 1.5 g   2) 3.0 g   3) 5.1 g   4) 6.0 g

52. How much of a 32 g sample of ^{60}Co will remain unchanged after 21.08 years?
    1) 1.0 g   2) 2.0 g   3) 4.0 g   4) 8.0 g

53. If 10.0 g of P-32 sample remains after 3 half-life periods, what was the original mass of the sample?
    1) 80.0 g   2) 30.0 g   3) 20.0 g   4) 3.33 g

54. A sample of ^{99}Tc decays to 0.5 grams in 1.49 x 10^6 years. What was the mass of the original sample?
    1) 32 g   2) 8 g   3) 128 g   4) 64 g

55. What fraction of the radioactive waste Strontium-90 will remain unchanged after 5 half-life periods of decaying?
    1) $^1/_{32}$ 2) $^1/_{16}$ 3) $^1/_8$ 4) $^1/_5$

56. Approximately what fraction of ^{99}Tc will remain unchanged after 8.52 x 10^5 years?
    1) $^1/_2$ 2) $^1/_8$ 3) $^1/_{16}$ 4) $^1/_4$

57. A sample of radioisotope Cr-51 decays to $^1/_8$th its original mass in 84 days. What is the half-life of Cr-51?
    1) 14 days   2) 28 days   3) 56 days   4) 84 days

58. Which radioisotope will decay the most over a period of 100 days?
    1) ^{32}P   2) ^{131}I   3) ^{198}Au   4) ^{222}Rn

59. A sample of which radioisotope will decay the least over a period of 100 years?
    1) 5 g of Co-60   2) 5 g of H-3   3) 5 g of Kr-85   4) 5 g of Sr-90

60. Which radioisotope is used in diagnoses of thyroid disorders?
    1) N-14   2) C-12   3) I-131   4) Fe-56

61. Geological dating can be done by comparing mineral remains of which two isotopes?
    1) U-238 and U-235   3) U-238 and Pb-206
    2) U-238 and Co-60   4) C-14 and Pb-206

62. Which radioisotope is used as a tracer to follow the course of a chemical reaction?
    1) Fe-53   2) U-238   3) C-12   4) C-14

Topic Mastery / Constructed Response

Using information provided on Reference Table N, write a balanced decay equation for these two radioisotopes.

63. Uranium-233   64. Krypton-85

65. Write a balanced nuclear equation for:
    Alpha absorption by ^{14}N with neutron emission

66. Write a balanced nuclear equation for:
    Neutron absorption by ^{209}Bi with alpha emission

67. Explain why it is more difficult to cause an artificial transmutation with an alpha particle than with a neutron.

Base your answers to questions 68 through 69 on the information below, the Reference Tables for Chemistry, and your knowledge of chemistry.

Radioactivity and radioactive isotopes have the potential for both benefiting and harming living organisms. One use of radioactive isotopes is in radiation therapy as a treatment for cancer. Cesium-137 is sometimes used in radiation therapy. A sample of cesium-137 was left in an abandoned clinic in Brazil in 1987. Cesium-137 gives off a blue glow because of its radioactivity. The people who discovered the sample were attracted by the blue glow and had no idea of any danger. Hundreds of people were treated for overexposure to radiation, and four people died.

68. Suppose a 40-gram sample of iodine-131 and a 40-gram sample of cesium-137 were both abandoned at the clinic in 1987. Explain why the sample of iodine-131 would not pose as great a radiation risk to people as the sample of cesium-137 would.

69. If 12.5 grams of the original sample of cesium-137 remained after 90.6 years, what was the mass of the original sample?

A U-238 atom decays to a Pb-206 atom through a series of steps. Each point on the graph below represents a nuclide and each arrow represents a nuclear decay mode.

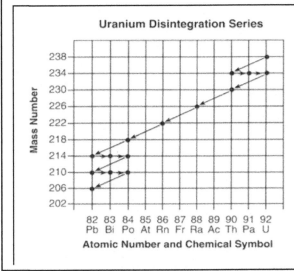

Uranium Disintegration Series

70. Explain why the U-238 disintegration series ends with the nuclide Pb-206.

71. Based on this graph, what particle is emitted during the nuclear decay of a Po-218 atom?

72. Based on this graph, what is the mass of the particle emitted during the nuclear decay of Bi-214?

Lab Safety

During lab experiments, appropriate safety procedures must be observed.

Some important safety guidelines that must be followed are:

- Wear protective goggles at all times.
- No eating or drinking in the lab, or out of lab equipment.
- No running in the lab.
- Tie back long hair.
- Roll up long sleeves.
- Know locations of lab safety equipment.
- When lighting a Bunsen burner, strike a match first, then turn on the gas.
- When diluting an acid, pour the acid slowly into water while stirring. Never add water to acid.
- Always follow the instructions of your teacher.

Laboratory Equipments

	Beaker	Measuring volume of a liquid.
	Test Tube	Placing a substance for observation or to conduct experiment.
	Evaporating dish	Heating a substance.
	Crucible	Heating a substance.
	Evaporated dish	Drying a wet solid. Covering up glassware while heating.
	Tongs	Holding an object over heat, or removing a heated glassware from heat.
	Buret	Dispensing an exact volume of a liquid. Often used in titration experiment.
	Erlenmeyer flask	Measuring volume of a liquid.
hottest part of a flame	**Bunsen burner**	A heat source for laboratory experiments. Requires propane gas.

Significant Figures

Significant figures in a number include all digits that are known for certain plus one estimated digit.

Rules for determining number of significant figures

Significant figures in a number can be determined using Atlantic – Pacific rule.	**405** has **3** significant figures
If a decimal is <u>A</u>bsent in a number (whole number) · Start counting with the first nonzero from <u>At</u>lantic (right) side of the number	**4050** has **3** significant figures
· Count toward the Pacific (left)	**200** has **1** significant figure
· Stop counting with the last non zero digit.	
How many you counted is the number of significant figures in that number.	**02** has **1** significant figure
If a decimal is <u>P</u>resent in a number (decimal fraction) · Start counting with the first nonzero from <u>Pa</u>cific (left) side of the number	0.00**36** has **2** significant figures
· Count toward the Atlantic (right), and count all numbers (including zeros) once you have started counting	0.0**936** has **3** significant figures
How many you counted is the number of significant figures in that number.	0.0**9360** has **4** significant figures
	200. has 3 significant figures
In Summary: *All zeros to start a number* are never counted as significant.	**0.013** has 2 significant figures
All zeros between two real numbers are always counted as significant.	**1040** has 3 significant figures
Zeros at the end of a number are significant only if the number contains a decimal point.	**1.040** has 4 significant figures

Significant Figure in Calculations

When Multiplying or Dividing

Limit or round answer so it has the same number of significant figures as the factor with the **least number** of significant figures.

Example 1

How much heat is absorbed by a 17 gram sample of ice to melt? Answer must have the correct number of significant figures.

Heat = mass x H_f

Heat = 17 x 334

Heat = 5678 J

Heat = 5700 J

17 is the factor with the least number of significant figures: 2

5678 (calculator result) has 4 significant figures. It MUST be rounded and limited to 2 significant figures.

5700 (answer) is rounded and limited to 2 significant figures.

Example 2

What is the density of an unknown substance if a 42.6 cm³ sample has a mass of 22.43 g?

$$Density = \frac{mass}{volume}$$

$$Density = \frac{22.43 \text{ g}}{42.6 \text{ cm}^3} = 0.527 \frac{g}{cm^3}$$

42.6 is the factor with the least number of significant figures: 3

0.527 (answer) also has 3 significant figures

When Adding or Subtracting

Limit or round answer so it has the same number of decimal places as the factor with the **least number of decimal places** (numbers after the decimal point).

Example 3

What is the sum of 0.31, 1.310 and 1.3205 to the correct number of significant figures?

0.31 + 1.310 + 1.3205 = 2.9405 = **2.94**

0.31 is the factor with the least number of decimal places: **2**

2.**9405** (calculator result) has **4** decimal places. It must be rounded and limited to 2 decimal places.

2.**94** (answer) has **2** decimal places.

Reading Measuring Equipment

- All laboratory measurements should include a value and unit.
- Measurements should be given to the right significant figures.
- A measurement has the correct number of significant figures when it includes all digits known with certainty, and one estimated digit determined between two of the smallest unit markings on the measuring equipment.

Mass Measurement

Triple-Beam Balance	An equipment for measuring mass of a substance.
Grams(g)	A unit of measurement for mass.

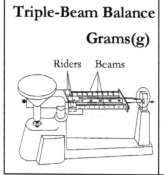

Riders   Beams

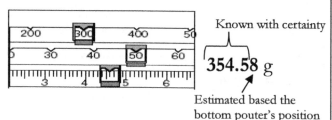

Known with certainty

354.58 g

Estimated based the bottom pouter's position

Volume Measurement

Graduated Cylinder	An equipment for measuring volume of a liquid.
Milliliters (mL)	A unit of measurement for volume.
Meniscus	The curve surface of a liquid in a graduated cylinder. • Accurate volume of a liquid should be read at eye level with the bottom of the meniscus.

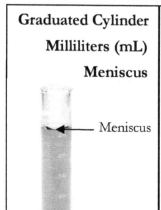

— Meniscus

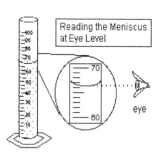

Reading the Meniscus at Eye Level

eye

Known with certainty

66.1°C

Estimated based on the bottom of the meniscus level.

Temperature Measurement

Thermometer	An equipment for measuring temperature.
Celsius	A unit of measurement for temperature.. • Accurate reading should be at eye level with the top of the red liquid inside the thermometer.

Known with certainty

44.7°C

Estimated based on the level being between the two smallest markings.

Accuracy, Precision, and Uncertainty in Measurements

Accuracy describes the closeness of a measured value to a known or true measurement.

Precision describes the closeness of several measurements of the same substance or material.

For an example: If the temperature of a sample of water is known to be 42.3°C. Accurate and precise measurements of the same water sample are given below:

Accurate temperature measurement: 42.4°C
Accurate and precise measurements: 42.4°C, 42.6°C, 42.2°C.

Inaccurate temperature measurement: 45.3°C
Inaccurate but precise measurements: 45.3°C, 45.4°C, 45.0°C

Inaccurate and imprecise measurements: 45.3°C, 49.8°C, 37.9°C

Uncertainty describes the best estimate of how far a measured quantity is from the true or known value. All measuring devices have allowable level of uncertainty.

• ± value (usually half the measuring unit) is used to represent the uncertainty of a measuring device.
• The smaller the ± of a measuring device, the higher its precision.

Example:
If the thermometer used in measuring the above water sample is scaled at 1.0°C interval:

• The estimated uncertainty of the thermometer will be ±0.5°C.
• The known temperature of the water can be recorded as 42.3 ±0.5°C.
• All temperature measurements that are 0.5°C lower or greater than 42.3°C can be claimed as accurate.

Percent Error

An expression of the difference between the experimental (measured) and actual (accepted) values of a measurement.

• Percent error should always be positive
• The smaller the percent error, the more accurate the measured value.
• Human errors and imprecision of the measuring equipment are common causes of high percent errors in lab experiments.

$$\% \text{ Error} = \frac{\text{Measured} - \text{Accepted}}{\text{Accepted}} \times 100$$

Example:
A student calculated the percent by mass of water in a hydrate sample as 16.2 %. What is the student's percent error if the actual percent of water is 14.7 %?

$$\% \text{ Error} = \frac{16.2 - 14.7}{14.7} \times 100$$

$$\% \text{ Error} = \frac{1.5}{14.7} \times 100 = \boxed{10\%}$$

Practice Questions

Answer the following multiple choice questions.

1. Which of the following statements in a student's laboratory report is an observation?
   1) Metal A will also react with an acid
   2) Metal A has luster
   3) Metal A is an alkali metal
   4) Metal A will conduct electricity

2. A student investigated the physical and chemical properties of a sample of an unknown gas and then identified the gas. Which statement represents a conclusion rather than an experimental observation?
   1) The gas is carbon dioxide
   2) The gas is colorless
   3) When the gas is bubbled into limewater, the liquid becomes cloudy
   4) When placed in the gas, a flaming splint stops burning

3. A student wishes to prepare approximately 100 mL of an aqueous solution of 6 M HCl using 12 M HCl. Which procedure is correct?
   1) Adding 50 mL of 12 M HCl to 50 mL of water while stirring the mixture steadily
   2) Adding 50 mL of 12 M HCl to 50 mL of water, and then stirring the mixture steadily
   3) Adding 50 mL of water to 50 mL of 12 M HCl while stirring the mixture steadily
   4) Adding 50 mL of water to 50 mL of 12 M HCl , and then stirring the mixture steadily

4. A student determined in the laboratory that the percent by mass of water in $CuSO_4 \cdot 5H_2O$ is 40.0%. If the accepted value is 36%, what is the percent error?
   1) 0.11 %   2) 1.1 %   3) 11 %   4) 4.0 %

5. A student found the boiling point of a liquid to be 80.4°C . If the liquid's actual boiling point is 80.6°C, the experimental percent error is equal to

   1) $\dfrac{80.6 - 80.4}{80.6} \times 100$

   2) $\dfrac{80.6 - 80.4}{80.4} \times 100$

   3) $\dfrac{80.5 - 80.4}{80.5} \times 100$

   4) $\dfrac{80.5 - 80.4}{80.4} \times 100$

6.

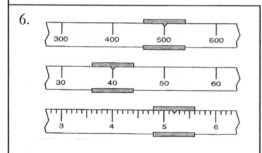

What is the total mass reading of the triple beam balance?

   1) 540.20 g   3) 540.52 g
   2) 545.20 g   4) 545.52 g

7.

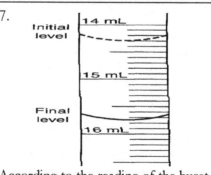

According to the reading of the buret, what is the total volume of the liquid used?

   1) 1.10 mL   3) 1.30 mL
   2) 1.40 mL   4) 1.45 mL

8. Which mass measurement contains four significant figures?
   1) 0.086 g   2) 0.431 g   3) 1003 g   4) 3870 g

9. Which measurement contains three significant figures?
   1) 0.03 g   2) 0.030 g   3) 0.035 g   4) 0.0351 g

10. Which volume measurement is expressed to two significant figures?
    1) 20 mL   2) 202 mL   3) 220 mL   4) 0.2 mL

11. Which measurement has the greatest number of significant figures?
    1) 44000 g   2) 404 g   3) 40.44 g   4) 0.40004 g

12. The mass of a solid is 3.60 g and its volume is 1.8 cm³. What is the density of
    the solid, expressed to the correct number of significant figures?
    1) 12 g/cm³   2) 2.0 g/cm³   3) 0.5 g/cm³   4) 0.50 g/cm³

13. Which quantity expresses the sum of 22.1 g + 375.66 g + 5400.132 g to
    the correct number of significant figures?
    1) 5800 g   2) 5798 g   3) 5797.9 g   4) 5797.892 g

14. The volume of a gas sample is 22 L at STP. The density of the gas is 1.35 g/ L.
    What is the mass of the gas sample, expressed to the correct number of
    significant figures?
    1) 30. g   2) 30.0 g   3) 16.7 g   4) 2.56 g

15. A student calculates the density of an unknown solid. The mass is 10.04 grams,
    and the volume is 8.21 cubic centimeters. How many significant figures should
    appear in the final answer?
    1) 1   2) 2   3) 3   4) 4

16. The density of a solid is 1.235 g/mL and its volume is 40.2 mL. A student
    calculating the mass of the solid should have how many significant figures in the
    final answer?
    1) 1   2) 2   3) 3   4) 4

17. Which set of laboratory equipment would most likely be used with a crucible?

    1)   2)   3)   4)

18. The two pieces of lab equipment shown below are

    1) Round bottom flask and a crucible   3) Evaporating dish and a beaker
    2) Round bottom flask and a watch glass 4) Evaporating dish and a watch glass

16 Days of Question Sets for
Regents and Final Exams Practice

The following section contains day-by-day practice question sets
for preparing for any end-of-the-year chemistry exam.

1. Which of these terms refers to matter that could be heterogeneous?
    1) Element   2) Mixture   3) Compound   4) Solution

2. One similarity between all mixtures and compounds is that both
    1) Are heterogeneous   3) Combine in definite ratios
    2) Are homogeneous   4) Consist of two or more substances

3. Which correctly describes particles of a substance in the gas phase?
    1) Particles are arranged in a regular geometric pattern and are far apart
    2) Particles are in a fixed rigid position and are close together
    3) Particles move freely in a straight path
    4) Particles move freely and are close together.

4. When a substance evaporates, it is changing from
    1) Liquid to gas   2) Gas to liquid   3) Solid to gas   4) Gas to solid

5. Energy that is stored in chemical substances is called
    1) Potential energy   3) Kinetic energy
    2) Activation energy   4) Ionization energy

6. The specific heat capacity of water is 4.18 J/ g·K Adding 4.18 Joules of heat to a 1-gram sample of water will cause the water to
    1) Change from solid to liquid   3) Change its temperature 1K
    2) Change from liquid to solid   4) Change its temperature 4.18 K

7. Real gases differ from ideal gases because the molecules of real gases have
    1) Some volume and no attraction for each other
    2) Some volume and some attraction for each other
    3) No volume and no attraction for each other
    4) No volume and some attraction for each other

8. Under which two conditions do real gases behave most like an ideal gas?
    1) High pressure and low temperature   3) High pressure and high temperature
    2) Low pressure and high temperature   4) Low pressure and low temperature

9. At constant pressure, the volume of a confined gas varies
    1) Directly with the Kelvin temperature   3) Directly with the mass of the gas
    2) Indirectly with the Kelvin temperature   4) Indirectly with the mass of the gas

10. Under which conditions would a volume of a given sample of a gas decrease?
    1) Decrease pressure and increase temperature
    2) Decrease pressure and decrease temperature
    3) Increase pressure and decrease temperature
    4) Increase pressure and increase temperature

11. Which statement describes a chemical property of iron?
    1) Iron can be flattened into sheets.
    2) Iron conducts electricity and heat.
    3) Iron combines with oxygen to form rust.
    4) Iron can be drawn into a wire.

12. Which sample at STP has the same number of molecules as 5 liters of $NO_2(g)$ at STP?
    1) 5 grams of $H_2(g)$ 3) 5 moles of $O_2(g)$
    2) 5 liters of $CH_4(g)$ 4) 5×10^{23} molecules of $CO_2(g)$

13. Which substance can be decomposed by a chemical change?
     1) Ammonia   2) Potassium   3) Aluminum   4) Helium

14. The graph below represents the relationship between temperature and time as heat
     is added at a constant rate to a substance, starting when the substance is a solid
     below its melting point

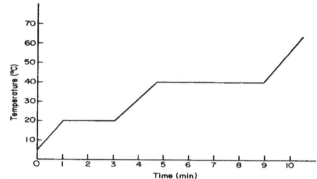

During which time period (in minutes) does the substance's average kinetic energy
remain the same?
     1) 0 − 1   2) 1 − 3   3) 3 - 5   4) 9 − 10

15. Molecules of which substance have the lowest average kinetic energy?
     1) NO(g) at 20°C   3) NO_2 at 35 K
     2) NO_2(g) at -30°C   4) N_2O_3 at 110 K

16. At STP, the difference between the boiling point and the freezing point of water in
     the Kelvin scale is
     1) 373   2) 273   3) 180   4) 100

17. How much heat is needed to change a 5.0 gram sample of water from 65°C to 75°C?
     1) 210 J   2) 14 J   3) 21 J   4) 43 J

18. A real gas will behave most like an ideal gas under which conditions of temperature
     and pressure?
     1) 0°C and 1 atm   2) 0°C and 2 atm 3) 273°C and 1 atm   4) 273°C and 2 atm

19. A 2.0 L sample of O_2(g) at STP had its volume changed to 1.5 L. If the temperature
     of the gas was held constant, what is the new pressure of the gas in kilopascals ?
     1) 3.0 kPa   2) 152 kPa   3) 101.3 kPa   4) 135 kPa

20. A gas occupies a volume of 6 L at 3 atm and 70°C. Which setup is correct for
     calculating the new volume of the gas if the temperature is changed to 150°C and
     the pressure is dropped to 1.0 atm?

1) 6 x $\dfrac{3 \quad x \quad 150}{1 \quad x \quad 70}$ 3) 6 x $\dfrac{3 \ x \ 423}{1 \ x \ 343}$

2) 6 x $\dfrac{3 \ x \ 80}{1 \ x \ 150}$ 4) 6 x $\dfrac{3 \ x \ 343}{1 \ x \ 423}$

21. Given the balanced particle-diagram equation:

Key
○ = an atom of an element
● = an atom of a different element

Which statement describes the type of change and the chemical properties of the product and reactants?

1) The equation represents a physical change, with the product and reactants having different chemical properties.
2) The equation represents a physical change, with the product and reactants having identical chemical properties.
3) The equation represents a chemical change, with the product and reactants having different chemical properties.
4) The equation represents a chemical change, with the product and reactants having identical chemical properties.

Constructed Response

Base your answers to questions 22 to 25 on the diagram of a molecule of nitrogen shown below.

     represents one molecule of nitrogen.

22. Draw a particle model that shows at least six molecules of nitrogen gas.

23. Draw a particle model that shows at least six molecules of liquid nitrogen.

24. Describe, in terms of particle arrangement, the difference between nitrogen gas and liquid nitrogen.

25. Good models should reflect the true nature of the concept being represented. What is the limitation of two-dimensional models?

Base your answers to questions 26 through 28 on the information and diagrams below.

Cylinder A contains 22.0 grams of $CO_2(g)$ and Cylinder B contains $N_2(g)$. The volumes, pressures, and temperatures of the two gases are indicated under each cylinder.

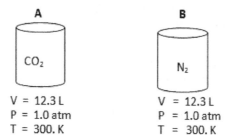

A

CO_2

$V = 12.3 L$
$P = 1.0 atm$
$T = 300. K$

B

N_2

$V = 12.3 L$
$P = 1.0 atm$
$T = 300. K$

26. How does the number of molecules of $CO_2(g)$ in cylinder A compare to the number of molecules of $N_2(g)$ in container B? Your answer must include both $CO_2(g)$ and $N_2(g)$.

27. The temperature of $CO_2(g)$ is increased to 450. K and the volume of cylinder A remains constant. Show a correct numerical setup for calculating the new pressure of $CO_2(g)$ in cylinder A.

28. Calculate the new pressure of $CO_2(g)$ in cylinder A based on your setup.

Base your answers to questions 29 through 33 on the information below.

A substance is a solid at 15°C. A student heated a sample of the substance and recorded the temperature at one-minute intervals in the data table below.

Time (min)	0	1	2	3	4	5	6	7	8	9	10	11	12
Temperature (°C)	15	32	46	53	53	53	53	53	53	53	53	60	65

29. On the grid, mark an appropriate scale on the axis labeled " Temperature (°C) ." An appropriate scale is one that allows a trend to be seen.

30 . Plot the data from the data table. Circle and connect the points.

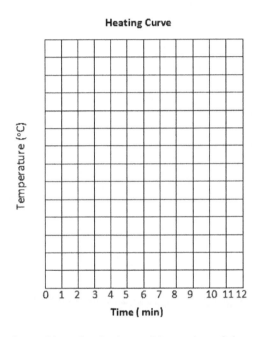

Heating Curve

Temperature (°C)

0 1 2 3 4 5 6 7 8 9 10 11 12

Time (min)

31. Based on the data table, what is the melting point of the substance?

32. What is the evidence that the average kinetic energy of the particles of the substance is increasing during the first three minutes?

33. The heat of fusion for this substance is 122 joules per gram. How many joules of heat are needed to melt 7.50 grams of this substance at its melting point ?

1. Which determines the order of placement of the elements on the modern Periodic Table?
   1) Atomic mass
   2) Atomic number
   3) The number of neutrons, only
   4) The number of neutrons and protons

2. The elements located in the lower left corner of the Periodic Table are classified as
   1) Metals
   2) Nonmetals
   3) Metalloids
   4) Noble gases

3. The strength of an atom's attraction for the electrons in a chemical bond is measured by the
   1) density
   2) ionization energy
   3) heat of reaction
   4) electronegativity

4. What is a property of most metals?
   1) They tend to gain electrons easily when bonding.
   2) They tend to lose electrons easily when bonding.
   3) They are poor conductors of heat.
   4) They are poor conductors of electricity.

5. A metal, M, forms an oxide compound with the general formula M_2O. In which group on the Periodic Table could metal M be found?
   1) Group 1   2) Group 2   3) Group 16   4) Group 17

6. Which halogen is correctly paired with its phase at STP?
   1) Br is a liquid   2) F is a solid   3) I is a gas   4) Cl is a liquid

7. As the elements in Group 1 of the Periodic Table are considered in order of increasing atomic number, the atomic radius of each successive element increases. This is primarily due to an increase in the number of
   1) Neutrons in the nucleus
   2) Unpaired electrons
   3) Valence electrons
   4) Electron shells

8. When elements within Period 3 are considered in order of decreasing atomic number, ionization energy of each successive element generally
   1) Increases due to an increase in atomic size
   2) Increases due to a decrease in atomic size
   3) Decreases due to an increase in atomic size
   4) Decreases due to a decrease in atomic size

9. Which set of characteristics is true of elements in Group 2 of the Periodic Table?
   1) They all have two energy levels and have different chemical characteristics
   2) They all have two energy levels and share similar chemical characteristics
   3) They all have two valence electrons and share similar chemical properties
   4) They all have two valence electrons and have different chemical properties

10. At STP, solid carbon can exist as graphite or as diamond. These two forms of carbon have
    1) The same properties and the same crystal structures
    2) The same properties and different crystal structures
    3) Different properties and the same crystal structures
    4) Different properties and different crystal structures

11. Which grouping of circles, when considered in order from the top to the bottom, best represents the relative size of the atoms of Li, Na, K, and Rb, respectively?

1)   2)   3)   4)

12. Elements strontium and beryllium both form a bond with fluorine with similar chemical formulas. The similarity in their formulas is due to
    1) Strontium and beryllium having the same number of kernel electrons
    2) Strontium and beryllium having the same number of valence electrons
    3) Strontium and beryllium having the same number of protons
    4) Strontium and beryllium having the same molecular structure

13. The element antimony is a
    1) Metal   2) Nonmetal   3) Metalloid   4) Halogen

14. Which of these elements in Period 2 is likely to form a negative ion?
    1) Oxygen   2) Boron   3) Neon   4) Lithium

15. Which of these characteristics best describes the element sulfur at STP?
    1) It is brittle   2) It is malleable   3) It has luster   4) It is ductile

16. Which of these elements has the highest thermal and electrical conductivity?
    1) Iodine   2) Carbon   3) Phosphorus   4) Iron

17. Chlorine will bond with which metallic element to form a colorful compound?
    1) Aluminum   2) Sodium   3) Strontium   4) Manganese

18. According to the Periodic Table, which sequence correctly places the elements in order of increasing atomic size?
    1) $Na \rightarrow Li \rightarrow H \rightarrow K$ 3) $Te \rightarrow Sb \rightarrow Sn \rightarrow In$
    2) $Ba \rightarrow Sr \rightarrow Ca \rightarrow Mg$ 4) $H \rightarrow He \rightarrow Li \rightarrow Be$

19. Which of these elements has stronger metallic characteristics than aluminum?
    1) He   2) Mg   3) Ga   4) Si

20. Which element has a greater tendency to attract electrons than phosphorus?
    1) Silicon   2) Arsenic   3) Boron   4) Sulfur

21. Which element has the greatest density at STP?
    1) barium   2) magnesium   3) beryllium   4) radium

22. An element that is malleable and a good conductor of heat and electricity could have an atomic number of
    1) 16   2) 18   3) 29   4) 35

23. Sodium atoms, potassium atoms, and cesium atoms have the same
    1) Atomic radius   3) First ionization energy
    2) Total number of protons   4) Oxidation state

24. When the elements in Group 1 are considered in order from top to bottom, each successive element at standard pressure has
    1) a higher melting point and a higher boiling point
    2) a higher melting point and a lower boiling point
    3) a lower melting point and a higher boiling point
    4) a lower melting point and a lower boiling point

25. Elements Q, X, and Z are in the same group on the Periodic Table and are listed in order of increasing atomic number. The melting point of element Q is –219°C and the melting point of element Z is –7°C. Which temperature is closest to the melting point of element X?
    1) –7°C   2) –101°C   3) –219°C   4) –226°C

Constructed Response

Base your answers to questions 26 through 29 on the information below.

> A metal, M, was obtained from compound in a rock sample. Experiments have determined that the element is a member of Group 2 on the Periodic Table of the Elements.

26. What is the phase of element M at STP?

27. Explain, in terms of electrons, why element M is a good conductor of electricity.

28. Explain why the radius of a positive ion of element M is smaller than the radius of an atom of element M.

29. Using the element symbol M for the element, write the chemical formula for the compound that forms when element M reacts with Iodine.

Element	Atomic Number	Electronegativity
Beryllium	4	1.6
Boron	5	2.0
Carbon	6	2.6
Fluorine	9	4.0
Lithium	3	1.0
Oxygen	8	3.4

Electronegativity (y-axis)

Atomic Number (x-axis)

30. On the grid, set up a scale for electronegativity on the y-axis and atomic number on the x-axis. Plot the data by drawing a best-fit line.

31. Using the graph, predict the electronegativity of nitrogen.

32. For these elements, state the trend in electronegativity in terms of atomic number.

1. Which conclusion was a direct result of the gold foil experiment?
   1) An atom is composed of at least three types of subatomic particles.
   2) An atom is mostly empty space with a dense, positively charged nucleus.
   3) An electron has a positive charge and is located inside the nucleus.
   4) An electron has properties of both waves and particles.

2. In the wave-mechanical model of the atom, orbitals are regions of the most probable locations of
   1) protons   2) positrons   3) neutrons   4) electrons

3. What is the charge and mass of an electron?
   1) Charge of +1 and a mass of 1 amu   3) Charge of +1 and a mass of 1/1836 amu
   2) Charge of -1 and a mass of 1 amu   4) Charge of -1 and a mass of 1/1836 amu

4. Which phrase describes an atom?
   1) a positively charged electron cloud surrounding a positively charged nucleus
   2) a positively charged electron cloud surrounding a negatively charged nucleus
   3) a negatively charged electron cloud surrounding a positively charged nucleus
   4) a negatively charged electron cloud surrounding a negatively charged nucleus

5. Which total mass is the smallest?
   1) the mass of 2 electrons
   2) the mass of 2 neutrons
   3) the mass of 1 electron plus the mass of 1 proton
   4) the mass of 1 neutron plus the mass of 1 electron

6. Which statement concerning elements is true?
   1) Different elements must have different numbers of isotopes.
   2) Different elements must have different numbers of neutrons.
   3) All atoms of a given element must have the same mass number.
   4) All atoms of a given element must have the same atomic number.

7. Which value of an element is calculated using both the mass and the relative abundance of each of the naturally occurring isotopes of this element?
   1) Atomic number   2) Atomic mass   3) Half-life   4) Molar volume

8. Which sequence represents a correct order of historical developments leading to the modern model of the atom?
   1) Atom is a hard sphere $\rightarrow$ atom is mostly empty space $\rightarrow$ electrons exist in orbitals outside the nucleus
   2) Atom is a hard sphere $\rightarrow$ electrons exist in orbitals outside the nucleus $\rightarrow$ atom is mostly empty space
   3) Atom is mostly empty space $\rightarrow$ atom is a hard sphere $\rightarrow$ electrons exist in orbitals outside the nucleus
   4) Atom is empty space $\rightarrow$ electrons exist in orbitals outside the nucleus $\rightarrow$ atom is a hard sphere

9. An atom is electrically neutral because the
   1) number of protons equals the number of electrons
   2) number of protons equals the number of neutrons
   3) ratio of the number of neutrons to the number of electrons is 1:1
   4) ratio of the number of neutrons to the number of protons is 2:1

10. How do the energy and the most probable location of an electron in the third shell of an atom compare to the energy and the most probable location of an electron in the first shell of the same atom?
    1) In the third shell, an electron has more energy and is closer to the nucleus.
    2) In the third shell, an electron has more energy and is farther from the nucleus.
    3) In the third shell, an electron has less energy and is closer to the nucleus.
    4) In the third shell, an electron has less energy and is farther from the nucleus.

11. During a flame test, ions of a specific metal are heated in the flame of a gas burner. A characteristic color of light is emitted by these ions in the flame when the electrons
    1) gain energy as they return to lower energy levels
    2) gain energy as they move to higher energy levels
    3) emit energy as they return to lower energy levels
    4) emit energy as they move to higher energy levels

12. A particle of an atom contains 26 protons, 23 electrons, and 56 neutrons. What will be the correct atomic number for this particle?
    1) 26   2) 23   3) 56   4) 33

13. An atom with 21 neutrons and 40 nucleons has
    1) A nuclear charge of +19   3) A mass number of 61
    2) A nuclear charge of +40   4) A mass number of 19

14. Which element could have a mass number of 86 atomic mass units and 49 neutrons in its nucleus?
    1) In   2) Rb   3) Rn   4) Au

15. Which correctly represents two isotopes of element X?

    1) $^{226}_{91}X$ and $^{226}_{91}X$ 3) $^{227}_{91}X$ and $^{227}_{90}X$

    2) $^{226}_{91}X$ and $^{227}_{91}X$ 4) $^{226}_{90}X$ and $^{227}_{91}X$

16. Which atom is an isotope of oxygen?

    1) $^{14}_{7}N$ 2) $^{16}_{8}N$ 3) $^{14}_{7}O$ 4) $^{17}_{8}O$

17. What is the total number of nucleons in the nuclide $^{65}_{30}Zn$?

    1) 65   2) 30   3) 35   4) 95

18. In which pair of atoms do the nuclei contain the same number of neutrons?
    1) Calcium-40 and Calcium-42   3) Bromine – 83 and Krypton - 83
    2) Chlorine-35 and Sulfur- 34   4) Iodine – 127 and Bromine – 80

19. Which is a ground state electron configuration of an atom in the fourth period of the periodic table
    1) 2 – 8 – 4   3) 2 – 8 – 18 – 18 – 4
    2) 2 – 8 – 18 – 4   4) 2 – 4

20. The total number of electrons found in the electron configuration of a neutral chromium atom is
    1) 24   2) 6   3) 13   4) 52

21. The highest amount of energy will be emitted by an electron when it moves from the
    1) 4th to 1st electron shell   3) 1st to 5th electron shell
    2) 1st to 4th electron shell   4) 5th to 4th electron shell

22. What is the total number of electrons in a Cr^{3+} ion?
    1) 3   2) 21   3) 24   4) 27

23. Which symbol represents a particle with a total of 10 electrons?
    1) N   2) Al   3) N^{3+} 4) Al^{3+}

24. Which electron configuration represents an atom of aluminum in an excited state?
    1) 2-7-4   2) 2-8-3   3) 2-7-7   4) 2-8-6

25. Element X has two isotopes. If 72.0% of the element has an isotopic mass of 84.9 amu, and 28.0% of the element has an isotopic mass of 87.0 amu, the average atomic mass of element X is numerically equal to

    1) (72.0 + 84.9) x (28.0 + 87.0)   3) $\dfrac{(72.0 \times 84.9)}{100} + \dfrac{(28.0 \times 87.0)}{100}$

    2) (72.0 - 84.9) x (28.0 + 87.0)   4) $\dfrac{(72.0 \times 84.9)}{100} - \dfrac{(28.0 \times 87.0)}{100}$

26. The diagram below represents the nucleus of an atom

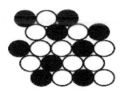

Key	
●	= proton
○	= neutron

What are the atomic number and mass number of this atom?
1) The atomic number is 9 and the mass number is 19.
2) The atomic number is 9 and the mass number is 20.
3) The atomic number is 11 and the mass number is 19.
4) The atomic number is 11 and the mass number is 20.

Constructed Response

Base your answers to questions 27 through 29 on the information below.

In the modern model of the atom, each atom is composed of three major subatomic (or fundamental) particles.

27. Name the subatomic particles contained in the nucleus.

28. State the charge associated with each type of subatomic particle contained in the nucleus of the atom.

29. What is the sign of the net charge of the nucleus?

Base your answers to questions 30 through 32 on the data table below, which shows three isotopes of neon.

Isotope	Atomic Mass (atomic mass units)	Percent Natural Abundance
^{20}Ne	19.99	90.9 %
^{21}Ne	20.99	0.3 %
^{22}Ne	21.99	8.8 %

30. Based on the atomic mass and the natural abundances shown in the data table show a correct numerical set-up for calculating the average atomic mass of neon.

31. Based on natural abundances, the average atomic mass of neon is closest to which whole number?

32. In terms of atomic particles, state one difference between these three isotopes of neon.

Base your answers to questions 33 and 34 on the diagram below, which shows bright-line spectra of selected elements.

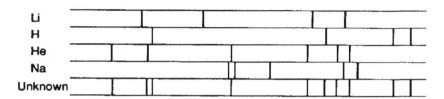

33. Explain, in terms of excited state, energy transitions, and ground state, how a bright-line spectrum is produced.

34. Identify the two elements in the unknown spectrum.

Base your answers to questions 35 and 36 on the diagram below, which represents an atom of magnesium-26 in the ground state.

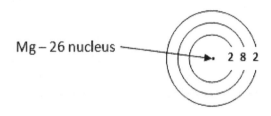

35. Write an appropriate number of electrons in each shell to represent a Mg – 26 atom in an excited state. Your answer may include additional shells.

36. What is the total number of valence electrons in an atom of Mg-26 in the ground state?

252

1. Atoms bond due to the interaction between
   1) Protons and neutrons
   2) Protons and electrons
   3) Neutrons and electrons
   4) Neutrons and positrons

2. Which statement describes what occurs as two atoms of bromine combine to become a molecule of bromine?
   1) Energy is absorbed as a bond is formed.
   2) Energy is absorbed as a bond is broken.
   3) Energy is released as a bond is formed.
   4) Energy is released as a bond is broken.

3. Which particles may be gained, lost, or shared by an atom when it forms a chemical bond?
   1) protons   2) electrons   3) neutrons   4) nucleons

4. The amount of potential energy in chemical bonds of substances depends on
   1) The composition of the substances only
   2) The structure of the substances only
   3) Both the composition and the structure of the substances
   4) Neither the composition nor the structure of the substances

5. Which type of bond results when one or more valence electrons are transferred from one atom to another?
   1) a hydrogen bond
   2) an ionic bond
   3) a nonpolar covalent bond
   4) a polar covalent bond

6. Which type of bonding is found in all molecular substances?
   1) covalent bonding
   2) hydrogen bonding
   3) ionic bonding
   4) metallic bonding

7. Two nonmetal atoms of the same element share electrons equally. The resulting molecule is
   1) Polar, only
   2) Nonpolar, only
   3) Either polar or nonpolar
   4) Neither polar nor nonpolar

8. Which best describes the shape and charge distribution in polar molecules?
   1) Asymmetrical shape with equal charge distribution
   2) Asymmetrical shape with unequal charge distribution
   3) Symmetrical shape with equal charge distribution
   4) Symmetrical shape with unequal charge distribution

9. Which characteristic is a property of molecular substances?
   1) Good heat conductivity
   2) Good electrical conductivity
   3) Low melting point
   4) High melting point

10. The degree of polarity of a chemical bond in a molecule of a compound can be predicted by determining the difference in the
    1) melting points of the elements in the compound
    2) densities of the elements in the compound
    3) electronegativities of the bonded atoms in a molecule of the compound
    4) atomic masses of the bonded atoms in a molecule of the compound

11. A solid substance is an excellent conductor of electricity. The chemical bonds in this substance are most likely
    1) ionic, because the valence electrons are shared between atoms
    2) ionic, because the valence electrons are mobile
    3) metallic, because the valence electrons are stationary
    4) metallic, because the valence electrons are mobile

12. Given the reaction at 101.3 kilopascals and 298 K:

     hydrogen gas + iodine gas   →   hydrogen iodide gas .

     This reaction is classified as
     1) endothermic, because heat is absorbed   3) exothermic, because heat is absorbed
     2) endothermic, because heat is released   4) exothermic, because heat is released

13. Atom X and atom Y bond to form a compound. The electron configuration of X
     and Y are 2 – 8. Which two atoms could be X and Y ?
     1) X could be magnesium and Y could be sulfur
     2) X could be magnesium and Y could be oxygen
     3) X could be calcium and Y could be sulfur
     4) X could be calcium and Y could be oxygen

14. Atoms in which compound are held together by ionic bonds?
     1) CH_4 2) $AlCl_3$ 3) H_2O 4) NH_3

15. Which formula contains nonpolar covalent bonds?
     1) NH_3 2) H_2O 3) O_2 4) $NaCl$

16. The atoms of which substance are held together by metallic bonds?
     1) $H_2(g)$ 2) $H_2O(l)$ 3) $SiC(s)$ 4) $Fe(s)$

17. Which compound contains both ionic and covalent bonds?
     1) Ammonia   3) Methane
     2) Lithium sulfate   4) Potassium chloride

18. The C – Cl bond in CCl_4 is best described as
     1) Ionic, because electrons are transferred
     2) Ionic, because electrons are shared
     3) Covalent, because electrons are transferred
     4) Covalent, because electrons are shared

19. Which structural formula represents a polar molecule?
     1) H – H   2) Na – H   3) H – Br   4) O = O

20. Which pair of atoms forms a bond that is the least covalent?
     1) Ba and I   2) Br and Cl   3) K and Cl   4) P and I

21. An atom of nitrogen is most stable when it bonds with
     1) One sodium atom   3) One aluminum atom
     2) One magnesium atom   4) One calcium atom

22. Based on bond type, which compound has the highest melting point?
     1) CH_3OH 2) C_6H_{14} 3) $CuCl_2$ 4) CCl_4

23. Which of the following has the lowest boiling point?
     1) He   2) Xe   3) Ne   4) Kr

24. Which electron-dot symbol represents a nonpolar molecule?

     1)   2) H : Cl :   3)   4)

25. Molecules in a sample of $NH_3(g)$ are held closely together by intermolecular forces
     1) existing between ions   3) caused by different numbers of neutrons
     2) existing between electrons   4) caused by unequal charge distribution

26. Which Lewis electron-dot diagram correctly represents a hydroxide ion?

     1) [:Ö:H]⁻   2) [:O:H:]⁻   3) [:Ö::H]⁻   4) [:O:H:]⁻

Base your answers to questions 27 through 31 on your knowledge of chemical bonding and on the Lewis electron-dot diagrams of H_2S, CO_2, and F_2 below.

$$H:\ddot{S}: \qquad :\ddot{O}::C::\ddot{O}: \qquad :\ddot{F}:\ddot{F}:$$
$$H$$

27. Which atom, when bonded as shown, has the same electron configuration as an atom of argon?

28. Explain, in terms of structure and/or distribution of charge, why CO_2 is a nonpolar molecule.

29. Explain, in terms of electronegativity, why a C = O bond in CO_2 is more polar than an F – F bond in F_2 .

30. What is the total number of covalent bonds in a molecule of CO_2?

31. What is the shape and molecular polarity of H_2S?

Base your answers to questions 32 through 34 on the information below.

Carbon and oxygen are examples of elements that exist in more than one form in the same phase.

Graphite and diamond are two crystalline arrangements for carbon. The crystal structure of graphite is organized in layers. The bonds between carbon atoms within each layer of graphite are strong. The bonds between carbon atoms that connect different layers of graphite are weak because the shared electrons in these bonds are loosely held by the carbon atoms. The crystal structure of diamond is a strong network of atoms in which all the shared electrons are strongly held by the carbon atoms. Graphite is an electrical conductor, but diamond is not. At 25°C, graphite has a density of 2.2 g/cm³ and diamond has a density of 3.51 g/cm³.

The element oxygen can exist as diatomic molecules, O_2, and as ozone, O_3. At standard pressure the boiling point of ozone is 161 K.

32. Explain, in terms of electrons, why graphite is an electrical conductor and diamond is *not*. Your response must include information about *both* graphite and diamond.

33. Calculate the volume, in cm³, of a diamond at 25°C that has a mass of 0.200 grams. Your response must include *both* a correct numerical setup and the calculated result.

34. Explain, in terms of intermolecular forces, the difference in the boiling points of O_2 and O_3 at standard pressure. Your response must include information about *both* O_2 and O_3.

Chemical Bonding

Base your answers to questions 35 and 36 on the table and information below.

The table below shows some properties of three solids: X, Y, and Z

Properties	X	Y	Z
Melting Point (°C)	800	80	1200
Soluble in water	yes	no	no
Solid state conducts electricity	no	no	Yes
Liquid state conduct electricity	yes	no	yes

35. Classify solids X, Y, and Z as the following: Metallic, ionic, or molecular

    Solid X :_____

    Solid Y: _____

    Solid Z: _____

36. Explain, in terms of ions, why solid X would be able to conduct electricity when it dissolves in water.

37. Explain, in terms of intermolecular forces, why pure hydrogen has a lower boiling point than hydrogen bromide.

38. Explain, in terms of electronegativity difference, why the bond in H – Cl is more polar than the bond in H – I.

39. Explain, in terms of molecular polarity, why hydrogen chloride is more soluble than pure hydrogen in water under the same conditions of temperature and pressure.

1. A chemical formula is an expression of
   1) Qualitative composition, only
   2) Quantitative composition, only
   3) Both qualitative and quantitative composition
   4) Neither qualitative nor quantitative composition

2. A type of formula showing the simplest ratio in which atoms are combined is called
   1) A molecular formula   3) A structural formula
   2) An empirical formula   4) A condensed formula

3. Given the balanced equation representing a reaction:
   $$H^+(aq) \quad + \quad OH^-(aq) \rightarrow \quad H_2O(l) \quad + \quad 55.8\,kJ$$
   In this reaction there is conservation of
   1) mass, only   3) mass and charge, only
   2) mass and energy, only   4) mass, charge, and energy

4. Given a balanced chemical equation, it is always possible to determine
   1) Whether a reaction will or will not take place
   2) The conditions necessary for the reaction to take place
   3) The relative number of moles taking place in the reaction
   4) The physical state of the products and reactants

5. Which list consists of types of chemical formulas?
   1) atoms, ions, molecules   3) metals, nonmetals, metalloids
   2) empirical, molecular, structural   4) synthesis, decomposition, neutralization

6. Which list is composed only of types of chemical reactions?
   1) Synthesis, decomposition, single replacement
   2) Decomposition, evaporation, and double replacement
   3) Synthesis, decomposition, freezing
   4) Decomposition, melting, combustion

7. In the compound, $Ca_3(PO_4)_2$, what is the total number of phosphate ions in the formula?
   1) 3   2) 2   3) 8   4) 4

8. The total number of atoms in the hydrate $CuSO_4 \cdot 3H_2O$ is
   1) 9   2) 12   3) 15   4) 24

9. What is the ratio of ammonium ions to sulfate ions in the formula $(NH_4)_2SO_4$?
   1) 2 : 1   2) 1 : 2   3) 8 : 4   4) 4 : 1

10. Which formula is an empirical formula?
   1) H_2CO_3 2) $H_2C_2O_4$ 3) CH_3COOH 4) CH_2OHCH_2OH

11. Which two compounds have the same empirical formula?
   1) C_2H_2 and C_2H_4 2) CH_2 and C_3H_8 3) HO and H_2O 4) NO_2 and N_2O_4

12. Which is the correct formula for iron(II) sulfide?
   1) FeS 2) Fe_5O_3 3) Fe_2S_3 4) $Fe_2(SO_4)_2$

13. The correct name for $NaClO_4$ is sodium
   1) Chloride   2) Chlorate   3) Perchlorate 4) chlorite

14. Which formula is a binary compound?
   1) KOH 2) $NaClO_3$ 3) Al_2S_3 4) $Bi(NO_3)_3$

15. What is the formula of titanium(II) oxide?
    1) TiO   2) Ti_2O 3) TiO_2 4) Ti_2O_3

16. What is the simplest ratio of nitrogen to oxygen atoms in the compound nitrogen(IV) oxide?
    1) 1 : 2   2) 2 : 1   3) 2 : 4   4) 4 : 2

17. Which substance has a chemical formula with the same ratio of metal ions to nonmetal ions as in potassium sulfide?
    1) sodium oxide   3) sodium chloride
    2) magnesium oxide   4) magnesium chloride

18. A single replacement reaction is shown in which equation?
    1) $Ca(OH)_2$ + $2HCl$ → $CaCl_2$ + $2 H_2O$
    2) Ca + $2H_2O$ → H_2 + $Ca(OH)_2$
    3) $2 H_2$ + O_2 → $2H_2O$
    4) $2H_2O_2$ → $2H_2O$ + O_2

19. Which of these equations shows conservation of atoms?
    1) $2KBr$ → K + Br_2 3) $CuCO_3$ → CuO + CO_2
    2) $2KClO_3$ → $2KCl$ + $2O_2$ 4) $CaCO_3$ → CO_2 + $2CaO$

20. Which chemical equation is correctly balanced?
    1) $H_2(g)$ + $O_2(g)$ → $H_2O(g)$ 3) $2KCl(s)$ → $2K(s)$ + $Cl_2(g)$
    2) $N_2(g)$ + $H_2(g$ → $NH_3(g)$ 4) $2NaCl(s)$ → $Na(s)$ + $Cl_2(g)$

21. Given the equation:
    $$X   +   Cl_2   →   C_2H_5Cl   +   HCl$$
    Which molecule is represented by X?
    1) C_2H_4 2) C_2H_6 3) C_3H_6 4) C_3H_8

22. Given the unbalanced equation:
    $$\_Fe_2O_3   +   \_CO   →   \_Fe   +   \_CO_2$$
    When the equation is correctly balanced using the smallest whole-number coefficients, what is the coefficient of CO?
    1) 1   2) 2   3) 3   4) 4

23. What is the chemical formula for sodium sulfate?
    1) Na_2SO_3 2) Na_2SO_4 3) $NaSO_3$ 4) $NaSO_4$

24. Given the structural formula:

$$
\begin{array}{c}
\text{H} \quad \text{H} \quad \text{H} \quad \text{H} \\
| \quad | \quad | \quad | \\
\text{HO} - \text{C} - \text{C} - \text{C} - \text{C} - \text{OH} \\
| \quad | \quad | \quad | \\
\text{H} \quad \text{H} \quad \text{H} \quad \text{H}
\end{array}
$$

What is the empirical formula of this compound?
    1) CH_3O 2) $C_4H_{10}O_2$ 3) C_2H_5O 4) $C_8H_{20}O_4$

25. Which polyatomic ion contains the greatest number of oxygen atoms?
    1) acetate   2) carbonate   3) hydroxide   4) peroxide

Constructed Response

26. What is the correct formula for ammonium dichromate?

27. What is the correct IUPAC name for the formula BeO?

Base your answers to questions 28 through 30 on the equation below.

    ___ C_4H_6 + ___ O_2 → ___ CO_2 + ___ H_2O

28. Balance the equation above, using the smallest whole number coefficients.

29. What is the sum of all coefficients when the equation is balanced?

30. What type of chemical reaction is represented by the equation?

Base your answers to questions 31 through 34 on the information below.

    Arsenic is often obtained by heating the ore arsenopyrite, FeAsS. The decomposition of FeAsS is represented by the balanced equation below.

        $FeAsS(s)$ → $FeS(s)$ + $As(g)$

    In the solid phase, arsenic occurs in two forms. One form, yellow arsenic, has a density of 1.97 g/cm^3 at STP. The other form, gray arsenic, has a density of 5.78 g/cm^3 at STP. When arsenic is heated rapidly in air, arsenic(III) oxide is formed.

    Although arsenic is toxic, it is needed by the human body in very small amounts. The body of a healthy human adult contains approximately 5 milligrams of arsenic.

31. Convert the mass of arsenic found in the body of a healthy human adult to grams.

32. When heated, a 125.0-kilogram sample of arsenopyrite yields 67.5 kilograms of FeS. Determine the total mass of arsenic produced in this reaction.

33. Write the formula for the compound produced when arsenic is heated rapidly in air.

34. Explain, in terms of the arrangement of atoms, why the two forms of arsenic have different densities at STP.

Base your answers to questions 35 through 37 on the information below.

Antacids can be used to neutralize excess stomach acid.

Brand A antacids contain the acid-neutralizing agent magnesium hydroxide, $Mg(OH)_2$. It reacts with $HCl(aq)$ in the stomach according to the following equation:

$$HCl(aq) \ + \ Mg(OH)_2(aq) \ \rightarrow \ MgCl_2(aq) \ + \ H_2O(l)$$

Brand B antacids contain the acid-neutralizing agent sodium hydrogen carbonate.

35. Write the chemical formula for sodium hydrogen carbonate.

36. What type of reaction is shown in the above balanced equatio ?

37. Balance the equation below using the smallest whole-number coefficients.

   ___ $HCl(aq)$ +   ___ $Mg(OH)_2(aq)$ $\rightarrow$ ___ $MgCl_2(aq)$ +   ___ $H_2O(l)$

1. What is the total number of moles of hydrogen atoms in 4 moles of $(NH_4)_2SO_4$?
   1) 8   2) 10   3) 16   4) 32

2. How many different types of atoms are in the formula $Ba(OH)_2 \cdot 8H_2O$?
   1) 3   2) 2   3) 5   4) 8

3. What is the gram-formula mass of $Ca_3(PO_4)_2$?
   1) 248 g/mole   2) 263 g/mole   3) 279 g/mole   4) 310. g/mole

4. What is the approximate mass in grams of 0.5 moles of Co?
   1) 27   2) 29   3) 12   4) 59

5. The number of moles of H_2SO_4 that weighs 245 grams is equal to
   1) 0.4 mole   2) 1 mole   3) 2.5 moles   4) 3 moles

6. The number of moles of the element lead that will have a mass of 311 grams is equal to
   1) 2 moles   2) 1.5 moles   3) 0.67 mole   4) 1.0 mole

7. What is the total mass in grams of 0.75 moles of SO_2?
   1) 16 g   2) 24 g   3) 32 g   4) 48 g

8. The mass in grams of two moles of $(NH_4)_2CO_3$ is equal to
   1) 96 x 2   2) 108 x 2   3) $\dfrac{96}{2}$ 4) $\dfrac{2}{96}$

9. What is the percent composition of nitrogen in the compound NH_4NO_3?
   1) 35 %   2) 29 %   3) 18 %   4) 5.7 %

10. What is the approximate percent composition of $CaCO_3$?
    1) 48% Ca, 12% C and 40% O   3) 40% Ca , 12% C and 48% O
    2) 12% Ca, 48% C, and 40% O   4) 40% Ca , 48% C, and 12% O

11. In which compound is the percent by mass of oxygen greatest?
    1) BeO   2) MgO   3) CaO   4) SrO

12. A sample of a substance containing only magnesium and chlorine was tested in the
    laboratory and was found to be composed of 74.5% chlorine by mass. If the total
    mass of the sample was 190.2 grams, what was the mass of the magnesium?
    1) 24.3 g   2) 48.5 g   3) 70.9 g   4) 142 g

13. A student measured an 8.24 g sample of a hydrated salt and heated it until it had a
    constant mass of 6.20 g. What was the percent by mass of water in the hydrated salt?
    1) 14.1 %   2) 24.8 %   3) 32.9 %   4) 75.2 %

14. A compound has an empirical formula of CH_2Br and a molecular mass of 188 grams
    per mole. What is the molecular formula of this compound?
    1) CH_2Br 2) $C_2H_4Br_2$ 3) $C_3H_6Br_3$ 4) $CHBr_2$

15. A compound has a molar mass of 90. grams per mole and the empirical formula
    CH_2O. What is the molecular formula of this compound?
    1) CH_2O 2) $C_2H_4O_2$ 3) $C_3H_6O_3$ 4) $C_4H_8O_4$

16. Acetic acid has a formula of $HC_2H_3O_2$. What is the ratio by mass of hydrogen to carbon to oxygen in this formula?
    1) $2 : 1 : 1$ 2) $2 : 3 : 3$ 3) $1 : 6 : 8$ 4) $1 : 2 : 4$

17. A sample of a compound contains 65.4 grams of zinc, 12.0 grams of carbon, and 48.0 grams of oxygen. What is the mole ratio of zinc to carbon to oxygen in this compound?
    1) $1 : 1 : 2$ 2) $1 : 1 : 3$ 3) $1 : 4 : 6$ 4) $5 : 1 : 4$

18. Given the reaction;

$$2C_2H_6 \quad + \quad 7O_2 \quad \rightarrow \quad 4CO_2 \quad + \quad 6H_2O$$

    What is the ratio of moles of CO_2 produced to moles of C_2H_6 consumed?
    1) 2 to 1   2) 1 to 1   3) 3 to 2   4) 7 to 2

19. Given the balanced equation representing a reaction:
$$F_2(g) \quad + \quad H_2(g) \quad \rightarrow \quad 2HF(g)$$
    What is the mole ratio of $H_2(g)$ to $HF(g)$ in this reaction?
    1) $1 : 1$ 2) $1 : 2$ 3) $2 : 1$ 4) $2 : 3$

20. Given the balanced equation representing the reaction between propane and oxygen:
$$C_3H_8 \quad + \quad 5O_2 \rightarrow \quad 3CO_2 \quad + \quad 4H_2O$$
    According to this equation, which ratio of oxygen to propane is correct?

    1) $\dfrac{5 \text{ grams } O_2}{1 \text{ grams } C_3H_8}$ 2) $\dfrac{5 \text{ moles } O_2}{1 \text{ mole } C_3H_8}$ 3) $\dfrac{10 \text{ grams } O_2}{11 \text{ grams } C_3H_8}$ 4) $\dfrac{10 \text{ moles } O_2}{11 \text{ moles } C_3H_8}$

21. Given the reaction:

$$4Fe \quad + \quad 3O_2 \quad \rightarrow \quad 2Fe_2O_3$$

    To produce 3 moles of Fe_2O_3, how many moles of Fe must be reacted?
    1) 1.5 moles   2) 3 moles   3) 4 moles   4) 6 moles

22. Given the balanced equation representing a reaction:
$$C_3H_8(g) \quad + \quad 5O_2(g) \quad \rightarrow \quad 3CO_2(g) \quad + \quad 4H_2O(g)$$
    What is the total number of moles of $O_2(g)$ required for the complete combustion of 1.5 moles of $C_3H_8(g)$?
    1) 0.30 mol   2) 1.5 mol   3) 4.5 mol   4) 7.5 mol

23. According to the reaction below:

$$2SO_2(g) \quad + \quad O_2(g) \quad \rightarrow \quad 2 SO_3(g)$$

    What is the total number of liters of $O_2(g)$ that will react completely with 89.6 liters of SO_2 at STP?
    1) 44.8 L   2) 22.4 L   3) 1.0 L   4) 0.500 L

24. Given the reaction:

$$4Al(s) \quad + \quad 3O_2(g) \quad \rightarrow \quad 2Al_2O_3(s)$$

    What is the minimum number of grams of O_2 gas required to produce 102 grams of Al_2O_3?
    1) 32.0 g   2) 192 g   3) 96.0 g   4) 48.0 g

Base your answers to questions 25 through 27 on the information below.

Gypsum is a mineral that is used in the construction industry to make drywall (sheetrock). The chemical formula for this hydrated compound is $CaSO_4 \cdot 2H_2O$. A hydrated compound contains water molecules within the crystalline structures. Gypsum contains 2 moles of water for each 1 mole of calcium sulfate.

25. What is the gram-formula mass of $CaSO_4 \cdot 2H_2O$?

26. Show a correct numerical setup for calculating the percent composition by mass of water in this compound and record your result.

27. What is the IUPAC name for gypsum, $CaSO_4 \cdot 2H_2O$?

Base your answers to questions 28 through 30 on the information below.

The decomposition of sodium azide, $NaN_3(s)$, is used to inflate airbags. On impact, $NaN_3(s)$ is ignited by an electrical spark, producing $N_2(g)$ and Na. The $N_2(g)$ inflates the airbag.

28. An inflated airbag has a volume of $5.00 \times 10^4 \, cm^3$ at STP. The density of $N_2(g)$ at STP is $0.00125 g/cm^3$. What is the total number of grams of $N_2(g)$ in the bag?

29. What is the total number of moles present in a 52.0 gram sample of NaN_3. (Gram-formula mass = 65.0 grams/mole)

30. Balance the equation below with the smallest whole number coefficients.
    ___ NaN_3 $\rightarrow$ ___ Na + ___N_2

Base your answers to questions 31 and 32 on the balanced chemical equation below.
    $2H_2O \rightarrow 2H_2 + O_2$

31. What is the total number of moles of O_2 produced when 8 moles of H_2O is completely consumed?

32. How does the balanced chemical equation show the Law of Conservation of Mass?

Base your answers to questions 33 through 37 on the information below.

A hydrate is a compound that has water molecules within its crystal structure. The formula for the hydrate $CuSO_4 \cdot 5H_2O(s)$ shows that there are five moles of water for every one mole of $CuSO_4(s)$. When $CuSO_4 \cdot 5H_2O(s)$ is heated, the water within the crystals is released, as represented by the balanced equation below.

$$CuSO_4 \cdot 5H_2O(s) \rightarrow CuSO_4(s) + 5H_2O(g)$$

A student first masses an empty crucible (a heat-resistant container). The student then masses the crucible containing a sample of $CuSO_4 \cdot 5H_2O(s)$. The student repeatedly heat and masses the crucible and its contents until the mass is constant. The student's recorded experimental data and calculations are shown below.

Data and calculation before heating:

mass of $CuSO_4 \cdot 5H_2O(s)$ and crucible	21.37 g
– mass of crucible	19.24 g
mass of $CuSO_4 \cdot 5H_2O(s)$	2.13 g

Data and calculation after heating to a constant mass:

mass of $CuSO_4(s)$ and crucible	20.61 g
– mass of crucible	19.24 g
mass of $CuSO_4(s)$	1.37 g

Calculation to determine the mass of water:

mass of $CuSO_4 \cdot 5H_2O(s)$	2.13 g
– mass of $CuSO_4(s)$	1.37 g
mass of $H_2O(g)$	0.76 g

33. Identify the total number of significant figures recorded in the calculated mass of $CuSO_4 \cdot 5H_2O(s)$.

34. In the space below, use the student's data to show a correct numerical setup for calculating the percent composition of water by mass in the hydrate.

35. Explain why the sample in the crucible must be heated until the constant mass is reached.

36. How many moles of $CuSO_4$ is represented by the mass of $CuSO_4$ calculated by the student?

37. How many moles of water is represented by the mass of H_2O calculated by the student?

1. The process of recovering a salt from a solution by evaporating the solvent is known as
   1) Decomposition   2) Crystallization   3) Reduction   4) Filtration

2. Which changes will increase the solubility of a gas in water?
   1) Increase in pressure and increase in temperature
   2) Increase in pressure and decrease in temperature
   3) Decrease in pressure and increase in temperature
   4) Decrease in pressure and decrease in temperature

3. The solubility of a salt in a given volume of water depends largely on the
   1) Surface area of the salt crystals
   2) Pressure on the surface of the water
   3) Rate at which the salt and water are stirred
   4) Temperature of the water

4. A solution in which equilibrium exists between dissolved and undissolved particles is also a
   1) Saturated solution   3) Supersaturated solution
   2) Concentrated solution   4) Dilute solution

5. A student adds solid KCl to water in a flask. The flask is sealed with a stopper and thoroughly shaken until no more solid KCl dissolves. Some solid KCl is still visible in the flask. The solution in the flask is
   1) saturated and is at equilibrium with the solid KCl
   2) saturated and is not at equilibrium with the solid KCl
   3) unsaturated and is at equilibrium with the solid KCl
   4) unsaturated and is not at equilibrium with the solid KCl

6. Which phrase describes the molarity of a solution?
   1) liters of solute per mole of solution   3) moles of solute per liter of solution
   2) liters of solution per mole of solution   4) moles of solution per liter of solution

7. As a solute is added to a solvent, what happens to the freezing point and the boiling point of the solution?
   1) The freezing point decreases and the boiling point decreases
   2) The freezing point decreases and the boiling point increases
   3) The freezing point increases and the boiling point decreases
   4) The freezing point increases and the boiling point increases

8. As water is added to a solution, the number of dissolved ions in the solution
   1) Increases, and the concentration of the solution remains the same
   2) Decreases, and the concentration of the solution increases
   3) Remains the same, and the concentration of the solution decreases
   4) Remains the same, and the concentration of the solution remains the same

9. The depression of the freezing point is dependent on
   1) The nature of the solute   3) Hydrogen bonding
   2) The concentration of dissolved particles   4) The formula of the solute

10. The vapor pressure of H_2O is less than that of CS_2. The best explanation for this is that H_2O has
    1) Larger molecules   3) Stronger ionic bonds
    2) A larger molecular mass   4) Stronger intermolecular forces

11. A dilute, aqueous potassium nitrate solution is best classified as a
    1) homogeneous compound   3) heterogeneous compound
    2) homogeneous mixture   4) heterogeneous mixture

12. What happens when $Ca(NO_3)_2(s)$ is dissolved in water?
    1) NO_3^- ions are attracted to the oxygen atoms of water
    2) Ca^{2+} ions are attracted to the oxygen atoms of water
    3) Ca^{2+} ions are attracted to the hydrogen atoms of water
    4) No attractions are involved; the crystal just falls apart

13. A decrease in water temperature will increase the solubility of
    1) $C_6H_{12}O_6(s)$ 2) $NH_3(g)$ 3) $KCl(s)$ 4) $Br_2(l)$

14. Under which two conditions would water contain the least number of dissolved $SO_2(g)$ molecules?
    1) 101.3 kPa and 273 K   3) 60 kPa and 273 K
    2) 101.3 kPa and 546 K   4) 60 kPa and 546 K

15. According to Reference Table F, which of these compounds is soluble in water at STP?
    1) $ZnSO_4$ 2) $BaSO_4$ 3) $ZnCO_3$ 4) $BaCO_3$

16. At STP, which aqueous solution will contain the least amount of dissolved ions?
    1) $NaNO_3$ 2) Na_2SO_4 3) $Pb(NO_3)_2$ 4) $PbSO_4$

17. What is the mass of NH_4Cl that must dissolve in 200. grams of water at 50.°C to make a saturated solution?
    1) 104 g   2) 84 g   3) 42 g   4) 26 g

18. According to Reference Table G, which solution is a saturated solution at 30°C?
    1) 30 grams of $KClO_3$ in 100 grams of water
    2) 30 grams of $KClO_3$ in 200 grams of water
    3) 76 grams of NaCl in 100 grams of water
    4) 76 grams of NaCl in 200 grams of water

19. What amount of potassium chloride must be added to a solution made by dissolving 80 g of the solute in 200 grams of H_2O at 60°C to produce a saturated solution?
    1) 45 g   2) 160 g   3) 100 g   4) 10 g

20. One hundred grams of water is saturated with NH_4Cl at 50°C. If the temperature of the solution is decreased to 10°C, what amount of the solute will precipitate?
    1) 5 g   2) 17 g   3) 30 g   4) 50 g

21. Based on Reference Table G, a solution of $NaNO_3$ that contains 120 g of solute dissolved in 100 grams of H_2O at 50 °C is best described as
    1) Saturated   2) Unsaturated   3) Supersaturated

22. A solution containing 140 grams of potassium iodide in 100 grams of water at 20°C is best classified as
    1) Unsaturated and dilute   3) Saturated and dilute
    2) Unsaturated and concentrated   4) Supersaturated and concentrated

23. A saturated solution of which compound will be the least concentrated solution in 100 g of water at 40°C?
    1) SO_2 2) NaCl   3) $KClO_3$ 4) NH_4Cl

24. A 3.0 M HCl(aq) solution contains a total of
    1) 3.0 grams of HCl per liter of water   3) 3.0 moles of HCl per liter of solution
    2) 3.0 grams of HCl per mole of solution   4) 3.0 moles of HCl per mole of water

25. When 5 grams of KCl are dissolved in 50. grams of water at 25°C, the resulting mixture can be described as
    1) heterogeneous and unsaturated   3) homogeneous and unsaturated
    2) heterogeneous and supersaturated   4) homogeneous and supersaturated

26. According to Reference Table G, how does a decrease in temperature from 40°C to 20°C affect the solubility of $NH_3(g)$ and that of NH_4Cl?
    1) The solubility of NH_3 increases, and the solubility of NH_4Cl increases
    2) The solubility of NH_3 decreases, and the solubility of NH_4Cl increases
    3) The solubility of NH_3 increases, and the solubility of NH_4Cl decreases
    4) The solubility of NH_3 decreases, and the solubility of NH_4Cl decreases

27. A solution of NaCl contains 1.8 moles of the solute in 600 mL of solution. What is the concentration of the solution?
    1) 333 M   2) 0.003 M   3) 3 M   4) 0. 05 M

28. A student dissolved 48 grams of $(NH_4)_2CO_3$ in 2000 mL of water. What will be the molarity of this solution?
    1) 1 M   2) 2 M   3) 0.25 M   4) 0.5 M

29. How many moles of KNO_3 are required to make .50 liter of a 2 molar solution of KNO_3?
    1) 1.0   2) 2.0   3) 0.50   4) 4.0

30. What is the total mass of solute in 1000 grams of a solution having a concentration of 5 parts per million?
    1) 0.005 g   2) 0.05 g   3) 0.5 g   4) 5 g

31. If 0.025 grams of $Pb(NO_3)_2$ is dissolved in 100. grams of H_2O, what is the concentration of the resulting solution, in parts per million?
    1) 2.5×10^{-4} ppm   2) 4.0×10^3 ppm   3) 250 ppm   4) 2.5 ppm

32. The vapor pressure of a liquid is 0.92 atm at 60°C. The normal boiling point of the liquid could be
    1) 35°C   2) 45°C   3) 55°C   4) 65°C

33. Which sample, when dissolved in 1.0 liter of water, produces a solution with the lowest freezing point?
    1) 0.1 mol of C_2H_5OH 3) 0.2 mol of $C_6H_{12}O_6$
    2) 0.1 mol of LiBr   4) 0.2 mol of $CaCl_2$

34. A student prepares four aqueous solutions, each with a different solute. The mass of each dissolved solute is shown in the table below.

**Mass of Dissolved Solute
for Four Aqueous Solutions**

Solution Number	Solute	Mass of Dissolved Solute (per 100. g of H_2O at 20.°C)
1	KI	120. g
2	$NaNO_3$	88 g
3	KCl	25 g
4	$KClO_3$	5 g

Which solution is saturated?
1) 1   2) 2   3) 3   4) 4

Constructed Response

Base your answers to questions 35 and 36 on the information below.

A student is instructed to make 0.250 liter of a 0.200 M aqueous solution of $Ca(NO_3)_2$.

35. In order to prepare the described solution in the laboratory, two quantities must be measured accurately. One of these quantities is the volume of the solution. What other quantity must be measured to prepare this solution?

36. Show a correct numerical setup for calculating the total number of moles of $Ca(NO_3)_2$ needed to make 0.250 liter of the 0.200 M calcium nitrate solution.

Base your answers to questions 37 through 39 on the information below.

When cola, a type of soda pop, is manufactured, $CO_2(g)$ is dissolved in it.

On the set of axes to the right.

37. Label one of them "Solubility" and the other "Temperature."

38. Draw a line to indicate the solubility of $CO_2(g)$ versus temperature.

39. A capped bottle of soda contains $CO_2(g)$ under high pressure. When the cap is removed, how does pressure affect the solubility of the dissolved $CO_2(g)$?

Given the balanced equation for the dissolving of NH₄Cl(s) in water:

$$NH_4Cl(s) \quad \rightarrow \quad NH_4^+(aq) \quad + \quad Cl^-(aq)$$

40. A student is holding a test tube containing 5.0 milliliters of water. When a sample of $NH_4Cl(s)$ is placed in the test tube, the test tube feels colder to the student's hand. Describe the direction of heat flow between the test tube and the hand.

41. Using the key to the right, draw at least two water molecules in the box showing the correct orientation of each water molecule when it is near the Cl⁻ ion in the aqueous solution

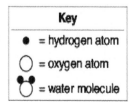

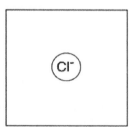

Base your answers to questions 42 through 45 on the information below.

Scientists who study aquatic ecosystems are often interested in the concentration of dissolved oxygen in water. Oxygen, O_2, has a very low solubility in water, and therefore its solubility is usually expressed in units of milligrams per 1000. grams of water at 1.0 atmosphere pressure. The graph below shows a solubility curve of oxygen in water.

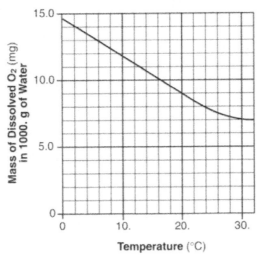

Temperature (°C)

42. A student determines that 8.2 milligrams of oxygen is dissolved in a 1000. gram sample of water at 15°C and 1.0 atmosphere of pressure. In terms of saturation, what type of solution is this sample?

43. Explain, in terms of molecular polarity, why oxygen gas has a low solubility in water. Your response must include both oxygen and water.

44. A student prepared a solution of oxygen by dissolving 6.0 mg of oxygen in 1000 grams of water at 20°C. Determine how many more milligrams of oxygen must be added to the solution to make it a saturated solution.

45. An aqueous solution has 0.007 grams of oxygen dissolved in 1000 grams of water. In the space below, calculate the dissolved oxygen concentration of this solution in parts per million. Your response should include both a correct numerical setup and calculated result.

1. When a solution of an acid is tested with pH paper, the result will be a pH
   1) Above 7, and the solution will conduct electricity
   2) Above 7, and the solution will not conduct electricity
   3) Below 7, and the solution will conduct electricity
   4) Below 7, and the solution will not conduct electricity

2. When a base is dissolved in water, it produces
   1) OH^- as the only negative ions in solution
   2) NH_4^+ as the only positive ions in solution
   3) CO_3^{2-} as the only negative ions in solution
   4) H^+ as the only positive ions in solution

3. As water is added to a 0.10 M NaCl aqueous solution, the conductivity of the resulting solution
   1) decreases because the concentration of ions decreases
   2) decreases, but the concentration of ions remains the same
   3) increases because the concentration of ions decreases
   4) increases, but the concentration of ions remains the same

4. A substance is classified as an electrolyte because
   1) it has a high melting point
   2) it contains covalent bonds
   3) its aqueous solution conducts an electric current
   4) its aqueous solution has a pH value of 7

5. The Arrhenius theory explains the behavior of
   1) acids and bases
   2) alcohols and amines
   3) acids and salts
   4) metals and nonmetals

6. Which statement describes an alternate theory of acids and bases?
   1) Acids and bases are both H^+ acceptors.
   2) Acids and bases are both H^+ donors.
   3) Acids are H^+ acceptors, and bases are H^+ donors.
   4) Acids are H^+ donors, and bases are H^+ acceptors.

7. According to the Arrhenius theory, an acid is a substance that
   1) changes litmus from red to blue
   2) changes phenolphthalein from colorless to pink
   3) produces hydronium ions as the only positive ions in an aqueous solution
   4) produces hydroxide ions as the only negative ions in an aqueous solution

8. Which substance is always produced in a reaction between an acid and a base?
   1) Water
   2) Hydrogen gas
   3) Oxygen gas
   4) A precipitate

9. The compound KOH(s) dissolves in water to yield
   1) hydroxide ions as the only negative ions
   2) hydroxide ions as the only positive ions
   3) hydronium ions as the only negative ions
   4) hydronium ions as the only positive ions

10. Which word equation represents a neutralization reaction?
    1) base + acid $\rightarrow$ salt + water
    2) base + salt $\rightarrow$ water + acid
    3) salt + acid $\rightarrow$ base + water
    4) salt + water $\rightarrow$ acid + base

11. Given the equation: $HCl(g) + H_2O(l) \rightarrow X(aq) + Cl^-(aq)$
    Which ion is represented by X?
    1) hydroxide
    2) hydronium
    3) hypochlorite
    4) perchlorate

12. Which two formulas represent Arrhenius acids?
    1) CH_3COOH and CH_3CH_2OH 3) $KHCO_3$ and $KHSO_4$
    2) $HC_2H_3O_2$ and H_3PO_4 4) $NaSCN$ and $Na_2S_2O_3$

13. Which compound releases hydroxide ions in an aqueous solution?
    1) CH_3COOH 2) HCl 3) CH_3OH 4) $LiOH$

14. Which aqueous solution could have a pH of 3?
    1) $H_2O(l)$ 2) $KOH(aq)$ 3) $CH_3OH(aq)$ 4) $H_2SO_4(aq)$

15. Which compound when dissolved in water will turn blue litmus red?
    1) CH_3OH 2) HBr 3) $C_6H_{12}O_6$ 4) $Ca(OH)_2$

16. Which is true of an aqueous solution of NH_4OH?
    1) It contains more OH^- ions than H^+ ions, and is a nonelectrolyte
    2) It contains more OH^- ions that H^+ ions, and is an electrolyte
    3) It contains more H^+ than OH^-, and is a nonelectrolyte
    4) It contains more H^+ than OH^-, and is an electrolyte

17. An example of a nonelectrolyte is
    1) $C_{12}H_{22}O_{11}(aq)$ 2) $K_2SO_4(aq)$ 3) $NH_4Cl(aq)$ 4) $HCl(aq)$

18. Which pH of a solution indicates the strongest base?
    1) 6   2) 7   3) 8   4) 9

19. When phenolphthalein is added to a solution, the solution stays colorless. What could be the pH of this solution?
    1) 2   2) 9   3) 11   4) 13

20. In a solution with a pH of 13, phenolphthalein will be
    1) pink, and litmus will be red   3) colorless, and litmus will be red
    2) pink, and litmus will be blue   4) colorless, and litmus will be blue

21. Which of these metals will not produce a reaction with sulfuric acid ?
    1) Ca   2) Au   3) Zn   4) Li

22. The pH of an aqueous solution changes from 4 to 3 when the hydrogen ion concentration in the solution is
    1) decreased by a factor of $4/3$ 3) increased by a factor of $3/4$
    2) decreased by a factor of 10   4) increased by a factor of 10

23. In the diagram below, which solution will cause the light bulb to glow?

    1) $C_6H_{12}O_6(aq)$ 2) $CO_2(aq)$ 3) $Cu(NO_3)_2(aq)$ 4) $C_2H_5OH(aq)$

24. Which equation represents a neutralization reaction?
    1) $4Fe(s) + 3O_2(g) \rightarrow 2Fe_2O_3(s)$
    2) $2H_2(g) + O_2(g) \rightarrow 2H_2O(l)$
    3) $HNO_3(aq) + KOH(aq) \rightarrow KNO_3(aq) + H_2O(l)$
    4) $AgNO_3(aq) + KCl(aq) \rightarrow KNO_3(aq) + AgCl(s)$

25. In the neutralization reaction:

    $$HC_2H_3O_2 + NH_4OH \rightarrow NH_4C_2H_3O_2 + H_2O$$

    The salt is
    1) NH_4OH 2) $HC_2H_3O_2$ 3) $NH_4C_2H_3O_2$ 4) H_2O

26. If 20 mL of 2.0 M KOH is exactly neutralized by 10 mL of HCl, the molarity of
    the HCl is
    1) 0.50 M   2) 2.0 M   3) 1.0 M   4) 4.0 M

27. How many milliliters of 3.0 M HCl are neutralized by 60 mL of 0.5 M $Ca(OH)_2$?
    1) 20 mL   2) 30 mL   3) 40 mL   4) 60 mL

Constructed Response

Base your answers to questions 28 through 30 on the information below.

A student was studying the pH difference in samples from two Adirondack streams.

The student measured a pH of 4 in stream A and a pH of 6 in stream B.

28. Identify one compound that could be used to neutralize the sample from stream A.

29. What is the color of bromthymol blue in the sample from stream A?

30. Compare the hydronium ion concentration in stream A to the hydronium ion
    concentration in stream B.

Base your answers to questions 31 through 33 on the information below.

A student titrates 60.0 mL of $HNO_3(aq)$ with 0.30 M NaOH(aq). Phenolphthalein is
used as the indicator. After adding 42.2 mL of NaOH(aq), a color change remains for
25 seconds, and the student stops the titration.

31. What color change does phenolphthalein undergo during this titration?

32. What is the concentration of the HNO_3 that was titrated?

33. Complete the equation below for the reaction that occurs during the titration.

    $HNO_3(aq) + NaOH(aq) \rightarrow$ _____ + _____

Base your answers to questions 34 through 37 on the graph below.

The graph shows the relationship between pH value and hydronium ion concentration for common aqueous solutions and mixtures.

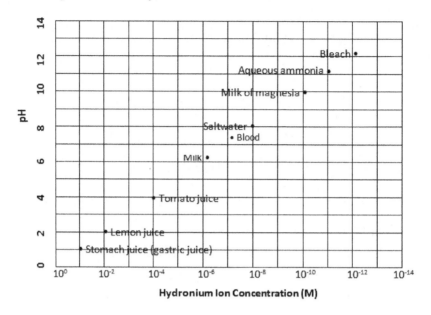

pH Versus Hydronium Ion Concentration

34. According to this graph, which mixture is approximately 100 times more acidic than milk of magnesia?

35. According to the graph, which mixture is approximately 10 times less acidic than aqueous ammonia?

36. What color is thymol blue when added to milk of magnesia?

37. What is the hydronium concentration of tomato juice?

1. Energy needed to start a chemical reaction is called
    1) Kinetic energy
    2) Activation energy
    3) Potential energy
    4) Ionization energy

2. Two particles collide with proper orientation. The collision will be effective if the particles have
    1) High activation energy
    2) High electronegativity
    3) Sufficient kinetic energy
    4) Sufficient potential energy

3. Which information about a chemical reaction is provided by a potential energy diagram?
    1) the oxidation states of the reactants and products
    2) the average kinetic energy of the reactants and products
    3) the change in solubility of the reacting substances
    4) the energy released or absorbed during the reaction

4. A catalyst works by
    1) increasing the potential energy of the reactants
    2) increasing the energy released during a reaction
    3) decreasing the potential energy of the products
    4) decreasing the activation energy required for a reaction

5. Why can an increase in temperature lead to more effective collisions between reactant particles and an increase in the rate of a chemical reaction?
    1) The activation energy of the reaction increases.
    2) The activation energy of the reaction decreases.
    3) The number of molecules with sufficient energy to react increases.
    4) The number of molecules with sufficient energy to react decreases.

6. A 1.0-gram sample of powdered Zn reacts faster with HCl than a single 1.0-gram piece of Zn because the surface atoms in powdered Zn have
    1) higher average kinetic energy
    2) lower average kinetic energy
    3) more contact with the H^+ ions in the acid
    4) less contact with the H^+ ions in the acid

7. In a reversible reaction, chemical equilibrium is attained when the
    1) rate of the forward reaction is greater than the rate of the reverse reaction
    2) rate of the reverse reaction is greater than the rate of the forward reaction
    3) concentration of the reactants reaches zero
    4) concentration of the products remains constant

8. The net energy released or absorbed during a reversible chemical reaction is equal to
    1) the activation energy of the endothermic reaction
    2) the activation energy of the exothermic reaction
    3) the difference between the potential energy of the products and the potential energy of the reactants
    4) the sum of the potential energy of the products and the potential energy of the reactants

9. Systems in nature tend to undergo changes toward
    1) Lower energy and higher entropy
    2) Lower energy and lower entropy
    3) Higher energy and lower entropy
    4) Higher energy and higher entropy

10. Increasing temperature on equilibrium reactions favors
    1) Exothermic reactions, only
    2) Endothermic reactions, only
    3) Both exothermic and endothermic reactions
    4) Neither exothermic nor endothermic reactions

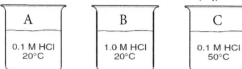

11. In each of the four beakers shown below, a 2.0-centimeter strip of magnesium ribbon reacts with 100 milliliters of HCl(aq) under the conditions shown.

A	B	C	D
0.1 M HCl 20°C	1.0 M HCl 20°C	0.1 M HCl 50°C	1.0 M HCl 50°C

In which beaker will the reaction occur at the fastest rate?
1) A   2) B   3) C   4) D

12. Based on the nature of the reactants in each equation, which reaction at 25°C will occur at the fastest rate?
1) $KI(aq)$ + $AgNO_3(aq)$ → $AgI(s)$ + $KNO_3(aq)$
2) $2C(s)$ + $O_2(g)$ → $2CO(g)$
3) $2SO_2(g)$ + $O_2(g)$ → $2SO_3(g)$
4) $NH_3(g)$ + $HCl(g)$ → $NH_4Cl(s)$

13. Given the reaction:
I + I → I_2 +   energy
This reaction has
1) $+\Delta H$ because the products have less energy than the reactants
2) $+\Delta H$ because the products have more energy than the reactants
3) $-\Delta H$ because the products have less energy than the reactants
4) $-\Delta H$ because the products have more energy than the reactants

14. Given the chemical change
$2H_2O(l)$ + 572 kJ   → $2 H_2(g)$ + $O_2(g)$
This reaction
1) Is endothermic and releases 572 kJ of heat energy
2) Is endothermic and absorbs 572 kJ of heat energy
3) Is exothermic and releases 572 kJ of heat energy
4) Is exothermic and absorbs 572 kJ of heat energy

15. Given the balanced equation:
$I_2(s)$ +   energy   → $I_2(g)$
As a sample of $I_2(s)$ sublimes to $I_2(g)$, the entropy of the sample
1) increases because the particles are less randomly arranged
2) increases because the particles are more randomly arranged
3) decreases because the particles are less randomly arranged
4) decreases because the particles are more randomly arranged

16. Which balanced equation represents a phase equilibrium?
1) $H_2(g)$ + $I_2(g)$ ↔ $2HI(g)$
2) $2NO_2(g)$ ↔ $N_2O_4(g)$
3) $Cl_2(g)$ ↔ $Cl_2(l)$
4) $3O_2(g)$ ↔ $2O_3(g)$

17. A potential energy diagram for a chemical reaction is given below.

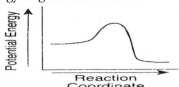

According to Reference Table I, which reaction could be represented by this potential energy diagram?

1) $2C(s) + 3H_2(g) \rightarrow C_2H_6(g)$ 3) $N_2(g) + O_2(g) \rightarrow 2NO(g)$
2) $2C(s) + 2H_2(g) \rightarrow C_2H_4(g)$ 4) $NH_4Cl(s) \rightarrow NH_4^+(aq) + Cl^-(aq)$

18. The potential energy diagram for a chemical reaction is shown below.

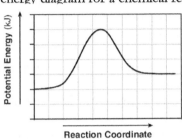

Each interval on the axis labeled "Potential Energy (kJ)" represents 40 kilojoules. What is the heat of reaction?

1) −120 kJ   2) −40 kJ   3) +40 kJ   4) +160 kJ

19. Given the equilibrium reaction below

$$N_2O_4 + 58.1 \text{ kJ} \leftrightarrow 2NO_2(g)$$

If heat is decreased on the reaction,

1) the rate of the forward reaction will increase, and equilibrium will shift to the right
2) the rate of the forward reaction will increase, and equilibrium will shift to the left
3) the rate of the reverse reaction will increase, and equilibrium will shift to the right
4) the rate of the reverse reaction will increase, and equilibrium will shift to the left

20. Given the reaction:
$$N_2(g) + O_2(g) + 182.6 \text{ kJ} \leftrightarrow 2NO(g)$$
Which change would cause an immediate increase in the rate of the forward reaction?
1) increasing the concentration of $NO(g)$
2) increasing the concentration of $N_2(g)$
3) decreasing the reaction temperature
4) decreasing the reaction pressure

21. Given the system at equilibrium:
$$2POCl_3(g) + \text{energy} \leftrightarrow 2PCl_3(g) + O_2(g)$$
Which changes occur when $O_2(g)$ is added to this system?
1) The equilibrium shifts to the right and the concentration of $PCl_3(g)$ increases.
2) The equilibrium shifts to the right and the concentration of $PCl_3(g)$ decreases.
3) The equilibrium shifts to the left and the concentration of $PCl_3(g)$ increases.
4) The equilibrium shifts to the left and the concentration of $PCl_3(g)$ decreases

Constructed Response

Base your answer to questions 22 through 25 on the potential energy diagram below.

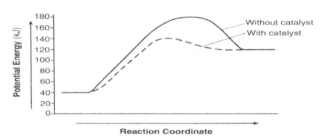

22. Explain, in terms of the function of a catalyst, why the curves on the potential energy diagram for the catalyzed and uncatalyzed reactions are different.

23. What is the activation energy for the forward reaction with the catalyst?

24. What is the heat of reaction for the reverse reaction without the catalyst?

25. What is the heat of the activated complex for the reaction with the catalyst?

Base your answers to questions 26 through 29 on the information below.

An investigation was conducted to study the effect of the concentration of a reactant on the total time needed to complete a chemical reaction. Four trials of the same reaction were performed. In each trial the initial concentration of the reactant was different. The time needed for the chemical reaction to be completed was measured. The data for each of the four trials are shown in the data table below.

Reactant Concentration and Reaction Time

Trial	Initial Concentration (M)	Reaction Time (s)
1	0.020	11
2	0.015	14
3	0.010	23
4	0.005	58

26. On the grid, mark an appropriate scale on the axis labeled "Reaction Time (s)." An appropriate scale is one that allows a trend to be seen.

27. On the same grid, plot the data from the table. Circle and connect the points .

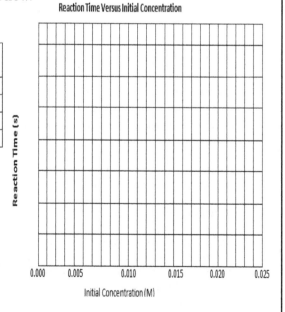

Reaction Time Versus Initial Concentration

28. State the effect of the concentration of the reactant on the rate of the chemical reaction.

29. In a different experiment involving the same reaction, it was found that an increase in temperature increased the rate of the reaction. Explain this result in terms of collision theory.

Base your answers to questions 30 through 32 on the information below.

Nitrogen gas, hydrogen gas, and ammonia gas are in equilibrium in a closed container at constant temperature and pressure. The equation below represents this equilibrium.

$$N_2(g) \ + \ 3H_2(g) \ \leftrightarrow \ 2NH_3(g)$$

The graph below shows the initial concentration of each gas, the changes that occur as a result of adding $H_2(g)$ to the system, and the final concentration when equilibrium is reestablished.

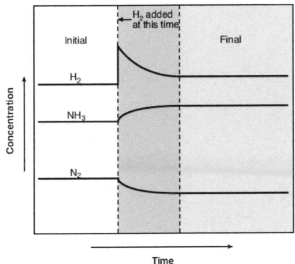

Concentration of Reaction Gases Versus Time

30. What information on the graph indicates that the system was initially at equilibrium?

31. Explain, in terms of Le Chatelier's Principle, why the final concentration of $NH_3(g)$ is greater than the initial concentration of $NH_3(g)$

32. Explain, in terms of collision theory, why the concentration of $H_2(g)$ begins to decrease immediately after more $H_2(g)$ is added to the system.

1. A compound that is classified as organic must contain the element
   1) Carbon   2) Nitrogen   3) Oxygen   4) Hydrogen

2. Compared with the rate of an inorganic reaction, the rate of an organic reaction is usually
   1) Faster, because organic compounds are ionic substances
   2) Faster, because organic compounds are molecular substances
   3) Slower, because organic compounds are ionic substances
   4) Slower, because organic compounds are molecular substances

3. A series of hydrocarbons in which each member of a group differs from the preceding member by one carbon is called
   1) A periodic series   3) An actinide series
   2) A homologous series   4) A lanthanide series

4. The total number of electrons shared between two adjacent carbon atoms in a saturated hydrocarbon is
   1) 1   2) 2   3) 3   4) 4

5. Which series of hydrocarbons contain unsaturated molecule, only?
   1) Alkane and benzene series   3) Alkene and alkyne series
   2) Alkyl and alkene series   4) Alkane and alkyne series

6. Each molecule of butane will contain a total of how many carbon atoms?
   1) 2   2) 4   3) 6   4) 8

7. The total number of electrons shared between two carbon atoms in a triple bond is
   1) 2   2) 3   3) 5   4) 6

8. As the length of the chain of carbon atoms in molecules of alkene series increases, the number of double bonds per molecule
   1) Increases   2) Decreases   3) Remains the same

9. The general formula for all alkyne molecules is
   1) C_nH_{2n} 2) C_nH_{2n+2} 3) C_nH_{2n-2} 4) C_nH_{2n+6}

10. Which functional group is found in all alcohols?
    1) –OH   2) – COOH   3) –CHO   4) – O –

11. Which IUPAC name ending is common for the class of organic compounds called aldehydes?
    1) –yl   2) –al   3) –ol   4) –one

12. Which is true of organic acids?
    1) They are non-electrolytes   3) They turn litmus blue
    2) They are weak electrolytes   4) They turn phenolphthalein pink

13. Two isomers must have the same
    1) Percent composition   3) Physical properties
    2) Arrangement of atoms   4) Chemical properties

14. The formation of large molecules from smaller molecules is an example of
    1) Saponification   3) Substitution
    2) Decomposition   4) Polymerization

15. What type of organic reaction describes the burning of a hydrocarbon in the presence of oxygen?
    1) Addition   3) Combustion
    2) Decomposition   4) Substitution

16. Each molecule of pentyne will contain a total of how many hydrogen atoms?
    1) 5 2) 8 3) 10 4) 12

17. Given the organic structure below,

$$H-\overset{\overset{\displaystyle H}{|}}{\underset{\underset{\displaystyle H}{|}}{C}}-\overset{\overset{\displaystyle H}{|}}{\underset{\underset{\displaystyle H}{|}}{C}}-OH$$

Which IUPAC name is possible for a compound with this structure?
    1) Methane 2) Ethanol 3) Propene 4) Butanol

18. Which two formulas are of compounds belonging to the alkane series?
    1) C_4H_6 and C_4H_8 3) C_2H_4 and C_4H_6
    2) $C_{11}H_{22}$ and $C_{11}H_{24}$ 4) C_8H_{18} and C_9H_{20}

19. Which set of IUPAC names are of compounds that are classified as alkenes?
    1) Methyl and ethyl 3) Ethane and pentene
    2) Ethene and decene 4) Ethyne and ethane

20. Which is an IUPAC name of a secondary alcohol?
    1) 1,2,-ethandiol 3) 1,2,3-propanetriol
    2) Propanol 4) 2-butanol

21. The formula of which compound represents an alcohol?
    1) CH_3CHO 2) CH_3CH_2OH 3) CH_3COOH 4) CH_3COOCH_3

22. A formula of which compound is an organic halide?
    1) $CH_3CH_2NH_2$ 3) $CH_3CH_2CH_2Br$
    2) CH_3OCH_3 4) HCl

23. A compound of which IUPAC name represents an aldehyde?
    1) Pentane 2) Butanoic 3) Propanol 4) Hexanal

24. The structure

$$H-\overset{\overset{\displaystyle H}{|}}{\underset{\underset{\displaystyle H}{|}}{C}}-\overset{}{\underset{\underset{\displaystyle OH}{|}}{C}}{=}O$$

is classified as an organic acid because it contains

    1) –OH groups 2) –COOH group 3) – C – C – bonds 4) C = O bond

25. The structure of which compound contains the functional group – O –
    1) Dimethyl ether 3) Propanone
    2) Methyl Butanoate 4) Ethanoic acid

26. The condensed formula that represents methyl propanoate is
    1) $CH_3CH_2COOCH_3$ 3) CH_3CH_2CHO
    2) CH_3COOH 4) CH_3CHO

27. Which compound is an isomer of butanoic acid, $CH_3CH_2CH_2COOH$?
    1) $CH_3CH_2CH_2CH_2OH$ 3) $CH_3CH_2CH_2CH_2COOH$
    2) $CH_3CH_2COOCH_3$ 4) $CH_3CH_2OCH_3$

28. Given the reaction below:

$$C_4H_8 \quad + \quad Cl_2 \quad \rightarrow \quad C_4H_8Cl_2$$

What type of reaction is represented by the equation?
1) Combustion   2) Substitution   3) Polymerization   4) Addition

29. Which formula correctly represents a compound formed from a reaction between C_2H_4 and Br_2?
1) 1,2-dibromoethene   2) 1,2-dibromoethane   3) Bromoethane   4) Bromoethene

30. Given the equation

$$C_2H_6 \quad + \quad F_2 \quad \rightarrow \quad X \quad + \quad HF$$

What is the name of compound X produced?
1) Ethene   2) Fluoroethane   3) 1,2-difluoroethane   4) Fluoropropane

Constructed Response

Base your answers to questions 31 through 33 on the information below.

Ethene (common name ethylene) is a commercially important organic compound. Millions of tons of ethene are produce by the chemical industry each year. Ethene is used in the manufacture of synthetic fibers for carpeting and clothing, and it is widely used in the making of polyethylene. Low-density polyethylene can be stretched into a clear, thin film that is used for wrapping food products and consumer goods. High-density polyethylene is molded into bottles for milk and other liquids. Ethene can also be oxidized to produce ethylene glycol, which is widely used in antifreeze for automobiles. The structural formula for ethylene glycol is:

$$
\begin{array}{c}
\text{H} \quad \text{H} \\
| \quad\quad | \\
\text{H} - \text{C} - \text{C} - \text{H} \\
| \quad\quad | \\
\text{OH} \quad \text{OH}
\end{array}
$$

At standard atmosphere pressure, the boiling point of ethylene glycol is 198°C, compared to ethene that boils at -104°C.

31. Explain, in terms of bonding, why ethene is an unsaturated hydrocarbon.

32. According to the information in the reading passage, state two consumer products manufactured from ethene.

33. Identify the type of organic reaction by which ethene is made into polyethylene.

Base your answers to questions 34 through 37 on the information and diagram below, and on your knowledge of chemistry.

Crude oil is a mixture of many hydrocarbons that have different numbers of carbon atoms. The use of fractionating towers allows the separation of this mixture based on the boiling points of the hydrocarbons.

To begin the separation process, the crude oil is heated to about 400°C in a furnace, causing many of the hydrocarbons of the crude oil to vaporize. The vaporized mixture is pumped into a fractionating tower that is usually more than 30 meters tall. The temperature of the tower is highest at the bottom. As vaporized samples of hydrocarbons travel up the tower, they cool and condense. The liquid hydrocarbons are collected on trays and removed from the tower. The diagram below illustrates the fractional distillation of the crude oil and the temperature ranges in which the different hydrocarbons condense.

Distillation of Crude Oil

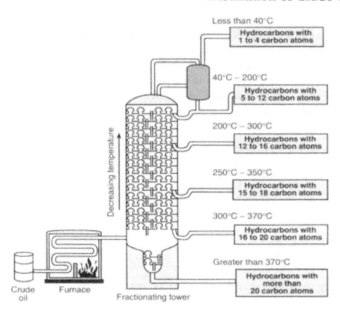

34. State the trend between the boiling point of the hydrocarbons contained in the crude oil and the number of carbon atoms in these molecules.

35. Describe the relationship between the strength of the intermolecular forces and the number of carbon atoms in the different hydrocarbon molecules.

36. Write the IUPAC name of one of the saturated hydrocarbons that leaves the fractionating tower at less than 40°C.

37. How many hydrogen atoms are present in one molecule of octane?

1. Which particles are gained and lost during a redox reaction?
   1) Protons   2) Electrons   3) Neutrons   4) Positrons

2. Which statement correctly describes a redox reaction?
   1) The oxidation half-reaction and the reduction half-reaction occur simultaneously
   2) The oxidation half-reaction occurs before the reduction half-reaction
   3) The oxidation half-reaction occurs after the reduction half-reaction
   4) The oxidation half-reaction occurs spontaneously but the reduction half-reaction does not

3. The sum of all oxidation numbers of atoms in a chemical formula must equal
   1) -1   2) 0   3) 1   4) 2

4. In an oxidation-reduction chemical reaction, reduction is a
   1) Gain of protons   3) Gain of electrons
   2) Loss of protons   4) Loss of electrons

5. What kind of reaction occurs in a voltaic cell?
   1) Non-spontaneous oxidation-reduction
   2) Spontaneous oxidation-reduction
   3) Non-spontaneous oxidation, only
   4) Spontaneous reduction, only

6. An electrolytic cell is different from a voltaic cell because in an electrolytic cell
   1) An electrical current is produced
   2) An electrical current causes a chemical reaction
   3) A redox reaction occurs
   4) A spontaneous reaction occurs

7. The negative electrode in a voltaic cell is the
   1) Cathode, where electrons are gained
   2) Cathode, where electrons are lost
   3) Anode, where electrons are gained
   4) Anode, where electrons are lost

8. What type of chemical reaction occurs in all electrochemical cells?
   1) Neutralization   3) Redox
   2) Double replacement   4) Hydrolysis

9. In any redox reaction, the substance that undergoes reduction will
   1) lose electrons and have a decrease in oxidation number
   2) lose electrons and have an increase in oxidation number
   3) gain electrons and have a decrease in oxidation number
   4) gain electrons and have an increase in oxidation number

10. In all redox reactions, there is conservation of
    1) Mass, but not charge   3) Both mass and charge
    2) Charge, but not mass   4) Neither mass nor charge

11. Which is true of a reducing agent in oxidation-reduction reactions?
    1) A reducing agent loses electrons, and is oxidized
    2) A reducing agent loses electrons, and is reduced
    3) A reducing agent gains electrons, and is oxidized
    4) A reducing agent gains electrons, and is reduced

12. What is the oxidation number of nitrogen in HNO_3?
    1) +5   2) +4   3) -3   4) -1

13. What is the oxidation number of hydrogen in LiH?
    1) 0   2) +1   3) +2   4) -1

14. What is the oxidation number of Cr in the polyatomic ion, $Cr_2O_7{}^{2-}$?
    1) +7   2) +6   3) -2   4) +2

15. In which substance does phosphorus have an oxidation number of +3?
    1) P_4O_{10} 2) PCl_5 3) $Ca_3(PO_4)_2$ 4) KH_2PO_3

16. Which equation represents an oxidation – reduction reaction?
    1) SO_2 + H_2O $\rightarrow$ H_2SO_3
    2) $SO_3{}^{2-}$ + $2H^+$ $\rightarrow$ H_2SO_4
    3) O_2 + $2H_2$ $\rightarrow$ $2H_2O$
    4) OH^- + H^+ $\rightarrow$ H_2O

17. In which oxidation number change would a species in a redox reaction gain the most number of electrons?
    1)   +3 to -1   3)   0 to +4
    2)   +6 to +3   4)   +3 to +7

18. Which half-reaction equation correctly represents a reduction reaction?
    1) Li^0 + e^- $\rightarrow$ Li^+
    2) Na^0 + e^- $\rightarrow$ Na^+
    3) $Br_2{}^0$ + $2e^-$ $\rightarrow$ $2Br^-$
    4) $Cl_2{}^0$ + e^- $\rightarrow$ $2Cl^-$

19. Consider the half-reaction equation below:
    $$Li^0   \rightarrow   Li^+   +   e^-$$
    The Li^0 is
    1) Oxidized, and is the reducing agent
    2) Oxidized, and is the oxidizing agent
    3) Reduced, and is the reducing agent
    4) Reduced, and is the oxidizing agent

20. In the oxidation-reduction reaction below,

    $$2Al   +   3Ni^{2+}   \rightarrow   2Al^{3+}   +   3Ni$$

    Which species acts as an oxidizing agent?
    1) Al   2) Al^{3+} 3) Ni   4) Ni^{2+}

21. In the reaction,
    $$Mg   +   ZnCl_2   \rightarrow   MgCl_2   +   Zn$$

    Which is true of the magnesium?
    1) It is oxidized by losing electrons
    2) It is oxidized by gaining electrons
    3) It is reduced by losing electrons
    4) It is reduced by gaining electrons

22. Given the cell diagram below

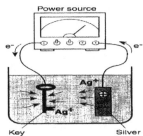

Which statement best describes the key in this diagram?
1) It acts as the anode, and is negative
2) It acts as the anode, and is positive
3) It acts as the cathode, and is negative
4) It acts as the cathode, and is positive

23. Given the reaction:

$$Mg(s) \quad + \quad FeSO_4(aq) \quad \rightarrow \quad Fe(s) \quad + \quad MgSO_4(aq)$$

The reaction would most likely occur in
1) A voltaic cell, and will produce energy
2) An electrolytic cell, and will produce energy
3) A voltaic cell, and will absorb energy
4) An electrolytic cell, and will absorb energy

24. Given a cell diagram below:

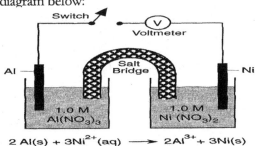

$$2\,Al(s) + 3Ni^{2+}(aq) \longrightarrow 2Al^{3+} + 3Ni(s)$$

When the switch is closed, which species will be oxidized in this electrochemical cell?
1) Al^{3+} ions   2) Al atoms   3) Ni^{2+} ions   4) Ni atoms

25. Consider the reaction below:

$$2H_2O \quad + \quad electricity \quad \rightarrow \quad 2H_2 \quad + \quad O_2$$

In which type of cell would this reaction most likely occur?
1) A voltaic, because it releases energy
2) An electrolytic, because it releases energy
3) A voltaic, because it absorbs energy
4) An electrolytic, because it absorbs energy

26. Which ion is most easily reduced?
1) Zn^{2+} 2) Mg^{2+} 3) Pb^{2+} 4) Na^+

27. Which element is likely to be obtained from the electrolytic process of the fused salt?
1) Br   2) Cu   3) H   4) K

28. In an electrolytic cell, which ion would migrate through solution to the positive electrode?
1) a hydrogen ion
2) a fluoride ion
3) an ammonium ion
4) a hydronium ion

Base your answers to questions 29 through 31 on the diagram and balanced equation below, which represents the electrolysis of molten NaCl.

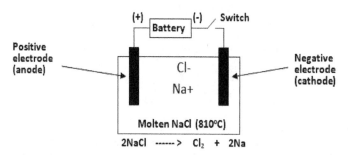

29. Write the balanced half-reaction for the reduction that occurs in this electrolytic cell.

30. What is the purpose of the battery in this electrolytic cell?

31. When the switch is closed, which electrode will attract the sodium ions?

Base your answers to questions 32 and 33 on the equation below.

$$4Al(s) \quad + \quad 3O_2(g) \quad \rightarrow \quad 2Al_2O_3(s)$$

32. Write a balanced oxidation half-reaction equation for this reaction.

33. What is the oxidation number of oxygen in Al_2O_3?

Base your answers to questions 34 through 39 on the following redox reaction, which occurs spontaneously.

$$Zn \quad + \quad Cr^{3+} \quad \rightarrow \quad Zn^{2+} \quad + \quad Cr$$

34. State what happens to the number of protons in a Zn atom when it changes to Zn^{2+} as the redox reaction occurs.

35. Which half-reaction occurs at the anode?

36. Which species loses electrons and which species gains electrons?

37. Write the half-reaction for the oxidation that occurs.

38. Write the half-reaction for the reduction that occurs.

39. Balance the redox equation using the smallest whole-number coefficients.

$$\_\_\_ Zn \quad + \quad \_\_\_\_ Cr^{3+} \quad \rightarrow \quad \_\_\_ Zn^{2+} \quad + \quad \_\_\_ Cr$$

Nuclear Chemistry

1. Which process converts an atom from one element to another when the nucleus of an atom is bombarded with high-energy particles?
   1) Artificial transmutation
   2) Addition polymerization
   3) Natural transmutation
   4) Condensation polymerization

2. Spontaneous decay of certain elements in nature occurs because these elements have a
   1) Disproportionate ratio of electrons to protons
   2) Disproportionate ratio of neutrons to protons
   3) High reactivity with oxygen
   4) Low reactivity with oxygen

3. The energy released by a nuclear reaction results primarily from
   1) Breaking of bonds between atoms
   2) Formation of bonds between atoms
   3) Conversion of mass into energy
   4) Conversions of energy into mass

4. An electron has a charge identical to that of
   1) A positron   2) A beta particle   3) An alpha particle   4) A proton

5. Which nuclear emission symbol has neither mass nor charge?
   1) α   2) β-   3) β+   4) γ

6. Which list is showing the particles arranged in order of decreasing penetrating power?
   1) Gamma → Beta → Alpha
   2) Beta → Gamma → Alpha
   3) Alpha → Beta → Gamma
   4) Gamma → Alpha → Beta

7. Which nuclear emission moving through an electric field would be attracted toward a positive electrode?
   1) Gamma radiation   2) Proton   3) Beta Particle   4) Alpha particle

8. When an alpha particle is emitted by an atom, the atomic number of the atom
   1) Increases by 2
   2) Increases by 4
   3) Decreases by 2
   4) Decreases by 4

9. Cobalt-60 and Iodine-131 are radioactive isotopes that are used in
   1) Dating geologic formations
   2) Industrial measurements
   3) Medical procedures
   4) Nuclear power

10. One benefit of nuclear fission reactions is
    1) Nuclear reaction meltdowns
    2) Storage of waste materials
    3) Biological exposure
    4) Production of energy

11. Diagnostic injections of radioisotopes used in medicine normally have
    1) Short half-lives and are quickly eliminated from the body
    2) Short half-lives and are slowly eliminated from the body
    3) Long half-lives and are quickly eliminated from the body
    4) Long half-lives and are slowly eliminated from the body

12. A beta or an alpha particle may be spontaneously emitted from
    1) A ground-state atom
    2) A stable nucleus
    3) An excited electron
    4) An unstable nucleus

13. Which Group 18 element is naturally radioactive and has no known stable isotope?
    1) Ar   2) Rn   3) Xe   4) Kr

14. Which notation of a radioisotope is correctly paired with the notation of its emission particle?
    1) $^{32}_{15}P$ and $^{0}_{+1}e$ 2) $^{226}_{88}Ra$ and $^{0}_{-1}e$ 3) $^{239}_{90}Pu$ and $^{4}_{2}He$ 4) $^{3}_{1}H$ and $^{0}_{+1}e$

15. Artificial transmutation is represented by which nuclear equation?

1) $^{238}_{92}U + ^{4}_{2}He \rightarrow ^{241}_{94}Pu + ^{1}_{0}n$ 3) $^{235}_{92}U + ^{1}_{0}n \rightarrow ^{87}_{35}Br + ^{146}_{57}La + 3\,^{1}_{0}n$

2) $^{16}_{7}N \rightarrow ^{16}_{8}O + ^{0}_{-1}e$ 4) $^{2}_{1}H + ^{1}_{1}H \rightarrow ^{3}_{2}He$

16. Given the nuclear reaction

$$^{19}_{10}Ne \rightarrow ^{0}_{+1}e + ^{19}_{9}F$$

    The reaction is an example of
1) Fission   3) Fusion
2) Natural transmutation   4) Artificial transmutation

17. Given the nuclear equation below

$$^{121}_{53}I \rightarrow X + ^{121}_{52}Te$$

    The reaction is best described as
1) Beta decay   3) Positron emission
2) Artificial transmutation   4) Alpha decay

18. Exactly how much time elapses before 16 grams of potassium-42 decays, leaving 2 grams of the original isotope?
    1) 98.88 hours   2) 24.72 hours   3) 37.08 hours   4) 49.44 hours

19. A radioactive isotope of an element decays from 20 grams to 5 grams in 8 minutes. What is the half-life of this radioisotope?
    1) 15 minutes   2) 4 minutes   3) 10 minutes   4) 20 minutes

20. The half-life of a radioisotope is 20.0 minutes. What is the total amount of a 10 g sample of this isotope remaining after 1 hour?
    1) 1.25 g   2) 2.50 g   3) 3.33 g   4) 5.00 g

21. Approximately what fraction of an original ^{60}Co sample remains unchanged after 21 years?
    1) $^{1}/_{2}$ 2) $^{1}/_{4}$ 3) $^{1}/_{8}$ 4) $^{1}/_{16}$

22. A sample of which radioisotope will have the greatest remaining amount after 100 years of decaying?
    1) 5 g of Co-60   2) 5 g of H-3   3) 5 g of Kr-85   4) 5 g of Sr-90

23. Radioactive dating of the remains of organic materials can be done by comparing the ratio of which two isotopes?
    1) Uranium -235 to Uranium -238   3) Nitrogen-14 to Nitrogen-16
    2) Carbon-14 to Carbon-12   4) Hydrogen-2 to Hydrogen-3

24. If 8.0 grams of a sample of ^{60}Co existed in 1990, in what year was the remaining amount of ^{60}Co in the sample 0.50 grams?
    1) 1995   2) 2000   3) 2006   4) 2011

25. If 3.0 grams of ^{90}Sr in a rock sample remained in 1989, approximately how many grams of ^{90}Sr were present in the original rock sample in 1931?

    1) 9.0 g   2) 12. g   3) 3.0 g   4) 6.0 g

Base your answers to questions 26 through 29 on the information below, which relates the numbers of neutrons and protons for specific nuclides of C, N, Ne, and S.

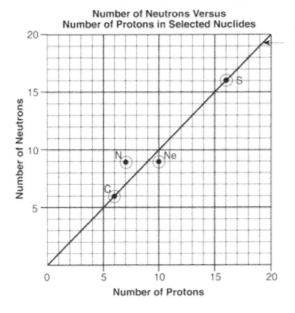

This line connects the points where the neutron-to-proton ratio is 1 : 1

26. Based on your Reference Tables, complete the nuclear decay equation for Ne-19.

$$^{19}Ne \rightarrow \underline{\hspace{1cm}} + \underline{\hspace{1cm}}$$

27. Using the point plotted on the graph for nitrogen, what is the neutron-to-proton ratio of this nuclide?

28. Explain, in terms of atomic particles, why S-32 is a stable nuclide.

29. What is the mass number of the carbon isotope represented on the graph?

Base your answers to questions 30 to 32 on the information and table below.

Some radioisotopes use tracers to make it possible for doctors to see the images of internal body parts and observe their functions. The table below lists information about three radioisotopes and the body part each radioisotope is used to study.

Medical uses of Some Radioisotopes

Radioisotope	Half-life	Decay Mode	Body Part
^{24}Na	15 hours	Beta	Circulatory system
^{59}Fe	44.5 days	Beta	Red blood cells
^{131}I	8.1 days	Beta	Thyroid

30. It could take up to 60. hours for a radioisotope to be delivered to the hospital from the laboratory where it is produced. What fraction of an original sample of ^{24}Na remains unchanged after 60 hours?

31. Complete the equation for the nuclear decay of the radioisotope used to study red blood cells. Include both atomic number and the mass number for each missing particle.

$$^{59}\text{Fe} \rightarrow \underline{\hspace{1.5cm}} + \underline{\hspace{1.5cm}}$$

32. A patient at a clinic was injected with a 100 mg sample of iodine-131 during a routine thyroid function test. How much of the original iodine-131 will remain in the patient's body after approximately 48 days?

Days 13 through 16

Practice Regents Exams

NYS Regents Chemistry
The Physical Setting
June 2014 and January 2014 Exams

survivingchem.com

Part A: Answer all questions in this part

Directions (1 – 30): For each statement or question, write on the separate answer sheet the number of the word or expression that, of those given, best completes the statement or answers the question. Some questions may require the use of the Reference tables for Physical Setting/Chemistry.

1 Compared to the charge of a proton, the charge of an electron has
   (1) a greater magnitude and the same sign
   (2) a greater magnitude and the opposite sign
   (3) the same magnitude and the same sign
   (4) the same magnitude and the opposite sign

2 Which atom has the largest atomic radius?
   (1) potassium   (3) francium
   (2) rubidium   (4) cesium

3 In the wave-mechanical model of the atom, an orbital is defined as
   (1) a region of the most probable proton location
   (2) a region of the most probable electron location
   (3) a circular path traveled by a proton around the nucleus
   (4) a circular path traveled by an electron around the nucleus

4 When an excited electron in an atom moves to the ground state, the electron
   (1) absorbs energy as it moves to a higher energy state
   (2) absorbs energy as it moves to a lower energy state
   (3) emits energy as it moves to a higher energy state
   (4) emits energy as it moves to a lower energy state

5 Which polyatomic ion is found in the compound represented by the formula $NaHCO_3$?
   (1) acetate   (3) hydrogen sulfate
   (2) hydrogen carbonate   (4) oxalate

6 The atomic mass of magnesium is the weighted average of the atomic masses of
   (1) all of the artificially produced isotopes of Mg
   (2) all of the naturally occurring isotopes of Mg
   (3) the two most abundant artificially produced isotopes of Mg
   (4) the two most abundant naturally occurring isotopes of Mg

7 Which element has atoms that can form halide ions?
 (1) iodine
 (2) silver
 (3) strontium
 (4) xenon

8 Two forms of solid carbon, diamond and graphite, differ in their physical properties due to the differences in their
 (1) atomic numbers
 (2) crystal structures
 (3) isotopic abundances
 (4) percent compositions

9 Which quantity can be calculated for a solid compound, given only the formula of the compound and the Periodic Table of the Elements?
 (1) the density of the compound
 (2) the heat of fusion of the compound
 (3) the melting point of each element in the compound
 (4) the percent composition by mass of each element in the compound

10 Which terms identify types of chemical reactions?
 (1) decomposition and sublimation
 (2) decomposition and synthesis
 (3) deposition and sublimation
 (4) deposition and synthesis

11 The greatest amount of energy released per gram of reactants occurs during a
 (1) redox reaction
 (2) fission reaction
 (3) substitution reaction
 (4) neutralization reaction

12 Which element has atoms with the strongest attraction for electrons in a chemical bond?
 (1) chlorine
 (2) nitrogen
 (3) fluorine
 (4) oxygen

13 Compared to the physical and chemical properties of the compound NO_2, the compound N_2O has
   (1) different physical properties and different chemical properties
   (2) different physical properties and the same chemical properties
   (3) the same physical properties and different chemical properties
   (4) the same physical properties and the same chemical properties

14 Which phrase describes a molecule of CH_4, in terms of molecular polarity and distribution of charge?
   (1) polar with an asymmetrical distribution of charge
   (2) polar with a symmetrical distribution of charge
   (3) nonpolar with an asymmetrical distribution of charge
   (4) nonpolar with a symmetrical distribution of charge

15 Which sample of copper has atoms with the *lowest* average kinetic energy?
   (1) 10. g at 45°C   (3) 30. g at 25°C
   (2) 20. g at 35°C   (4) 40. g at 15°C

16 Which change results in the formation of different substances?
   (1) burning of propane
   (2) melting of $NaCl(s)$
   (3) deposition of $CO_2(g)$
   (4) solidification of water

17 Which substance can *not* be broken down by a chemical change?
   (1) ammonia   (3) propanal
   (2) ethanol   (4) zirconium

18 According to Table *I*, which equation represents a change resulting in the greatest quantity of energy released?
   (1) $2C(s)$ + $3H_2(g) \rightarrow C_2H_6(g)$
   (2) $2C(s)$ + $2H_2(g) \rightarrow C_2H_4(g)$
   (3) $N_2(g)$ + $3H_2(g) \rightarrow 2NH_3(g)$
   (4) $N_2(g)$ + $O_2(g) \rightarrow 2NO(g)$

19 Which element is a liquid at STP?

(1) bromine   (3) francium

(2) cesium   (4) iodine

20 Which statement describes a reversible reaction at equilibrium?

(1) The activation energy of the forward reaction must equal the activation energy of the reverse reaction.

(2) The rate of the forward reaction must equal the rate of the reverse reaction.

(3) The concentration of the reactants must equal the concentration of the products.

(4) The potential energy of the reactants must equal the potential energy of the products.

21 Given the balanced equation representing a reaction:

$$O_2 \rightarrow O + O$$

What occurs during this reaction?

(1) Energy is absorbed as bonds are broken.

(2) Energy is absorbed as bonds are formed.

(3) Energy is released as bonds are broken.

(4) Energy is released as bonds are formed.

22 In terms of entropy and energy, systems in nature tend to undergo changes toward

(1) lower entropy and lower energy

(2) lower entropy and higher energy

(3) higher entropy and lower energy

(4) higher entropy and higher energy

23 Which term is defined as the difference between the potential energy of the products and the potential energy of the reactants in a chemical reaction?

(1) activation energy   (3) heat of fusion

(2) thermal energy   (4) heat of reaction

24 What is the atomic number of the element whose atoms bond to each other in chains, rings, and networks?
(1) 10   (3) 6
(2) 8   (4) 4

25 How many pairs of electrons are shared between two adjacent carbon atoms in a saturated hydrocarbon?
(1) 1   (3) 3
(2) 2   (4) 4

26 Given the balanced equation representing a reaction:
$$4Al(s) + 3O_2(g) \rightarrow 2Al_2O_3(s)$$
As the aluminum loses 12 moles of electrons, the oxygen
(1) gains 4 moles of electrons   (3) loses 4 moles of electrons
(2) gains 12 moles of electrons   (4) loses 12 moles of electrons

27 Which compound is an electrolyte?
(1) CH₃CHO   (3) CH₃COOH
(2) CH₃OCH₃   (4) CH₃CH₂CH₃

28 Which statement describes one acid-base theory?
(1) An acid is an H^+ acceptor, and a base is an H^+ donor.
(2) An acid is an H^+ donor, and a base is an H^+ acceptor.
(3) An acid is an H– acceptor, and a base is an H– donor.
(4) An acid is an H– donor, and a base is an H– acceptor.

29 Which compounds are classified as Arrhenius acids?
(1) HCl and NaOH   (3) NH₃ and H₂CO₃
(2) HNO₃ and NaCl   (4) HBr and H₂SO₄

30 Which statement describes the stability of the nuclei of potassium atoms?
(1) All potassium atoms have stable nuclei that spontaneously decay.
(2) All potassium atoms have unstable nuclei that do not spontaneously decay.
(3) Some potassium atoms have unstable nuclei that spontaneously decay.
(4) Some potassium atoms have unstable nuclei that do not spontaneously decay.

Part B – 1:   Answer all questions in this part.

Directions (31 – 50): For each statement or question, write on the separate answer sheet the number of the word or expression that, of those given, best completes the statement or answers the question. Some questions may require the use of the Reference Tables for Physical Setting/Chemistry.

31 Which notations represent different isotopes of the element sodium?
   (1) ^{32}S and ^{34}S
   (2) S^{2-} and S^{6+}
   (3) Na^+ and Na^0
   (4) ^{22}Na and ^{23}Na

32 Which electron configuration represents the electrons in an atom of Ga in an excited state?
   (1) 2-8-17-3
   (2) 2-8-17-4
   (3) 2-8-18-3
   (4) 2-8-18-4

33 Which statement describes the general trends in electronegativity and first ionization energy as the elements in Period 3 are considered in order from Na to Cl?
   (1) Electronegativity increases, and first ionization energy decreases.
   (2) Electronegativity decreases, and first ionization energy increases.
   (3) Electronegativity and first ionization energy both increase.
   (4) Electronegativity and first ionization energy both decrease.

34 What is the gram-formula mass of $Fe(NO_3)_3$?
   (1) 146 g/mol
   (2) 194 g/mol
   (3) 214 g/mol
   (4) 242 g/mol

35 Given the balanced equation representing a reaction:
   $$Al_2(SO_4)_3 \ + \ 6NaOH \rightarrow 2Al(OH)_3 \ + \ 3Na_2SO_4$$
   The mole ratio of NaOH to $Al(OH)_3$ is
   (1) 1:1
   (2) 1:3
   (3) 3:1
   (4) 3:7

36 Which equation represents a single replacement reaction?

(1) $2H_2O_2 \rightarrow 2H_2O + O_2$

(2) $2H_2 + O_2 \rightarrow 2H_2O$

(3) $H_2SO_4 + Mg \rightarrow H_2 + MgSO_4$

(4) $HCl + KOH \rightarrow KCl + H_2O$

37 The accepted value for the percent by mass of water in a hydrate is 36.0%. In a laboratory activity, a student determined the percent by mass of water in the hydrate to be 37.8%. What is the percent error for the student's measured value?

(1) 5.0%   (3) 1.8%

(2) 4.8%   (4) 0.05%

38 The boiling points, at standard pressure, of four compounds are given in the table below.

Boiling Points of Four Compounds

Compound	Boiling Point (°C)
H_2O	100.0
H_2S	−59.6
H_2Se	−41.3
H_2Te	−2.0

Which type of attraction can be used to explain the unusually high boiling point of H_2O?

(1) ionic bonding

(2) hydrogen bonding

(3) polar covalent bonding

(4) nonpolar covalent bonding

39 Which formula represents a molecule with the most polar bond?

(1) CO   (3) HI

(2) NO   (4) HCl

40 The graph below represents the uniform heating of a substance from the solid to the gas phase.

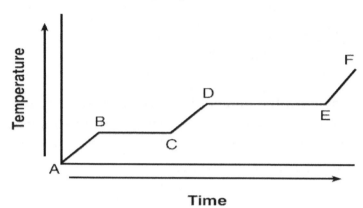

Which line segment of the graph represents boiling?
(1) $\overline{AB}$ (3) $\overline{CD}$
(2) $\overline{BC}$ (4) $\overline{DE}$

41 A 1-gram sample of a compound is added to 100 grams of $H_2O(\ell)$ and the resulting mixture is then thoroughly stirred. Some of the compound is then separated from the mixture by filtration. Based on Table F, the compound could be
(1) AgCl   (3) NaCl
(2) $CaCl_2$ (4) $NiCl_2$

42 At standard pressure, the total amount of heat required to completely vaporize a 100.-gram sample of water at its boiling point is
(1) $2.26 \times 10 \text{ J}$ (3) $2.26 \times 10^3 \text{ J}$
(2) $2.26 \times 10^2 \text{ J}$ (4) $2.26 \times 10^5 \text{ J}$

43 A sample of helium gas is in a sealed, rigid container. What occurs as the temperature of the sample is increased?
(1) The mass of the sample decreases.
(2) The number of moles of gas increases.
(3) The volume of each atom decreases.
(4) The frequency of collisions between atoms increases.

44 Given the equation representing a reaction at equilibrium:

$$2SO_2(g) + O_2(g) \rightarrow 2SO_3(g) + heat$$

Which change causes the equilibrium to shift to the right?

(1) adding a catalyst

(2) adding more $O_2(g)$

(3) decreasing the pressure

(4) increasing the temperature

45 Given the formula representing a compound:

```
    H   H   H       H
    |   |   |       |
H – C – C – C = C – C – H
    |   |       |   |
    H   H       H   H
```

What is a chemical name of this compound?

(1) 2-pentene   (3) 3-pentene

(2) 2-pentyne   (4) 3-pentyne

46 What is the oxidation number of manganese in $KMnO_4$?

(1) +7   (3) +3

(2) +2   (4) +4

47 When the pH of an aqueous solution is changed from 1 to 2, the concentration of hydronium ions in the solution is

(1) decreased by a factor of 2

(2) decreased by a factor of 10

(3) increased by a factor of 2

(4) increased by a factor of 10

48 What is the color of the indicator thymol blue in a solution that has a pH of 11?

(1) red   (3) pink

(2) blue   (4) yellow

49 Which formulas represent compounds that are isomers of each other?

```
    H              H  H
    |              |  |
H − C − H  and  H − C − C − H
    |              |  |
    H              H  H
        (1)
```

```
    H  H  H               H       H  H
    |  |  |               |       |  |
H − C − C − C − OH  and  H − C − O − C − C − H
    |  |  |               |       |  |
    H  H  H               H       H  H
            (3)
```

```
    H                    H
    |                    |
HO − C − H  and    H − C − OH
    |                    |
    H                    H
        (2)
```

```
    H  OH H              OH H
    |  |  |              |  |
H − C − C − C − H  and  H − C − C − H
    |  |  |              |  |
    H  H  H              H  H
        (4)
```

50 One beneficial use of radioisotopes is
   (1) detection of disease
   (2) neutralization of an acid spill
   (3) decreasing the dissolved $O_2(g)$ level in seawater
   (4) increasing the concentration of $CO_2(g)$ in the atmosphere

Part B-2: Answer all questions in this part

Directions (51-65): Record your answers in the spaces provided in your answer booklet. Some questions may require the use of the Reference Tables for Physical Setting/Chemistry.

51 Draw a Lewis electron-dot diagram for a molecule of bromomethane, CH_3Br. [1]

52 Explain, in terms of atomic structure, why Group 18 elements on the Periodic Table rarely form compounds. [1]

53 Explain, in terms of electrons, why the radius of a potassium atom is larger than the radius of a potassium ion in the ground state. [1]

54 Identify the type of bonding in solid potassium. [1]

Base your answers to questions 55 through 56 on the information below.

A 2.50-liter aqueous solution contains 1.25 moles of dissolved sodium chloride. The dissolving of $NaCl(s)$ in water is represented by the equation below.

$$NaCl(s) \xrightarrow{H_2O} Na^+(aq) \ + \ Cl^-(aq)$$

55 Determine the molarity of this solution. [1]

56 Compare the freezing point of this solution to the freezing point of a solution containing 0.75 mole NaCl per 2.50 liters of solution. [1]

Base your answers to questions 57 through 58 on the information below.

A 1.00-mole sample of glucose, C6H12O6, completely reacts with oxygen, as represented by the balanced equation below.

$$C_6H_{12}O_6(s) \ + \ 6O_2(g) \rightarrow 6CO_2(g) + \ 6H_2O(\ell \ ) + energy$$

57 Write the empirical formula for glucose. [1]

58 Using the axes *in your answer booklet,* complete the potential energy curve for the reaction of glucose with oxygen. [1]

Base your answers to questions 59 through 61 on the information below.

Ethane, C2H6, has a boiling point of -89°C at standard pressure. Ethanol, C2H5OH, has a much higher boiling point than ethane at standard pressure. At STP, ethane is a gas and ethanol is a liquid.

59 Identify the class of organic compounds to which ethanol belongs. [1]

60 A liquid boils when the vapor pressure of the liquid equals the atmospheric pressure on the surface of the liquid. Based on Table *H*, what is the boiling point of ethanol astandard pressure? [1]

61 Compare the intermolecular forces of the two substances at STP. [1]

Base your answers to questions 62 through 65 on the information below.

An operating voltaic cell has zinc and iron electrodes. The cell and the unbalanced ionic equation representing the reaction that occurs in the cell are shown below.

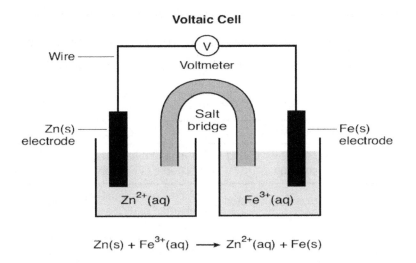

Voltaic Cell

$$Zn(s) + Fe^{3+}(aq) \longrightarrow Zn^{2+}(aq) + Fe(s)$$

62 Identify the subatomic particles that flow through the wire as the cell operates. [1]

63 Balance the equation *in your answer booklet* for the redox reaction that occurs in this cell, using the smallest whole-number coefficients. [1]

64 Identify *one* metal from Table *J* that is more easily oxidized than Zn. [1]

65 Explain, in terms of Zn atoms and Zn ions, why the mass of the Zn electrode *decreases* as the cell operates. [1]

Part C: Answer all questions in this part.

Directions (66-84): Record your answers in the spaces provided in your answer booklet. Some questions may require the use of the Reference Tables for Physical Setting/Chemistry.

Base your answers to questions 66 through 69 on the information below.

A student compares some models of the atom. These models are listed in the table below in order of development from top to bottom.

Models of the Atom

Model	Observation	Conclusion
Dalton model	Matter is conserved during a chemical reaction.	Atoms are hard, indivisible spheres of different sizes.
Thomson model	Cathode rays are deflected by magnetic/electric fields.	Atoms have small, negatively charged particles as part of their internal structure.
Rutherford model	Most alpha particles pass straight through gold foil but a few are deflected.	An atom is mostly empty space with a small, dense, positively charged nucleus.
Bohr model	Unique spectral lines are emitted by excited gaseous elements.	Packets of energy are absorbed or emitted by atoms when an electron changes shells.

66 State the model that first included electrons as subatomic particles. [1]

67 State *one* conclusion about the internal structure of the atom that resulted from the gold foil experiment. [1]

68 Using the conclusion from the Rutherford model, identify the charged subatomic particle that is located in the nucleus. [1]

69 State *one* way in which the Bohr model agrees with the Thomson model. [1]

Base your answers to questions 70 through 72 on the information below.

Paintball is a popular recreational activity that uses a metal tank of compressed carbon dioxide or nitrogen to launch small capsules of paint. A typical tank has a volume of 508 cubic centimeters. A 340.-gram sample of carbon dioxide is added to the tank before it is used for paintball. At 20.°C, this tank contains both $CO_2(g)$ and $CO_2(\ell)$. After a paintball game, the tank contains only $CO_2(g)$.

70 Determine the total number of moles of CO_2 added to the tank before it is used for paintball. [1]

71 In the box *in your answer booklet*, use the key to draw a particle diagram to represent the two phases of CO_2 in a newly filled tank. Your response must include *at least six* molecules of CO_2 in *each* phase. [1]

72 After the paintball game, the tank has a gas pressure of 6.1 atmospheres and is at 293 K. If the tank is heated to 313 K, the pressure in the tank will change. Show a numerical setup for calculating the pressure of the gas in the tank at 313 K. [1]

Base your answers to questions 73 through 75 on the information below.

Many breads are made by adding yeast to dough, causing the dough to rise. Yeast is a type of microorganism that produces the catalyst zymase, which converts glucose, $C_6H_{12}O_6$, to ethanol and carbon dioxide gas. The balanced equation for this reaction is shown below.

$$C_6H_{12}O_6(aq) \xrightarrow{\text{zymase}} 2C_2H_5OH(aq) + 2CO_2(g)$$

73 Draw a structural formula for the ethanol formed during this reaction. [1]

74 Describe how the catalyst, zymase, speeds up this reaction. [1]

75 Determine the total mass of ethanol produced when 270. grams of glucose react completely to form ethanol and 132 grams of carbon dioxide. [1]

Base your answers to questions 76 through 79 on the information below.

During a laboratory activity, a student places 25.0 mL of HCl(aq) of unknown concentration into a flask. The student adds four drops of phenolphthalein to the solution in the flask. The solution is titrated with 0.150 M KOH(aq) until the solution appears faint pink. The volume of KOH(aq) added is 18.5 mL.

76 What number of significant figures is used to express the concentration of the KOH(aq)? [1]

77 Complete the equation *in your answer booklet* for the neutralization reaction that occurs during the titration. [1]

78 Determine the concentration of the HCl(aq) solution, using the titration data. [1]

79 Describe *one* laboratory safety procedure that should be used if a drop of the KOH(aq) is spilled on the arm of the student. [1]

_____

Base your answers to questions 80 through 82 on the information below.

A few pieces of dry ice, $CO_2(s)$, at -78°C are placed in a flask that contains air at 21°C. The flask is sealed by placing an uninflated balloon over the mouth of the flask. As the balloon inflates, the dry ice disappears and no liquid is observed in the flask.

80 State the direction of heat flow that occurs between the dry ice and the air in the flask. [1]

81 Write the name of the process that occurs as the dry ice undergoes a phase change in the flask. [1]

82 Compare the entropy of the CO_2 molecules in the dry ice to the entropy of the CO_2 molecules in the inflated balloon. [1]

Base your answers to questions 83 through 85 on the information below.

Illuminated EXIT signs are used in public buildings such as schools. If the word EXIT is green, the sign may contain the radioisotope tritium, hydrogen-3. The tritium is a gas sealed in glass tubes. The emissions from the decay of the tritium gas cause a coating on the inside of the tubes to glow.

83 State, in terms of neutrons, how an atom of tritium *differs* from an atom of hydrogen-1. [1]

84 Determine the fraction of an original sample of tritium that remains unchanged after 24.62 years. [1]

85 Complete the nuclear equation *in your answer booklet* for the radioactive decay of tritium, by writing a notation for the missing product. [1]

PHYSICAL SETTING

CHEMISTRY

June 24, 2014 — 9:15 to 12:15 p.m., only

ANSWER BOOKLET

Student . . . . Sex: ☐ Male ☐ Female

Teacher . . . .

School . . . . Grade . . . .

Record your answers for Part B–2 and Part C in this booklet

Part B–2

51

52 _____

_____

_____

53 _____

_____

_____

54 _____

55 _____**M**

56 _____

_____

57 _____

58

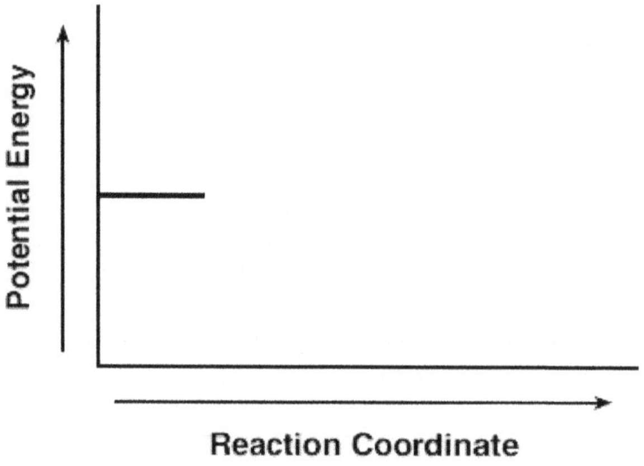

59 _____

60 _____°C

61 _____

_____

_____

62 _____

63 ___Zn(s) + ___Fe³⁺(aq) → ___Zn²⁺(aq) + ___Fe(s)

63 ___$Zn(s)$ + ___$Fe^{3+}(aq)$ → ___$Zn^{2+}(aq)$ + ___$Fe(s)$

64 _____

65 _____

_____

_____

Part C

66 _____

67 _____

_____

68 _____

69 _____

_____

70 _____ mol

71

Key
◯ = CO_2 molecule

72

73

74 _____

_____

75 _____ **g**

76 _____

77   KOH(aq) + HCl(aq) → _____

78 _____**M**

79 _____

_____

_____

80 _____

_____

81 _____

82 _____

_____

83 _____

_____

84 _____

85   $_{1}^{3}\text{H}$ $\rightarrow$ $_{-1}^{0}\text{e}$ +   _____

Part A: Answer all questions in this part

Directions (1 – 30): For each statement or question, write on the separate answer sheet the number of the word or expression that, of those given, best completes the statement or answers the question. Some questions may require the use of the Reference tables for Physical Setting/Chemistry.

1 What is the approximate mass of a proton?
(1) 1 u
(3) 1 g
(2) 0.0005 u
(4) 0.0005 g

2 An electron in a sodium atom gains enough energy to move from the second shell to the third shell. The sodium atom becomes
(1) a positive ion
(2) a negative ion
(3) an atom in an excited state
(4) an atom in the ground state

3 Which particle has *no* charge?
(1) electron
(3) positron
(2) neutron
(4) proton

4 Which quantity represents the number of protons in an atom?
(1) atomic number
(2) oxidation number
(3) number of neutrons
(4) number of valence electrons

5 The element sulfur is classified as a
(1) metal
(3) nonmetal
(2) metalloid
(4) noble gas

6 The elements in Group 2 have similar chemical properties because each atom of these elements has the same
(1) atomic number
(2) mass number
(3) number of electron shells
(4) number of valence electrons

7 What is formed when two atoms of bromine bond together?
   (1) a monatomic molecule
   (2) a diatomic molecule
   (3) a heterogeneous mixture
   (4) a homogeneous mixture

8 Gold can be flattened into an extremely thin sheet. The malleability of gold is due to the
   (1) radioactive decay mode of the isotope Au-198
   (2) proton-to-neutron ratio in an atom of gold
   (3) nature of the bonds between gold atoms
   (4) reactivity of gold atoms

9 Which term represents the attraction one atom has for the electrons in a bond with another atom?
   (1) electronegativity
   (2) electrical conductivity
   (3) first ionization energy
   (4) mechanical energy

10 Salt water is classified as a
   (1) compound because the proportion of its atoms is fixed
   (2) compound because the proportion of its atoms can vary
   (3) mixture because the proportion of its components is fixed
   (4) mixture because the proportion of its components can vary

11 Which substance can *not* be broken down by a chemical change?
   (1) ammonia   (3) ethane
   (2) arsenic   (4) propanal

12 Some physical properties of two samples of iodine-127 at two different temperatures are shown in the table below.

Selected Physical Properties of Iodine-127 Samples at 1 atm

Sample	Sample Temperature (K)	Description	Density (g/cm³)
1	298	dark-gray crystals	4.933
2	525	dark-purple gas	0.006

These two samples are two different
(1) mixtures   (3) phases of matter
(2) substances   (4) isotopes of iodine

13 Powdered iron is magnetic, but powdered sulfur is *not*. What occurs when they form a mixture in a beaker at room temperature?
(1) The iron retains its magnetic properties.
(2) The iron loses its metallic properties.
(3) The sulfur gains magnetic properties.
(4) The sulfur gains metallic properties.

14 Which property is a measure of the average kinetic energy of the particles in a sample of matter?
(1) mass   (3) pressure
(2) density   (4) temperature

15 According to the kinetic molecular theory, which statement describes the particles of an ideal gas?
(1) The gas particles are arranged in a regular pattern.
(2) The force of attraction between the gas particles is strong.
(3) The gas particles are hard spheres in continuous circular motion.
(4) The collisions of the gas particles may result in the transfer of energy.

16 The concentration of a solution can be expressed in
(1) milliliters per minute
(2) parts per million
(3) grams per kelvin
(4) joules per gram

17 Two hydrogen atoms form a hydrogen molecule when
(1) one atom loses a valence electron to the other atom
(2) one atom shares four electrons with the other atom
(3) the two atoms collide and both atoms gain energy
(4) the two atoms collide with sufficient energy to form a bond

18 Which type of formula represents the simplest whole-number ratio of atoms of the elements in a compound?
(1) molecular formula   (3) empirical formula
(2) condensed formula   (4) structural formula

19 The coefficients in a balanced chemical equation represent
(1) the mass ratios of the substances in the reaction
(2) the mole ratios of the substances in the reaction
(3) the total number of electrons in the reaction
(4) the total number of elements in the reaction

20 Systems in nature tend to undergo changes toward
(1) lower energy and higher entropy
(2) lower energy and lower entropy
(3) higher energy and higher entropy
(4) higher energy and lower entropy

21 Which formula represents an organic compound?
(1) CaH_2 (3) H_2O_2
(2) C_4H_8 (4) P_2O_5

22 Which class of organic compounds contains nitrogen?
(1) aldehyde   (3) amine
(2) alcohol   (4) ether

23 Which term identifies a type of organic reaction?
(1) deposition   (3) esterification
(2) distillation   (4) sublimation

24 Which compound is classified as a hydrocarbon?
(1) butanal   (3) 2-butanol
(2) butyne   (4) 2-butanone

25 In an oxidation-reduction reaction, the number of electrons lost is
   (1) equal to the number of electrons gained
   (2) equal to the number of protons gained
   (3) less than the number of electrons gained
   (4) less than the number of protons gained

26 Which substance is an electrolyte?
   (1) $C_6H_{12}O_6(s)$ (3) $NaOH(s)$
   (2) $C_2H_5OH(\ell)$ (4) $H_2(g)$

27 Which energy conversion must occur in an operating electrolytic cell?
   (1) electrical energy to chemical energy
   (2) electrical energy to nuclear energy
   (3) chemical energy to electrical energy
   (4) chemical energy to nuclear energy

28 Which compound yields H_ ions as the only positive ions in an aqueous solution?
   (1) KOH   (3) CH_3OH
   (2) NaOH   (4) CH_3COOH

29 Which statement describes the relative masses of two different particles?
   (1) A neutron has less mass than a positron.
   (2) A beta particle has less mass than a neutron.
   (3) An alpha particle has less mass than a positron.
   (4) An alpha particle has less mass than a beta particle.

30 Which term represents a type of nuclear reaction?
   (1) condensation
   (2) vaporization
   (3) single replacement
   (4) natural transmutation

Part B – 1: Answer all questions in this part.

Directions (31 – 50): For each statement or question, write on the separate answer sheet the number of the word or expression that, of those given, best completes the statement or answers the question. Some questions may require the use of the Reference tables for Physical Setting/Chemistry.

31 Which ion has the *smallest* radius?
(1) O^{2-} (3) Se^{2-}
(2) S^{2-} (4) Te^{2-}

32 Equal amounts of ethanol and water are mixed at room temperature and at 101.3 kPa. Which process is used to separate ethanol from the mixture?
(1) distillation   (3) filtration
(2) reduction   (4) ionization

33 A sample of a substance has these characteristics:
• melting point of 984 K
• hard, brittle solid at room temperature
• poor conductor of heat and electricity as a solid
• good conductor of electricity as a liquid or in an aqueous solution

This sample is classified as
(1) a metallic element
(2) a radioactive element
(3) a molecular compound
(4) an ionic compound

34 Given the balanced equation representing a reaction:

$$N_2 + energy \rightarrow N + N$$

Which statement describes this reaction?
(1) Bonds are broken, and the reaction is endothermic.
(2) Bonds are broken, and the reaction is exothermic.
(3) Bonds are formed, and the reaction is endothermic.
(4) Bonds are formed, and the reaction is exothermic.

35 When lithium reacts with bromine to form the compound LiBr, each lithium atom
(1) gains one electron and becomes a negatively charged ion
(2) gains three electrons and becomes a negatively charged ion
(3) loses one electron and becomes a positively charged ion
(4) loses three electrons and becomes a positively charged ion

36 A beaker with water and the surrounding air are all at 24°C.
After ice cubes are placed in the water, heat is transferred from
(1) the ice cubes to the air
(2) the beaker to the air
(3) the water to the ice cubes
(4) the water to the beaker

37 A sample of chlorine gas is at 300. K and 1.00 atmosphere.
At which temperature and pressure would the sample behave more like an ideal gas?
(1) 0 K and 1.00 atm
(2) 150. K and 0.50 atm
(3) 273 K and 1.00 atm
(4) 600. K and 0.50 atm

38 When a sample of a gas is heated in a sealed, rigid container from 200. K to 400. K, the pressure exerted by the gas is
(1) decreased by a factor of 2
(2) increased by a factor of 2
(3) decreased by a factor of 200.
(4) increased by a factor of 200.

39 The bright-line spectra produced by four elements are represented in the diagram below.

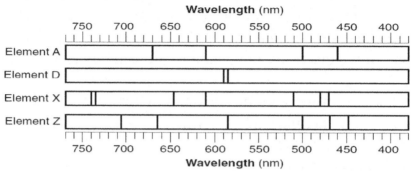

Given the bright-line spectrum of a mixture formed from two of these elements:

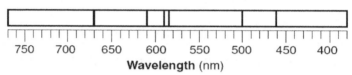

Which elements are present in this mixture?

(1) *A* and *D*　　　　　(3) *Z* and *D*
(2) *A* and *X*　　　　　(4) *Z* and *X*

40 The graph below represents the relationship between time and temperature as heat is added at a constant rate to a sample of a substance.

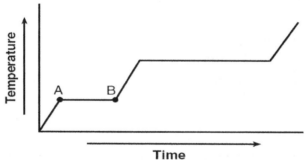

During interval *AB*, which energy change occurs for the particles in this sample?

(1) The potential energy of the particles increases.
(2) The potential energy of the particles decreases.
(3) The average kinetic energy of the particles increases.
(4) The average kinetic energy of the particles decreases.

41 Given the potential energy diagram for a reversible chemical reaction:

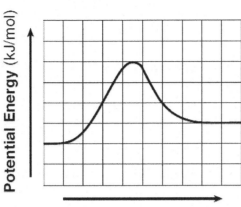

Each interval on the axis labeled "Potential Energy (kJ/mol)" represents 10. kilojoules per mole. What is the activation energy of the forward reaction?

(1) 10. kJ/mol   (3) 40. kJ/mol
(2) 30. kJ/mol   (4) 60. kJ/mol

42 Which condensed structural formula represents an unsaturated compound?

(1) $CH_3CHCHCH_3$ (3) CH_3CH_3
(2) $CH_3CH_2CH_3$ (4) CH_4

43 Which element reacts spontaneously with 1.0 M HCl(aq) at room temperature?

(1) copper   (3) silver
(2) gold   (4) zinc

44 Given the balanced ionic equation:

$$3Pb^+(aq) \ + \ 2Cr(s) \rightarrow 3Pb(s) \ + \ 2Cr^{3+}(aq)$$

What is the number of moles of electrons gained by 3.0 moles of lead ions?

(1) 5.0 mol   (3) 3.0 mol
(2) 2.0 mol   (4) 6.0 mol

45 What is the amount of heat energy released when 50.0 grams of water is cooled from 20.0°C to 10.0°C?
(1) 5.00×10^2 J
(3) 1.67×10^5 J
(2) 2.09×10^3 J
(4) 1.13×10^6 J

46 What occurs at one of the electrodes in both an electrolytic cell and a voltaic cell?
(1) Oxidation occurs as electrons are gained at the cathode.
(2) Oxidation occurs as electrons are lost at the anode.
(3) Reduction occurs as electrons are gained at the anode.
(4) Reduction occurs as electrons are lost at the cathode.

47 Given the balanced equation representing a reaction:
$$H_2O(\ell) + HCl(g) \rightarrow H_3O^+(aq) + Cl^-(aq)$$
According to one acid-base theory, the $H_2O(\ell)$ molecules
(1) accept H^+ ions
(3) donate H^+ ions
(2) accept OH^- ions
(4) donate OH^-ions

48 When an atom of the unstable isotope Na-24 decays, it becomes an atom of Mg-24 because the Na-24 atom spontaneously releases
(1) an alpha particle
(3) a neutron
(2) a beta particle
(4) a positron

49 Which balanced equation represents nuclear fusion?
(1) $^3_1H \rightarrow \ ^3_1He + \ ^0_{-1}e$

(2) $^{235}_{92}U \rightarrow \ ^{231}_{90}Th + \ ^4_2He$

(3) $^2_1H + \ ^2_1H \rightarrow \ ^4_2He$

(4) $^{235}_{92}U + \ ^1_0n \rightarrow \ ^{90}_{38}Sr + \ ^{143}_{54}Xe + 3^1_0n$

50 Which reaction releases the greatest amount of energy per kilogram of reactants?
(1) $^1_0n + \ ^{235}_{92}U \rightarrow \ ^{141}_{56}Ba + \ ^{92}_{36}Kr + 3^1_0n$

(2) $2C + H_2 \rightarrow C_2H_2$

(3) $C_3H_8(g) + 5O_2(g) \rightarrow 3CO_2(g) + 4H_2O(\ell)$

(4) $NaOH(aq) + HCl(aq) \rightarrow NaCl(aq) + H_2O(\ell)$

Part B-2: Answer all questions in this part

Directions (51-65): Record your answers in the spaces provided in your answer booklet. Some questions may require the use of the Reference Tables for Physical Setting/Chemistry.

Base your answers to questions 51 through 54 on the information below.

The diagram below represents three elements in Group 13 and three elements in Period 3 and their relative positions on the Periodic Table.

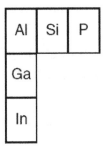

Some elements in the solid phase exist in different forms that vary in their physical properties. For example, at room temperature, red phosphorus has a density of 2.16 g/cm^3 and white phosphorus has a density of 1.823 g/cm^3.

51 Identify the element from the diagram that will react with chlorine to form a compound with the general formula $XCl4$. [1]

52 Consider the Period 3 elements in the diagram in order of increasing atomic number. State the trend in electronegativity for these elements. [1]

53 Compare the number of atoms per cubic centimeter in red phosphorus with the number of atoms per cubic centimeter in white phosphorus. [1]

54 Identify *one* element from the diagram that will combine with phosphorus in the same ratio of atoms as the ratio in aluminum phosphide. [1]

Base your answers to questions 55 through 57 on the information below.

The compounds KNO3 and NaNO3 are soluble in water.

55 Compare the entropy of 30. grams of solid KNO3 at 20.°C with the entropy of 30. Grams of KNO3 dissolved in 100. grams of water at 20.°C. [1]

56 Explain why the total thermal energy of a sample containing 22.2 grams of NaNO3 dissolved in 200. grams of water at 20.°C is greater than the total thermal energy of a sample containing 11.1 grams of NaNO3 dissolved in 100. grams of water at 20.°C. [1]

57 Compare the boiling point of a NaNO3 solution at standard pressure to the boiling point of water at standard pressure. [1]

Base your answers to questions 58 through 61 on the information below.

Ethene and hydrogen can react at a faster rate in the presence of the catalyst platinum. The equation below represents a reaction between ethene and hydrogen.

$$\underset{H}{\overset{H}{\diagdown}}C=C\underset{H}{\overset{H}{\diagup}} \;+\; H-H \longrightarrow \begin{array}{c} H \;\; H \\ | \;\;\; | \\ H-C-C-H \\ | \;\;\; | \\ H \;\; H \end{array}$$

58 Determine the molar mass of the product. [1]

59 State the number of electrons shared between the carbon atoms in one molecule of the reactant ethene. [1]

60 Explain, in terms of activation energy, why the catalyzed reaction occurs at a faster rate. [1]

61 Explain why the reaction is classified as an addition reaction. [1]

Base your answers to questions 62 through 63 on the information below.

In a titration, 50.0 milliliters of 0.026 M HCl(aq) is neutralized by 38.5 milliliters of KOH(aq).

62 In the space *in your answer booklet*, show a numerical setup for calculating the molarity of the KOH(aq). [1]

63 Complete the equation *in your answer booklet* for the neutralization by writing the formula of the missing product. [1]

Base your answers to questions 64 through 65 on the information below.

Table sugar, sucrose, is a combination of two simple sugars, glucose and fructose. The formulas below represent these simple sugars.

Glucose   Fructose

64 Identify the functional group that appears more than once in the fructose molecule. [1]

65 Explain, in terms of atoms and molecular structure, why glucose and fructose are isomers of each other. [1]

Part C: Answer all questions in this part.

Directions (66-85): Record your answers in the spaces provided in your answer booklet. Some questions may require the use of the Reference Tables for Physical Setting/Chemistry.

Base your answers to questions 66 through 70 on the information below.

Baking soda, $NaHCO_3$, can be commercially produced during a series of chemical reactions called the Solvay process. In this process, $NH_3(aq)$, $NaCl(aq)$, and other chemicals are used to produce $NaHCO_3(s)$ and $NH_4Cl(aq)$.

To reduce production costs, $NH_3(aq)$ is recovered from $NH_4Cl(aq)$ through a different series of reactions. This series of reactions can be summarized by the overall reaction represented by the unbalanced equation below.

$$NH_4Cl(aq) + CaO(s) \rightarrow NH_3(aq) + H_2O(\ell) + CaCl_2(aq)$$

66 Write a chemical name for baking soda. [1]

67 Determine the percent composition by mass of carbon in baking soda (gram-formula mass = 84 grams per mole). [1]

68 State the color of bromcresol green in a sample of $NH_3(aq)$. [1]

69 Determine the mass of NH_4Cl that must be dissolved in 100. grams of H_2O to produce a saturated solution at 70.°C. [1]

70 Balance the equation *in your answer booklet* for the overall reaction used to recover $NH_3(aq)$, using the smallest whole-number coefficients. [1]

Base your answers to questions 71 through 75 on the information below.

Rubbing alcohol is a product available at most pharmacies and supermarkets. One rubbing alcohol solution contains 2-propanol and water. The boiling point of 2-propanol is 82.3°C at standard pressure.

71 Explain, in terms of electronegativity differences, why a C–O bond is more polar than a C–H bond. [1]

72 Identify a strong intermolecular force of attraction between an alcohol molecule and a water molecule in the solution. [1]

73 Determine the vapor pressure of water at a temperature equal to the boiling point of the 2-propanol. [1]

74 Explain, in terms of charge distribution, why a molecule of the 2-propanol is a polar molecule. [1]

75 In the space *in your answer booklet*, draw a structural formula for the 2-propanol. [1]

Base your answers to questions 76 through 77 on the information below.

Silver-plated utensils were popular before stainless steel became widely used to make eating utensils. Silver tarnishes when it comes in contact with hydrogen sulfide, H2S, which is found in the air and in some foods. However, stainless steel does *not* tarnish when it comes in contact with hydrogen sulfide.

76 In the space *in your answer booklet*, draw a Lewis electron-dot diagram for the compound that tarnishes silver. [1]

77 In the ground state, an atom of which noble gas has the same electron configuration as the sulfide ion in Ag2S? [1]

Base your answers to questions 78 through 81 on the information below.

Common household bleach is an aqueous solution containing hypochlorite ions. A closed container of bleach is an equilibrium system represented by the equation below.

$$Cl_2(g) + 2OH^- (aq) \rightleftarrows ClO^- (aq) + Cl^-(aq) + H_2O(\ell)$$

78 Compare the rate of the forward reaction to the rate of the reverse reaction for this system. [1]

79 State the change in oxidation number for chlorine when the $Cl_2(g)$ changes to Cl^- (aq) during the forward reaction. [1]

80 Explain why the container must be closed to maintain equilibrium. [1]

81 State the effect on the concentration of the ClO^- ion when there is a *decrease* in the concentration of the OH^- ion. [1]

Iodine has many isotopes, but only iodine-127 is stable and is found in nature. One radioactive iodine isotope, I-108, decays by alpha particle emission. Iodine-131 is also radioactive and has many important medical uses.

82 Determine the number of neutrons in an atom of I-127. [1]

83 Explain, in terms of protons and neutrons, why I-127 and I-131 are different isotopes of iodine. [1]

84 Complete the equation *in your answer booklet* for the nuclear decay of I-108. [1]

85 Determine the total time required for an 80.0-gram sample of I-131 to decay until only 1.25 grams of the sample remains unchanged. [1]

PHYSICAL SETTING

CHEMISTRY

Wednesday, January 29, 2014 — 1:15 to 4:15 p.m., only

ANSWER BOOKLET

☐ Male

Student . . . . Sex: ☐ Female

Teacher . . . .

School . . . . Grade . . . .

Record your answers for Part B–2 and Part C in this booklet

Part B–2

51 _____

52 _____

_____

53 _____

_____

54 _____

55 _____

_____

56 _____

_____

_____

57 _____

_____

58 _____ **g/mol**

59 _____

60 _____

_____

_____

61 _____

_____

_____

62

63 KOH(aq) + HCl(aq) → _____ (aq) + $H_2O(\ell)$

64 _____

65 _____

_____

_____

Part C

66 _____

67 _____%

68 _____

69 _____**g**

70 ___ NH_4Cl + ___ CaO → ___ NH_3 + ___ H_2O + ___ $CaCl_2$

71 _____

_____

_____

72 _____

73 _____**kPa**

74 _____

_____

_____

75

76

77 _____

78 _____

_____

79 _____ to _____

80 _____

_____

_____

81 _____

_____

82 _____

83 _____

_____

_____

84 $^{108}_{53}I \rightarrow {}^{4}_{2}He$ + _____

85 _____ d

C Reference Tables for Physical Setting/CHEMISTRY
2011 Edition

Table A
Standard Temperature and Pressure

Name	Value	Unit
Standard Pressure	101.3 kPa 1 atm	kilopascal atmosphere
Standard Temperature	273 K 0°C	kelvin degree Celsius

Table B
Physical Constants for Water

Heat of Fusion	334 J/g
Heat of Vaporization	2260 J/g
Specific Heat Capacity of $H_2O(\ell)$	4.18 J/g•K

Table C
Selected Prefixes

Factor	Prefix	Symbol
10^3	kilo-	k
10^{-1}	deci-	d
10^{-2}	centi-	c
10^{-3}	milli-	m
10^{-6}	micro-	μ
10^{-9}	nano-	n
10^{-12}	pico-	p

Table D
Selected Units

Symbol	Name	Quantity
m	meter	length
g	gram	mass
Pa	pascal	pressure
K	kelvin	temperature
mol	mole	amount of substance
J	joule	energy, work, quantity of heat
s	second	time
min	minute	time
h	hour	time
d	day	time
y	year	time
L	liter	volume
ppm	parts per million	concentration
M	molarity	solution concentration
u	atomic mass unit	atomic mass

Table E
Selected Polyatomic Ions

Formula	Name	Formula	Name
H_3O^+	hydronium	CrO_4^{2-}	chromate
Hg_2^{2+}	mercury(I)	$Cr_2O_7^{2-}$	dichromate
NH_4^+	ammonium	MnO_4^-	permanganate
$C_2H_3O_2^-$ CH_3COO^- } acetate		NO_2^-	nitrite
		NO_3^-	nitrate
CN^-	cyanide	O_2^{2-}	peroxide
CO_3^{2-}	carbonate	OH^-	hydroxide
HCO_3^-	hydrogen carbonate	PO_4^{3-}	phosphate
$C_2O_4^{2-}$	oxalate	SCN^-	thiocyanate
ClO^-	hypochlorite	SO_3^{2-}	sulfite
ClO_2^-	chlorite	SO_4^{2-}	sulfate
ClO_3^-	chlorate	HSO_4^-	hydrogen sulfate
ClO_4^-	perchlorate	$S_2O_3^{2-}$	thiosulfate

Table F
Solubility Guidelines for Aqueous Solutions

Ions That Form *Soluble* Compounds	Exceptions	Ions That Form *Insoluble* Compounds*	Exceptions
Group 1 ions (Li^+, Na^+, etc.)		carbonate (CO_3^{2-})	when combined with Group 1 ions or ammonium (NH_4^+)
ammonium (NH_4^+)		chromate (CrO_4^{2-})	when combined with Group 1 ions, Ca^{2+}, Mg^{2+}, or ammonium (NH_4^+)
nitrate (NO_3^-)			
acetate ($C_2H_3O_2^-$ or CH_3COO^-)		phosphate (PO_4^{3-})	when combined with Group 1 ions or ammonium (NH_4^+)
hydrogen carbonate (HCO_3^-)		sulfide (S^{2-})	when combined with Group 1 ions or ammonium (NH_4^+)
chlorate (ClO_3^-)		hydroxide (OH^-)	when combined with Group 1 ions, Ca^{2+}, Ba^{2+}, Sr^{2+}, or ammonium (NH_4^+)
halides (Cl^-, Br^-, I^-)	when combined with Ag^+, Pb^{2+}, or Hg_2^{2+}		
sulfates (SO_4^{2-})	when combined with Ag^+, Ca^{2+}, Sr^{2+}, Ba^{2+}, or Pb^{2+}		

*compounds having very low solubility in H_2O

Table G
Solubility Curves at Standard Pressure

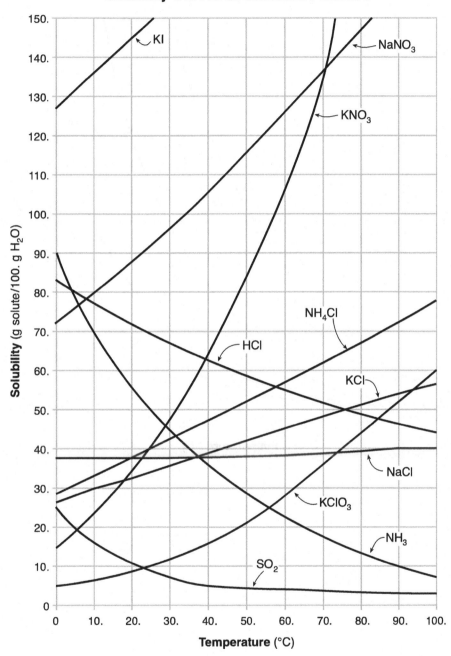

Table H
Vapor Pressure of Four Liquids

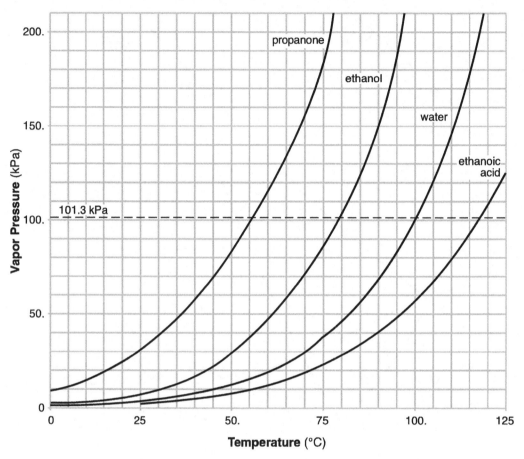

Table I
Heats of Reaction at 101.3 kPa and 298 K

Reaction	ΔH (kJ)*
$CH_4(g) + 2O_2(g) \longrightarrow CO_2(g) + 2H_2O(\ell)$	−890.4
$C_3H_8(g) + 5O_2(g) \longrightarrow 3CO_2(g) + 4H_2O(\ell)$	−2219.2
$2C_8H_{18}(\ell) + 25O_2(g) \longrightarrow 16CO_2(g) + 18H_2O(\ell)$	−10943
$2CH_3OH(\ell) + 3O_2(g) \longrightarrow 2CO_2(g) + 4H_2O(\ell)$	−1452
$C_2H_5OH(\ell) + 3O_2(g) \longrightarrow 2CO_2(g) + 3H_2O(\ell)$	−1367
$C_6H_{12}O_6(s) + 6O_2(g) \longrightarrow 6CO_2(g) + 6H_2O(\ell)$	−2804
$2CO(g) + O_2(g) \longrightarrow 2CO_2(g)$	−566.0
$C(s) + O_2(g) \longrightarrow CO_2(g)$	−393.5
$4Al(s) + 3O_2(g) \longrightarrow 2Al_2O_3(s)$	−3351
$N_2(g) + O_2(g) \longrightarrow 2NO(g)$	+182.6
$N_2(g) + 2O_2(g) \longrightarrow 2NO_2(g)$	+66.4
$2H_2(g) + O_2(g) \longrightarrow 2H_2O(g)$	−483.6
$2H_2(g) + O_2(g) \longrightarrow 2H_2O(\ell)$	−571.6
$N_2(g) + 3H_2(g) \longrightarrow 2NH_3(g)$	−91.8
$2C(s) + 3H_2(g) \longrightarrow C_2H_6(g)$	−84.0
$2C(s) + 2H_2(g) \longrightarrow C_2H_4(g)$	+52.4
$2C(s) + H_2(g) \longrightarrow C_2H_2(g)$	+227.4
$H_2(g) + I_2(g) \longrightarrow 2HI(g)$	+53.0
$KNO_3(s) \xrightarrow{H_2O} K^+(aq) + NO_3^-(aq)$	+34.89
$NaOH(s) \xrightarrow{H_2O} Na^+(aq) + OH^-(aq)$	−44.51
$NH_4Cl(s) \xrightarrow{H_2O} NH_4^+(aq) + Cl^-(aq)$	+14.78
$NH_4NO_3(s) \xrightarrow{H_2O} NH_4^+(aq) + NO_3^-(aq)$	+25.69
$NaCl(s) \xrightarrow{H_2O} Na^+(aq) + Cl^-(aq)$	+3.88
$LiBr(s) \xrightarrow{H_2O} Li^+(aq) + Br^-(aq)$	−48.83
$H^+(aq) + OH^-(aq) \longrightarrow H_2O(\ell)$	−55.8

*The ΔH values are based on molar quantities represented in the equations.
A minus sign indicates an exothermic reaction.

Table J
Activity Series**

Most Active	Metals	Nonmetals	Most Active
	Li	F_2	
	Rb	Cl_2	
	K	Br_2	
	Cs	I_2	
	Ba		
	Sr		
	Ca		
	Na		
	Mg		
	Al		
	Ti		
	Mn		
	Zn		
	Cr		
	Fe		
	Co		
	Ni		
	Sn		
	Pb		
	H_2		
	Cu		
	Ag		
Least Active	Au		Least Active

**Activity Series is based on the hydrogen standard. H_2 is *not* a metal.

Table K
Common Acids

Formula	Name
HCl(aq)	hydrochloric acid
HNO_2(aq)	nitrous acid
HNO_3(aq)	nitric acid
H_2SO_3(aq)	sulfurous acid
H_2SO_4(aq)	sulfuric acid
H_3PO_4(aq)	phosphoric acid
H_2CO_3(aq) or CO_2(aq)	carbonic acid
CH_3COOH(aq) or $HC_2H_3O_2$(aq)	ethanoic acid (acetic acid)

Table L
Common Bases

Formula	Name
NaOH(aq)	sodium hydroxide
KOH(aq)	potassium hydroxide
$Ca(OH)_2$(aq)	calcium hydroxide
NH_3(aq)	aqueous ammonia

Table M
Common Acid–Base Indicators

Indicator	Approximate pH Range for Color Change	Color Change
methyl orange	3.1–4.4	red to yellow
bromthymol blue	6.0–7.6	yellow to blue
phenolphthalein	8–9	colorless to pink
litmus	4.5–8.3	red to blue
bromcresol green	3.8–5.4	yellow to blue
thymol blue	8.0–9.6	yellow to blue

Source: *The Merck Index*, 14th ed., 2006, Merck Publishing Group

Table N
Selected Radioisotopes

Nuclide	Half-Life	Decay Mode	Nuclide Name
^{198}Au	2.695 d	β^-	gold-198
^{14}C	5715 y	β^-	carbon-14
^{37}Ca	182 ms	β^+	calcium-37
^{60}Co	5.271 y	β^-	cobalt-60
^{137}Cs	30.2 y	β^-	cesium-137
^{53}Fe	8.51 min	β^+	iron-53
^{220}Fr	27.4 s	α	francium-220
^{3}H	12.31 y	β^-	hydrogen-3
^{131}I	8.021 d	β^-	iodine-131
^{37}K	1.23 s	β^+	potassium-37
^{42}K	12.36 h	β^-	potassium-42
^{85}Kr	10.73 y	β^-	krypton-85
^{16}N	7.13 s	β^-	nitrogen-16
^{19}Ne	17.22 s	β^+	neon-19
^{32}P	14.28 d	β^-	phosphorus-32
^{239}Pu	2.410×10^4 y	α	plutonium-239
^{226}Ra	1599 y	α	radium-226
^{222}Rn	3.823 d	α	radon-222
^{90}Sr	29.1 y	β^-	strontium-90
^{99}Tc	2.13×10^5 y	β^-	technetium-99
^{232}Th	1.40×10^{10} y	α	thorium-232
^{233}U	1.592×10^5 y	α	uranium-233
^{235}U	7.04×10^8 y	α	uranium-235
^{238}U	4.47×10^9 y	α	uranium-238

Source: *CRC Handbook of Chemistry and Physics*, 91st ed., 2010–2011, CRC Press

Table O
Symbols Used in Nuclear Chemistry

Name	Notation	Symbol
alpha particle	^4_2He or $^4_2\alpha$	α
beta particle	$^0_{-1}\text{e}$ or $^0_{-1}$ ▬▬▬▬▬	$-$
gamma radiation	$^0_0\gamma$	γ
neutron	^1_0n	n
proton	^1_1H or ^1_1p	p
positron	$^0_{+1}\text{e}$ or $^0_{+1}\beta$	β^+

Table P
Organic Prefixes

Prefix	Number of Carbon Atoms
meth-	1
eth-	2
prop-	3
but-	4
pent-	5
hex-	6
hept-	7
oct-	8
non-	9
dec-	10

Table Q
Homologous Series of Hydrocarbons

Name	General Formula	Examples	
		Name	Structural Formula
alkanes	C_nH_{2n+2}	ethane	H H $\quad\mid\ \ \mid$ H—C—C—H $\quad\mid\ \ \mid$ H H
alkenes	C_nH_{2n}	ethene	H H $\diagdown\quad\diagup$ C=C $\diagup\quad\diagdown$ H H
alkynes	C_nH_{2n-2}	ethyne	H—C≡C—H

Note: n = number of carbon atoms

Table R
Organic Functional Groups

Class of Compound	Functional Group	General Formula	Example
halide (halocarbon)	$-F$ (fluoro-) $-Cl$ (chloro-) $-Br$ (bromo-) $-I$ (iodo-)	$R-X$ (X represents any halogen)	$CH_3CHClCH_3$ 2-chloropropane
alcohol	$-OH$	$R-OH$	$CH_3CH_2CH_2OH$ 1-propanol
ether	$-O-$	$R-O-R'$	$CH_3OCH_2CH_3$ methyl ethyl ether
aldehyde	$\overset{\displaystyle O}{\overset{\displaystyle \|}{-C}}-H$	$R-\overset{\displaystyle O}{\overset{\displaystyle \|}{C}}-H$	$CH_3CH_2\overset{\displaystyle O}{\overset{\displaystyle \|}{C}}-H$ propanal
ketone	$\overset{\displaystyle O}{\overset{\displaystyle \|}{-C}}-$	$R-\overset{\displaystyle O}{\overset{\displaystyle \|}{C}}-R'$	$CH_3\overset{\displaystyle O}{\overset{\displaystyle \|}{C}}CH_2CH_2CH_3$ 2-pentanone
organic acid	$\overset{\displaystyle O}{\overset{\displaystyle \|}{-C}}-OH$	$R-\overset{\displaystyle O}{\overset{\displaystyle \|}{C}}-OH$	$CH_3CH_2\overset{\displaystyle O}{\overset{\displaystyle \|}{C}}-OH$ propanoic acid
ester	$\overset{\displaystyle O}{\overset{\displaystyle \|}{-C}}-O-$	$R-\overset{\displaystyle O}{\overset{\displaystyle \|}{C}}-O-R'$	$CH_3CH_2\overset{\displaystyle O}{\overset{\displaystyle \|}{C}}OCH_3$ methyl propanoate
amine	$\overset{\displaystyle \|}{-N}-$	$R-\overset{\displaystyle R'}{\overset{\displaystyle \|}{N}}-R''$	$CH_3CH_2CH_2NH_2$ 1-propanamine
amide	$\overset{\displaystyle O}{\overset{\displaystyle \|}{-C}}-\overset{\displaystyle \|}{N}H$	$R-\overset{\displaystyle O}{\overset{\displaystyle \|}{C}}-\overset{\displaystyle R'}{\overset{\displaystyle \|}{N}}H$	$CH_3CH_2\overset{\displaystyle O}{\overset{\displaystyle \|}{C}}-NH_2$ propanamide

Note: R represents a bonded atom or group of atoms.

Periodic Table of the Elements

KEY

Atomic Mass → 12.011 — −4 ← Selected Oxidation States

Symbol → **C** +2 +4

Relative atomic masses are based on $^{12}C = 12$ (exact)

Atomic Number → 6

Electron Configuration → 2-4

Note: Numbers in parentheses are mass numbers of the most stable or common isotope.

Period	Group 1	Group 2	Group 3	4	5	6	7 Group	8	9	10	11	12	Group 13	14	15	16	17	18
1	1.00794 +1 −1 **H** 1 1																	4.00260 0 **He** 2 2
2	6.941 +1 **Li** 3 2-1	9.01218 +2 **Be** 4 2-2											10.81 +3 **B** 5 2-3	12.011 −4 +2 +4 **C** 6 2-4	14.0067 −3 −2 −1 +1 +2 +3 +4 +5 **N** 7 2-5	15.9994 −2 **O** 8 2-6	18.9984 −1 **F** 9 2-7	20.180 0 **Ne** 10 2-8
3	22.98977 +1 **Na** 11 2-8-1	24.305 +2 **Mg** 12 2-8-2											26.98154 +3 **Al** 13 2-8-3	28.0855 −4 +2 +4 **Si** 14 2-8-4	30.97376 −3 +3 +5 **P** 15 2-8-5	32.065 −2 +4 +6 **S** 16 2-8-6	35.453 −1 +1 +5 +7 **Cl** 17 2-8-7	39.948 0 **Ar** 18 2-8-8
4	39.0983 +1 **K** 19 2-8-8-1	40.08 +2 **Ca** 20 2-8-8-2	44.9559 +3 **Sc** 21 2-8-9-2	47.867 +2 +3 +4 **Ti** 22 2-8-10-2	50.9415 +2 +3 +4 +5 **V** 23 2-8-11-2	51.996 +2 +3 +6 **Cr** 24 2-8-13-1	54.9380 +2 +3 +4 +7 **Mn** 25 2-8-13-2	55.845 +2 +3 **Fe** 26 2-8-14-2	58.9332 +2 +3 **Co** 27 2-8-15-2	58.693 +2 +3 **Ni** 28 2-8-16-2	63.546 +1 +2 **Cu** 29 2-8-18-1	65.409 +2 **Zn** 30 2-8-18-2	69.723 +3 **Ga** 31 2-8-18-3	72.64 +2 +4 **Ge** 32 2-8-18-4	74.9216 −3 +3 +5 **As** 33 2-8-18-5	78.96 −2 +4 +6 **Se** 34 2-8-18-6	79.904 −1 +1 +5 **Br** 35 2-8-18-7	83.798 0 +2 **Kr** 36 2-8-18-8
5	85.4678 +1 **Rb** 37 2-8-18-8-1	87.62 +2 **Sr** 38 2-8-18-8-2	88.9059 +3 **Y** 39 2-8-18-9-2	91.224 +4 **Zr** 40 2-8-18-10-2	92.9064 +3 +5 **Nb** 41 2-8-18-12-1	95.94 +6 **Mo** 42 2-8-18-13-1	(98) +4 +6 +7 **Tc** 43 2-8-18-13-2	101.07 +3 **Ru** 44 2-8-18-15-1	102.906 +3 **Rh** 45 2-8-18-16-1	106.42 +2 +4 **Pd** 46 2-8-18-18	107.868 +1 **Ag** 47 2-8-18-18-1	112.41 +2 **Cd** 48 2-8-18-18-2	114.818 +3 **In** 49 2-8-18-18-3	118.71 +2 +4 **Sn** 50 2-8-18-18-4	121.760 −3 +3 +5 **Sb** 51 2-8-18-18-5	127.60 −2 +4 +6 **Te** 52 2-8-18-18-6	126.904 −1 +1 +5 +7 **I** 53 2-8-18-18-7	131.29 0 +2 +4 +6 **Xe** 54 2-8-18-18-8
6	132.905 +1 **Cs** 55 2-8-18-18-8-1	137.33 +2 **Ba** 56 2-8-18-18-8-2	138.9055 +3 **La** 57 2-8-18-18-9-2	178.49 +4 **Hf** 72 *18-32-10-2	180.948 +5 **Ta** 73 *18-32-11-2	183.84 +6 **W** 74 *18-32-12-2	186.207 +4 +6 +7 **Re** 75 *18-32-13-2	190.23 +3 +4 **Os** 76 *18-32-14-2	192.217 +3 +4 **Ir** 77 *18-32-15-2	195.08 +2 +4 **Pt** 78 *18-32-17-1	196.967 +1 +3 **Au** 79 *18-32-18-1	200.59 +1 +2 **Hg** 80 *18-32-18-2	204.383 +1 +3 **Tl** 81 *18-32-18-3	207.2 +2 +4 **Pb** 82 *18-32-18-4	208.980 +3 +5 **Bi** 83 *18-32-18-5	(209) +2 +4 **Po** 84 *18-32-18-6	(210) **At** 85 *18-32-18-7	(222) 0 **Rn** 86 *18-32-18-8
7	(223) +1 **Fr** 87 *18-32-18-8-1	(226) +2 **Ra** 88 *18-32-18-8-2	(227) +3 **Ac** 89 *18-32-18-9-2	(261) +4 **Rf** 104	(262) **Db** 105	(266) **Sg** 106	(272) **Bh** 107	(277) **Hs** 108	(276) **Mt** 109	(281) **Ds** 110	(280) **Rg** 111	(285) **Cn** 112	(284) **Uut** 113**	(289) **Uuq** 114	(288) **Uup** 115	(292) **Uuh** 116	(?) **Uus** 117	(294) **Uuo** 118

140.116 +3 +4 **Ce** 58	140.908 +3 **Pr** 59	144.24 +3 **Nd** 60	(145) +3 **Pm** 61	150.36 +2 +3 **Sm** 62	151.964 +2 +3 **Eu** 63	157.25 +3 **Gd** 64	158.925 +3 **Tb** 65	162.500 +3 **Dy** 66	164.930 +3 **Ho** 67	167.259 +3 **Er** 68	168.934 +3 **Tm** 69	173.04 +2 +3 **Yb** 70	174.9668 +3 **Lu** 71
232.038 +4 **Th** 90	231.036 +4 +5 **Pa** 91	238.029 +3 +4 +5 +6 **U** 92	(237) +3 +4 +5 +6 **Np** 93	(244) +3 +4 +5 +6 **Pu** 94	(243) +3 +4 +5 +6 **Am** 95	(247) +3 **Cm** 96	(247) +3 **Bk** 97	(251) +3 **Cf** 98	(252) +3 **Es** 99	(257) +3 **Fm** 100	(258) +2 +3 **Md** 101	(259) +2 +3 **No** 102	(262) +3 **Lr** 103

* denotes the presence of (2-8-) for elements 72 and above

** The systematic names and symbols for elements of atomic numbers 113 and above will be used until the approval of trivial names by IUPAC.

Source: *CRC Handbook of Chemistry and Physics*, 91st ed., 2010–2011, CRC Press

Table S
Properties of Selected Elements

Atomic Number	Symbol	Name	First Ionization Energy (kJ/mol)	Electro-negativity	Melting Point (K)	Boiling* Point (K)	Density** (g/cm³)	Atomic Radius (pm)
1	H	hydrogen	1312	2.2	14	20.	0.000082	32
2	He	helium	2372	—	—	4	0.000164	37
3	Li	lithium	520.	1.0	454	1615	0.534	130.
4	Be	beryllium	900.	1.6	1560.	2744	1.85	99
5	B	boron	801	2.0	2348	4273	2.34	84
6	C	carbon	1086	2.6	—	—	—	75
7	N	nitrogen	1402	3.0	63	77	0.001145	71
8	O	oxygen	1314	3.4	54	90.	0.001308	64
9	F	fluorine	1681	4.0	53	85	0.001553	60.
10	Ne	neon	2081	—	24	27	0.000825	62
11	Na	sodium	496	0.9	371	1156	0.97	160.
12	Mg	magnesium	738	1.3	923	1363	1.74	140.
13	Al	aluminum	578	1.6	933	2792	2.70	124
14	Si	silicon	787	1.9	1687	3538	2.3296	114
15	P	phosphorus (white)	1012	2.2	317	554	1.823	109
16	S	sulfur (monoclinic)	1000.	2.6	388	718	2.00	104
17	Cl	chlorine	1251	3.2	172	239	0.002898	100.
18	Ar	argon	1521	—	84	87	0.001633	101
19	K	potassium	419	0.8	337	1032	0.89	200.
20	Ca	calcium	590.	1.0	1115	1757	1.54	174
21	Sc	scandium	633	1.4	1814	3109	2.99	159
22	Ti	titanium	659	1.5	1941	3560.	4.506	148
23	V	vanadium	651	1.6	2183	3680.	6.0	144
24	Cr	chromium	653	1.7	2180.	2944	7.15	130.
25	Mn	manganese	717	1.6	1519	2334	7.3	129
26	Fe	iron	762	1.8	1811	3134	7.87	124
27	Co	cobalt	760.	1.9	1768	3200.	8.86	118
28	Ni	nickel	737	1.9	1728	3186	8.90	117
29	Cu	copper	745	1.9	1358	2835	8.96	122
30	Zn	zinc	906	1.7	693	1180.	7.134	120.
31	Ga	gallium	579	1.8	303	2477	5.91	123
32	Ge	germanium	762	2.0	1211	3106	5.3234	120.
33	As	arsenic (gray)	944	2.2	1090.	—	5.75	120.
34	Se	selenium (gray)	941	2.6	494	958	4.809	118
35	Br	bromine	1140.	3.0	266	332	3.1028	117
36	Kr	krypton	1351	—	116	120.	0.003425	116
37	Rb	rubidium	403	0.8	312	961	1.53	215
38	Sr	strontium	549	1.0	1050.	1655	2.64	190.
39	Y	yttrium	600.	1.2	1795	3618	4.47	176
40	Zr	zirconium	640.	1.3	2128	4682	6.52	164

Atomic Number	Symbol	Name	First Ionization Energy (kJ/mol)	Electro-negativity	Melting Point (K)	Boiling* Point (K)	Density** (g/cm³)	Atomic Radius (pm)
41	Nb	niobium	652	1.6	2750.	5017	8.57	156
42	Mo	molybdenum	684	2.2	2896	4912	10.2	146
43	Tc	technetium	702	2.1	2430.	4538	11	138
44	Ru	ruthenium	710.	2.2	2606	4423	12.1	136
45	Rh	rhodium	720.	2.3	2237	3968	12.4	134
46	Pd	palladium	804	2.2	1828	3236	12.0	130.
47	Ag	silver	731	1.9	1235	2435	10.5	136
48	Cd	cadmium	868	1.7	594	1040.	8.69	140.
49	In	indium	558	1.8	430.	2345	7.31	142
50	Sn	tin (white)	709	2.0	505	2875	7.287	140.
51	Sb	antimony (gray)	831	2.1	904	1860.	6.68	140.
52	Te	tellurium	869	2.1	723	1261	6.232	137
53	I	iodine	1008	2.7	387	457	4.933	136
54	Xe	xenon	1170.	2.6	161	165	0.005366	136
55	Cs	cesium	376	0.8	302	944	1.873	238
56	Ba	barium	503	0.9	1000.	2170.	3.62	206
57	La	lanthanum	538	1.1	1193	3737	6.15	194
			Elements 58–71 have been omitted.					
72	Hf	hafnium	659	1.3	2506	4876	13.3	164
73	Ta	tantalum	728	1.5	3290.	5731	16.4	158
74	W	tungsten	759	1.7	3695	5828	19.3	150.
75	Re	rhenium	756	1.9	3458	5869	20.8	141
76	Os	osmium	814	2.2	3306	5285	22.587	136
77	Ir	iridium	865	2.2	2719	4701	22.562	132
78	Pt	platinum	864	2.2	2041	4098	21.5	130.
79	Au	gold	890.	2.4	1337	3129	19.3	130.
80	Hg	mercury	1007	1.9	234	630.	13.5336	132
81	Tl	thallium	589	1.8	577	1746	11.8	144
82	Pb	lead	716	1.8	600.	2022	11.3	145
83	Bi	bismuth	703	1.9	544	1837	9.79	150.
84	Po	polonium	812	2.0	527	1235	9.20	142
85	At	astatine	—	2.2	575	—	—	148
86	Rn	radon	1037	—	202	211	0.009074	146
87	Fr	francium	393	0.7	300.	—	—	242
88	Ra	radium	509	0.9	969	—	5	211
89	Ac	actinium	499	1.1	1323	3471	10.	201
			Elements 90 and above have been omitted.					

*boiling point at standard pressure
** density of solids and liquids at room temperature and density of gases at 298 K and 101.3 kPa
- no data available
Source: CRC Handbook for Chemistry and Physics 91st ed., 2010-2011, CRC Press

Table T
Important Formulas and Equations

Density	$d = \dfrac{m}{V}$	d = density $\quad$ m = mass $\quad$ V = volume
Mole Calculations	number of moles = $\dfrac{\text{given mass}}{\text{gram-formula mass}}$	
Percent Error	% error = $\dfrac{\text{measured value} - \text{accepted value}}{\text{accepted value}} \times 100$	
Percent Composition	% composition by mass = $\dfrac{\text{mass of part}}{\text{mass of whole}} \times 100$	
Concentration	parts per million = $\dfrac{\text{mass of solute}}{\text{mass of solution}} \times 1\,000\,000$ $\quad$ molarity = $\dfrac{\text{moles of solute}}{\text{liter of solution}}$	
Combined Gas Law	$\dfrac{P_1V_1}{T_1} = \dfrac{P_2V_2}{T_2}$	P = pressure $\quad$ V = volume $\quad$ T = temperature
Titration	$M_AV_A = M_BV_B$	M_A = molarity of H^+ $\quad$ M_B = molarity of OH^- $\quad$ V_A = volume of acid $\quad$ V_B = volume of base
Heat	$q = mC\Delta T$ $\quad$ $q = mH_f$ $\quad$ $q = mH_v$	q = heat $\quad$ H_f = heat of fusion $\quad$ m = mass $\quad$ H_v = heat of vaporization $\quad$ C = specific heat capacity $\quad$ ΔT = change in temperature
Temperature	$K = {}^\circ C + 273$	K = kelvin $\quad$ ${}^\circ C$ = degree Celsius

DET 609 ADU

Reference Tables for Physical Setting/Chemistry – 2011 Edition

A

Absolute Zero (5)
0 K or -273°C; the temperature at which all molecular movements stop.

Accelerator (208)
a device which gives charged particles sufficient kinetic energy to penetrate the nucleus.

Acid, Arrhenius (121 – 122)
a substance that produces H^+ (hydrogen ion, proton) or H_3O^+ (hydronium) ion as the only positive ion in solutions.

Acid , Alternate Theory (122)
a substance that donates H^+ (hydrogen ion, proton) in acid-base reactions.

Activated complex (142)
a high energy substance formed during a chemical reaction.

Activation energy (138)
minimal amount of energy needed to start a reaction.

Addition reaction (172 – 173)
organic reaction that involves the adding of hydrogen atoms (or halogen atoms) to a double or a triple bond.

Addition polymerization (172, 174)
the joining of monomers (small unit molecules) with double bonds to form a polymer (a larger unit) molecule.

Alcohol (165 – 166, 169)
an organic compound containing the hydroxyl group (-OH) as the functional group.

Aldehyde (167, 169)
an organic compound containing $-\overset{\overset{\displaystyle O}{\|}}{C}-H$ as the functional group.

Alkali metal (23, 25)
an element in Group 1 of the Periodic Table.

Alkaline Earth metal (23, 25)
an element in Group 2 of the Periodic Table.

Alkalinity (121)
describes how basic a solution is

Alkane (163, 164)
a saturated hydrocarbon with all single bonds and a general formula of C_nH_{2n+2}

Alkene (163, 164)
an unsaturated hydrocarbon with a double bond and a general formula of C_nH_{2n}

Alkyl group (170)
a hydrocarbon group (found as a side chain) that contains one less H atom than an alkane with the same number of C atoms.

Alkyne 163, 164
an unsaturated hydrocarbon with a triple ($\equiv$) bond and a general formula of C_nH_{2n-2} .

Allotropes   (20)
two or more different forms of the same element that have different formulas, structures, and properties.

Alpha decay   (210, 215)
a nuclear decay that releases an alpha particle.

Alpha particle (208)
a helium nucleus, ^4_2He

Amide (167, 169)
an organic compound formed from a reaction of an organic acid with an amine.

Amine   (167, 169)
an organic compound that has $-\overset{|}{N}-$ (nitrogen) as its functional group.

Amino acid   (167)
an organic compound containing an amine (- NH_2 -) and a carboxyl (-COOH) group.

Anode (190)
an electrode (site) where oxidation occurs in electrochemical (voltaic and electrolytic) cells. In voltaic cells, the anode is negative. In electrolytic cells, the anode is positive.

Aqueous solution (103)
a homogeneous mixture made with water as the solvent.

Artificial Transmutation   (210, 215)
converting (transforming) a stable element to a radioactive unstable element by bombarding (hitting) the stable nucleus with a high energy particle.

Asymmetrical molecule   (58, 62)
a molecule that has a polarized structure because of an uneven charge distribution.

Atom (33, 35)
the basic or the smallest unit of an element that can be involved in chemical reactions.

Atomic mass (39, 88)
the weighted average mass of an element's naturally occurring isotopes.

Atomic mass unit (39)
one-twelfth (1/12th) the mass of a carbon-12 atom.

Atomic number   (35, 36)
the number of protons in the nucleus of an atom.

Atomic radius (size) (21, 27)
half the distance between adjacent nuclei of identical bonded atoms.

Avogadro's law (hypothesis)   (10)
equal volumes of all gases under the same pressure and temperature contain equal numbers of molecules.

Avogadro's number (87, 92)
quantity of particles in one mole of a substance; 6.02×10^{23}

B

Base, Arrhenius (121, 122)
a substance that produces OH⁻(hydroxide) ions as the only negative ions in solutions.

Base, Alternate Theory (122)
a substance that accepts H^+ (hydrogen ion, proton) in acid-base reactions.

Battery (189)
an example of a voltaic cell. It uses a redox reaction to produce electricity.

Beta particle (208)
a high-speed electron , $_{-1}^{0}e$, released from an atomic nucleus during a nuclear decay.

Beta decay (211, 215)
a nuclear decay that releases a beta particle.

Binary compound (76, 78)
a chemical substance composed of two different elements chemically combined.

Boiling point (6, 113)
the temperature of a liquid at which the vapor pressure of the liquid is equal to the atmospheric pressure. Boiling point of water = 100°C at 1 atm pressure.

Boyle's Law (11)
describes behavior of a gas at constant temperature: At constant temperature, volume of a gas varies indirectly with the pressure.

Bronsted-Lowry acid and bases (see acid and base alternate theory) (118)

C

Calorimeter (7)
a device used in measuring heat energy change during a physical and a chemical process.

Catalyst (138)
a substance that speeds up a reaction by providing an alternate, lower activation energy pathway.

Cathode (190)
an electrode (site) where reduction occurs in electrochemical cells.
In voltaic cells, the cathode is positive. In electrolytic cells, the cathode is negative.

Charles' Law (11)
describes behavior of gases at constant pressure: At constant pressure, the volume of a gas is directly proportional to its Kelvin (absolute) temperature.

Chemical bonding (55)
the simultaneous attraction of two nuclei to electrons.

Chemical change (13, 79)
the changing of composition of one or more substances during chemical reactions.

Chemical formula (73)
expression of qualitative and quantitative composition of pure substances.

Chemical property (13)
a characteristic of a substance based on its interaction with other substances.

Chemistry (1)
the study of the composition, properties, changes, and energy of matter.

Coefficient (93)
a number (usually a whole number) in front of a formula that indicates how many moles (or units) of that substance.

Collision Theory (137)
for a chemical reaction to occur, reacting particles must collide effectively.

Combined gas law (11) $\dfrac{P_1 V_1}{T_1} = \dfrac{P_2 V_2}{T_2}$

Combustion (172, 174)
an exothermic reaction of a substance with oxygen to produce H_2O , CO_2 , and energy

Compound (1)
a substance composed of two or more different elements chemically combined in a definite ratio
a substance that can be separated (decomposed) only by chemical methods.

Concentrated solution (108, 110)
a solution containing a large amount of dissolved solute relative to the amount of solvent.

Condensation (4)
exothermic phase change of a substance from gas (vapor) to a liquid.

Condensation polymerization (172, 174)
the joining of monomers (small unit molecules) into a polymer (a large unit molecule) by the removal of water.

Conductivity (21)
ability of an electrical current to flow through a substance.
Conductivity of electrolytes (soluble substances) in aqueous and liquid phase is due to mobile ions. Conductivity of metallic substances is due to mobile valence electrons.

Conjugate acid-base pair (133)
species in acid-base reactions that differ by just one hydrogen atom

Coordinate covalent bond (59)
a type of covalent bond in which one atom provides both shared electrons with H^+

Covalent bond (58)
a bond formed by the sharing of electrons between nonmetal atoms.

Cracking (172)
the breaking of a large hydrocarbon molecule into smaller molecules.

Crystallization (104)
a process of recovering a solute from a solution (mixture) by evaporation (or boiling).

D

Dalton's law of partial pressures (10)
total pressure of a gas mixture is the sum of all the individual gas pressures.

Decomposition (80)
chemical reaction in which a compound is broken down into simpler substances.

Density (21)
mass per unit volume of a substance ; $\text{Density} = \dfrac{\text{mass}}{\text{volume}}$

Deposition   (4)
an exothermic phase change by which a gas changes to a solid.

Diatomic molecule (element)   (25, 58)
a molecule consisting of two identical atoms. Examples; O_2 and H_2

Dihydroxy alcohol   (166)
an alcohol with two –OH groups

Dilute solution   (108)
a solution containing little dissolved solute in comparison to the amount of solvent.

Dipole (aka polar)   (58)
a molecule with positive and negative ends due to uneven charge distributions.

Distillation   (2)
a process by which components of a homogeneous mixture can be separated by differences in boiling points.

Double covalent bond (=)   (163)
the sharing of two pairs of electrons (four total electrons) between two atoms.

Double replacement   (80)
a chemical reaction that involves the exchange of ions.

Ductile (21)
ability (property) of a metal to be drawn into a thin wire.

E

Effective collision   (137)
a collision in which the particles collide with sufficient kinetic energy, and at appropriate angle.

Electrochemical cell   (1)
a system in which there is a flow of electrical current while a chemical reaction is taking place. Voltaic and electrolytic cells are the two most common types of electrochemical cells.

Electrode (189)
a site at which oxidation or reduction can occur in electrochemical cells.
The anode (oxidation site) and cathode (reduction site) are the two electrodes of electrochemical cells.

Electrolysis (189, 190, 194)
a process by which electrical current forces a nonspontaneous redox reaction to occur.
Electrolysis of water: $2H_2O$ + electricity $\rightarrow$ $2 H_2$ + O_2

Electrolyte   (127)
a substances that dissolves in water to produce an aqueous solution that conducts electricity. Conductivity of an electrolyte is due to mobile ions in solutions.

Electrolytic cell   (189, 192, 194)
an electrochemical cell that requires an electrical current to cause a nonspontaneous redox reaction to occur.

Electron (36)
a negatively charge subatomic particle found surrounding the nucleus (in orbitals) of an atom.

Electron configuration (40, 47)
distribution of electrons in electron shells (energy levels) of an atom.

Electron-dot diagram (41, 65, 66, 67)
a diagram showing the symbol of an atom and dots equal to the number of valence electrons.

Electronegativity (21, 28)
a measure of an atom's ability (tendency) to attract electrons during chemical bonding.

Electrolytic reduction (192)
the use of an electrolytic cell to force an ion to gain electrons and form a neutral atom.

Electroplating (193)
use of an electrolytic cell to coat a thin layer of a metal onto another surface.

Element (1)
a substance composed of atoms of the same atomic number.
a substance that cannot be decomposed (broken down) into simpler substances.

Empirical formula (74, 91)
a formula showing atoms combined in the simplest whole number ratio.

Empty space theory (33, 34)
Rutherford's gold foil experimental conclusion that an atom is mostly empty space.

Endothermic (4, 7, 140)
a process that absorbs energy.
Products of endothermic reactions always have more energy than the reactants.

Energy
ability to do work; can be measured in joules or calories.

Entropy (144)
a measure of the disorder or randomness of a system.
Entropy increases from solid to liquid to gas and with an increase in temperature

Equilibrium (145 – 149)
a state of a system when the rates (speeds) of opposing processes (reactions) are equal.

Equilibrium expression / Equilibrium constant (157)
the ratio of the molar concentrations of the products to reactants of an equilibrium reaction. Liquids and solids are excluded from equilibrium expressions.

Ester (168, 169)
an organic compound with $-\overset{\displaystyle O}{\overset{\displaystyle \|}{C}}-O$ $(-COO-)$ as the functional group.

Esterification (172, 173)
an organic reaction between an alcohol and organic acid to produce an ester.

Ether (166, 169)
an organic compound with $-O-$ as the functional group.

Ethene (164)
first member of the alkene hydrocarbons with a formula of C_2H_4

$$\overset{\displaystyle H}{\diagdown}\underset{\displaystyle H}{\diagup}C = C\overset{\displaystyle H}{\diagup}\underset{\displaystyle H}{\diagdown}$$

Ethyne (164)
first member of the alkyne hydrocarbons with a formula of C_2H_2 $H - C \equiv C - H$

Evaporation (4)
an endothermic phase change by which a liquid changes to gas (vapor)

Excited state (42)
a state of an atom in which electrons are at higher electron shells (energy levels)

Exothermic (4, 7, 140)
a process that releases energy.
Products of exothermic reactions always have less energy than the reactants.

F

Fermentation (172, 174)
an organic reaction in which sugar is converted to alcohol (ethanol, C_2H_5OH) and carbon dioxide.

Filtration (2, 104)
a process that is used to separate a heterogeneous liquid mixture that is composed of substances with different particle sizes.

Fission (212, 213, 215)
the splitting of a large nucleus into smaller nuclei fragments in a nuclear reaction. Mass is converted to huge amounts of energy during fission.

Formula (73)
symbols and subscripts used to represent the composition of a substance.

Formula mass (88)
total mass of all the atoms in one unit of a formula.

Freezing (solidification) (4)
an exothermic phase change by which a liquid changes to a solid.

Frequency (54)
the number of completed waves of a radiation that passes a point per second (Hertz)

Freezing point (solid/liquid equilibrium) (5, 145)
the temperature at which both solid and liquid phases of a substance can exist at equilibrium. The freezing point and melting point of a substance are the same.

Functional group (165)
an atom or a group of atoms that replaces a hydrogen atom in a hydrocarbon.

Fusion (nuclear change) (212, 214, 215)
the joining of two small nuclei to make a larger nucleus in a nuclear reaction.

Fusion (melting) phase change (4, 8)
endothermic phase change by which a solid changes to liquid.

G

Gamma ray (208)
high-energy rays similar to X-rays that are released during nuclear decay.
A gamma ray has zero mass and zero charge, ${}^{0}_{0}\gamma$

Gaseous phase (3)
a phase of matter with no definite shape and no definite volume.

Gay-Lussac's law (11)
at constant volume, pressure of a gas varies directly with the Kelvin temperature

Geological dating (221)
determining the age of a rock or mineral by comparing amounts of Uranium-238 to Lead-206 in a sample.

Graham's Law of Effusion (18)
the rates at which gases travel is inversely proportional to their molar masses

Gram-formula mass (88)
Mass of one mole of a substance expressed in grams.
the total mass of all atoms in one mole of a substance.

Ground state (42)
a state of an atom in which all electrons of the atom occupy the lowest available levels.

Group (family) (20)
the vertical column of the Periodic Table.
Elements in the same group have the same number of valence electrons and share similar chemical properties.

H

Haber process (80)
a chemical reaction that produces ammonia from nitrogen and hydrogen.
$$N_2 \quad + \quad 3H_2 \rightarrow \quad 2NH_3 \quad (\text{Haber process equation}).$$

Half-life (217)
the length of time it takes for a sample of a radioisotope to decay to half its original mass (or atoms)

Half-reaction (186)
a reaction that shows either the oxidation or the reduction part of a redox reaction.

Halide (165, 169)
a compound that contains a halogen (Group 17) atom.

Halogen (23, 25)
an element found in Group 17 of the Periodic Table.

Heat (7)
a form of energy that can flow (or transfer) from one substance (or area) to another.
Joules and calories are two units commonly used to measure the quantity of heat.

Heat of fusion (8)
the amount of heat needed to change a unit mass of a solid to a liquid at its melting point.. Heat of fusion for water is 334 Joules per gram.

Heat of reaction (ΔH) (141)
amount of heat absorbed or released during a reaction.
the difference between the heat energy of the products and the heat energy of the reactants. ΔH = heat of products − heat of reactants.

Heat of vaporization   (8)
the amount of heat needed to change a unit mass of a liquid to vapor (gas) at its boiling point.   Heat of vaporization for water is 2260 Joules per gram.

Heterogeneous   (2)
a mixture in which substances in the mixture are not uniformly or evenly mixed.

Homogeneous   (2)
a type of mixture in which substances in the mixture are uniformly and evenly mixed. Solutions are homogeneous mixtures.

Homologous series   (163)
a group of related compounds in which one member differs from the next member by a set number of atoms.

Hydrate   (73, 91)
an ionic compound containing a set number of water molecules within its crystal structure.
$CuSO_4 \cdot 5H_2O$ is an example formula of a hydrate. This hydrate contains five moles of water.

Hydrocarbon   (163)
an organic compound containing only hydrogen and carbon atoms.

Hydrogen bonding   (64)
attraction of a hydrogen atom to an oxygen, nitrogen, or fluorine atom of another molecule. Hydrogen bonding exists (or is strongest) in H_2O (water), NH_3 (ammonia), and HF (hydrogen fluoride).

Hydrogen ion (H$^+$)   (122)
a hydrogen atom that has lost its only electron. H^+ is a proton.
The only positive ion produced by all Arrhenius acids in solution.

Hydrolysis   (133)
a reaction of a salt in water to produce either an acidic, basic, or neutral solution.

Hydronium ion   **(H$_3$O$^+$)**   (122)
a polyatomic ion formed when H_2O (a water molecule) combines with H^+ (hydrogen ion). Ion formed by all Arrhenius acids in solutions.

Hydroxide ion (OH$^-$)   (122)
the only negative ion produced by Arrhenius bases in solutions.

Hydroxyl group (–OH)   (165)
a functional group found in compounds of alcohols.
NOTE: Hydroxyl ions do not ionize

I

Ideal gas   (9)
a theoretical gas that has all the characteristics described by the kinetic molecular theory.

Ideal gas law (18)
$PV = nRT$. Describes an ideal gas behavior by relating moles, pressure, volume and absolute temperature of the gas.

Immiscible liquids   (105)
two liquids that do not mix well with each other.

Indicator (123)
any substance that changes color in the presence of another substance.
Acid-base indicators are used to determine if a substance is an acid or a base.

Insoluble (105, 107)
a solute substance with low solubility (doesn't dissolve well) in a given solvent.

Intermolecular forces (63, 64)
weak forces of attraction between molecules of molecular substances in the liquid and solid phase

Ion (44)
a charged (+ or -) particle.

Ionic bond (57)
a bond formed by the transfer of one or more electrons from a metal to a nonmetal.
An ionic bond is formed by electrostatic attraction of a positive ion to a negative ion.

Ionic compound (substance) (57)
compounds that are composed of positive and negative particles.
$NaCl$, $NaNO_3$, and ammonium chloride are examples of ionic substances.

Ionic radius (21)
the size of an ion as measured from the nucleus to the outer energy level of that ion.

Ionization energy (21, 28)
energy needed to remove the most loosely bound valence electron from an atom.

Isomers (170, 171)
organic compounds with the same molecular formula but different structural formulas.

Isotopes (38)
atoms of the same element with the same number of protons but different numbers of neutrons. Isotopes have the same atomic number but different mass numbers.

J - K

Joules (7)
a unit for measuring the amount of heat energy.

Kelvin (K) (5)
a unit for measuring temperature. A Kelvin temperature unit is always 273 higher than the equivalent temperature in Celsius. (K = °C + 273)

Ketone (171)
an organic compound containing $-\overset{\overset{\displaystyle O}{\|}}{C}-$ or $(-CO-)$, a carbonyl functional group.

Kinetic energy (5)
energy due to motion or movement of particles in a substance.
Average kinetic energy of particles determines temperature of a substance.

Kinetic molecular theory (ideal gas law) (9)
a theory that is used to explain behavior of gas particles.

Kinetics (137)
the study of rates and mechanisms of reactions

L

Law of conservation (80)
In a chemical reaction, mass, atoms, charges, and energy are conserved (neither created nor destroyed).

Law of definite composition (1)
atoms of a compound are in a fixed ratio.

Le Chatelier's principle   (147)
a chemical or physical process will shift at equilibrium to compensate for added stress.

Lewis electron-dot diagram (41, 65, 66, 67)
a diagram showing the symbol of an atom and dots equal to the number of its valence electrons.

Limiting reagent   (100)
a reactant in a reaction that is completely used up first.

Liquid   (3)
a phase of matter with definite volume but no definite shape (takes the shape of the container).

Luster   (21)
a property that describes the shininess of a metallic element

M

Malleability   (21)
ability (or property) of a metal to be hammered into a thin sheet.

Mass number   (37)
the total number of protons and neutrons in the nucleus of an atom.

Matter   (1)
anything that has mass and volume (occupied space).

Melting point (solid/liquid equilibrium)   (5, 145)
the temperature at which both the solid and the liquid phases of a substance can coexist. The melting point of water is 0°C or 273 K.

Metal   (21, 22, 23)
an element that tends to lose electrons and form a positive ion during chemical reactions. The majority of the elements (about 75%) are metals.

Metallic bond   (59. 60)
bonding in metals described as "positive ions immersed in a sea of mobile electrons"

Metalloid (21, 22, 23)
an element with both metallic and nonmetallic properties (characteristics).

Mixture   (1)
a physical combination of two or more substances that can be homogeneous or heterogeneous. Mixtures can be separated by physical methods.

Molar mass (88)
mass in grams of one mole of a formula.

Molar volume (92)
volume of one mole of a gas at STP is equal to 22.4 liters.

Molarity (112)
concentration of a solution expressed in moles of solute per liter of solution.

$$\text{Molarity} = \frac{\text{moles of solute}}{\text{liter of solution}}$$

Mole   (87)
unit of quantity of particles (atoms, molecules, ions, electrons) in a substance
1 mole = 6.02 x 10^{23} particles.

Molecular formula   (74, 91)
a formula showing the actual composition (or ratio of atoms) in a substance.

Molecule (58)
the smallest unit of a covalent (molecular) substance that has the same properties of the substance.
A molecule could be one nonmetal atom (He, Ne) or a group of nonmetal atoms ($C_6H_{12}O_6$, HCl, H_2O) covalently bonded

Molecular substance (covalent substance)   (58, 60)
a substance composed of molecules
H_2O, CO_2, O_2, NH_3, and $C_6H_{12}O_6$ are examples of molecular substances.

Monomer   (172, 174)
an individual unit of a polymer.

Multiple covalent bond (170)
a double or a triple covalent bond formed by the sharing of more than two electrons.

N

Network covalent bond   (59)
covalent bonding with absence of discrete particles in network solid substances

Neutralization   (126)
a reaction of an acid with a base to produce water and a salt.

Neutron   (36)
a subatomic particle with no charge, found in the nucleus of an atom .

Noble gas   (23, 25)
an element found in Group 18 of the Periodic Table.

Nonmetal (21, 22, 23)
an element that tends to gain electrons and forms negative ions, or shares electrons to form a covalent bond.

Nonpolar covalent bond   (58, 60)
a bond formed by the equal sharing of electrons between two identical nonmetal atoms (or of the same electronegativity).

Nonpolar substance   (58, 60)
a substance whose molecules have symmetrical shape and even charge distribution.

Nucleons   (36)
particles in the nucleus that include protons and neutrons.

Nucleus   (35)
the small, dense, positive core of an atom containing protons and neutrons.

O

Octet rule   (55)
when an atom has a stable configuration with eight electrons in the valence shell.

Orbital   (40, 46)
a region in an atom where electrons are likely to be found (or located).

Orbital notation   (47)
a diagram showing arrangements of electrons in orbitals of atoms.

Organic acid (168, 169)
a compound containing –COOH or $-\overset{\overset{\displaystyle O}{\displaystyle \|}}{C}-OH$ as its functional group.

Organic chemistry (161)
the study of carbon and carbon based compounds.

Oxidation (185, 186)
the loss of electrons by an atom during a redox reaction.
Oxidation leads to an increase in oxidation state (number) of a substance.

Oxidized substance (Reducing agent) (185)
a substance that loses electrons in a redox reaction.
a substance whose oxidation number (state) increases after a redox reaction

Oxidizing agent (Reduced substance) (185)
a substance that is reduced (gains electrons) in a redox reaction.
a substance whose oxidation number (state) decreases after a redox reaction

Oxidation number/ Oxidation state (183, 184)
a charge an atom has or appears to have

Ozone (20)
O_3, an allotrope (a different molecular form) of oxygen

P

Parts per million (112)
concentration of a solution expressed as the ratio of mass of solute per
million parts of a solution.
$$\text{Part per million (ppm)} \; = \; \frac{\text{mass of solute}}{\text{mass of solution}} \; \times \; 1\,000\,000$$

Percent composition (90, 91)
composition of a compound as the percentage by mass of each element
compared to the total mass of the compound.
$$\text{Percent composition} \; = \; \frac{\text{mass of part}}{\text{mass of whole}} \; \times \; 100$$

Period (20)
the horizontal rows of the Periodic Table
Elements in a period have the same number of occupied electron shells (or energy levels).

Periodic law (20)
states that properties of elements are periodic functions of their atomic numbers.

pH (123)
values that indicate the strength of an acid or a base. pH values ranges from $0 - 14$.
pH value is determined from how many H^+ ions are in a solution.

Phase change diagram (6)
a diagram showing changes in a substance as it is being heated or cooled over time.

Phase equilibrium (145)
a state of balance when the rates of two opposing (opposite) phase changes are equal.

Physical change (13, 79)
a change that does not change the composition of a substance.
Phase changes and dissolving are examples of physical changes.

Physical properties (13)
characteristics of a substance that can be observed or measured without changing the
chemical composition of the substance

Polar covalent bond (58)
a bond formed by the unequal sharing of electrons between two different nonmetal atoms.

Polyatomic ion (76)
group of two or more atoms with excess positive or negative charges (See Table E).

Polymer (172, 174)
an organic compound composed of chains of monomers (smaller units).

Polymerization (172, 174)
an organic reaction by which monomers (small units of molecules) are joined together to make a polymer (a larger unit molecule) .

Positron (208)
a positively charge particle similar in mass to an electron. $_{+1}^{0}e$

Positron decay (emission) (211)
a nuclear decay that releases a positron

Potential energy (6, 56,)
stored energy in chemical substances.
Amount of potential energy depends on composition and the structure of a substance.

Potential energy diagram (143)
a diagram showing the changes in potential energy of substances during a reaction.

Precipitate (111)
a solid that forms out of a solution

Primary alcohol (166)
an alcohol with an –OH functional group attached to an end carbon.

Product (79)
a substance that remains (or forms) after a chemical reaction is completed.
Products are placed to the right of an arrow in equations.

Proton (35)
a subatomic particle with a positive charge found in the nucleus of an atom.
The number of protons in an atom is equal to the atomic number of the element.

Pure substance (1)
a type of matter with the same composition and properties in all samples.
Elements and compounds are pure substances.

Q

Qualitative (73)
indicates the types of atom that is in a chemical formula.

Quanta (42)
specific amounts of energy absorbed or released by an electron as it changes from one level to another.

Quantum theory (46)
describes location and behavior of electrons in sets of four quantum numbers

Quantitative (73)
indicates the number of each atom in a formula.

R

Radioisotope (209)
an unstable isotope of an element that is radioactive and can decay.

Rate (137)
a measure of the speed (how fast) a reaction occurs.

Reactant (79, 142)
the starting substance in a chemical reaction.
Reactants are shown (or placed) to the left of the arrow in equations.

Redox (183)
a reaction that involves oxidation and reduction.

Reduction (185, 186)
the gaining of electrons during a redox reaction.
Reduction leads to a decrease in oxidation number (state) of a substance

Reduced substance (oxidizing agent) (185)
a substance that gains electrons during a redox reaction .
a substance whose oxidation number (state) decreases after a reaction

Reducing agent (oxidized substance) (185)
the substance that is oxidized (loses electrons) in a redox reaction.
a substance whose oxidation number (state) increases after a redox reaction.

S

Saponification (172, 174)
organic reaction that produces soap and glycerol (a trihydroxy alcohol).

Salt (126, 127)
a product of a neutralization reaction.
an ionic substance.

Salt bridge (190)
allows for ions to flow (migrate) between the two half cells of voltaic cells.

Saturated hydrocarbon (163)
alkane hydrocarbon with only single bonds between the carbon atoms.

Saturated solution (108)
a solution containing the maximum amount of dissolved solute possible at a given temperature.

Secondary alcohol (166)
an alcohol in which the –OH is bonded to a carbon atom that is already bonded to two other carbon atoms.

Single covalent bond (163)
a covalent bond formed by the sharing of just two electrons (or one pair of electrons).

Single replacement (80)
a reaction in which a more reactive element replaces the less reactive element of a compound.

Solid (3)
a phase of matter with definite shape and definite volume

Solubility (105)
a measure of the extent to which a solute will dissolve in a given solvent at a specified temperature.

Soluble (105, 107)
a substance with high solubility.

Solute (103)
the substance that is being dissolved.
When a salt dissolves in water, the solute is the salt.

Solution (103)
a homogeneous mixture of substances in the same physical state.

Solvent (103)
the substance (usually a liquid) that is dissolving the solute.
Water is the solvent in all aqueous solutions.

Specific heat capacity (7)
amount of heat needed to change the temperature of a one gram sample of a substance by one ºC or one K.

Spectral lines (bright-line spectrum) (43)
band of colors produced as electrons go from excited (high) to ground (low) state.

Spontaneous reaction (158)
a reaction that will occur under a given set of conditions
a reaction that proceeds in the direction of lower energy and greater entropy

Stoichiometry (87)
the study and calculations of relative quantities of substances in formulas and equations.

STP (12)
standard temperature (0ºC , 273 K) and pressure (1 atm, 101.3 kPa)

Stress (146, 147, 148, 149)
a change in temperature, pressure, or concentration in a reaction at equilibrium.

Sublimation (4)
an endothermic phase change from solid to gas.

Subscript (73)
a whole number written next to a chemical symbol to indicate the number of atoms.

Substitution reaction (172, 173)
an organic reaction of an alkane with a halogen to produce a halide.
a reaction in which a halogen atom replaces a hydrogen atom of an alkane (saturated) hydrocarbon.

Supersaturated solution (108)
a solution containing more solute than would normally dissolve at that given temperature.

Symmetrical molecule (58, 62)
a molecule that has a nonpolarized structure due to an even charge distribution.

Synthesis (80)
a chemical reaction in which two or more substances combine to make one substance.

T

Temperature   (5, 12)
the measure of the average kinetic energy of particles in a substance.
Temperature and average kinetic energy are directly related.

Tertiary alcohol   (166)
an alcohol in which the –OH is bonded to a carbon atom that is already bonded to
three other carbon atoms.

Thomson, J.J.   (33, 34)
conducted cathode ray experiment that led to the discovery of electrons

Titration   (126)
a process used in determining the concentration of an unknown solution by reacting it
with a solution of known concentration.

Tracer   (221)
a radioisotope used to track a chemical reaction.

Transition element   (23, 25)
an element found in Groups 3 – 12 of the Periodic Table.

Transmutation   (207)
the changing or converting of a nucleus of one atom into a nucleus of a different atom

Trihydroxy alcohol   (166)
an alcohol with three –OH (hydroxyl) groups.

Triple covalent bond   (163)
a covalent bond resulting from the sharing of three pairs of electrons (six total
electrons).

U - W

Unsaturated hydrocarbon   (163)
organic compound containing double or triple bonded carbon atoms.

Unsaturated solution   (108)
a solution containing less dissolved solute than can be dissolved at a given temperature.

Valence electrons   (41)
the electrons in the outermost electron shell (energy level) of an atom.

Vapor   (113)
a gas form of a substance that is normally a liquid at room temperature.

Vapor pressure   (113)
the pressure exerted by vapor (evaporated particles) on the surface of the liquid.

Vaporization (evaporation)   (4)
phase change of a substance from liquid to gas state at its boiling point.

Voltaic cell   (189, 191, 194)
an electrochemical cell in which electrical energy is produced from a spontaneous
redox chemical reaction.

Wave-mechanical model (electron-cloud model)   (33)
the current model of an atom that places electrons in orbitals.
The orbital is described as the most probable region of finding electrons in an atom.

Surviving Chemistry Books
Available in Hard Copy and eBook
Instant Online Preview
Visit SurvivingChem.com

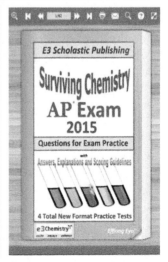

Made in United States
North Haven, CT
23 July 2022

21581658R00209